A NAZI SPY CHIEF'S CONFESSIONS— SELF-JUSTIFICATION . . . OR TRUTH?

HITLER'S SECRET SERVICE

(Original Title: *The Labyrinth*)

The Memoirs of
WALTER SCHELLENBERG

Introduction by
ALAN BULLOCK

Translated by
LOUIS HAGEN

A JOVE / HBJ BOOK

Copyright © 1956 by Harper & Brothers
Published by arrangement with Harper & Row, Publishers

First Jove/HBJ edition published December 1977

Library of Congress Catalog Card Number: 56-8761

Printed in the United States of America

Jove/HBJ books are published by Jove Publications, Inc. (Harcourt Brace Jovanovich), 757 Third Avenue, New York, N.Y.
10017

CONTENTS

v

INTRODUCTION
by
ALAN BULLOCK

WALTER SCHELLENBERG'S memoirs would be worth reading, if for nothing else, as a first-rate collection of spy stories. For the text does not belie the promise of the chapter headings: the plot to kidnap the Duke of Windsor, the affair of the Vietinghoff brothers, the Polish agent K—— and the spy ring in the Manchoukuoan Embassy, the capture of the British Secret Service agents at Venlo, and the hunting down of the Communist *Rote Kapelle* organization. All these are episodes not from fiction but from the history of the last twenty years and they are described by the man who became the head of Hitler's Foreign Intelligence Service.

When the Nazis came to power at the end of January 1933, Walter Schellenberg was a young man of twenty-two looking for a job. Three years at the University of Bonn, during the course of which he changed from the study of medicine to that of law, had left him with few qualifications. Like thousands of other German university students he had only his wits to rely on at a time when jobs were more difficult to get than ever before. Like thousands of others in the same situation he joined the Nazi party, neither from conviction nor against it, but as the obvious avenue to success.

Making the most of his education, Schellenberg took care to join the black-shirted SS—in the SS one found "the better type of people"—and leaped at the chance of a job in the SD, the intelligence and security service set up within the SS by Heydrich, another young man on the make.

For the rest of his career (it was over by the age of thirty-five) this was Schellenberg's world, the world of the Secret Service and the Secret Police, a world in which nothing was too fantastic to happen, in which normality

7

of behavior or simplicity of motive were curiosities and nothing was taken at face value, a world in which lies, bribes, blackmail and false papers, treachery and violence were part of the daily routine.

All this, the spurious glamour of the spy and the secret agent, Schellenberg enjoyed to the full. In writing his memoirs after the war and reliving his exploits, he was able to recapture temporarily the sense of excitement and activity, the deprivation of which he felt as acutely as a drug addict. When he comes to describe the room he occupied as head of the German Foreign Intelligence Service he writes with unconcealed pride: "Microphones were everywhere, hidden in the walls, under the desk, even in one of the lamps, so that every conversation and every sound was automatically recorded. . . . My desk was like a small fortress. Two automatic guns were built into it which could spray the whole room with bullets. All I had to do in an emergency was to press a button and both guns would fire simultaneously. At the same time I could press another button and a siren would summon the guards to surround the building and block every exit. . . . Whenever I was on missions abroad I was under standing orders to have an artificial tooth inserted which contained enough poison to kill me within thirty seconds if I were captured. To make doubly sure, I wore a signet ring in which, under a large blue stone, a gold capsule was hidden containing cyanide."

Hollywood could not have asked for more, but the point which it is only too easy to miss is that Schellenberg was not exaggerating when he wrote this. The Third Reich was a gangster empire. Its rulers behaved in a manner which continually brings to mind the actors in a third-rate film, and it was in the hectic atmosphere described by Schellenberg that decisions of the greatest importance were taken even when they involved the "final solution" of the Jewish problem or the invasion of Russia.

What Schellenberg gives us is a picture of the Nazis seen, not by the Opposition, not by the generals or by politicians like Papen and Schacht, anxious to underline their disapproval, but by one of themselves. This is the value of his book as a piece of historical evidence, for none of those who have so far published their memoirs of this period were in as good a position to know and to have seen at first hand what took place at the center of power.

To appreciate this, it is necessary to examine the position of the organization in which Schellenberg made his career, the SD, the Sicherheitsdienst or Security Service of the SS.

When Hitler appointed Heinrich Himmler as Reichsfuehrer SS in January 1929, the SS was no more than Hitler's private bodyguard, numbering less than three hundred men. By January 1933 it had grown to fifty-two thousand and formed a *corps d'élite* within the private army of the brown-shirted SA. In the notorious purge of June 30, 1934, when Roehm, the leader of the SA, was murdered, Himmler's SS was given the job of carrying out the arrests and executions, and a month later was rewarded with the status of an independent organization. Within the SS itself a separate intelligence and security service (the SD) had been organized as early as 1931 and in the summer of 1934 the SD, under Himmler's chief lieutenant Heydrich, was recognized as the sole intelligence and counter-intelligence agency of the Party.

For fifteen months after Hitler came to power, a bitter fight[1] was waged between Goering, as Minister-President of Prussia, and Himmler, nominally chief of police in Bavaria but also Reichsfuehrer of the SS, for control of the Prussian Gestapo or Secret State Police. Here too the formidable combination of Himmler and Heydrich proved successful and, from Goering's reluctant concession of control over the Prussian Gestapo to Himmler in April 1934, the latter went on to become chief of the entire German police in July 1936.

This double position, as chief of the state police and at the same time Reichsfuehrer of the SS (a position independent of the state), enabled Himmler to build up a private empire which by the later years of the war threatened to overshadow state, Party, and armed forces alike.

Himmler achieved this, not by force of personality (of which he possessed little), but by virtue of the unique position which the security police must hold in a dictatorship. The power of a totalitarian regime rests on twin

---

[1] Described by two witnesses on the losing side: Rudolf Diels, *Lucifer ante Portas*, Interverlag A.G., Zurich, 1949, and H. B. Gisevius, *To the Bitter End*, Houghton Mifflin, Boston, 1947.

foundations: propaganda and terror. The instrument of terror in Hitler's Germany was the Reichsicherheitshauptamt, the Main Security Office, set up in September 1939 to bring into a single organization the State Security Police (SIPO and Gestapo) and the SS Sicherheitsdienst.

The Main Security Office (RSHA) was the creation of Reinhard Heydrich, Himmler's sinister lieutenant, whose portrait is for the first time drawn at full length in these pages. It concentrated under the control of half a dozen men (of whom Schellenberg became one) all the powers of spying and intelligence, interrogation and arrest, torture and execution on which dictatorship ultimately depends. Its work was divided among seven sections, of which only four need be mentioned here. AMT III, under the direction of Otto Ohlendorf, dealt with intelligence work in Germany and the occupied countries; its counterpart was AMT VI which dealt with foreign intelligence. AMT IV, the old Gestapo, under the direction of Heinrich Mueller, was set up "to combat opposition to the state"; AMT V, under the direction of Arthur Nebe, controlled the Criminal Police (Kripo) whose duty was to combat crime.

AMT IV, to which Schellenberg was first assigned, had many ramifications.[2] Schellenberg, as head of the AMT IV E, was entrusted with counter-espionage work for the Gestapo in Germany and the occupied countries. In June 1941, at the time of the invasion of Russia, he took over and reorganized AMT VI, the Foreign Intelligence Service. Finally in the summer of 1944, on the liquidation of the Abwehr, the Intelligence Service of the German High Command (which, under Admiral Canaris and General Oster, had been used as a cover for the underground opposition to Hitler), Schellenberg assumed the additional responsibility for the German Military Intelligence and so achieved his ambition of a unified Foreign Intelligence Service.

Schellenberg was never one of the Nazi leaders. His picture rarely appeared in the papers, his name was unfamiliar. He belonged to the "back-room boys," the tech-

---

[2] "RSHA, AMT IV A 4B was responsible for the rounding up, transportation, shooting, and gassing to death of at least three million Jews." Edward Crankshaw, *Gestapo*, Putnam, London, 1956.

nicians of dictatorship, and he is the only member of
that highly important group to have written his memoirs.
Fortunately, Schellenberg was far more interested in describing what he had seen and done than in constructing
an apology. He had a gift for drawing a portrait. Mueller,
Ribbentrop, Kaltenbrunner, Canaris, and Himmler himself
are all brought to life and given that touch of humanity
without which the fantastic element in their actions and
utterances remains unconvincing. None of them made so
deep an impression on Schellenberg as Heydrich, and the
pages in which he describes his relationship with Heydrich, "the man with an iron heart," are among the best
in the book.

The inner politics of Nazi Germany (as of every dictatorship) were dominated by a fierce and incessant struggle
for power not only between rival organizations—the Main
Security Office, the Foreign Office, the Propaganda Ministry, the High Command, and the Nazi party—but also
within each organization itself. Schellenberg was adept at
both forms of intrigue, and needed to be if he were to
survive. Since he was constantly in the company and in
the confidence of Heydrich and Himmler, he provides
valuable evidence on the steady engrossing of power by
the SS leaders. His worst enemies were to be found in his
own Main Security Office, Kaltenbrunner (Heydrich's successor) and "Gestapo" Mueller. Only the continued favor
of Himmler enabled Schellenberg to escape their attempts
to destroy him.

Schellenberg's responsibility was the organization of
intelligence work abroad and this meant that he was also
in a good position to follow the course and consequences
of Hitler's policy toward the enemy, toward Germany's
allies and the occupied countries. Two areas with which
he was especially concerned were Occupied Russia and
the Far East; in both cases his memoirs add considerably
to our knowledge. He describes in some detail the steps
taken to place German agents behind the Russian lines
and to prevent the counter-penetration of Communist
agents into Germany. He saw the opportunities which
were being missed in Russia through Hitler's obstinate
adherence to a policy of indiscriminate brutality, and
he provides some interesting information on Japanese
attempts to mediate between Germany and the Soviet

Union. From these doubts sprang his own ambitious scheme (formed as early as 1942, according to his own account) to bring about a compromise peace through his influence over Himmler.

On certain subjects Schellenberg maintains a discreet silence. He barely mentions the concentration camps or the mass murders of the Jews, although both were the responsibility of Himmler and the SS. Nor has he more than a sentence or two about the German opposition to Hitler and the plot of July 20, 1944, about which he must have known a good deal if only because of the part the liquidation of the plot played in his plans to secure control of the Abwehr.

The concluding episode, in which for the only time he tried directly to influence the course of major events by persuading Himmler to initiate independent negotiations for peace, is already well known.[3] But Schellenberg's own account illuminates more vividly than any other the atmosphere of unreality in which the Nazi leaders were living in the last months of the war and the bankruptcy of their leadership. Even the suggestion of independent action was enough to plunge Himmler into a nervous crisis and Schellenberg at one stage brought in an astrologer to stiffen the timid resolution of the Reichsfuehrer SS. Never surely has a man amassed such power and been so completely incapable of using it in anything more than a subordinate capacity. No wonder that Hitler, the most suspicious of men, never felt his own position threatened by Himmler's accumulation of offices. For the reasons I have given I believe that Schellenberg's memoirs, quite apart from the interest of the narrative, have considerable value as historical evidence. We must turn now to examine their authenticity.

On the German collapse, Schellenberg found shelter with Count Bernadotte in Sweden and used the time, at Bernadotte's suggestion, to prepare a report on the negotiations in which he had been involved during the last months of the war. This is the so-called Trosa Memorandum, named from the Swedish village in which it was

---

[3] Cf. H. R. Trevor-Roper, *The Last Days of Hitler*, Macmillan, London, 1950; Count Bernadotte, *The Curtain Falls*, Knopf, New York, 1945, and *The Kersten Memoirs*, Hutchinson, London, 1956.

written, and it provides the basis of the account given in the later chapters of the memoirs. Schellenberg's extradition, however, was soon requested by the Allied Powers and he returned to Germany in June 1945 to stand his trial at Nuremberg. The preparation of his defense and his interrogation by Allied officers provided a further occasion for recalling the events of his career.

Schellenberg appeared only as a witness in the trial of the major war criminals, Goering, Ribbentrop, and the other Nazi leaders.[4] His own trial did not begin until January 1948, when he was brought before an American military tribunal in the Wilhelmstrasse Case, *The United States of America vs. Ernst von Weizsaecker et al.*[5] Among the twenty defendants, besides von Weizsaecker and Schellenberg, were Wilhelm Keppler, Bohle, Lammers, Darré, Meissner, and Schwerin von Krosigk. All of them had held prominent, although not the leading, positions in the Nazi regime, either as State Secretaries, minor Ministers, or heads of government departments. The charges against them were comprehensive and the proceedings protracted. The indictment covered eight counts, from the planning of aggressive war and crimes against humanity to membership in criminal organizations. The hearings lasted fifteen months and judgment was not delivered until April 1949.

Schellenberg was acquitted on all but two charges. He was a member of the SS and the SD which the International Military Tribunal had declared to be criminal organizations during the Nuremberg trial of the major war criminals, and the department (AMT VI) of which he was head was found guilty of complicity in the execution without trial of a number of Russian prisoners recruited for Operation "Zeppelin."[6] The court considered that Schellenberg's guilt was mitigated by his efforts to aid prisoners in the concentration camps in the later stages of the war, whatever the motives from which he had acted. He was sentenced to six years' imprisonment

---

[4] His evidence is to be found in *The Trial of German Major War Criminals*, Part 3, pp. 290-98, H.M.S.O., London, 1946-1952.

[5] *Trials of War Criminals before the Nuremberg Military Tribunal under Control Council*, No. 10, vols. xii, xiii, xiv, H.M.S.O., London, 1947-1949.

[6] See page 261.

(to run from June 1945), one of the lightest sentences imposed by the court.

Schellenberg had not been long in prison after the trial when he had to undergo a serious operation and soon afterward, early in June 1951, he was released as an act of clemency. He took refuge in Switzerland and while there began work on the memoirs which he had now contracted to write for a well-known Berne firm of publishers, Scherz Verlag. Before long, however, Schellenberg was discovered by the Swiss police and asked to leave the country. He moved over the frontier to Italy and settled at the little town of Pallenza on the shores of Lake Maggiore.

In the summer of 1951, Herr Alfred Scherz invited Herr Harpprecht, a young German journalist, to help in editing the memoirs. Herr Harpprecht[7] accepted the invitation and arrived at Pallenza at the end of August 1951. He found Schellenberg a sick and unhappy man. Harpprecht's description is worth quoting at some length: "Thin and of medium height, correctly dressed, with not one single feature out of the ordinary, he could have been taken for an amiable lawyer or a moderately successful businessman. His politeness was too forced to be perfect, in spite of his natural charm. His voice was soft but the negligence with which he formulated his phrases was not always convincing.

"It appeared that Schellenberg aimed at winning his partner in a conversation during the very first minutes. You had the impression that his large bright eyes were asking how you liked this Walter Schellenberg, the former chief of the German Intelligence, and whether he was still able to impress his surroundings as he had in the past. If he encountered opposition in an argument he showed himself capable of suddenly giving way. With a disarming smile he started yielding to his opponent's point of view, capitulating on terms which he tried to negotiate fairly and gently.

"This marked degree of receptiveness explains his unusual gift of intellectual adaptability which no doubt had been one of the secrets of his career. His particular talent

---

[7] Herr Harpprecht has since published, under the *nom-de-plume* Stefan Brant, a full-length account of the revolt of June 17-18, 1953, translated into English as *The East German Rising* (Thames & Hudson, 1955).

of assimilation ultimately produced an impression of unreliability, while his almost feminine sensibility made him
as moody as a film star no longer sure of success."

Although Schellenberg was in continual pain and deeply worried about finding the money to meet his expenses,
Herr Harpprecht believes that his bitterest humiliation was
the fact that no one any longer regarded him as interesting
and that the Italian police did not even bother to keep a
watch on him. He particularly resented the fact that it
should have been General Gehlen (the former chief of
the German High Command Section "Foreign Armies
East") and not he who was invited by the Americans to
organize an intelligence service against the Russians. In
compensation Schellenberg created his own world of make-
believe, hinting at messages from exiled heads of states,
financial aid from big business, and constant surveillance
by English and French agents who watched every step he
took. Even a simple journey to Milan was surrounded with
an air of mystery.

In such a frame of mind it was natural that Schellenberg should attach great importance to his memoirs, of
which he had already made a draft close on a thousand
pages long. In reliving the triumphs of his past career he
found relief from the shabby obscurity of the present.
Herr Harpprecht's task was to put the draft into order
and help fill the gaps in his memory. The work had already been interrupted by a visit to Spain (during which
Schellenberg was reconciled to his old enemy, Otto Skorzeny, at that time living in Madrid) and it was now
further delayed by a rapid deterioration in Schellenberg's
health.

For some time Schellenberg had been aware that another operation was essential if he was to secure any relief
from the disease of the liver from which he was suffering.
He put off this operation too long, was admitted to hospital too late for the doctors to save his life and died in
the Clinica Fornaca, Turin, on the last day of March 1952.

In the early summer of the same year Frau Schellenberg returned from Pallenza to Düsseldorf, taking with her
the ms. of the memoirs. In Düsseldorf she met Dr. Werner
Best, who had once been a collaborator of her husband's
in the SS and later became the German governor of Occupied Denmark. At that time Best was working in the offices of Dr. Achenbach, one of the foreign policy experts

of the present Free Democratic party and the Ruhr lawyer
who acted as defense counsel for Werner Naumann, Goebbels' former lieutenant, when the latter was arrested by the
British occupation authorities in January 1953.

On Best's advice Frau Schellenberg gave up the idea of
publication through a Swiss firm and decided to offer the
memoirs to a German publisher. In fact, all that appeared
was a brief sensationalized account in the Munich illus-
trated magazine *Quick* (*Die Grosse Mörder-GMBH*) based
on incidents in the memoirs without revealing Schellenberg's identity. The articles, which bore every sign of having been written up by a "ghost," were described as the
reminiscences of a high-ranking SS officer, the mysterious
"Colonel Z."

The reasons for this anonymity are not clear. It is possible that the publishers of *Quick* believed that the Swiss
firm of Alfred Scherz might still possess some claim to the
copyright or that Frau Schellenberg was influenced by
threats against herself and her children. In the end the
full ms. of the still unpublished memoirs was bought by
the present publisher, Mr. André Deutsch, from *Quick*
Verlag in Munich.

When it reached London, packed in a large suitcase,
the manuscript was in complete disorder. Mr. Deutsch was
able to check parts of it with material left by Schellenberg with the Swedish firm of Norstedt Verlag and to
show it to Dr. Goverts—a partner of Scherz und Goverts
Verlag—who had been in touch with Schellenberg and his
wife as early as 1950. Finally he invited Herr Harpprecht
to come over to England and inspect the manuscript. Herr
Harpprecht spent a week examining the material in detail.
He was able to point to numerous notes on the ms. made
in his own hand and to satisfy himself that this was the
original draft on which he had worked with Schellenberg
in 1951.

In the summer of 1955 I was asked to read the English
translation of the manuscript. At that time I had no knowledge of how it had come into Mr. Deutsch's hands, but I
was satisfied that the internal evidence pointed to the conclusion that these were Schellenberg's memoirs. They were
obviously written by someone with intimate knowledge of
the SD, the Main Security Office, and the German Intelligence Service; they were consistent with other accounts of
the events and personalities they described, yet sufficiently

independent to make it unlikely that they had been compiled at second hand. My conclusion was strengthened by the reflection that, if anyone had had the patience and the knowledge to forge so full an account, he would have fathered it on someone better known than Schellenberg and given it a more sensational character.

All this amounts to less than certainty, but my own belief is that Schellenberg wrote (or supplied the material for collaborators like Herr Harpprecht to write) the original draft and that the translation which follows has been made from that draft. It is not a translation of the complete manuscript, for length alone has made some abridgment necessary and other omissions and additions may well have been made since the original left Schellenberg's hands in 1952. Nor would it be wise to accept Schellenberg as a trustworthy witness where his evidence cannot be corroborated. Naturally enough he presents his own part in these events in as favorable a light as possible and often with some exaggeration of his own importance.

These qualifications are important, but much the same might be said of many other volumes of historical memoirs. They do not, I believe, substantially impair the value and interest of what follows. For Schellenberg, with all his faults (and they are plain enough to need no underlining), had two rare qualities in a writer of memoirs. For the most part he limits himself to describing events of which he has first-hand knowledge, and he is comparatively free from that passion for tortuous self-justification which disfigures so many German memoirs of these years. What drove him to write was the desire to recapture, not to disown, the sensations of power and importance. It is this lack of self-consciousness, damning as a revelation of character, which makes him the more valuable as an historical witness.

St. Catherine's Society
Oxford
August, 1956

1. THE MAKINGS OF A NAZI

Early years—Effects of the social crisis—The SS and the SD—A meeting of Party leaders—The night of the Roehm purge—Secret orders from Berlin—At the Ministry of the Interior—Heydrich's influence on my situation —Preparation and use of intelligence reports

IN THIS book I shall try to describe the development, organization, and activities of the German Secret Service under the National Socialist regime. During the whole of the regime I was closely connected with this organization and it seemed as though from my earliest youth various influences had been at work to turn me toward this particular field of service for my country and my people.

I was born in 1910, early enough to know the terrors of the First World War. We lived in Saarbruecken, and when I was only seven I had my first experience of an air raid when the French bombed the town. The hard winter of that year, the hunger, the cold, and the misery, will always remain in my memory.

The French occupied the Saar after the defeat of 1918, and our family business—my father was a piano manufacturer—suffered through the subsequent economic decline of the region. By 1923 things were so bad that my father decided to move to Luxembourg where there was another branch of the business. Thus, very early in life, I made contact with the world outside Germany and gained a knowledge of western Europe, and especially of France and the French.

I was the youngest of seven children. During my early years it was the personality of my mother, who gave us a Christian upbringing, which influenced me most. My father was too much occupied by the demands of his business, and it was not until later that his more liberal philosophy and outlook began to affect my way of thinking.

I was attending the Reform-Realgymnasium, a school that prepared pupils for university matriculation, giving special attention to languages and science. A history professor who greatly influenced my intellectual development awoke in me an interest in the Renaissance and the political and cultural currents that stemmed from that period. I was fascinated by the problems of the relationship between peoples and nations and the political and economic forces that arise from this relationship. My family's position in the Saar and in Luxembourg had also given me a personal interest in these matters, particularly with regard to foreign affairs.

In the summer of 1929, I entered the University of Bonn. During the first two years I studied medicine and then changed over to law, which both my father and I agreed would serve as the best basis either for a commercial career or for a career in the Foreign Service. It was also with my father's approval that, instead of joining the Union of Catholic Students, I joined one of the student corps that had, as so many of them did, a code of honor and dueling.

Meanwhile the world economic crisis had struck Germany and the widespread misery that came upon the German people affected my family and myself. Our finances had become increasingly strained, and in order to continue my studies I had been forced to ask for state grants. My position was no better after I had passed my final examination. In Germany it was customary to serve a period of apprenticeship, similar to that of an articled clerk in England, before taking up a legal career. Government grants were also available for such purposes as this, and I applied for one.

This was in the spring of 1933, the year when Hitler came to power. The judge who dealt with my application suggested that my chances of securing the grant would increase appreciably if I were a member of the Nazi party and one of its formations, the SA or the SS.

At the University I had not paid much attention to the political questions of the day, but I was certainly not unaware of the severity of the social crisis—there were now six million unemployed in Germany—and there was no sign of any help coming from the outside world to encourage the democratic elements of the Weimar Republic. After the Nazis' rise to power, the mass of the people came to believe that the more forceful approach of the new regime would lead to a solution of their internal problems as well as of the problem of Germany's position among the nations. It was my own financial difficulties, however, which decided me to join the Party, though I cannot say that I reached this decision with any great reluctance or difficulty. It was obvious that a vigorous program was needed which would overcome the worst social injustices of the Weimar Republic and bring about equal status for Germany among the nations, as well as a revision of the Versailles Treaty. It seemed to me only just that Germany should strive for those rights which every sovereign nation, and especially France, has always fought to secure for itself.

At this time thousands of people with widely differing backgrounds were rushing to join the National Socialist movement, though often for widely different reasons. I was certain, as were the majority of these people, that Hitler was a political realist and that having gained power he would now drop the more extreme and unreasonable aspects of his program—such as the measures against the Jews. These might have been useful to gain adherents in the past, but they certainly could not serve as principles on which to run a modern state.

All young men who joined the Party had to join one of its formations as well. The SS was already considered an "élite" organization. The black uniform of the Fuehrer's special guard was dashing and elegant, and quite a few of my fellow-students had joined. In the SS one found the "better type of people" and membership in it brought considerable prestige and social advantages, while the beer-hall rowdies of the SA were beyond the pale. In those days they represented the most extreme, violent, and fanatical elements of the Nazi movement.

I cannot deny that at the age of twenty-three such things as social prestige and, shall we say, the glamour of a smart uniform played quite a large part in my choice. However, I found the reality considerably less glamorous than I had imagined. The monotonous military drill that formed the chief activity of the ordinary SS did not appeal to me. We had to report for duty three evenings a week, and on Saturdays and Sundays there were long and arduous cross-country marches, often with a full pack.

These were supposed to temper the young Nazi manhood for the great tasks that lay ahead.

However, I soon managed to secure a more suitable form of activity. It had been realized that the SS would have to offer more to the students of a university town than merely marching and drill, and I was presently assigned to the task of conducting indoctrination talks and giving lectures, mostly of an historical nature, dealing with the development of Germanic law and at the same time directly attacking the Catholic Church. These lectures were for both students and workers and soon became quite popular. It was my first lecture, to which I gave an outspoken anti-Catholic bias, that first aroused the attention of the chief of the SD, Reinhard Heydrich.

One evening I noticed at the back of the audience two older men dressed in SS uniforms without any special insignia. At the end of the lecture they introduced themselves: both were professors at Bonn University, one a philologist, the other an educationalist. They said they had found my lecture very interesting and wanted to talk to me about other fields of activity in the SS.

It was from these two professors that I first heard about the existence of the SD. Within it, they explained, there was the Internal Security Section which concerned itself with matters inside Germany, and the Foreign Security Section which dealt with information from abroad. Both were highly secret institutions and their function was to gather information that could help the government to form policy or to evaluate the results of policy decisions already taken.

They asked me whether I would like to join one of these departments, I having told them of my keen interest in foreign affairs and foreign policy. They explained, however, that before I could get into foreign secret service work I would have to put in a spell at the Ministry of the Interior. They suggested that I should continue with my legal career, my status with the SD remaining a purely "honorary" one without obligations on either side, and meanwhile, I would be freed from all other duties for the SS. I had no hesitation in agreeing to join the SD and enrolled immediately. But I still had to do one last spell of duty as an SS guard, and a fateful and unforgettable one it turned out to be.

The date was June 30, 1934. We were sent to guard the

fashionable Hotel Dreesen at Bad Godesberg. All day strange and disquieting rumors had reached my unit. There were said to be plots, divisions in the Party, and impending disasters. It was whispered that the highest leaders of the Party were coming to the hotel, and I was posted outside the French windows that led from the terrace to the dining room, from which point I could look down over the valley of the Rhine to the mountains beyond. Inside the dining room preparations had been made for a conference, and before long "they" arrived; it seemed the rumors were true. In the dining room were assembled the highest leaders of the Nazi movement; among them I recognized Hitler, Goebbels, and Goering. I could see their changes of expressions and the movement of their lips, though I could not hear what they said.

Meanwhile, black clouds had been gathering over the valley and now the storm broke. As the rain poured down, I pressed myself back into the shelter of the building. Lightning forked across the sky, illuminating the scene with a weird and frightening glow. From time to time Hitler would come to the window and stand staring at the tempest with unseeing eyes. He was clearly laboring under the burden of weighty and difficult decisions.

After dinner the meeting was resumed, then finally with a brusque gesture Hitler brought the discussion to an end: a decision had been made. At once the huge black Mercedes cars drove up and Hitler and his companions got in. Trucks arrived for the guards and we clambered inside, then roared after the car into the night toward the airport at Hangelar near Bonn, where waiting aircraft took off for Munich as soon as the leaders were aboard.

The great purge of Roehm and his followers in the SA had begun.

Roehm's activities in setting up a private militia may have constituted a threat to the state, but this was only the pretext for the monstrous blood bath that Hitler's orders let loose among his own followers that night. The moving force behind the scenes was the General Staff of the Wehrmacht. They had maneuvered Goering into forcing a showdown. Their purpose was the elimination of the more unreliable elements among the Nazis, in particular the radical wing led by Gregor Strasser, who took the socialist aspect of National Socialism too seriously. General Schleicher, however, who had preceded Hitler as

Chancellor, was in no way connected with Roehm or Strasser, and really had nothing to do with the affair. He was shot on the express orders of Hitler himself because he knew too much of the shady financial transactions by means of which Hitler came to power.

In the ambitious Himmler, and the still more ambitious Reinhard Heydrich, Hitler found willing executioners, each of whom seized the opportunity to build up his own power. June 30 marked the ascendancy within the Nazi structure of the SS, whose black uniform with the death's-head insignia I now wore. It was also a crucial step upward for Heydrich. The ruthless cruelty displayed by him that night filled even the most hardened of the Nazi veterans with fear.

I soon started my secret work for the SD. The information I had to obtain concerned academic matters and political and personal relationships at various universities. I was told to go to the lodgings of a Professor H——, a professor of surgery at the University, who would personally hand me my orders. They came in sealed green envelopes directly from the central office of the SD in Berlin. I never received any acknowledgments, however, of my written reports and was left with a feeling of working in the dark; the whole thing began to appear mysterious and unreal.

All the same, I much enjoyed the long conversations with Professor H——, whom I had to visit once or twice a week. Often we talked until late at night. He was an erudite man with a remarkable store of general knowledge and had collected a magnificent library, especially of literature dealing with secret service work.

Sometimes I received orders from a gentleman who looked like a commercial traveler and who always received me in a small hotel. I also established contact with a Mr. K—— S——. He was a highly gifted man who had formerly been a Jesuit Father, and impressed me as the most able and intelligent of these three men. He never asked me for written reports, but sought by questioning and conversing with me to form his own picture of the information I brought him.

After a while, Professor N——, the educationalist who had recruited me into the SD, called on me again and suggested that I should move to Frankfurt to continue my training for the State Law Examination at the Police

Headquarters. This move, which occurred in 1934, brought with it considerable financial advantages. At Frankfurt I always seemed to be assigned to the most interesting and important cases, and I got the impression that my movements were being plotted as though by an unseen hand. I had to investigate the highest Party functionaries suspected of administrative misconduct. Twice I went to Berlin to make reports in person to the Minister of the Interior, Dr. Frick, who supplied me with the necessary documents to enable me to assert myself against the Gauleiters—the district bosses.

Violent quarrels were raging at this time between Frick, Guertner, who was Minister of Justice, and the Gauleiter, or District Chief, of Nuremberg, Julius Streicher. Two SS men had each been sentenced to ten years' imprisonment because one of them had killed a Jew with a hammer. I was convinced that the other was innocent, as apparently he had only lent the hammer to the first man without knowing for what purpose it was wanted. I therefore went into the prison one night and unlocked the door of the man's cell so that he could escape. This "breach of the law" caused the Minister of Justice to remonstrate violently with Streicher.

Presently, without any warning I was sent to France for four weeks, with orders to discover the political views of a certain professor at the Sorbonne, whom I had once mentioned in one of my reports. Shortly after my return from France I was called to Berlin to continue my training in the Ministry of the Interior. I reported to the Personnel Bureau of the Ministry, and was directed to see Dr. Schafer, the Personnel Director of the Gestapo, who handed me a meticulous printed schedule of my future work and activities, including all the places I should have to visit for further instruction and information.

It was an extremely interesting period for me. Officials at all levels were most friendly and courteous and every door was opened to me as though some unseen power was working silently through the complex channels of this huge machine.

One day I was told to report to the chief of Department II [Secret Political Police], SS Oberfuehrer Mueller, who was virtually chief of the Gestapo. Mueller was dry and laconic. Short and broad, with the squarish skull of a peasant and a jutting forehead, he had tense, narrow lips and penetrating brown eyes, hooded by nervously twitching eyelids. His hands were wide and massive, with fingers as square as a matchbox.

This man, who had started his career as an ordinary detective in Munich, was to play a very important role in my life. Although he had worked his way up to the top, he could never forget his origin. He once said to me in his crude Bavarian accent, "One really ought to drive all the intellectuals into a coal mine and then blow it up." Any form of real conversation with him was almost impossible; it consisted on his part almost entirely of coldly phrased questions and was largely an interrogation. Yet all the while he sought to establish an atmosphere of frankness, and by his broad Bavarian speech to suggest a natural geniality. Our first conversation ended by his saying, "Heydrich likes your reports. You've only been sent to us as a matter of routine. Actually you'll work in the main office of the SD, which comes under the Party rather than the government. A pity—I could make better use of you in my department." In spite of the friendly gesture with which he said good-by, his eyes and expression remained quite cold. At that time I did not know the extent of his resentment of the SD.

At last some light had been thrown on the mystery of my advancement. Mueller had said it was Heydrich who was interested in me. So the dreaded chief of the SD himself had been the unseen force guiding me like a pawn on a chessboard through all the channels of the Nazi secret police service.

The next day I presented myself at the Central Bureau of the SD. An SS Oberfuehrer whom I had already met in Frankfurt explained to me the mission of the SD and its aims. The SD was the chief organ of the information service of the Party. Its task was to inform the top Party leaders of all opposition movements and forces at home and abroad. It covered the administration, the Party, industry, the theater, journalism, the police—in fact there was no sphere that was not under the watchful eye of the SD, no place where it did not seek out the first signs of opposition among movements or individuals "hostile to the state."

This tremendous administrative problem was the concern of SS Oberfuehrer Dr. Mehlhorn, and in the ensuing period I worked chiefly with him. This man had built up for Heydrich the machinery with which he could secretly survey every sphere of German life. The material was collected all over Germany by the SD district organizations, which corresponded to the administrative divisions of the country. Each organization had its "honorary" agents—trusted informants placed strategically in all walks of life, in every profession and industry. They were usually men of wide experience in their own fields and were thus in a position to furnish very valuable information, giving special attention to reports on public opinion and reactions to legislation, decrees and other measures taken by the government.

From this material a fortnightly situation report was prepared in the Berlin headquarters to give the leader of Germany a detailed and accurate picture of public opinion.

A file was prepared for each individual whose name appeared in these reports, and the reports cross-indexed against their subject matter. A huge, circular table was constructed on which the files were placed. This table was electrically driven and by pressing a button one man seated at the controls could bring any one of 500,000 cards within easy reach. Up to this time only the information service dealing with Germany had been organized so thoroughly.

The spadework done by Mehlhorn during the preceding years served as a pedestal for Heydrich's power. It was only to be expected that a man of Heydrich's character would discard him as soon as he had served his purpose. Heydrich instigated proceedings against Mehlhorn before a "Court of Honor" in 1937, which led to his dismissal from the service. However, he was sent on a journey round the world and given the task of reporting to Hitler on global developments. His reports on the Far Eastern situation were of substantial and lasting value to the political leadership, but those on the situation and on trends in the United States were utterly misleading, so that an entirely wrong picture of the American scene was presented to Hitler.

2. UNDER HEYDRICH'S ORDERS

Impressions of Heydrich—The case against General von Fritsch—Himmler the mystic—Heydrich's position endangered—"Salon Kitty"—My relations with Frau Heydrich—Her husband's attempts to trap me—My marriage "assisted"

NOT LONG after I had begun my work at headquarters I was called to my first interview with Heydrich, the formidable chief of the SD. It was with considerable apprehension that I walked over to the Gestapo building where he had his office. Now perhaps I would find out what plans he had for me.

When I entered his office Heydrich was sitting behind his desk. He was a tall, impressive figure with a broad, unusually high forehead, small restless eyes as crafty as an animal's and of uncanny power, a long predatory nose, and a wide full-lipped mouth. His hands were slender and rather too long—they made me think of the legs of a spider. His splendid figure was marred by the breadth of his hips, a disturbingly feminine effect which made him appear even more sinister. His voice was much too high for so large a man and his speech was nervous and staccato and, though he scarcely ever finished a sentence, he always managed to express his meaning quite clearly.

My first interview was fairly easygoing. He began by speaking about my family and then about music—Heydrich himself was an accomplished violinist and often gave evenings of chamber music at his home. He asked me many questions about my legal training, and in particular whether I still intended to try to become an associate of X——, a noted barrister in Düsseldorf. He thought this a good idea and said it was important that trained lawyers, less "fossilized" than those of the previous generation and with open minds toward the new state, should enter public life. But this was only a conventional introduction to our talk, and when he began to speak of the organization and extension of the counter-espionage system in Germany and the Political Secret Service abroad, a tone of seriousness and urgency came into his voice and I felt he was trying to inspire a similar response in me.

He never once forgot, however, that he was talking to a subordinate, and sharply criticized certain aspects of my work, warning me against a tendency toward legalistic formality. After an hour and a half he brought the interview to an end, and I walked out of his office overwhelmed by the strength of his personality to an extent that I have never experienced before or since.

When I really got to know Heydrich during the years that followed, I never changed my first opinion of him. This man was the hidden pivot around which the Nazi regime revolved. The development of a whole nation was guided indirectly by his forceful character. He was far superior to all his political colleagues and controlled them as he controlled the vast intelligence machine of the SD.

In order to understand this man, whom I met when he was nearing the peak of his career, one must recall something of his antecedents. After the end of the First World War he joined the German Navy as an officer candidate, then served in the cruiser *Berlin* as a cadet with the future Admiral Canaris as his commanding officer. He was promoted to the rank of lieutenant, but because of his personal conduct and especially his affairs with women he had to appear before an officers' Court of Honor and was forced to apply for his release from the service.

Penniless and unemployed, he at last succeeded in 1931, through SS friends in Hamburg, in obtaining an introduction to Himmler, who in order to try him out assigned to him the drafting of a plan of organization for what was to become the Party's "security service" (SD).

Heydrich had an incredibly acute perception of the moral, human, professional, and political weaknesses of others and he also had the ability to grasp a political situation in its entirety. His unusual intellect was matched by the ever-watchful instincts of a predatory animal, always alert to danger and ready to act swiftly and ruthlessly. Whatever his instinct pinpointed as useful, he adopted, exploited, and then, if necessary, dropped with equal swiftness. Whatever seemed redundant or to offer the slightest threat or inconvenience was thrown out.

He was inordinately ambitious. It seemed as if, in a

pack of ferocious wolves, he must always prove himself the strongest and assume the leadership. He had to be the first, the best, in everything, regardless of the means, whether by deceit, treachery, or violence. Untouched by any pangs of conscience and assisted by an ice-cold intellect, he could carry injustice to the point of extreme cruelty.

Toward his assistants and colleagues and toward the higher Party leaders, such as Rudolf Hess, Hitler's deputy, Martin Bormann, chief of the Reich Chancellery, and the Gauleiters, he operated on the principle of "divide and rule," and even applied this to his relations with Hitler and Himmler. The decisive thing for him was always to know more than others, to know everything about everyone, whether it touched on the political, professional, or most intimate personal aspects of their lives, and to use this knowledge and the weaknesses of others to render them completely dependent on him, from the highest to the lowest. It was this that enabled him to hold and manipulate the balance of power in a milieu full of intrigue and crosscurrents of personal ambition, rivalry, and animosity, while he himself remained in the background. He was a master at playing antagonists off one against the other, feeding each one, under an oath of strict secrecy, with detrimental information about his rival, and getting still more damaging information in return. Heydrich was, in fact, the puppet master of the Third Reich.

He made Hitler dependent on him by fulfilling all his most insane schemes, thus making himself indispensable. He supplied Himmler with brilliant ideas so that he could shine in conferences with Hitler, Hess, Bormann, and the General Staff, and yet would do this so tactfully that Himmler never suspected that these ideas were not his own.

Heydrich's only weakness was his ungovernable sexual appetite. To this he would surrender himself without inhibition or caution, and the calculated control which characterized him in everything else he did left him completely. But in the end he always regained sufficient mastery over himself to prevent serious repercussions.

In February 1938, Heydrich found himself in conflict with the Commander-in-Chief of the German Army, General von Fritsch. One of the shadier characters in his service, Chief Inspector Meisinger, a former Munich po-

lice detective, brought Heydrich what he considered to be
conclusive evidence that General von Fritsch had been
guilty of serious moral offenses. It was quite likely that
Heydrich was delighted to accept at its face value incriminating evidence against the Commander-in-Chief of the
German Army. Be that as it may, he passed the material
on to Himmler and Hitler without checking its validity. By
the time he realized that Meisinger had made a serious
mistake it was too late, and he decided to maintain the
accusation before his superiors. He was willing, in fact,
that the General should be unjustly accused as long as his
own mistake could be covered up.

But the Court of Honor summoned by the Reichswehr,
over which Goering presided—one result of this affair was
serious tension between Goering and Heydrich—brought
the truth to light. The chief witness for the prosecution
gave certain evidence about homosexual practices, but it
was evidence that concerned not von Fritsch the General,
but a cavalry officer called von Frisch—an incredible
blunder to have made. The court established the innocence
of General von Fritsch beyond any doubt. Yet in spite of
this Hitler used the incident to force von Fritsch to resign
"for reasons of ill-health." Von Brauchitsch, later promoted to Field Marshal, replaced him as Commander-in-
Chief of the Army.

During the von Fritsch case I witnessed for the first
time some of the rather strange practices resorted to by
Himmler through his inclination toward mysticism. He
assembled twelve of his most trusted SS leaders in a room
next to the one in which von Fritsch was being questioned
and ordered them all to concentrate their minds on exerting a suggestive influence over the General that would
induce him to tell the truth. I happened to come into the
room by accident, and to see these twelve SS leaders
sitting in a circle, all sunk in deep and silent contempla-
tion, was indeed a remarkable sight.

The SS organization had been built up by Himmler on
the principles of the order of the Jesuits. The service
statutes and spiritual exercises prescribed by Ignatius Loy-
ola formed a pattern which Himmler assiduously tried to
copy. Absolute obedience was the supreme rule; each and
every order had to be accepted without question.

The "Reichsfuehrer SS"—Himmler's title as the supreme head of the SS—was intended to be the counter-

part of the Jesuits' "General of the Order," and the whole structure of the leadership was adopted from these studies of the hierarchic order of the Catholic Church.

A medieval castle near Paderborn in Westphalia was reconstructed and adapted to serve as a kind of SS monastery, the so-called "Webelsburg." Here the secret Chapter of the Order assembled once a year. Each member had his own armchair with an engraved silver name plate, and each had to devote himself to a ritual of spiritual exercises aimed mainly at mental concentration.

Himmler was born in 1900, son of a daughter of a Savoyard greengrocer and a former tutor at the Bavarian Court. He was brought up in the strictest observance of the Catholic faith but soon drifted away from the Church, possibly out of hatred of his despotic father, though not until after his father's death did he dare to leave the Church. His father had intended him to become a farmer, but, having served as an ensign in the First World War, he joined the Hitler movement after Germany's defeat. Already in 1926 he was Reichsfuehrer der Schutzstaffel (SS) or chief of the Security Echelon—Hitler's bodyguard.

Before the sitting of the Court of Honor that was to try Genral von Fritsch, I was told to report to Heydrich and to arm myself with a service pistol and an ample supply of ammunition. When I arrived, Heydrich invited me to dine with him in his office. On the way to dinner he said, "I've heard you're an excellent shot with a pistol." I said that I was.

We sat down, Heydrich, his adjutant, and I, and ate in silence. Though I was mystified by the whole affair I was careful not to ask questions, for Heydrich was obviously in a state of extreme tension. After dinner he took a large number of aspirins. Then suddenly he said, without any preamble, "If they don't start marching from Potsdam during the next hour and a half, the greatest danger will have passed."

Gradually he became more relaxed and then began to explain. Through informants within the army, Heydrich had learned that officers of the General Staff, outraged at the shameful proceedings against their popular Commander-in-Chief, were contemplating the strongest countermeasures, and that the officers in Potsdam had even discussed a resort to force against the regime. Heydrich knew that if they were going to strike they would do so that night. He had, of course, taken the fullest security precautions but remained so nervous that, knowing of my prowess as a marksman, he wanted me near him that evening.

Some time after one o'clock in the morning I was allowed to go. Walking out of the building with me, the adjutant said softly, "There has been no evidence of great heroism tonight." I shook my head.

This affair certainly damaged Heydrich's position for a time and it took all his skill and cunning to re-establish himself. He immediately replaced "M," appointing Dr. Best as Investigating Criminal Director of the Gestapo.

From the first Heydrich had been impressed by my work and my reports, and as our working relationship progressed and I grew to know him better I began to be aware of his intentions. Basically, his attitude toward me was the same as to all his subordinates. It was a sort of cat-and-mouse game, played in terms of trickery and deception, Heydrich always playing the part of the cat, never resting until he had got the mouse completely in his power, to be struck down at the slightest sign of escape.

In my case, he met with no success at first. Outside my work I came to be of some personal value to Heydrich as a means toward social contacts in spheres which he would not otherwise have got into—the intellectual and cultural circles of Berlin society. His wife, a cool Nordic beauty, not without pride and ambition of her own, yet completely enslaved by Heydrich, was glad to find in me someone who could satisfy her hunger for the better things of life—her longing for more intelligent and cultivated society in the world of literature and art.

When Heydrich first became aware of his wife's cultural aspirations, he was suspicious. But in spite of the subservience to which he had reduced her, Frau Heydrich retained a strong personality. Eventually Heydrich gave in with a good grace and took up riding, went to concerts and the theater, which the three of us enjoyed together, and began to frequent the best circles in Berlin society.

Unknown to me, however, he was using this new relationship between his wife and me to set a trap. We would spend afternoons or evenings playing bridge, in what he called "the dear intimacy of the family circle," where he would act the part of the devoted husband, and the very next evening I would get a telephone call from him—his voice now assuming a suggestive leer—saying, "This evening we must go out together—in mufti. We'll have dinner somewhere, and then 'go places.' "

During dinner his conversation would become obscene. He would try to make me drunk as we prowled from bar to bar, but I always excused myself on the grounds of not feeling quite up to the mark, and he never succeeded.

One evening he conceived the idea that it might be a good thing for the SD to set up an establishment where important visitors from other countries could be "entertained" in a discreet atmosphere and where they would be offered seductive feminine companionship. In such an atmosphere the most rigid diplomat might be induced to unbend and reveal useful information.

Not long afterward I received orders from Heydrich to establish such an "institution," as the increasing number of visiting foreign diplomats and their entourages made some such place almost a social necessity. The establishment was to be called "Salon Kitty."

Through an apparently innocuous businessman, a large house was rented in a fashionable district of Berlin. The furnishing and decoration were supervised by a leading architect, and then the technical specialists went to work. Double walls were built for the incorporation of microphones. These were connected by automatic transmission to tape recorders which would record every word spoken throughout the house. Three of our department's technical experts, bound by oath, were put in charge of this apparatus. The ostensible owner of the house was provided with the necessary domestic and catering staff for the establishment to be able to offer the best service, food, and drink.

The next problem was to find hostesses. I refused to have anything to do with this. As I pointed out to Heydrich, my department supplied only the most valuable of women agents and I could not afford to assign them to such work.

One of Heydrich's underlings, Arthur Nebe, chief of the Criminal Police, who for many years had worked in the vice squad, agreed to take on the task. From all the great cities of Europe he recruited the most highly qualified and cultivated ladies of the demimonde, and I regret to say that quite a few ladies from the upper crust of German society were only too willing to serve their country in this manner.

"Salon Kitty" certainly brought results—the most surprising information was yielded by some of the guests. They were mainly diplomatic secrets which Heydrich, with his usual astuteness, would use against Ribbentrop and his Foreign Ministry, for no one, not even Ribbentrop himself, knew to whom the "Salon Kitty" really belonged. One of the biggest catches was the Italian Foreign Minister, Count Ciano, who went there with other important diplomats.

Heydrich, of course, missed no opportunity for what he described as a "personal inspection" of the establishment, but on these occasions I was given special orders to turn off the listening and recording apparatus. Out of this came one of Heydrich's characteristic intrigues.

Having told Himmler about "Salon Kitty" and of the importance of the information picked up there, he went on to complain that during one of his "inspections" I had not turned off the recording apparatus, in spite of strict orders to do so. Afterward he called me into his office and said, "I don't know how Himmler has got hold of the information, but he says that in spite of my orders you had the listening apparatus on when I inspected 'Salon Kitty.'"

This plan misfired, however, as I immediately got sworn statements, which I put before Heydrich, from the entire technical staff, showing that I had carried out his orders.

His next plot against me was more dangerous. There was a conference of SS and police leaders on the island of Fehmarn in the Baltic Sea. Heydrich's wife came from the island, where they owned a lovely summer villa. After the conference, Heydrich, who had been a fighter pilot, flew back to Berlin in his own plane. I, still having one free day, remained there. In the afternoon Frau Heydrich asked me to drive her to the Ploener Lake. It was a harmless excursion. We had coffee and talked about art, literature, and concerts—in fact, all those things which interested her so much and which she had so little opportunity to talk about at other times. Before it grew dark we drove back.

Four days later in Berlin I was told by SS Gruppen-fuehrer Mueller, chief of the Gestapo, that Heydrich wanted us to go out with him "in mufti." I thought it was going to be one of his usual escapades and accepted the invitation without a thought, although at that time I was not exactly on good terms with Mueller. As is often the case with people who continually feel their lives to be in danger, I was superstitious and had a rather uncomfortable premonition about the evening. But I found Heydrich at his most charming and this feeling was soon dissipated. He did not want to hear, as he usually did, about the latest espionage cases, but said that for once we would not speak of service matters at all.

After supper at a well-known restaurant, we went to an obscure bar near the Alexanderplatz. I noticed that the barman looked a most sinister individual. Mueller ordered the drinks and handed me mine. Our conversation was casual, mainly about Heydrich's private plane, until suddenly Mueller said to me, "Well, how was it at the Ploener Lake? Did you have a good time?" I looked at Heydrich; his face was very pale. I quickly pulled myself together and asked him if he wanted to know about my excursion with his wife.

In a cold, sibilant voice, he said, "You have just drunk some poison. It could kill you within six hours. If you tell me the complete and absolute truth, I'll give you an antidote—but I want the truth."

I did not believe a word of it—Heydrich was quite capable of making just such a grisly joke with a perfectly straight face—and yet . . . I felt the tension within me expanding till it seemed as though my heart was about to burst. But I had nothing to hide, and speaking as calmly as I could I told him truthfully about the events of that afternoon.

Mueller listened to what I had to say very carefully. Once he interrupted me: "After you had coffee, you went for a walk with the chief's wife. Why do you hide that? You must realize surely that you were being watched all the time?"

Again, as truthfully as I could, I described our fifteen-minute walk and the conversation that took place.

After I had finished, Heydrich sat motionless and withdrawn for several minutes. At last he looked at me with glittering eyes, and said, "Well, I suppose I must believe you, but you will give me your word of honor that you won't attempt this sort of escapade again."

By this time I had managed to get hold of myself and I said, quite aggressively, "A word of honor secured in this sort of way is just an extortion. First I must ask you to let me have the antidote"—it was always best to be on the safe side in dealings with Heydrich—"then I'll give you my word of honor. As a former naval officer would you consider it honorable to act in any other way?"

Heydrich eyed me narrowly. He hated an appeal to his honor, but he nodded, and I was given—somewhat to my surprise—a dry martini. Was it my imagination, or did it taste peculiar? Certainly it seemed to have an added dash of bitters. I gave Heydrich my word of honor, then in view of what had passed between us I begged to be excused. But he wouldn't hear of it, and we had to continue the evening's merrymaking. Once more he had failed to entrap me.

In the end it was entirely by my own doing that I put myself in his power. In 1940 I was engaged to be married for the second time, and as a member of the SS I had to submit *Ahnenpapiere* or racial heredity certificates. Then I discovered that my fiancée's mother was Polish. To get official approval for such a marriage was bound to be difficult, for I knew only too well how the Party leadership felt by now about Poland. So at the end of one of my routine reports to Heydrich I asked him for his help in a personal matter and told him of my difficulty. Rather to my surprise, he agreed to do all he could to persuade Himmler to give his official permission. He told me to send him all the heredity documents of my fiancée's family and to include two photographs of her.

Within four days I received a copy of an order from Himmler to the *Rasse und Siedlungshauptamt* [the Race and Settlement Office], giving me official permission to marry. Heydrich handed me the order with his best wishes. (He also returned my fiancée's photographs, on which Himmler had colored her lipstick and eyebrows with green pencil and added a note describing them as "exaggerated.") I wondered what had induced them both to grant me this special dispensation.

I had been married about six months when one day my secretary handed me a folder marked *"Geheime Reichssache"* [Secret Business in the Reich]. This was the highest secret classification then in use, employed, mainly, for communications between the chiefs of departments. But as at least eighty such folders went through my hands every day, I opened this one as a matter of course. There lay a secret report from the State Police in Posen addressed personally to Mueller, the Gestapo chief. It was a detailed surveillance report on my wife's family in Poland. Among other things it contained a reference to my mother-in-law's sister, who was married to a Jewish millowner. Heydrich had finally succeeded in gaining a hold over me, and through a strange twist of fate it was I who had given him the means. Now he was satisfied and stopped all other efforts to entrap me.

But in tracing the course of Heydrich's machinations against me I have gone ahead of my narrative, and must return to 1937.

3. THE REICHSWEHR AND THE RED ARMY

A grim trade—Collaboration between German and Russian Staffs—Opposition from General Hoffman and Rechberg—Suspicion of Marshal Tukhachevsky—The Russo-German Pact foreshadowed—Sale of Tukhachevsky's dossier to Stalin's envoy

AT THE beginning of 1937 I was instructed to prepare for Heydrich a study of the past relations between the Reichswehr and the Red Army. The man who brought me the assignment was a country gentleman from Pomerania named Jahnke, who for many years had been a key figure in the German Secret Service. Later I had a chance to look into his personal files—three crates full of them—and to acquaint myself with the life story of this remarkable man.

Jahnke was the son of a Pomeranian landowner. Before the First World War he emigrated to America and drifted about there until he finally joined the border police of the United States Immigration Service. His duties brought him into contact with Chinese groups in San Francisco (the Chinatown of that city is said to be the largest in the Occidental world) and through these contacts Jahnke established himself in the strangest trade. The Chinese, whose religion embraces what amounts almost to a worship of their native land, wanted to ship home to China the bodies of relatives who had died in the United States, but for hygienic reasons the United States authorities had forbidden this practice. Jahnke had the brilliant idea of having zinc boxes made that would serve as airtight containers for wooden coffins. These he shipped to Shanghai and Hong Kong without any difficulty and for every dead Chinese thus returned to the land of his fathers Jahnke received one thousand dollars. Within a short time he was a very rich man. So grateful were the Chinese that with the most solemn rites they made him a member of the family of the great Sun Yat-sen. This, of course, provided

Jahnke with the best possible contacts in China. (Madame Chiang Kai-shek, for instance, is a member of this family.) Later he also developed valuable contacts with the Japanese Secret Service.

During the First World War, Jahnke worked for the German Secret Service. The great strikes of the dock and transport workers in the east coast harbors of the United States resulted from his activities. When later he returned to Germany, he became Rudolf Hess's expert on intelligence and espionage. Politically he was interested only in questions of major importance. He was a big, heavy man with the thick skull of a Pomeranian peasant, and when he sat opposite you, impassive, with his eyes half closed, he gave an impression of reticence and cunning. He liked to live in great style.

After I had assembled my material I made a verbal report to Heydrich at his hunting lodge—it was almost in the nature of an historical lecture. The subject was one that grew in importance in the later years of the Nazi regime: the basic conflict in German policy between an orientation toward western Europe, and toward Russia.

Surprisingly enough, the greatest support within Germany for a policy of co-operation with Soviet Russia came from the army officers of the General Staff. Since 1923 there had been collaboration on the training of officers and in the exchange of technical information between the German and Red armies. In addition, in exchange for certain patents Germany was allowed to build up her output of arms inside the Soviet Union. At the same time it was Stalin's policy to support German nationalism in the hope of turning Germany against the Western *bourgeoisie*, and accordingly he directed the German Communist party to regard not the National Socialist party of Hitler but the Social Democrats as their chief enemy.

The chief center of opposition to the pro-Russian party of the German General Staff was among the German industrialists, who hoped for a union of the civilized powers against the dangers of Bolshevism. Under the leadership of General Hoffman, who had headed the German delegation at Brest-Litovsk and had negotiated the armistice of 1918, and Arnold Rechberg, a leading German industrialist, many efforts had been made for a fusion of European political, military, and industrial powers against the common enemy. For a time General Ludendorff had

lent his support to the plan, but on Hoffman's death in
1927 Ludendorff lost faith in the Western Allies, and it
became impossible to carry through such a policy against
the opposition of the German General Staff.

This, in brief, was the background of the report I made
to Heydrich in 1937, little realizing at that time the
historic decisions which it foreshadowed.

Heydrich had received information from a White Russian emigré, General Skoblin, that Tukhachevsky, Marshal of the Soviet Union, was plotting with the German
General Staff to overthrow the Stalin regime.

Heydrich at once grasped the tremendous importance
of this piece of intelligence. If used correctly, a blow
could be struck at the leadership of the Red Army from
which it would not recover for many years.

Jahnke was of a different opinion. He warned Heydrich
that Skoblin might be playing a double game, and that the
information might have been concocted by the Russians
and passed on by Skoblin on Stalin's orders. Jahnke
thought Stalin had a double purpose in this: he wanted to
weaken the German General Staff by arousing Heydrich's
suspicions against them, and, at the same time, would be
able to act against the Soviet military clique, of which
Tukhachevsky was the head. Jahnke thought that because
of internal problems in the Soviet government, Stalin did
not wish to initiate proceedings against the generals himself and would prefer that the incriminating material
should come from abroad.

Heydrich remained unconvinced by Jahnke's subtle reasoning. Indeed, his suspicions were turned against Jahnke,
whose viewpoint, he felt, was motivated by loyalty toward
the General Staff. Heydrich at once placed Jahnke under
house arrest for three months.

Meanwhile Heydrich submitted Skoblin's information
on Tukhachevsky to Hitler. The material itself was not
complete. It contained no documentary proof of active
participation by the German Army leaders in Tukhachevsky's conspiracy. Heydrich recognized this, and himself
added fictitious material aimed at incriminating the German generals. He felt himself justified in this if he could
thereby weaken the growing strength of the Red Army
which was threatening the superiority of the Reichswehr.
It must be remembered that Heydrich was convinced of
the authenticity of Skoblin's information, and in view of

what subsequently happened I think he was proved right. His forgeries were therefore merely to strengthen and lend further conviction to information that was in itself valid.

Hitler at this moment was faced with the momentous decision whether to align himself with the Western Powers or against them. And it was within this larger decision that he had also to make up his mind how to use the material that Heydrich had brought him. On the one hand, support for Tukhachevsky might have meant the end of Russia as a world power—but failure would have involved Germany in war; on the other hand, to unmask Tukhachevsky might be helping Stalin to strengthen his forces, or might equally well push him into destroying a large part of his General Staff. Hitler finally decided against Tukhachevsky and intervened in the internal affairs of the Soviet Union on Stalin's side.

This decision to back Stalin instead of Tukhachevsky and the generals determined the whole course of German policy until 1941 and can be rightly regarded as one of the most fateful decisions of our time. It eventually brought Germany into a temporary alliance with the Soviet Union and encouraged Hitler to attack the West before turning against Russia. Once Hitler had made his decision, Heydrich, of course, supported him.

Hitler expressly ordered that the German Army Staff should be kept from knowing anything of the contemplated move against Tukhachevsky, fearing that the Soviet Marshal might be forewarned by them. So one night Heydrich dispatched two special squads to break into the secret archives of the General Staff and of the Abwehr, the Army Intelligence Service, run by Admiral Canaris. Burglary experts from the headquarters of the Criminal Police accompanied the squads. In three places they found and removed material concerning the collaboration of the German General Staff and the Red Army. Important material was also found in Admiral Canaris' files. To conceal the break-in, fires were started which soon destroyed all evidence of it. In the resulting confusion the special squads escaped safely and unnoticed.

It has been claimed that the material assembled by Heydrich to implicate Tukhachevsky consisted largely of forgeries. Actually, very little of it was forged, indeed no more than was necessary to fill in certain gaps. This is corroborated by the fact that the entire and remarkably voluminous dossier was made ready and presented to Hitler within the brief space of four days.

After careful consideration it was decided to contact Stalin through the following channels: one of our diplomatic agents, who worked under SS Standartenfuehrer Boehme, was a German emigrant living in Prague. Through him, Boehme made contact with a trusted friend of Dr. Benes, then President of the Czechoslovak Republic. Dr. Benes at once wrote a personal letter to Stalin, whose reply came back to Heydrich through the same channels, asking him to establish contact with a certain member of the Soviet Embassy in Berlin. We did so, and the Russian at once flew to Moscow and returned accompanied by a personal envoy of Stalin, who presented special credentials from Jezhov, then chief of the GPU.

Stalin asked what price we had set on the material. Neither Hitler nor Heydrich had considered that there would be any financial prospects in the affair. However, to preserve appearances, Heydrich asked for three million gold roubles—which Stalin's emissary, after no more than a cursory examination of the documents, paid at once.

The material against Tukhachevsky was handed over to the Russians in the middle of May 1937. As is known, the trial of Tukhachevsky was held in secret. The court was composed chiefly of Soviet Marshals and Red Army leaders. The indictment was prepared by a Military Council and the prosecutor was Andrei Vishinsky.

Tukhachevsky and his fellow-conspirators were arrested on the evening of June 4, 1937. After he had made an unsuccessful attempt at suicide, the trial began at ten o'clock on June 11; it ended at nine o'clock the same evening. According to the *Tass* dispatches of that day, all the defendants confessed their guilt. Practically no other details of the case were made public. Vishinsky's summing up for the prosecution took barely twenty minutes. He demanded expulsion of the defendants from the Red Army and their death by shooting. Sentence was executed four hours later. On Stalin's orders, Marshal Bluecher (who himself fell a victim to one of the later purges) commanded the firing squad. Of the judges of the court, only Voroshilov and Budienny survive today.

I personally had to destroy most of the three million roubles paid to us by the Russians, for it was all in bills of high denominations, the numbers of which had obviously been listed by the GPU. Whenever one of our agents tried to use them inside the Soviet Union, he was arrested within a remarkably short time.

Thus the affair of Marshal Tukhachevsky was a preparatory step toward the *rapprochement* between Hitler and Stalin. It was the turning point that marked Hitler's decision to secure his eastern front by an alliance with Russia, while preparing to attack the West.

4. THE OCCUPATION OF AUSTRIA AND CZECHOSLOVAKIA

Preparations for the Anschluss—Hitler's reception in Vienna—A bomb on the route—Hitler's visit to Mussolini—Security precautions in Italy—Attitude of the Sudeten Germans—Secret order for the dismemberment of Czechoslovakia—Germany assumes "protectorship" over the Czechs

AT THE beginning of 1938 I was instructed to assemble and edit all the reports that were to be submitted to Hitler on the attitude of Italy toward the contemplated annexation of Austria and its incorporation into the German Reich. Great importance was also attached, of course, to the attitude of the other Western Powers toward this matter. The decisive event was the resignation of Anthony Eden. We soon learned that his successor at the Foreign Office, Lord Halifax, did not view the Anschluss of Austria with hostility. This attitude must have influenced Hitler's decision considerably.

The intelligence material from Austria itself was so plentiful that the main problem was how to cope with it. The thousands of Nazis who had recently fled from Austria provided us with all the contacts we needed.

On February 12, 1938, Kurt von Schuschnigg, the Austrian Chancellor, conferred with Hitler at Obersalzberg. He promised to limit and repress the activities of the anti-German "Fatherland Front." When it proved obvious, as it soon did, that he could not see his way to carrying out this promise, Hitler decided to force the pace. To forestall invasion by the German Army, Schuschnigg resigned on March 11. Seyss-Inquart, the leader of the Austrian Nazis, at once took over the government. The order to march was given to the German Army by Hitler.

The same night that the German Army marched into Austria, March 11, I was ordered to fly to Vienna with

Himmler. We had with us a company of Waffen SS, the purely military formation of the SS, and some members of the so-called "Austrian Legion" which had been formed in Germany.

We took off from Berlin-Tempelhof in two large transports. It was a rather unpleasant flight. Both aircraft were badly overloaded and weather conditions were difficult. Most of the way we lost sight of the ground and also lost radio contact with Vienna.

During the flight Himmler discussed with me various administrative problems which had arisen in connection with the setting up of the new "Ostmark"—as Austria was officially called from then on. We had gone aft in the plane to be further away from the engine noise and Himmler was leaning against a door when I noticed that the safety catch was not on. At any moment the door might have opened under the weight of his body. I quickly grasped him by his coat and jerked him away. He glared at me furiously, but when I showed him the door was unlatched he thanked me and said that if the opportunity ever arose he would be happy to do as much for me.

We finally landed in Vienna at four o'clock in the morning. The administrative change-over to German rule was taking place at that very moment and the government of Dr. Seyss-Inquart was firmly established. The Bundeshaus, the seat of the Central Government of the Austrian Confederacy, was a scene of tremendous activity. There was a continual round of conferences and meetings. In the anterooms and corridors excited men were haggling for those government posts which had not yet been filled.

A huge crowd filled the square in front of the building. Police duties had already been taken over by the Austrian SA and SS, wearing white armbands. Almost unnoticed by the crowds, Dr. Miklas, the President of the Austrian Republic, and Skubl, the Minister of Police, left the building bent and dejected.

Meanwhile, Heydrich had arrived. I reported to him on the situation and he told me to secure all the files and documents of the chief of the Austrian Secret Service, Colonel Ronge. The papers that I found were not very up-to-date, though there was some interesting material on deciphering codes. Colonel Ronge himself expressed his willingness to work in future for the German Secret Service.

During the next fortnight I had to work out draft laws and decrees—in particular, those concerned with the police and the security system—providing for the administrative integration of the Ostmark into the Reich. I also had to suggest the necessary changes of personnel in these departments. It was a rather heavy task and was not made any easier by continual interruptions.

Hitler's reception in Vienna was a great personal triumph. Never, except perhaps during his Italian visit, have I seen such tremendous, enthusiastic, and joyous crowds. Shortly before his arrival, without any warning I found myself put in charge of the security measures for his tour of Vienna. For the following twelve hours I was to be solely and completely responsible for the Fuehrer's safety.

As minute-to-minute reports of his progress came through by telephone to the central police bureau, a huge map was marked with little white flags to show the course of his tour. The security measures in all districts seemed to be working perfectly when suddenly a report came in that three suspected persons had been arrested at a bridge. They had admitted that the bridge was mined and that they were there to set off the charge. I was asked whether Hitler's route should be changed and a new one prepared. I knew how much he disliked having to change a set program, so in view of this information the responsibility of letting him proceed weighed very heavily upon me. He was due at the bridge in eight minutes. If only I could reach it before him, and make certain that everything was safe. . . .

I placed another official temporarily in charge of the command post and drove rapidly to the spot. It took me a few minutes to examine the explosive charges and try to make sure that they had been made harmless. As far as I could see, everything looked all right. I could now hear Hitler's entourage approaching and the next moment his car was on the bridge. He passed over it safely and with a feeling of immense relief I returned to the central bureau. That evening I was very glad to turn my responsibilities back to Mueller.

In spite of reports of increasing tension between Hitler and Mussolini over the annexation of Austria, the Duce had acquiesced. Soon after his triumphal entry into Vienna, Hitler therefore paid Mussolini a visit in Italy to show

the world that the friendship and unity of purpose between them remained unbroken.

I flew ahead with Mueller to prepare the security measures for the visit. The Italian authorities proved extremely
co-operative; we had only to express a wish in order for it
to be fulfilled. They made the greatest effort to impress us
with their efficiency, their Fascist discipline, the potency of
their weapons, and with displays of grandiose pomp and
tradition.

Their security preparations were thorough and far-
reaching. On certain streets along the proposed route of
Hitler's tour they had erected wooden posts moored in
concrete with heavy iron chains stretched between them.
In view of the excitability of the Latin temperament, this
precaution, as we soon saw, was not exaggerated. My men
drove along the route repeatedly and made searches in all
the houses overlooking it, while the Italians secured signed
guarantees from all the householders that they would be
responsible for the actions of everyone inside their houses.

The Italians also arrested over six thousand suspicious
persons and placed them in preventive custody. Border
control and control of passports within Italy were tight-
ened up, and to supplement these precautions I placed
about eighty of my ablest detectives at key points along
the various routes of Hitler's tour. I also assigned them to
the banquets and various other entertainments planned in
Rome, Naples, and Florence.

I wished to take advantage of this opportunity to com-
bine the arrangement of security measures with an attempt to get a fuller picture of the intelligence situation in
Italy. So I selected five hundred of the best linguists in the
SD and sent them into Italy as tourists. They were organized in the well-known system of cells of three, which I
had adopted from the Russians. Their chief mission was to
look out for anything which might seem suspicious in
connection with Hitler's visit and report it at once. They
were also to note and report on all evidence of popular
feeling in Italy and of the attitude of the Italian people
toward the Fascist regime. When these reports were assembled later I had a comprehensive picture of the situation in Italy.

Hitler's visit passed off without any serious incident. He
rode through the streets of the Italian cities by the side of
Mussolini, and the adoring populace cheered themselves

hoarse. The Via Triumphalis was floodlit as brightly as if it were midday, and the Colosseum had been turned into a sea of colored flame. There was only one anxious moment in Rome: Hitler and Mussolini had left their car to admire the beauties of an ancient fountain and the crowd in a frenzy of adulation broke through the police cordon. My agents, whom I had placed as observers at this point, reported to me over the telephone that they had lost sight of Hitler in the confusion. I suffered several extremely anxious minutes till the *carabinieri* drove the crowd back and re-established control of the situation.

In Naples there was one rather embarrassing incident. Hitler was to accompany the King of Italy in inspecting a guard of honor. As the Fuehrer was to attend a gala performance at the San Carlo Opera immediately afterward, he changed into evening clothes before the inspection and thus walked along the ranks of the guard in tails. The King, however, walked beside him in uniform. As a result of this, Hitler immediately dismissed the chief protocol officer, von Buelow Schwandte.

When Hitler left Italy on May 28, we were all convinced that the military alliance he desired was a foregone conclusion. On the day of his return he delivered an address lasting two hours to the highest leaders of the Party, the state, and the army. He ordered the strengthening of the Luftwaffe, the formation of new army units, and the beginning of the construction of the new western defense wall—the Siegfried Line, which was built under the direction of the engineer, Todt. Hitler spoke openly of the necessity of strengthening Germany's military preparedness to the point where, within two or three months, she would be ready to deal with any contingency of war. "Then," Hitler said, "we will shatter Czechoslovakia!"

Secret Service work in Czechoslovakia was placed under the direction of the political branch of the SD. As in Austria, conditions were again favorable for the establishment of contacts. The Sudeten German party of Konrad Henlein, at this point, only demanded autonomy for the Poles, Hungarians, and Slovaks, also contributed valuable information. The intelligence material was so plentiful that in order to handle all the incoming messages special telegraph lines running direct to Berlin had to be installed at two points on the German-Czech frontier.

Heydrich had a special department whose task it was to

maintain a continual check on the Sudeten German party
and on Henlein, for the Party was by no means united in
its aims, nor at that time completely under Hitler's control. The Nazi wing of the Party, led by Karl Hermann
Frank, who was later Minister of State of the Protectorate
of Bohemia-Moravia, pursued a policy that aimed at the
entire destruction of the Czechoslovak Republic, while
Henlein, at this point, only demanded autonomy for the
three million Sudeten Germans. But, after considerable
pressure from Heydrich and other German quarters, Henlein capitulated completely to Hitler's demands at the
conference held in July 1938.

There was a serious divergence of opinion between
Berlin and the leaders of the Sudeten German party regarding the much-discussed fact-finding and mediation
mission of Lord Runciman. The British Secret Service was
quite well informed about this and one of their agents,
Colonel Christie, who had already conferred several times
with Henlein, met him again at the beginning of August
1938, in Zurich. I received a special order from Heydrich
to investigate their conversations, and to keep Henlein
under close observation. This surveillance was to be carried out in such a way that Henlein should be aware of
it—for the chief purpose was to remind him of his prom-
ises to Hitler.

When Colonel Christie saw how completely the Sudeten
leader had given way to Hitler's demands, he was astonished. At their meeting Henlein declared that to wait any
longer would be impossible, both for the Sudeten German
party and for Hitler, and if necessary the problem would
have to be solved by force. It was at this time that Hitler
made his famous Nuremberg speech, threatening the
Czechoslovak government and rejecting any solution based
on the establishment of an autonomous Sudeten state.

There followed the historic visit of Neville Chamberlain
to Berchtesgaden on September 15, 1938, the British-
German conference at Godesberg, and then—Munich.

The preparations for taking over the administration of
the Sudeten territories were carried out mainly at the
Hotel Dreesen in Dresden. I was sent there and for eight
days helped prepare the necessary decrees and draft legislation.

Already in the first days of October 1938, it became
quite clear to me from various remarks made by Heydrich

that Hitler was aiming at the total destruction of Czechoslovakia, and would not be satisfied with the far-reaching economic concessions which the Prague government had granted him.

In January 1939, Hitler called Heydrich and other chief officials of the Secret Service to a conference at which he gave the following secret order: "The foreign policy of Germany demands that the Czechoslovak Republic be broken up and destroyed within the next few months—if necessary by force of arms. To prepare and facilitate the moves against Czechoslovakia, it appears expedient to support and stimulate the endeavors of the Slovaks in their movement for autonomy. After that it will be quite easy for Germany to deal with the remaining Czech portion of the Republic."

Hitler stressed the secret nature of this order; for the time being no other department of the Foreign Office, army, or Party, was to know of it. The order was carried out by the Secret Service, and both intelligence and political operations were planned in detail and with the usual care. Each step that was worked out was first submitted to Hitler for his approval.

Our main points of contact were with the heterogeneous currents of the Slovak nationalist movement, and after unsuccessful negotiations with various Slovak groups within the Czechoslovak government we finally established an understanding with an opposition group led by Dr. Joseph Tiso.

In March, Hitler decided the time had come to move against Czechoslovakia. During the night of March 12, two representatives of the German Secret Service had a final and decisive conference with Dr. Tiso. He declared himself ready to proclaim the sovereignty of Slovakia under German protection, and on March 13, was flown to Berlin in a special aircraft of the German Secret Service.

Meanwhile, to provoke a deepening of the tension between the Slovaks and the central government, terrorist squads of the German Secret Service had been sent into Slovakia.

Hitler was able to complete the discussions with Dr. Tiso on the proclamation of Slovak autonomy before the arrival of Dr. Hacha, President of the Czechoslovak Republic, who, when he visited Hitler, was faced with a *fait accompli*.

On March 14, Dr. Tiso proclaimed the founding of the autonomous Slovak Republic, and the next day Hitler and Hacha signed the well-known agreement establishing the protectorate of Greater Germany over the Czech people. This was followed immediately by the peaceful occupation of Czechoslovakia by German troops.

In order to be the first to arrive at the Hradshin, the ancient and historic castle in Prague, Hitler, with his entourage and SS guards, raced through the night at breakneck speed over icy roads, passing the advancing German columns on the way. When we got there I had to select suitable offices and *lebensraum* for Hitler in the castle.

The SD and the German Security Police at once took over control of the police, working very closely, however, with their Czech colleagues. The Czech police force was an exceptional organization, the men having been most carefully selected and given excellent training. This greatly impressed Himmler. "Exceptional human material!" he exclaimed. "I shall take them all into the Waffen SS."

Some important documents of the Czechoslovak Military and Political Secret Service were secured, and life very quickly returned to normal.

5. ACTIVE ESPIONAGE

My first "field trip"—An assessment of Dakar—Practical problems of espionage—Prelude to the sinking of the Royal Oak—The case of Lieutenant-Colonel Sosnovski— A Polish spy ring uncovered

DURING the summer of 1938, Hitler's thoughts were turning more and more to the approaching war with the West. He discussed the situation with Himmler, who in turn discussed it with Heydrich, and Heydrich with me. Hitler spoke contemptuously of President Roosevelt, and called America "a Jewish rubbish heap." He was sure that once the war had started Germany would overrun the West, but he did concede the possibility that Great Britain, together with the United States, might attempt a counter-attack against the European Continent from North Africa. But he concluded that the west coast of Africa hardly offered sufficient harbor facilities for such an action; nor did North Africa provide a suitable hinterland for the deployment of modern machines of war.

It was this last point of Hitler's rambling exposition that turned out to be of immediate consequence to me. Himmler, always eager to see directives for concrete action in Hitler's remarks, at once decided, in consultation with Heydrich, to survey the situation of the West African coastal region and its harbors. And so in the autumn of 1938, I was given my first job of active espionage. Heydrich wanted me to compile a full report on the harbor at Dakar, the chief French naval station in Africa. No one, he warned me, not even my immediate family, must know of my assignment. It would be officially camouflaged— ostensibly I would be going on a "business trip" round Germany for about eighteen days. I promised Heydrich that no one should know the true nature of my job, and until this moment I have never revealed it.

Heydrich wanted me to find out about the condition

and nature of the harbor installations and whether they could be extended and enlarged fairly easily. He also wanted me to secure from the harbor authorities charts, maps, statistics, and, in fact, whatever documents I could lay hands on. He gave me a Leica camera specially designed for the job, a Dutch passport (I was given the identity of the son of a Dutch diamond merchant who had just wound up his business affairs in Germany), and a large amount in foreign currencies. Everything had been most carefully prepared—my itinerary, the flight schedule, and addresses of contacts in Madrid and Lisbon. Finally I boarded the plane for Spain.

During the long flight I went over the details of my mission and tried to prepare myself mentally for the task ahead. In the beginning I had accepted the assignment with great enthusiasm, but now I began to have misgivings.

At the airport I met my first unexpected difficulty. The specially constructed Leica aroused intense interest among the customs officers and it required much explanation, reinforced by considerable financial outlay, to get the camera through.

My contact in Lisbon was one of Jahnke's collaborators—a Japanese—and a close friendship quickly developed between us, which in later years proved extremely valuable. When we discussed the practical problems of my mission, my Japanese friend advised me not to take the Leica, no matter how good it might be, but instead to get another camera in Dakar. He also emphasized that on missions of this nature it was best to work as quickly as possible and never to carry large sums of money. As I discussed my plans with him they had to undergo one revision after another. My first encounter with the practical realities of this type of work made me realize that things were quite different on the spot to what they had seemed from behind a desk in Berlin.

On arriving at Dakar, I went to stay, as arranged, with a Portuguese family of Jewish descent. My host was a merchant in the gold and diamond trade, and both he and his partner in Lisbon were working for us. He had been informed of my mission through "business correspondence" with Lisbon and had prepared everything for my arrival.

After five days of hard work, my Portuguese host was

able to secure valuable details of the harbor facilities from the port authorities. These were posted at once to Lisbon, disguised in business correspondence as descriptions of wares and samples. I no longer remember the exact sum the partners spent for us in Lisbon and Dakar, but it was a very considerable amount.

Carefully arranged lunches in a small intimate circle brought me into contact with key men from marine underwriters' firms, and Portuguese and French shipowners. Through them I gained a very good picture of the general situation, and casual remarks dropped at these luncheons provided me with much useful information about the harbor at Dakar.

The idea of taking photographs still troubled me. Although by this time I had managed to overcome my first fears and inhibitions, I was still nervous in the streets and in the glance of every casual passer-by I sensed the sharp, searching eye of a *Sûreté* agent.

This apprehension, the climate, and the unfamiliar surroundings completely exhausted me, and each night I lay awake pursued by all the mistakes I had made during the day. In the end, my thoughts would weave themselves into a restless, dream-laden sleep, from which I would awake toward dawn unrefreshed and bathed in sweat.

However uneasy I might feel about the task, the most essential part of my assignment was the taking of the photographs, and it could no longer be put off. My host therefore arranged for me to make an "excursion" to the waterfront with his family. We visited various parts of the harbor, and I took the sort of "family shots" a tourist would naturally take. But the family group was always posed in such a way that whatever installation or structure I was interested in would form the background. Or, if I wanted to photograph a certain detail, they would stand closely round me so as to screen my actions.

The films, when developed in Berlin, showed quite good results, in fact some of the photographs were excellent and together with my report they gave us quite a lot of information.

I was very happy after nine days to be back in Lisbon with my Japanese friend.

I had smuggled the films out concealed in a bandage on my upper thigh, where I had inflicted a small scratch with a razor blade. The gauze of the bandage was soaked with blood, and the films, which were hermetically wrapped, made quite a bump, so that the whole thing looked like a swollen and infected wound and aroused a good deal of sympathy among the customs officials and border guards.

I made a verbal report on my trip to Heydrich which took me fully two hours, and the next day submitted a detailed report in writing together with the photographs. On the whole, everyone was very satisfied.

This experience had given me much food for thought. I determined that in future, when ordering and preparing Secret Service operations, I must never lose sight of the practical problems that confronted my agents in the field and I decided that the worst thing was to try to prepare and carry out Secret Service work under pressure. An intelligence network has to be built up step by step. On foreign soil it must be nurtured like a plant and allowed to take root. Only then will there be a healthy growth and a plentiful harvest.

But the German leaders refused to proceed in this manner. Hitler wanted to force everything, for he, and only he, "had been appointed by providence to conduct this war." The overwhelming number of problems he tackled simultaneously resulted in a forced, unorganic development in all phases of German life. Looking back, one can only be amazed that the immense war effort of the German people was possible at all.

This is what I wrote in my report after returning from Dakar: "In Secret Service work one must never be rash. The careful selection and developing of above-average collaborators is decisive. In order to work in a foreign country they must be virtually natives, and must acquire a 'valid' profession unless there is some other natural explanation for their presence in the country in question. Only after one or two years should the first trial assignments be given. Certain specialists should be used only in time of great crisis or in war. Valuable intelligence contacts, especially in political circles, should be patiently cultivated over periods of years and should not be exploited until the decisive moment. These channels can also be very useful for launching false reports to mislead the enemy. . . . "

For men like Jahnke such generalities about Secret Service work constitute the most obvious commonplaces, but in the confusion and pressure of wartime they are often forgotten. And so in Germany it was impossible to speak of the organic growth of the German Secret Service; its operational basis only began to be laid at the outbreak of the Second World War and its organization unified only in the last year of the war. On the whole, the work consisted of a series of relatively impressive improvisations. The surprisingly high average of the service's effectiveness can only be accounted for by the ruthless expenditure that went on of human life and resources.

How important intelligently planned long-range preparatory work can be—and how rewarding in the end—is shown by the successful operation of the German U-boat commander, Captain Prien, against the British naval base at Scapa Flow in October 1940. The success of this operation was made possible by careful preparatory work over a period of fifteen years. Alfred Wehring had been a captain in the German Imperial Navy and later joined the military sector of the Secret Service. After the First World War he became a traveler for a German watch factory. Working all the time under orders from the Secret Service, he learned the watchmaker's trade thoroughly in Switzerland. In 1927, under the name of Albert Oertel and with a Swiss passport, he settled in England. In 1932 he became a naturalized British subject, and soon afterward opened a small jewelry shop at Kirkwall in the Orkneys, near Scapa Flow, whence from time to time he sent us reports on the movements of the British Home Fleet.

It was in the beginning of October 1939 that he sent us the important information that the eastern approach to Scapa Flow through the Kierkesund was not closed off by anti-submarine nets but only by hulks lying relatively far apart. On the receipt of this information Admiral Doenitz ordered Captain Prien to attack any British warship in Scapa Flow.

Prien immediately altered course for the Orkneys and during the night of October 14 nosed his way carefully past the obstructions into the inner channel. Among other warships at anchor was the *Royal Oak*. Prien fired his torpedoes, and was already on his way back to the open sea before the British even knew what was happening.

The sinking of this battleship took less than fifteen minutes—but fifteen years of patient and arduous work by Alfred Wehring had been the necessary foundation for this supremely successful mission.

Another example of the value of careful preparation occurred just before the Second World War. I was put in charge of one of the most famous espionage cases concerning a Lieutenant Colonel Sosnovski. The incident that brought the matter to the attention of German Counter-Espionage took place one foggy morning just after the streams of officers and office workers had entered the Operations Department of the German War Ministry in the Bendlerstrasse. It was a very small incident: a girl who was the chief secretary to a high General Staff officer, a colonel in the Operations Department, was late for work. But it caused the Ministry porter to notice her because whereas she had previously been punctual, poorly dressed, and modest, she was now smartly dressed and was no longer modest or punctual. This gave the old porter food for thought.

Several days later, when he was making his nightly round, he noticed a light in one of the offices and looking in found Fraulein von N—— still sitting at her typewriter. She was startled when he came in but quickly recovered herself and complained about the amount of work she had to do. The porter noticed the elegant shoes, the fur coat on the hanger, the open safe, and the frightened expression of Fraulein von N——.

The next morning he went to the Colonel and reported what he had seen. At first the Colonel was irritated, then he remembered the contents of his safe, which held the latest plans for operations against Czechoslovakia and Poland, statistics on the present state and strength of the various armaments of the Wehrmacht, descriptions and plans of new weapons, production figures, and so on.

During the next few days the Colonel watched his secretary with a new awareness. On three different days he returned to his office late in the evening and checked the contents of his safe. Everything was in perfect order. But on the fourth night the last ten pages of an important operational study were missing. He had been working on this plan and Fraulein von N—— still had some revisions to type. But that did not give her the right to leave the document out of the safe. Even though he found the ten pages back in the safe the next morning, he was still reluctant to face the full implications of his discovery. However, he decided that he must report her, and it was finally agreed that she should be put under strict surveillance.

By the end of the week fourteen of Fraulein von N——'s friends were under continual observation. Without their realizing it, the net was closing about them. Soon we had enough evidence to proceed against all the German nationals involved, and indeed it would have been quite simple to arrest them, but it was Lieutenant Colonel Sosnovski in whom we were chiefly interested. To justify the arrest of a Polish national we had to catch him red-handed.

One of the things that our surveillance had disclosed was that Sosnovski had established contact with the French Secret Service. One of our agents got into touch with Sosnovski, pretending to be an agent of the *Deuxième Bureau*. Sosnovski took the bait, and expressed his willingness to sell him secret German military documents.

And so, the next day, in exchange for a sizable sum he delivered this material to our man in the first-class waiting room of a Berlin railway station. Within a few seconds of the exchange both Sosnovski and the agent were arrested—the arrest of our agent was necessary, of course, to preserve the pretense and enable us to use the "confession" of the provocateur to break down the suspect.

All the other members of the ring were arrested in various parts of Berlin within the next ten minutes. Now began a round of interrogations and examinations which continued without interruption throughout several days and nights. And at length the full story emerged.

Sosnovski was a strikingly handsome man, tall, well built, and with great charm and good manners. After becoming an officer in the Polish Army, he had been assigned to Military Intelligence and had been sent to Germany to get information about German armaments, and especially to secure authentic plans of the German General Staff.

In Berlin he began to move in diplomatic circles and the higher strata of German society. He exercised a great influence over women and sought to have as many love affairs as possible, always with a view to gaining secret information.

Finally he found the instrument he had been looking for in Fraulein von B——, who was a secretary at the OKH, the Supreme Command of the German Army. She belonged to the impoverished Prussian nobility. Her father, who had been a high officer in the Imperial German Army, was dead, and she lived with her mother in very straitened circumstances. Soon after she met Sosnovski an affair developed between them which on her part was completely sincere.

Shortly afterward Sosnovski met a friend and colleague of hers, Fraulein von N——, and the three of them spent much time together in fashionable restaurants, bars, and night clubs where Sosnovski entertained them lavishly. He gave them the most magnificent presents and was systematically getting them accustomed to a much higher standard of life than either of them had been able to enjoy before.

Very soon he started an affair with Fraulein von N——, though without Fraulein von B——'s knowledge.

Fraulein von B—— introduced Sosnovski to her family. He treated her mother with chivalry and tact, and soon restored their household to its former splendor. Their debts were paid and they were at least able to maintain the sort of life that their social position demanded. The old lady hoped one day to see this dashing and wealthy officer as her son-in-law, and, in spite of the high moral principles of her class, she did not even object to his spending the night at her house. The closer his emotional ties with her daughter, the more certain the old lady felt of the future.

Meanwhile jealousy had begun to arise between the two young women. This could have been dangerous. However, Sosnovski managed to control the situation with such skill that in the end each was content with a share of his love, jealousy binding them ever more strongly to him.

Sosnovski chose his moment and then revealed himself to the two women. He told them that he was a Polish secret agent. He described the difficulties of his situation and showed them messages from his superiors in Warsaw, expressing their displeasure with his failure and their determination to recall him from Berlin to return to active duty with the Polish Army. The two women could not bear the thought of losing him, and, playing upon their fears, he told each of them separately that if he could bring his assignment to a successful conclusion, he would marry her and they would spend their lives together abroad with the money he would receive for his services.

Both the girls agreed to work for him (Fraulein von

B—— also worked at the headquarters of the General Staff, though not in such an important position as Fraulein von N——), and during the nights of love-making he instructed them in their duties. They both began to bring home documents overnight for Sosnovski to photograph, and soon the home of Fraulein von N—— became the favorite meeting place of several of the most charming women in Berlin society, with connections of a political, military, or economic sort. Among these ladies Sosnovski began a further series of liaisons.

At first Warsaw found the material he sent them excellent and the authorities were delighted. But as the information he delivered grew increasingly important and more and more startling, his superiors began to grow suspicious. The material seemed too good to be true, and they arrived at the conclusion that Sosnovski was being fed with false information by the German Secret Service. When he finally brought two trunks full of vitally important documents to Warsaw, his superiors would not accept their validity and told him that he had been duped by the Germans. They permitted him, however, to sell the material to other intelligence services and the *Deuxième Bureau,* recognizing its importance, bought part of it. British Intelligence also participated in the purchase. Large sums were offered to Sosnovski for further information, and only when he was arrested did Warsaw realize their mistake. But by then it was too late.

A trial followed the arrest of the spy ring. Fraulein von B—— and Fraulein von N—— were both condemned to death. A last appeal for clemency on their behalf was rejected by Hitler. They were executed and died with their devotion to Sosnovski still unbroken.

One of the circle of ladies with whom Sosnovski had also begun a liaison reacted quite differently. She was the owner of a small but elegant millinery shop in the West End of Berlin. As her complicity in this affair was slight, Counter-Espionage requested the court to separate her case from that of the others and to stop all proceedings against her. We felt that we could use her. It was pointed out to the lady that proceedings against her could be reopened at any time if she should show herself to be uncooperative. But this precaution proved unnecessary. For when the truth was revealed to her and she learned, to her great surprise, of the trial and fate that had befallen her two friends, her former attachment turned into the fiercest hatred for Sosnovski, and she determined to take the most ruthless revenge on the Polish Secret Service. Under our instructions she continued to work for the Poles, who, after checking her carefully, took her back into their service. She became one of our most valuable and trusted collaborators and delivered at least ten Polish agents into our hands. Sosnovski himself was exchanged for several of our agents whom the Poles had arrested.

As a consequence of the affair, the German General Staff was forced to reshape its plans, and it took us a considerable time to recover from this setback.

6. THE INVASION OF POLAND

The Gleiwitz radio plot—Aboard Himmler's special train—
His criticism of my reports—Hitler visits the front line—
Warsaw in ruins—Counteracting espionage in the Ruhr—
Another Polish ring brought to book

IT WAS August 26, 1939, and an oppressive heat lay over Berlin. In the afternoon Dr. Mehlhorn telephoned and asked me whether I would be free that evening. He wanted to talk to me urgently about a personal matter and did not think it wise to call on me at my office. So at eight o'clock we met in a small discreet restaurant. It was really a rendezvous run by my Counter-Espionage Department, and from the cook to the head watier, the whole staff were specially selected agents in my employ.

I noticed immediately that Mehlhorn seemed deeply troubled and depressed. I did not press him with questions, however, but let him take his time. He did not speak while we ate and I waited patiently.

After dinner we drove through the West End. In those days Berlin was a beautiful city at the height of its power and wealth. The bright and elegant shop windows, the dazzling confusion of colored signs, the endless streams of traffic, the bustling crowds, all these were part of the gay and energetic life of peacetime.

I was going to take Mehlhorn to a small bar and was looking for a parking space when he asked me to keep on driving. He needed fresh air, he said, and wanted to get away from the crowds. So we headed toward Wannsee, a lake between Berlin and Potsdam. There I parked the car and we got out and started to walk. Presently Mehlhorn relaxed and began to talk, but more as though he were speaking to himself than to me. From time to time a cool breeze came from the lake and sighed in the old trees. Then there would be silence again, except for the voice of my friend. He spoke rapidly in abrupt, fragmentary sentences and almost without a pause.

"There's going to be war. It can't be prevented any longer. Hitler made his decision long ago; you must have known it. Everything's ready. Even if the Western powers or Poland make a last-minute shot at conciliation—even if Italy intercedes, it won't change Hitler's basic plan. At the very most it might mean a slight delay, that's all."

His voice grew more excited as he told me that Heydrich had asked him to come to his office, and, surprisingly, had confided to him one of Hitler's secret orders. Before September 1, if possible, an absolutely irreproachable cause for war had got to be created, one that would stand in history as a complete justification, and would brand Poland in the eyes of the world as the aggressor against Germany. It had therefore been planned to dress troops in Polish uniforms and attack the Gleiwitz radio transmitter. Hitler had assigned Heydrich and Admiral Canaris, chief of Army Intelligence, to carry out this operation. However, Canaris was so repelled by the order that he had managed to withdraw and Heydrich alone was in charge of it. Heydrich had explained to Mehlhorn the details of the plan. The Polish uniforms were to be supplied at Keitel's command by the OKW—the Supreme Command of the Armed Forces.

I asked Mehlhorn where they would get the Poles who were to wear these uniforms. "That's just it," Mehlhorn replied. "That's the devilish thing about this plan; the 'Poles' will be convicts from the concentration camps. They're going to be armed with proper Polish weapons, but most of them will just be mown down, of course. They've been promised that any who get away with it will have their freedom immediately. But who's going to believe such a promise?"

Mehlhorn paused. Then he said, "Heydrich has put me in command of the attack." He gripped my arm hard. "What am I to do?" he asked. "Heydrich has given me this assignment to get rid of me. I know it. He wants my death! What can I do?"

Now it was my turn to be silent. What advice could I possibly give? Finally I said, "The whole thing is insane. One can't make world history by tactics of that kind. The thing couldn't possibly be kept secret, not for long anyway. Somewhere, somehow, it'll all come out. You must keep clear of it though. Try to talk your way out. Make some excuse—say you're ill—or just simply refuse. Whatever happens through your refusing that sort of order, it'll be preferable to the consequences of your carrying it out."

The next day Mehlhorn faced up to the most difficult crisis of his career. He had the guts to refuse the assignment, excusing himself on the grounds of his health which would prevent him from carrying out such an exacting job with the one hundred per cent efficiency required to guarantee its success.

Heydrich refused to accept this excuse at first, but Mehlhorn stood his ground in face of all Heydrich's threats. Luckily Heydrich was greatly overburdened with work at this time, and finally accepted his refusal. But ten minutes later Heydrich gave orders that Mehlhorn was to be assigned to a difficult and subordinate post in the east.

At ten o'clock on September 1, 1939, Hitler addressed the Reichstag and the German people. When I heard his justification for the German advance into Poland, which had begun that morning—"Numerous Polish attacks on German territory, among others an attack by regular Polish troops on the Gleiwitz transmitter"—I must admit I could still hardly believe my ears.

Just over four hours earlier Hitler had given orders for the offensive against Poland to begin. The Second World War had started.

On September 3 three special trains left Berlin for Poland: one was the Fuehrer's, aboard which were Hitler, General Keitel, Major General Jodl, and the entire staff of the three Wehrmacht sections; another was "Special Train Goering," carrying the Air Marshal and his Staff; the third was "Special Train Heinrich" with Himmler, von Ribbentroop, and Dr. Lammer, Secretary of the Reich Chancellery, aboard.

I had been assigned to Himmler's train as the representative of the Reichssicherheithauptamt (RSHA)—the Supreme National Security Board, set up not long before under the joint control of Himmler and Heydrich. This was a top-level committee for the co-ordination and direction of the various police departments of the state and the police and intelligence departments of the Party (SD). I had been appointed head of Department IV E (Counter-[Espionage/Inland] within this new organization, and it was as its representative that I was to serve on Himmler's train. Himmler wanted a qualified person in his entourage to deal with the courier mail arriving every day, and to maintain the closest and speediest communications by courier, wireless, and telephone between the special trains and Heydrich in Berlin. Also, someone had to be at hand who could deal on the spot with urgent intelligence matters.

When Heydrich told me of this appointment he added, "I want you to be most careful—the floor is damned slippery. You will have to work in continual contact with Himmler's Chief of Staff, Gruppenfuehrer Wolff— Himmler can't live without his little Wolffie. Wolff's adjutants are a pretty unpleasant lot, but don't pay too much attention to them—their barks are worse than their bites." (Knowing Heydrich, I realized from this how deep was his aversion to Wolff.) "And, most important," Heydrich went on, "is the need for you to get to know the Reischsfuehrer of the SS personally. And I'm giving you my own secretary—you'll find that you'll have quite a bit of work to do on this trip."

The past days had been exhausting, and now there was this assignment which did not please me at all. It would take me away from my new task, the direction of the Counter-Espionage department, which I had just taken over and in which I had become completely absorbed.

On the other hand, my interest grew increasingly once I realized the opportunities the assignment offered. I would be at the Supreme Command post, where I would get to know and watch those actually in control of this mighty machine.

My reception on "Special Train Heinrich" was courteous but noticeably cool. I was kept rather at a distance, almost as if I were an interloper. I decided that my best bet, anyhow to start with, would be to remain unnoticed and keep in the background as much as possible, then slowly and naturally to become part of this new environment. But unfortunately the secretary Heydrich had placed at my disposal made this difficult. She was extremely efficient and diplomatic—but she was well over six feet tall. She stood out above the crowd like a lighthouse, and for me to remain unnoticed while I was with her was hardly possible.

I had presented myself to Himmler and Wolff, his Chief

of Staff, on the first day. The second day I made my first report to Himmler at eleven o'clock. I confess I felt somewhat nervous and ill at ease. He sat so that I could not see his eyes behind their glistening pince-nez, and his face remained an impenetrable mask. At the end I was curtly dismissed.

Every day it was the same. I never knew whether he agreed with the opinion I was expressing, whether I was proceeding in the right manner, or even whether he was at all interested in what I was saying. After several days, however, I realized that this was precisely his purpose; he wanted me to find my own way.

Now it became increasingly clear to me that my assignment to this inner circle had a purpose quite different from the one mentioned by Heydrich. I was being put through a planned and thorough testing process, and this "putting me through my paces" seemed to amuse Himmler especially.

This man Himmler, whom I now faced every day, was, after Hitler, the most powerful man in the Reich, yet I could not describe him otherwise than as the archetype of the German schoolmaster. No smile could be more apt. He was like a schoolmaster who graded the lessons of his pupils with finicky exactitude, and for each answer would have liked to enter a mark in his classbook. His whole personality expressed bureaucratic precision, industry, and loyalty. However, to judge Himmler only from this studiously preserved façade would be misleading, as I was to find out later on.

In the meantime, "Special Train Heinrich" had brought us to Breslau, and from there we rolled on in the direction of Kattowitz and into Poland. The earlier reserve of my new colleagues had relaxed as I gradually gained their confidence and by this time I was greeted with friendly "Hullos" whenever I entered the "work carriage."

The rattling of typewriters and the loud voices of those who were dictating created an almost unbearable din even when the train was standing still, but it grew quite intolerable on top of the noise of the wheels. So I made myself a work table, using a crate covered by a blanket, in the spacious sleeper that had been reserved for me. Here I could do my work in peace.

The information and communications service aboard the special trains functioned with remarkable efficiency.

We had telegraph and wireless facilities, and at every stop we could get in touch immediately with any administrative office in the Reich.

I made reports to Himmler regularly. At first he was impatient about their length, although I was as brief as possible. Then I evolved a system by which I stated the recommendation or request at the beginning and then described briefly the pertinent details. Himmler expressed his approval of this form of reporting, but through Gruppenfuehrer Wolff—characteristically, not giving praise or blame directly to any individual.

Later I gained a further insight into this peculiarity of Himmler's behavior. In a way it was a type of cowardice—not that he was afraid to praise or blame; he could be pretty tough on occasions. But it really went against his nature to express an opinion; it was safer for someone else to be in the position of having been at fault. If time proved that some criticism had been wrong or blame misplaced, a subordinate could always be found to have erred. This system gave Himmler an air of aloofness, of being above ordinary conflicts. It made him the final arbiter. Only when he displayed the same characteristic in dealing with important political decisions did I realize its danger.

I continued to make my reports in this form, trying to keep them as brief as possible. It was really Himmler himself who now began to prolong the interviews by questioning and promoting discussion, and I realized that in line with all his actions he was pursuing a definite aim. He wanted to test my general education and background, and at the same time display the universality of his own interests and knowledge. I felt as though I were once more facing my old headmaster.

One incident will always remain in my memory. We were in the Posen area at that time. The "Fuehrer's Train" and Himmler's "Special Train Heinrich" were standing not far apart. Himmler was to appear for a "discussion of the general situation" with Hitler at eleven-thirty. I had finished giving him my report and as he was putting on his overcoat, his dear little Wolff came in. "The Reichsfuehrer SS will really have to hurry," he said, throwing a reproachful glance in my direction.

The train was standing on the open track and the bottom step of the carriage was some way from the ground, so to bridge this gap the train commander had put a crate beneath the carriage door. As Himmler stepped down, peering shortsightedly through his pince-nez, I saw his foot go through the top of the crate and he crashed headfirst to the ground, pince-nez, gloves, and peaked cap flying in all directions as he did so. Not without difficulty his legs was pulled out of the crate, his coat dusted, the peaked cap brushed, and the pince-nez restored. Then the group marched off, wrapped in the dark cloud of the enraged SS leader's displeasure. At lunch Wolff told me that I was to blame for everything, having delayed the Reichsfuehrer until he was late, and therefore in a state of nervous haste, and that both he himself and the Reichsfuehrer were most displeased with me.

After the meal Himmler asked me whether I had enough work to keep me busy. I replied that as a rule in the late afternoons and evenings I had some spare time.

"Then please prepare reports for me, very briefly, on the following subjects: (1) Militia or People's Army. (2) Will mass armies be decisive in the wars of the future, or will the decisive actions be carried out by smaller special-ized units of the ground forces, the air arm and the fleet? (3) The military tradition or Militarism? (4) Your own ideas on the new organization of the Counter-Espionage Department."

I felt as though I were taking my exams. I certainly had enough work to do now. There were also tours of the front-line areas, to which I had been invited and which I did not want to miss, as well as special assignments almost every day.

I spent as much time as possible in the Fuehrer's train, finding out all I could about what went on there. It was fascinating to be at the control panel of a great war machine operating at top speed. From this train the hand of the Nazi leadership intervened in all phases of German life and all sections of the nation.

I met many able and industrious men among the higher executives. They were all intelligent and conscientious, but none of them ever dreamed that their part in the govern-ment of Germany would be submitted to the scrutiny of history. Unfortunately for the German people—indeed, for the whole of Europe—the men at the top thought too much about history, or, rather, about the "making of history," in the fantastic context of Hitler's obsession with the creation of a so-called "Thousand Year Reich."

The special trains had meanwhile been moved to Zoppot, a seaside resort on the Baltic. From here numerous visits to the front lines were organized for Hitler, Himmler, and their immediate staffs. They visited many of the chief battlefields, usually driving right up to the front, which ran unevenly across the north Polish plains. Toward Posen the main bulk of the bravely fighting Polish Army was being encircled ever more tightly by a German pincer movement and broken up by Luftwaffe attacks. Within ten days the Poles were finished.

There was always the same spectacle along the country roads: great stretches of land to right and left were wholly untouched by the fury of war, villages, farmhouses, and churches all lay in deep peace. But on the roads the continuous traffic of war rolled along, lorries, armored cars, tanks, motorcycles, all moving toward the front. And in the opposite direction, the unending stream of prisoners, exhausted by battle, strain, and hunger, trudged apathetically toward the hard fate lying in store for them. Ambulances sped by bearing the wounded, both of friend and foe. Control points set up by the military police, and other obstacles, created huge traffic jams in which even the Fuehrer's column was sometimes forced to halt. Then there were those brief stretches of countryside where the battle line had held fast and the artillery and dive-bombers had ravaged the fields, mown down the trees, and razed the houses.

Never shall I forget the harbor town of Gdynia, which we entered shortly after its fall. I was deeply struck by the total destruction of the residential districts and I could not help asking myself why the Wehrmacht had carried the war into these parts. Until then I had had no real conception of what total war meant.

On these tours we usually started out for the front at nine or ten in the morning, and would return to the train toward nightfall. We had to supply our own provisions—sandwiches, thermos flasks of hot tea, and cognac to fortify us against the increasingly cold weather. As the SS adjutants were already overburdened with other duties, it was my job to secure these provisions.

One day we returned so early that a lot of our food and drink had hardly been touched. The next day we were called out early and the thermos flasks were not ready. I only had time to take what was left over from the previous day—a bottle of cognac, half full, and two packets of sandwiches, which I had placed near a window, hoping they would remain fresh overnight.

After driving for about two hours in the open car, Himmler asked for something to eat, so Gruppenfuehrer Wolff took a packet of sandwiches from me and they both began to eat. They had already got through the first packet when they happened to look at the second. The rest of the sandwiches were all covered with green mold. Himmler's face grew even greener as he tried desperately not to be sick. I quickly offered him some cognac—usually he did not drink; at the most two or three glasses of table wine—but he took a deep gulp and then, as he recovered, fixed me with a steely glance. I was prepared for the worst. "I notice you ate none of the sandwiches yourself." I hastened to explain, but there was a terrible look in his eyes as he thanked me for restoring his life with the cognac after having tried to poison him.

By this time the German armies were closing in on Warsaw and we went by plane to watch this last and most exciting phase of the campaign. We flew along the Vistula down to the Bug, over the so-called "Land of the Four Rivers": Pissa, Narew, Vistula, and San. Most of the countryside over which we flew appeared completely untouched by war.

After landing very near Warsaw, we inspected two heavily damaged Polish armored trains which had been put out of action by Stukas. Hitler climbed about among the wreckage, inspecting everything very closely. Three or four bombs had landed near the trains and had torn huge craters in the earth. After estimating the number of hits and near hits, he ordered that the bombsight of the Sukas should be improved. He personally measured the thickness of the train's armorplate with a ruler, and inspected the armament, the caliber of the guns, etc. He insisted on seeing everything for himself as he clambered about with Keitel running after him, puffing and sweating.

Dr. Morell, Hitler's personal physician, had come along on this flight at Hitler's request. For some of the time we had flown through very rough weather and Morell was extremely sick. I had always disliked him, but it was really pathetic to see this man sitting there, a picture of woe, looking green and helpless in spite of all his pills and injections.

Later we watched the artillery, who were still fully engaged, though the officers reporting on the situation said that the resistance of the defenders had greatly declined. Already German infantry spearheads had penetrated the outskirts of the city. Our artillery were firing one full salvo after another and the noise was deafening. From time to time Polish shells landed in our vicinity but Hitler paid no attention. He rejected well-meant suggestions that he should leave the zone of fire, insisting that he wanted to see everything for himself.

After three or four hours we returned to our planes. Hitler's aircraft had already taken off when we discovered that Dr. Morell was not with us. Finally he arrived accompanied by two soldiers. He was dripping with sweat and his escort told us they had found him in a small wood—literally in full flight. Obviously he was attempting to make a long detour in order to void the zone of fire and had lost his way.

Finally we took off. A great pall of smoke and dust lay over Warsaw as again and again fresh squadrons of bombers in close formation like swarms of hornets flew over the city raining death and destruction upon it.

On the way back Himmler asked me to join him at supper. We had a lengthy discussion about Dr. Morell and finally decided on his immediate and complete surveillance. Himmler also talked to me about our relations with the Russians. In accordance with secret clauses of our agreement with them of August 23, 1939, we were to occupy their zone on Poland on September 18. He also told me that we were turning over the Baltic States to the Russians and said that I should begin to consider security measures for the new frontier. He would like me to consider whether the Russians were likely now to decrease their intelligence activities or conduct them even more intensively. When I had reached an opinion I should make a report, giving my reasons.

I was astonished. "That question can be answered immediately," I said. "They will intensify their intelligence activities with all the means in their power. No doubt they will try to infiltrate their agents among the Baltic Germans and the other minority groups which are being repatriated."

On September 28, Heydrich arrived at our special train to supervise personally all security measures for Hitler's proposed visit to Warsaw.

Upon the capitulation of the city on September 29, we left the special trains for a few days, and traveled to Warsaw by road. Our three-day stay in the capital made one of the deepest and most disturbing impressions on me of all my war experiences. I was shocked at what had become of the beautiful city I had known—ruined and burned-out houses, starving and grieving people. The nights were already unpleasantly chilly and a pall of dust and smoke hung over the city and everywhere there was the sweetish smell of burned flesh. There was no running water anywhere. In one or two streets isolated resistance by Polish nationalist bands was being continued. Elsewhere everything was quiet. Warsaw was a dead city.

On October 1 a great military parade was held for Hitler. Afterward we went to the Warsaw airport, now repaired by our engineers and in use again. Two great tents had been erected for the leaders and their entourage, and we had a quick meal. Immediately afterward Hitler took off for Berlin.

I was able to drive back in my own car as it had been sent to Warsaw. In Berlin I spent two days discussing counter-espionage problems with my experts and looking over Polish Secret Service documents which had been captured. The amount of information collected by the Poles, especially concerning Germany's production of armaments, was quite astonishing. I decided therefore to leave immediately for Dortmund to study on the spot the problem of industrial security in the Ruhr area.

Dortmund is one of the centers of the German iron and steel industry and, after Essen and Düsseldorf, was the most important arsenal of the German war effort in the Ruhr. It was a typical industrial city, gray with smoke, crowded and filled with driving energy.

When I arrived I was thoroughly dismayed by the state in which I found our counter-espionage office. There were five special agents and several assistants and secretaries. One of the agents was entirely occupied in conducting a "paper war" with Berlin, useless scribbling which filled filing cabinets but did not catch spies. And these five specialists were responsible for the whole area around Dortmund with its population of three and a half million and almost four hundred industrial establishments engaged in secret war work.

The next few weeks were filled with meetings with the directors and managers of the war industries, and with the government and military inspection offices. I began to work out a program to deal with the problems in the area, and to rectify the shortcomings of our organization. I was about to go to Berlin to make a report on this when a most interesting investigation was brought to my attention. It concerned a work superintendent who had been employed by an armaments firm for eighteen years. He was born a Pole, but had spent most of his life in Germany and had acquired German nationality. He was an expert on the manufacture of gun barrels and was in charge of that department at the plant. He therefore had access to the blueprints and drawings of the newest anti-tank guns and also of new recoil mechanisms and guncarriages.

One evening two of the plant engineers happened to need a certain drawing. On going to the safe they found that the plans of the newest anti-tank gun were missing. On investigation they discovered that the Polish superintendent had taken the drawing home with him. They immediately informed the local counter-espionage office, who passed the information on to me. I ordered that the foreman be placed under surveillance at once and a check maintained on the contents of the safe so that we could know what blueprints were removed and for how long.

For four nights nothing was taken from the safe, but on the fifth night seven blueprints were missing. Meanwhile, a thorough investigation of the foreman's background had revealed the following information: he had been born near Kalish in Poland, had been apprenticed to an ironmonger, and had become a turner; he had worked in various ironworks in Upper Silesia and had settled in the Ruhr in 1924. His excellent references and his technical experience, as well as his ability to manage men, had soon gained him the confidence of his employers. He was extremely industrious and highly intelligent. He was married, had three children, and lived very quietly and respectably. From time to time he met some of his Polish compatriots, who also visited him at his house. According to his neighbors, they usually spoke Polish on these occasions. That, and the missing blueprints, were the only things that might rouse suspicion. His neighbors all agreed that he lived well within his means.

The night the seven blueprints were missing, the agents carrying out the investigation reported that two men had come to visit the superintendent at midnight and were still at his house. I decided that the time had come to act.

I myself directed the operation. After all the windows and doors of the house had been covered, we forced the door of the kitchen which was on the ground floor and rushed into the living room, where we found the three men. We had moved so swiftly that they had not even had time to rise from their chairs, but sat staring with terror into the muzzles of our pistols. The missing blueprints were lying in front of them on the table. We arrested all three of them, searched them, and then searched the house and arrested the remaining members of the family. During the first hours of cross-examination enough information was gained to justify some further arrests. All in all we picked up sixteen persons.

The superintendent had been working for the Polish Secret Service for the past eleven years and it was on their advice that he had adopted German nationality. He did not work for pay, but was motivated solely by patriotism, and it was the disaster that had befallen his country which had also brought about his own doom. He had always been appalled by the almost criminal optimism of his compatriots in their foolish underestimation of German military strength, and in order to correct this view he had sought, especially during the last months, to give Warsaw a clearer insight into the high quality and tremendous quantity of German arms production. When war began his contact with Warsaw had been broken off. But he had been told that a courier would get in touch with him to collect new material before the end of September, "no matter what the military or political situation might be at the time," so Warsaw had said.

Of the two other men we had arrested at the house, one was a distant relative who came at night to help him copy the drawings, the other an officer of the Polish Secret Service. He had had special training in industrial espionage, and traveled as the representative of a fictitious firm "selling" industrial oil and grease. Until the outbreak of war he had been in continual contact with an assistant of the Polish Military Attaché in Berlin, through whom the material was passed on to Warsaw.

On the evening that we descended on the house he and

the Polish superintendent had arranged to meet once more to agree on a plan for future activities. They had decided to cease all espionage work for the present and wait until they received further orders from the Polish underground army which was now being formed and with which the intelligence officer was already in touch. In view of the large Polish population working in the Ruhr area—numbering about 200,000 at the outbreak of the war—they might still be able to do valuable work. The superintendent also decided to try to establish connections with the Polish prisoners of war who were now being sent to work in the factories.

At the trial, experts gave evidence of the grave damage to Germany's military strength which the activities of the ring had inflicted. About one and a half trunks full of secret drawings had been shipped to Poland by them. Of the sixteen accused, all but two were found guilty of espionage on behalf of Poland, and, as their last criminal acts had been committed after the outbreak of war, the three chief defendants were sentenced to death.

I must confess that I was forced to admire the supreme calm with which this Polish patriot received the verdict. He had given his life and the happiness of his family for his country. When I parted from him his last words to me were, "Today Germany is triumphant—but in the end, who knows?"

7. THE VENLO INCIDENT

Contact with the British Secret Service—My identity changed—First meeting with Best and Stevens—The Dutch customs suspicious—Our second meeting and the Western Powers' proposals—Negotiations held up—The plan of abduction—Best and Stevens kidnaped

BACK IN Berlin I reported to Heydrich on my experiences in the Ruhr and pointed out how inadequate the few counter-espionage agents were in that enormously important area. Heydrich listened attentively. "You will have an opportunity of changing all that," he said, "but before you can get on with it I have another task for you. For several months now we have maintained a very interesting contact directly with British Intelligence. By placing misleading material in their hands, we have succeeded in penetrating their organization. The point has now arrived when we must decide whether we want to continue this game or break it off and be satisfied with what we have learned. I feel you are the right man to take over this affair and I want you to get all the material on it immediately and study it carefully—form your own opinions and then give me your recommendations."

I at once got hold of all the relevant documents which revealed the following situation:

For several years a German secret agent, F 479, had been working in the Netherlands. He had originally been a political refugee and by continuing to pose as one after he began working for us he was able to make contact with the British Secret Service. He pretended to have connections with a strong opposition group within the Wehrmacht, which greatly interested the British. His influence became so great that his reports were sent direct to London and through him we were able to infiltrate a continual stream of misleading intelligence. He had also built up a network of informants of his own and had managed to establish contact with the *Deuxième Bureau*.

After the outbreak of war, British Intelligence showed even greater interest in establishing contact with this alleged opposition group. They thought they might be able to exploit the activities of this officers' conspiracy to bring about the overthrow of the Hitler regime. At the time I was called in, this operation had reached a crucial stage; the British had been promised direct discussions with a high-ranking representative of the opposition group.

After careful study of the case, and long discussions with those who had been conducting it, I came to the conclusion that it would be advantageous to continue the game. I therefore decided to go to Holland myself to meet the agents of the British Secret Service, adopting for this purpose the identity of Hauptmann Schaemmel, of the Transport Department of the OKW. I had found out that there really was such a Hauptmann in the Transport Department and I saw to it that he was sent on an extensive journey in the eastern areas.

Having secured approval of my plans, I went to Düsseldorf, where I established residence in a small private house. These "lodgings" had been equipped, however, for Secret Service work, having direct telegraphic and telephonic connections with the central office in Berlin.

Berlin was meanwhile to contact our agent F 479 and instruct him to arrange a meeting between Hauptmann Schaemmel and the British agents. Unfortunately circumstances made it impossible for me to meet F 479 beforehand and discuss arrangements with him, so I had to leave everything to his skill and ingenuity. There was, of course, a considerable element of risk in this, but that is something which cannot be avoided in Secret Service work.

Further information was sent to me in Düsseldorf by airmail from Berlin and I studied it carefully. I had to master the story completely, memorize every detail of the fictitious conspiracy we had planned and the names and relationships between the various people, as well as all the available information on the British agents whom I was to meet. I had also secured an exact and detailed report on Hauptmann Schaemmel—his background, his way of life, his behavior and appearance—for instance, he always wore a monocle, so I had to wear one too, which was not difficult, as I am shortsighted in my right eye. The more inside knowledge of the group I possessed, the more chance I had of gaining the confidence of the British, for, of course, the smallest mistake would immediately arouse their suspicions.

On October 20 at six o'clock in the evening a message finally came through: "Meeting arranged for October 21 in Zutphen, Holland."

One of our agents was to accompany me. He knew the background of the affair well, for he had been in charge of Agent F 479 at various times. We made a final check of our passports and the registration papers of our car (the German customs and frontier police had been instructed not to ask us unnecessary questions). We had very little baggage and I took special care checking our clothes and laundry for any signs that might betray our identity. Neglect of small details of this kind can cause the best laid Secret Service plans to fail.

In the evening, I received a call, much to my surprise, from Heydrich. He told me that he had secured full authorization for me to carry on the "negotiations" in whatever manner I thought best. I had complete freedom of movement. Finally he said, "I want you to be very careful. It would be too stupid if something should happen to you. But in case anything does go wrong, I've alerted all posts along the frontier. I want you to call me immediately you get back."

I was surprised by this show of concern. However, I realized that it was based not so much on human feelings as on purely practical considerations.

Early in the morning on October 21 we drove to the Dutch border. It was a dark and rainy day. My companion drove while I sat beside him lost in thought. I could not suppress a feeling of uneasiness, more especially because I had had no chance to speak to F 479, and as we drew near the frontier this feeling of uncertainty increased.

The formalities at the German border were dispatched quickly and easily. The Dutch, however, were more troublesome, insisting on a thorough inspection, but in the end we were passed through without much difficulty.

When we arrived in Zutphen a large Buick was waiting for us at the appointed meeting place. The man sitting behind the wheel introduced himself as Captain Best, of British Intelligence. After a brief exchange of courtesies, I got in beside him and we drove off, my companion following in my car.

Captain Best, who, incidentally, also wore a monocle, spoke excellent German, and we very soon established friendly relations. Our common interest in music—the Captain apparently was a very good violinist—helped to break the ice. The conversation was so pleasant that after a little while I felt I could almost have forgotten the purpose of my journey. But though I may have appeared outwardly calm, I was inwardly tense as I waited for Captain Best to broach the matter that we were to discuss. But apparently he did not wish to do so until we got to Arnhem, where his colleagues, Major Stevens and Lieutenant Coppens, were to join us. When we arrived there, they got into the car and we drove on. The discussion took place while the Buick rolled through the Dutch countryside.

They accepted me apparently without reservations as the representative of a strong opposition group within the highest spheres of the German Army. I told them that the head of this group was a German general, but that I was not free to divulge his name at this stage of the negotiations. Our aim was the forcible removal of Hitler and the setting up of a new regime. My purpose in these conversations was to explore the attitude of the British government toward a new government controlled by the German Army and whether they would be willing to enter in a secret agreement with our group which would lead to a peace treaty once we were in power.

The British officers assured me that His Majesty's government were definitely interested in our enterprise and that their government attached the greatest importance to preventing a further extension of the war and to the attainment of peace. They would welcome the removal of Hitler and his regime. Furthermore, they offered us all the aid and support within their power. As far as any political commitments and agreements were concerned, they were not at this point authorized to enter into anything of the kind. However, if it were possible that the leader of our group, or any other German general, could be present at our next meeting, they believed they would be able to present a more binding declaration on the part of His Majesty's government. They assured me that they were in direct contact at all times with the Foreign Office and with Downing Street.

It was clear that I had definitely gained the confidence

of the British officers. We agreed to renew our conversations on October 30 at the central office of British Intelligence in The Hague. I promised them that I would be there to meet them at that time, and after we had had a meal together, we parted on the best of terms. The return journey and the frontier crossings were uneventful.

As soon as I arrived in Düsseldorf, I called Berlin to tell them of my return. They ordered me to report there in person at once and discuss further steps in the affair.

I arrived in Berlin in the evening and after a discussion which lasted late into the night it was left entirely to me to work out the further conduct of the negotiations. I was also given a free hand to choose suitable collaborators.

During the next few days I worked out my plans. I was accustomed to spend most of my free time in the peaceful atmosphere of the house of my best friend, Professor Max de Crinis, of Berlin University, and director of the Psychiatric Department of the famous Charité Hospital. It was a most pleasant and cultivated household, and for years I had been received there like a son. I had my own room and could come and go as I pleased.

That day, while I was working out my plans, de Crinis came to my room and insisted that I should go riding with him. The fresh air would clear my head. We were cantering briskly along when I was suddenly struck by an idea. I told de Crinis about the operation in Holland, and asked him whether he could come to The Hague with me. De Crinis, who was a colonel in the Medical Corps of the German Army, was born at Graz in Austria, and was considerably older than I. Elegant, stately, highly intelligent and cultured, he was ideally suited for the role I had in mind, and his slight Austrian accent would make him still more convincing. I would introduce him at our next meeting with the British as the right hand of the leader of our opposition group. De Crinis readily agreed to go with me, and in due course my plan was approved by the central office.

On October 29 de Crinis and I, and the agent who had accompanied me to the first meeting, left Berlin for Düsseldorf, where we spent the night and made our final preparations. I had decided that for the rest of the journey we would not talk about our mission, so that this was our final briefing.

De Crinis and I agreed upon a system of signs by which

I could communicate with him during the discussion with
the British: if I removed my monocle with my left hand it
meant that he was to stop talking at once and let me take
over the conversation; if I removed it with my right it
mean that I needed his support. The sign for an immediate breaking off of the conversation would be for me to
say that I had a headache.

Before we set out I carefully checked de Crinis' luggage. This time we had no difficulty in crossing the border.

At Arnhem we drove to a crossroads where we were to
meet our British friends at noon. When we reached the
spot at two minutes to twelve they had not arrived. We
waited half an hour without anything happening; the half
hour became three-quarters of an hour as we slowly drove
up and down the street, our nervousness increasing every
minute, and still nothing happened. De Crinis, unaccustomed to situations of this sort, was, of course, the most
nervous of us and I tried to calm him.

Suddenly we saw two Dutch policemen slowly approaching our car. One of them asked us in Dutch what
we were doing there. The agent who accompanied us replied that we were waiting for friends. The policeman
shook his head, climbed into our car, and ordered us to
drive to the police station. To all appearances it seemed
that we had fallen into a trap. The main thing now was to
keep calm and retain our self-control.

At the police station we were treated very politely, but
in spite of all our protests they searched our persons and
our luggage. They were very thorough about it, each article
of de Crinis' toilet kit, for instance, being examined with
great care. While they were doing this I was examining our
luggage even more carefully, for I suddenly realized that I
had been so preoccupied with de Crinis at Düsseldorf
that I failed to check the luggage of the agent who
accompanied us. His toilet kit lay open on a table near me
and now I saw to my horror that it contained a roll of
aspirin tablets wrapped in the official German Army pack-
ing with a label on which was printed "SS Sanitaetshaupt-
tamt" [Main Medical Office of the SS].

I pushed my own luggage, which had already been
examined, closer to the toilet kit, at the same time glancing round to see whether I was observed. Quickly I
grabbed the roll of aspirins and at the same moment

dropped a hairbrush under the table. As I bent down to pick it up I put the tablets into my mouth. They were truly "bitter pills" and some of the paper that was round them stuck in my throat, so that I had to drop the hairbrush again and pretend to search for it under the table while I tried to choke everything down. Fortunately all this passed unnoticed.

Then the interrogation began: Where did we come from? Where were we going? Who were these friends we were to meet? What sort of business were we going to discuss? I replied that I refused to answer anything until we had had an opportunity to consult a lawyer. I also complained forcibly about the manner in which we were being treated. They were going too far, there was no possible justification for all this; they had seen that our papers and our luggage were in order, and they had no right to detain us. I became intentionally rude and arrogant and it seemed to work. Several of the policemen became visibly unsure of themselves, but the others were determined to continue the examination. We had been wrangling for almost an hour and a half when suddenly the door opened and Lieutenant Coppens came in. He showed the policemen some papers—I tried to see what they were, but did not manage to get a look at them—whereupon the attitude of the police changed at once. With the most profound apologies they released us.

When we came out of the police station we saw Captain Best and Major Stevens sitting in the Buick. They explained that it had all been a terrible mistake. They had waited for us at the wrong crossroads and then had spent a long time looking for us. Again and again they apologized, saying what a painfully embarrassing misunderstanding the whole thing had been.

It was immediately clear to me, of course, that the whole affair had been arranged by them. They had used the arrest, the search, and the examination as an excellent means of checking us over to reassure themselves about our identity. I felt that we had better be prepared for further tests of one sort or another.

After a fast drive, we reached The Hague, where we went to a large room in the offices of Major Stevens. Here our talks began, with Captain Best doing most of the talking. After a detailed and thorough discussion, we finally agreed on the following points:

The political overthrow of Hitler and his closest assistants was to be followed immediately by the conclusion of peace with the Western Powers. The terms were to be the restoration of Austria, Czechoslovakia, and Poland to their former status; the renunciation of Germany's economic policies and her return to the gold standard. The possibility of a return to Germany of the colonies she had held before the First World War was one of the most important subjects of our discussion. This has always been of special interest to me and I kept coming back to it again and again. I pointed out how vitally important it was to everyone that Germany should have a safety valve for her surplus population, otherwise German pressure against her borders in the east and in the west must continue to create an element of danger in Central Europe.

Our partners in the discussion recognized the validity of this, and agreed that a solution should be found to meet Germany's demands. They felt that a formula could be found that would secure for Germany the necessary economic rights and advantages and which could be reconciled politically with the present system of mandates.

At the conclusion of the discussion we set down these results in the form of an *aide-mémoire*. Major Stevens then went to inform London by telephone of our conclusions. After about half an hour he returned and stated that there had been a positive reaction in London, but that the agreement would still have to be discussed with Lord Halifax, the Foreign Minister. This would be done at once and we could count on a definite decision during the ment on our part would be necessary, which would rep-course of the evening. At the same time a binding agree-resent a definite and final decision of the German opposition and would also include a time limit.

The talks had lasted approximately three and a half hours. Toward the end I had developed a genuine headache, mainly because I had smoked too many strong English cigarettes and was not accustomed to them. While Major Stevens was speaking to London, I went to refresh myself in the washroom and let the cool water run over my wrists. I was standing there lost in thought when Captain Best, who had entered without my noticing, suddenly said in a soft voice behind me, "Tell me, do you always wear a monocle?"

It was fortunate that he could not see my face, for I could feel myself blushing. After a second I regained control of myself and replied calmly, "You know, I've been meaning to ask you the same question."

Afterward we drove to the villa of one of Best's Dutch associates where three comfortable rooms had been prepared for us. We rested for a while and then changed, for we had been invited to dinner at Best's home.

Best's wife, the daughter of a Dutch soldier, General Van Rees, was a well-known portrait painter and the conversation at dinner was pleasant and lively. Stevens came in later, explaining that his duties had detained him. He drew me aside and told me that he had received an affirmative reply from London; the whole thing was a great success.

Our agent, F 479, was also invited to the dinner, and for a few minutes I was able to talk to him undisturbed. He was very nervous and could hardly stand the tension any longer. I tried to reassure him and said that if he found a pretext to return to Germany, I would use all my influence to straighten things out for him with the authorities in Berlin.

The dinner was excellent. I have never tasted such marvelous oysters. Best made a brief and amusing after-dinner speech, to which de Crinis replied with all his Viennese charm. The general conversation after dinner proved most interesting and through it I gained a greater insight into the attitude of the British toward the war. They had not undertaken it lightly, and would fight to the bitter end. Indeed, if Germany were successful in invading Britain, they would carry on the war from Canada. We also talked of music and painting, and it was quite late when we drove back to the villa.

Unfortunately my headache had not left me, so before retiring I asked my host for some aspirins. Several minutes later a charming young lady came to my room with some tablets and a glass of lemonade. She began talking to me and asked a number of questions. I felt quite relieved when I finally managed to maneuver her out of my room without actually being impolite. After the strain and exertions of the day I was in no state of mind to satisfy her curiosity with safety.

In the morning I met de Crinis for a moment in the bathroom. He was beaming and said in his broadest Viennese dialect, "Well, well—these chaps really can make things move, can't they?"

There was an ample Dutch breakfast to fortify us for the homeward journey. At nine o'clock a car collected us to take us to a brief final meeting, which was held in the offices of a Dutch firm (in reality a cover firm of the British Secret Service) the *N.V. Handels Dienst Veer Het Continent*) [Continental Trade Service] at Nieuwe Uitleg No. 15. We were given an English transmitting and receiving set and a special code with which we could maintain contact with the English Secret Service Station at The Hague. The call number was O-N-4. Lieutenant Coppens gave us credentials that instructed the Dutch authorities to assist the bearers to call a secret telephone number in The Hague—I believe it was 556-331—to protect us against any recurrence of unpleasant incidents, such as that of the previous day. After we had agreed to arrange the time and place of the next meeting by wireless, Captain Best accompanied us to the border, which again we crossed without difficulty.

This time we did not stop in Düsseldorf but drove straight to Berlin. The next day I made my report and suggested that I should try to continue negotiations with the aim of going to London.

During the following week on three occasions the British asked us to fix a date for the next talks. We were in daily communication with them by wireless, over O-N-4, which functioned perfectly. But by November 6 no directive had been received from Berlin and I began to fear that we would lose contact with the British. I therefore decided to go ahead on my own initiative. I agreed to meet them on November 7, and we finally arranged a rendezvous in the café near the frontier at two o'clock in the afternoon.

At this meeting I explained to Best and Stevens that my trip to Berlin had taken longer than I had expected and that unfortunately the German opposition had been unable to reach a final decision. I then suggested that it might be best if I accompanied the General (the fictitious leader of the group) to London, where final discussions on the highest level could be held with the British government. The British agents saw nothing against this and said they could have a courier plane ready the next day at the Dutch airport of Schiphol, to take us to London. In the end we agreed that I would try to bring the leader of the German opposition to a meeting next day at the same time and place.

I returned to Düsseldorf, but there was still no directive from Berlin and no permission to continue the conversations. I sent an urgent request to Berlin, warning them that without a decisive step of one sort or another my situation was becoming untenable. I received the reply that Hitler had not yet made a decision, but was inclined to break off the negotiations. He felt that they had gone far enough already. Apparently any discussion about his overthrow, even though it was bogus, made the Fuehrer uncomfortable.

So I sat in Düsseldorf, feeling impotent and frustrated, but the game intrigued me so much that I decided to go ahead. I got through to The Hague by wireless and confirmed the meeting for the next day. I must confess that at that moment I had no idea what sort of story I would tell my British friends. I realized that I was placing myself in a very ticklish position. If I aroused their suspicions in any way they could easily have me arrested again; the whole affair might come to a most unpleasant end. But I was determined to go on with the negotiations at all costs. I was angry with Berlin, although I knew that they had good reason for being hesitant: Hitler had tentatively set November 14 as the date for his attack on the West. The bad weather prevailing at that time may have been the main reason for abandoning this plan, but Himmler admitted later that my negotiations with the British agents might have been a contributing factor.

I spent a sleepless night, all sorts of plans whirling confusedly through my mind.

At breakfast I glanced at the morning papers. The headlines proclaimed that the King of the Belgians and the Queen of the Netherlands had made a joint offer to attempt to negotiate between the belligerents. I breathed a sigh of relief—this was the solution to my immediate problem. I would simply tell the British agents at today's meeting that the German opposition had decided to wait and see how Hitler would respond to the Dutch-Belgian proposal. I would add that illness prevented the leader of the opposition from attending today's meeting, but that he would certainly be there tomorrow and would probably still wish to go to London. That was my plan for today's conversations.

In the morning I had a talk with the man I had selected to play the role of the General, the leader of our opposition group. He was an industrialist, but held a high honorary rank in the army and was a leader of the SS—in fact, he was admirably suited for the part.

In the afternoon I crossed the border once more. This time I had to wait for three-quarters of an hour in the café. I noticed that I was being watched very closely by several persons pretending to be harmless civilians; it was clear that the British had again become suspicious.

Finally they arrived. It was a rather short meeting this time, and I had no difficulty in presenting the situation to them as I had it planned that morning, thus explaining the delay. Their suspicions were entirely dissipated and when we said *au revoir* to each other the warm cordiality of the previous meetings had been reestablished.

Back in Düsseldorf that evening an SS leader called on me. He was in charge of a special detachment and had been sent by Berlin unobtrusively to safeguard my crossing of the frontier. He told me that in Berlin they were very worried about my safety. He had been ordered to block off the whole sector of the frontier and cover all Dutch border police in the area. If the Dutch had tried to arrest me the situation would have become very difficult, for his orders were that on no account was he to let me fall into the hands of the enemy and a serious incident might therefore have resulted.

It gave me a rather strange feeling to hear this, especially when I thought of my plans for the next day, and what might have happened if I had not been able to speak to this SS leader beforehand. I told him that tomorrow I might drive away with the British agents, as my purpose was to go to London. If I went with them voluntarily I would give him a sign. We also discussed the measures he should take in case my departure with the British was not voluntary. He assured me that the best men available had been selected from his detachment.

I then had another talk with the industrialist who was to go with me and pose as the leader of the opposition group. We went over all the details very carefully, and it was midnight before I went to bed.

I had taken a sleeping pill to insure myself against

another sleepless night and had sunk into a deep sleep when the insistent buzzing of the telephone awoke me. It was the direct line to Berlin. Drugged with sleep, I groped for the receiver and reluctantly grunted, "Hullo." At the other end I heard a deep, rather excited voice: "What did you say?" "Nothing so far," I replied. "Who am I speaking to?" The reply came sharply, "This is the Reichsfuehrer SS Heinrich Himmler. Are you there at last?" My consternation struggling with my sleepiness, I replied with the habitual, "Yes, sir." "Well, listen carefully," Himmler continued. "Do you know what has happened?" "No, sir," I said, "I know nothing." "Well, this evening, just after the Fuehrer's speech in the Beer Cellar[1] an attempt was made to assassinate him! A bomb went off. Luckily he'd left the cellar a few minutes before. Several old Party comrades have been killed and the damage is pretty considerable. There's no doubt that the British Secret Service is behind it all. The Fuehrer and I were already on his train to Berlin when we got the news. He now says—and this is an order—when you meet the British agents for your conference tomorrow, you are to arrest them immediately and bring them to Germany. This may mean a violation of the Dutch frontier, but the Fuehrer says that's of no consequence. The SS detachment that's been assigned to protect you—which, by the way, you certainly don't deserve, not after the arbitrary and self-willed way you've been behaving—this detachment is to help you to carry out your mission. Do you understand everything?" "Yes, Reichsfuehrer. But—" "There's no 'but,'" Himmler said sharply. "There's only the Fuehrer's order—which you will carry out. Do you now understand?" I could only reply, "Yes, sir." I realized it would be quite senseless to try to argue at this point.

Thus I was presented with a completely new situation and had to forget all about my great plan of continuing the negotiations in London.

I immediately roused the SS leader of the special detachment and explained the Fuehrer's order to him. He and his second-in-command were very doubtful about the plan and said it would be far from easy to carry it out.

---

[1] Every year, on November 8, the anniversary of Hitler's Munich *putsch* in 1923, he delivered a speech in the beer cellar where the *putsch* originated.

The terrain was not favorable for such an operation and for several days the whole Venlo sector of the frontier had been so thoroughly covered by Dutch border guards and secret police that it would hardly be possible to carry the thing off without some shooting; and once shooting began you could never tell where it would end. Our great advantage lay in the element of surprise. Both the SS leaders thought that if we waited until the British agents had joined me at the café and we had sat down to begin our talks it would be too late. The time to act would be the moment Best's Buick arrived. They had taken a good look at the car the previous day and were certain they would recognize it immediately. The moment the British arrived our SS cars would break through the frontier barrier at great speed, arrest the Britishers in the street and haul them out of their own car into ours. The driver of the SS car was skilled at driving backward, he would not even have to turn the car round, and this would give the SS men wider field of fire. At the same time, several men would advance to the right and left of the street to cover the flanks during the retreat.

The SS leaders suggested that I personally should take no part whatever in the affair, but should wait for the British in the café. When I saw their car approaching I should come out into the street as though to greet them. Then I was to get into my own car and immediately drive away.

This plan sounded fine and I agreed to it. However, I asked them to introduce me to the twelve men of the special detachment; I wanted all of them to get a good look at me. Captain Best, though he was slightly taller than I, was of about the same build, had a similar overcoat, and also wore a monocle, so I wanted to make certain that there would be no mistake.

Between one and two o'clock I crossed the frontier as usual. The agent who had accompanied me on previous trips was still with me, but I had left the man who was to play the General safely in the German customs office, for no one could say how the situation might develop.

At the café we ordered an *apéritif*. There was quite a crowd in the place and unusually heavy traffic in the street, many of them cyclists, as well as some strange-looking men in civilian clothes accompanied by police dogs. It seemed that our British friends had taken unusually thorough security measures for this meeting.

I must admit that I felt pretty nervous, especially as time went on and there was still no sign of them. I began to wonder whether they had prepared a similar trick to the one they played on us at Arnhem. It was already after three o'clock and we had been waiting more than an hour. Suddenly I started—a gray car was approaching at high speed. I wanted to go outside, but my companion grasped my arm and held me back. "That's not the car," he said. I was afraid that the leader of the SS detachment might also be misled, but everything remained quiet.

Having ordered a strong coffee, I had just taken the first sip and was glancing again at the clock—it was now nearly twenty past three—when my companion said, "Here they come." We stood up. I told the waiter that some friends were arriving and we went out into the street, leaving our coats in the café.

The big Buick was approaching at speed, then, braking hard, it turned off the road into the car park behind the café. I walked toward the car and was about ten yards from it when I heard the sound of the SS car approaching. Suddenly there were shots and we heard shouting.

The SS car, which had been parked behind the German customs house, had driven right through the barrier. The shots had been fired to add to the surprise and had reduced the Dutch frontier guards to such confusion that they ran about aimlessly and did nothing.

Captain Best was driving the Buick and Lieutenant Coppens was sitting beside him. Coppens jumped out of the car at once, at the same time drawing out a heavy service revolver which he pointed at me. I, being completely unarmed, jumped to one side and tried to present a less prominent target. At this moment the SS car came skidding around the corner into the car park. Coppens, recognizing it as the greater danger, turned and fired several shots into the windscreen. I saw the glass shatter and crystalline threads spreading from the bullet holes. It is strange how vividly one notices details on such an occasion and how indelibly they remain etched in one's memory. I was certain Coppens must have hit the driver and the SS leader sitting beside him. Yet it seemed like an eternity before anything else happened. Then suddenly I saw the lithe figure of the leader leap from the car. He had also drawn his pistol and a regular duel developed between him and Coppens. I had no time to move and found myself between them. Both men shot with deliberation, aiming carefully. Then Coppens slowly lowered his gun and sank down on his knees. I heard the leader shouting at me, "Will you get the hell out of this! God knows why you haven't been hit."

I turned and ran round the corner of the house toward my car. Looking back, I saw Best and Stevens being hauled out of the Buick like bundles of hay.

As I rounded the corner I suddenly found myself face to face with a huge SS subaltern whom I had not seen before. He grabbed hold of me and thrust a huge pistol under my nose. It was obvious that he mistook me for Captain Best. Later I learned that against my express orders he had been added to the special detachment just before they left and consequently did not know who I was.

I pushed him back violently, shouting, "Don't be stupid. Put that gun away!"

But he was obviously nervous and excited and he grabbed hold of me again. I tried to fight him off, whereupon he aimed his gun at me, but in the same second that he pulled the trigger his hand was knocked to one side and the bullet missed my head by about two inches. I owed my life to the second SS leader's alertness. He had noticed what was happening and intervened just in time.

I did not wait for any further explanations, but got into my car as quickly as I could and drove off, leaving it to the SS detachment to finish the operation.

The plan was for everyone to return to Düsseldorf as fast as they could. I got there in about half an hour and the SS leaders arrived about the same time. They reported to me as follows:

"Best and Stevens, as well as their Dutch driver, have been secured as ordered. From Lieutenant Coppens' papers it transpires that he is not British at all, but is an officer of the Dutch General Staff. His real name is Klop. Unfortunately he was seriously wounded during the shooting and is at present under medical care."

The other SS leader added, "I'm sorry that I had to shoot Coppens, but he fired first; it was a question of his life or mine. I turned out to be the better shot."

Coppens, or Klop, later died of his wound in a Düsseldorf hospital. Best, Stevens, and their driver were brought to Berlin.

Best and Stevens were held prisoner for the duration of the war and finally liberated in 1945. I tried several times to secure their freedom by having them exchanged for German POW's, but all these attempts were sharply rejected by Himmler, until finally in 1943 he forbade me ever to bring up the matter again. Mention of it would remind Hitler of Elser, the man who planted the bomb in the Beer Cellar. Hitler still believed that there were others behind Elser and considered it one of the greatest failures of the Gestapo that they were not able to uncover anything to prove this. Himmler had been glad that with the passing of time Hitler had forgotten the matter, and did not want to remind him of it by bringing up Best and Stevens, who were linked in Hitler's mind with the Beer Cellar affair.

8. INVESTIGATING THE BEER CELLAR EXPLOSION

*Hitler supervises the interrogation of Best and Stevens—
Confession of a suspect—Awards for the Venlo incident—
Hitler gives a dinner party—His assessment of the war
situation—My own views invited—An interview with
Elser, the suspect*

ON NOVEMBER 11, 1939, I left Düsseldorf and drove to Berlin. I was dissatisfied with the outcome of the Venlo incident and still felt it would have been better if I could have continued the negotiations as I had wished. In Berlin I found the atmosphere extremely tense. The special commission to investigate the attempt on Hitler's life had just returned from Munich. The central office of the Security Service was like a hornets' nest into which someone had poked a stick. The whole machinery of the Gestapo and the Criminal Police had been set in motion and all telegraph and telephone communications were blocked for any other business.

I made my report on what happened at Venlo and was ordered to report to Himmler the next day and to bring with me the two SS leaders who had taken part in the operation. On that occasion I again expressed my dissatisfaction with the outcome of the affair, but however much I disagreed with my orders I had carried them out successfully.

I was ordered to write a detailed report for Hitler on the negotiations and the final operation, and was also ordered to assign the ablest and most experienced counterespionage experts to the interrogation of the British intelligence officers, Best and Stevens.

These interrogations were begun the next day. I laid special stress on absolutely correct and humane treatment, and I was able to reassure myself that my men treated the prisoners in the best possible manner.

Unfortunately, orders began to come down from above

almost at once. Hitler demanded that every evening the reports of the day's interrogation be shown to him personally. This meant that these reports had to be retyped on a special typewriter equipped with type three times the normal size, as Hitler's eyes were weak and he could read only very large print. He began to issue detailed directives on the handling of the case to Himmler, Heydrich, and me and gave releases to the press. To my dismay, he became increasingly convinced that the attempt on his life had been the work of the British Intelligence, and that Best and Stevens, working together with Otto Strasser, were the real organizers of this crime.

Meanwhile a carpenter by the name of Elser had been arrested while trying to escape over the Swiss border. The circumstantial evidence against him was very strong, and finally he confessed. He had built an explosive mechanism into one of the wooden pillars of the Beer Cellar. It consisted of an ingeniously worked alarm clock which could run for three days and set off the explosive charge at any given time during that period. Elser stated that he had first undertaken the scheme entirely on his own initiative, but that later on two other persons had helped him and had promised to provide him with a refuge abroad afterward. He insisted, however, that the identity of neither of them was known to him.

I thought it possible that the "Black Front" organization of Otto Strasser might have something to do with the matter and that the British Secret Service might also be involved. But to connect Best and Stevens with the Beer Cellar attempt on Hitler's life seemed to me quite ridiculous. Nevertheless that was exactly what was in Hitler's mind. He announced to the press that Elser and the officers of the British Secret Service would be tried together. In high places there was talk of a great public trial, to be staged with the full orchestra of the propaganda machine, for the benefit of the German people. I tried to think of the best way to prevent this lunacy.

In the meantime new directives were continually being issued by Hitler. These made our work so much harder that often we were ready to tear our hair. For instance, within twenty-four hours he wanted a list of all the names of German émigrés in Holland whom the Abwehr [Military Intelligence] suspected of having relations with the British Secret Service, and so on.

Several days later at the Reich Chancellery, Hitler received the special detachment of the SS that had taken part in the Venlo operation. We marched into the courtyard in military formation and stood at attention while a guard of honor of the SS was drawn up in front of us. The whole thing was made into a solemn ceremony. We then marched into the Chancellery—it was the first time I had been there; the furnishings were excessively grandiose, but what I was most impressed by was the size of the rooms—and were conducted to Hitler's study, above the door of which hung a large portrait of Bismarck. Presently Hitler entered, affecting a firm, imperious stride, and placed himself in front of us as though he were about to give a command. At first he said nothing, but stared piercingly at each one of us in turn. Then he spoke. He said he was grateful for our achievement, both as individuals and as a group. He was especially pleased by our resolution, initiative, and courage. The British Secret Service had a great tradition. Germany possessed nothing comparable to it. Therefore each success meant the building up of such a tradition and required even greater determination. The traitors who would stab Germany in the back during this most decisive struggle must be ruthlessly destroyed. The cunning and perfidy of the British Secret Service was known to the world, but it would avail them little unless Germans themselves were ready to betray Germany. In recognition of our achievement and of the fact that the conflict on the secret front was just as important as armed combat on the field of battle, he would now present decorations to members of the German Secret Service for the first time in its history.

Four of the men of the special detachment received the Iron Cross, First Class, the rest the Iron Cross, Second Class. Hitler made the presentation in person, shaking each man's hand and adding a few appreciative words. Then he posted himself in front of us again in military fashion, and raised his right arm. The investiture was at an end.

We drove away in several cars while a company of Hitler's bodyguard presented arms. I must confess that at the time I was most impressed by the whole ceremony.

The next evening I was to report to Hitler at nine o'clock. Heydrich asked me to talk to Mueller before going and inform myself fully about the investigation of

Elser, so that I would be able to answer any questions Hitler might ask about this aspect of the affair.

Mueller was very pale and looked overworked. I tried to persuade him that it was a great mistake to try to establish a link between Best and Stevens and Elser, and finally he agreed, but said with a hopeless shrug, "After all, if Himmler and Heydrich cannot move Hitler on this point, you can hardly expect to be more successful. You'll only burn your fingers." I asked who he thought must be behind Elser. "I haven't been able to get anything at all out of him on that point," he said. "He either refuses to say anything or else tells stupid lies. In the end he always goes back to his original story; he hates Hitler because one of his brothers who had been a Communist sympathizer was arrested and put into a concentration camp. He liked tinkering with the complicated mechanism of the bomb and he liked the thought of Hitler's body being torn to pieces. The explosives and the fuse were given him by his anonymous friend in a Munich café." Mueller paused thoughtfully for a moment. "It is quite possible that Strasser and his 'Black Front' have something to do with this business." With his left hand Mueller massaged the knuckles of his right hand, which were red and swollen. His lips were compressed, and there was a malevolent expression in his small eyes. Then he said very softly but with great emphasis, "I've never had a man in front of me yet whom I did not break in the end."

I could not repress a shudder of revulsion. Mueller noticed it and said, "If Elser had been given some of the medicine he has had from me earlier on, he would never have tried this business."

That was Mueller, the little Munich police detective, who now had practically unlimited power.

I was very thoughtful that evening as I drove to the Reich Chancellery. I reported to Himmler and Heydrich, who were there already. We stood in the antechamber of the great dining room and waited for Hitler. Himmler had not yet read my report, and said he would try to read it before supper. I gave him a brief account of its contents and also of my conversation with Mueller. At the same time I reiterated all my arguments against a propaganda trial of Stevens, Best, and Elser. Both Himmler and Heydrich made rather long faces. They agreed that I was right, but their problem was how to explain this to their master. Obviously, they wanted me to go ahead and try my luck.

The others present had noticed that we were engaged in a serious discussion and their curiosity was aroused. Hess, Bormann, Major General Schmundt, and several others, came over and sought to join in the conversation, but the stony faces of Himmler and Heydrich warned them off.

Some time before this I had had a talk with Hess about intelligence problems. This evening he showed a marked interest in me and said to Himmler with a smile, "You know, Schellenberg and I had a discussion about political intelligence a few weeks ago. He showed me that a lawyer can sometimes have quite sensible ideas. As a matter of fact, I could use a lawyer like him myself."

Himmler merely nodded curtly, while I could see that Heydrich's ever-vigilant suspicions were immediately aroused. Indeed, the next day he asked me what I had discussed with Hess and was not satisfied until I had repeated to him the entire conversation.

Finally the door that led to Hitler's private apartment opened. He entered, walking very slowly and talking to one of his adjutants. He did not look up until he had reached the middle of the room. Then he shook hands with Hess, Himmler, and Heydrich, and finally with me. At the same time he measured me with a penetrating glance from head to foot. The others he greeted by raising his hand briefly. Then he strode into the dining room, accompanied by Hess and Himmler.

The adjutant quietly and quickly arranged the order in which we were to sit. On Hitler's right sat Himmler, then I, then Heydrich, and on his left Keitel and Bormann. Hess sat immediately opposite to him.

Hitler turned to me as soon as we had taken our places and said in his guttural voice, "I find your reports very interesting. I want you to go on with them." I nodded. There was a slight pause. Hitler's face looked rather red and swollen that day; I thought he must have a cold. As though he had read my thoughts he turned to me again and said, "I have a bad cold today. This low atmospheric pressure makes me uncomfortable too." Then, turning to Hess, he said, "Do you know, Hess, what the barometric pressure in Berlin is today? Only 739 mm. Just imagine! It's quite abnormal. It must upset people tremendously."

A subject of conversation having been found which

seemed to interest Hitler, everyone began talking about barometric pressure. But Hitler now sat withdrawn and did not say a word. It was quite obvious that he was not listening.

We had begun to eat, but Hitler was still waiting for his specially prepared meal. I was very hungry and helped myself generously. Meanwhile the conversation gradually died down. It is curious, I thought to myself, no one has anything to say; they are afraid to speak.

Then the silence was broken by Hitler turning to Himmler and saying, "Schellenberg does not believe that the two British agents are connected with Elser." "Yes, my Fuehrer," replied Himmler, "there is no possibility of any connection between Elser and Best and Stevens. I don't deny that British Intelligence may be connected with Elser through other channels. They may have made use of Germans—members of Strasser's 'Black Front,' for instance—but at the moment that's only hypothetical. Elser admits he was connected with two unknown men, but whether he was in touch with any political group we just don't know. They may have been Communists, agents of the British Secret Service, or members of the Black Front. There is only one other clue: our technical men are practically certain that the explosives and the fuses used in the bomb were made abroad."

Hitler remained silent for a moment. Then he turned to Heydrich. "That sounds quite possible, but what I would like to know is what type we are dealing with, from the point of view of criminal psychology? I want you to use every possible means to induce this criminal to talk. Use hypnosis, give him drugs—everything that modern science has developed in this direction. I've got to know who the instigators are, who stands behind this thing."

Not until now did Hitler turn toward his food. He ate hastily and not every elegantly—first, corn on the cob, over which he poured plenty of melted butter, then a huge plate of *kaiserschmarren*—a kind of Viennese pancake with raisins and sugar and a sweet sauce. While he was eating he remained silent. When he had finished he said to his aide, "I still haven't had that report Jodl was to send over."

The aide left the room and returned about two minutes later, bringing several typewritten sheets. He gave them to Hitler and handed him a large magnifying glass. While

Hitler studied the report the company round the table remained silent. Presently he said, as though he were thinking aloud, not addressing anyone in particular:

"The estimates of French steel production given in this report are quite correct in my opinion. The data on light and heavy guns—disregarding for the moment the armament of the Maginot Line—are probably also quite accurate. When I compare these figures to ours, it's quite obvious how superior we are to the French in these arms. They may still have a slight advantage in howitzers and heavy mortars, but even there we shall catch them up very quickly. And when I compare the reports on French tanks with our present strength—there our superiority is absolute. On top of this, we have new anti-tank guns and other automatic weapons—especially our new 105 mm. gun—not to mention the Luftwaffe. Our superiority is assured. No, no, I don't fear the French, not in the slightest." After having marked the report with a pencil, he handed it back to the aide. "Put it on my desk for tonight. I want to go over it again."

To the astonishment of the others I broke the ensuing silence by asking, in relation to Hitler's last remarks:

"And how, my Fuehrer, do you evaluate the strength of England's armaments? It is quite certain that England will fight, and in my opinion anyone who does not believe that is badly informed."

Hitler looked at me for a moment with astonishment. "For the moment," he said, "I am solely interested in the strength of the British Expeditionary Force on the Continent. Our entire Intelligence Service is working on this question at present. As far as Britain is concerned, don't forget that we have the stronger air force. We shall bomb their industrial centers out of existence with it."

"I cannot at present estimate the strength of Britain's anti-aircraft defenses," I said, "but we may be sure they'll be supported by their fleet, and that is certainly superior to ours."

"The support of their fleet in aircraft defense does not worry me," Hitler replied. "We shall take measures to divert the British Navy, and keep them busy. Our air force will sow mines all along the coasts of Britain. And don't forget one thing, my dear Schellenberg; I am going to build U-boats, and U-boats, and still more U-boats. This time Britain will not force us to our knees by starving us."

Then he asked suddenly, "What was your general impression during the conversations you had with those Englishmen in Holland—I mean before they were being interrogated?"

"My impression," I said, "was that Britain will fight this war as relentlessly and ruthlessly as she had fought all her wars; that even if we succeeded in occupying England, the government and the leaders would carry on the war from Canada. It will be a life and death struggle between brothers—and Stalin will be a smiling spectator."

At this point Himmler kicked me on the shin so violently that I could not continue, while Heydrich was glaring hard at me across the table. But I could not see why I should not speak freely, even to Hitler. And as though some devil were prompting me I could not help adding, "I don't know, my Fuehrer, if it was really necessary to change our policy toward Britain after the agreement at Godesberg."

The whole company were now looking at each other, horrified by my impudence. Heydrich had paled to the roots of his hair, while Himmler looked down at the table in front of him deeply embarrassed and played nervously with his bread.

Hitler stared fixedly at me for several seconds. But I looked him firmly in the eye. For quite a while he said nothing. The pause seemed interminable. Finally he said, "I hope you realize that it is necessary to see the situation in Germany as a whole. Originally I wanted to work together with Britain. But Britain has rejected me again and again. It is true, there is nothing worse than a family quarrel, and racially the English are in a way our relatives. As far as that goes, you may be right. It's a pity that we have to be locked in this death struggle, while our real enemies in the East can sit back and wait until Europe is exhausted. That is why I do not wish to destroy Britain and never shall"—here his voice became sharp and penetrating—"but they must be made to realize, and even Churchill must be made to realize, that Germany has the right to live too. And I will fight Britain until she has come down off her high horse. The time will come when they will be ready to reach an agreement with us. That is my real aim. You understand that?"

"Yes, my Fuehrer," I replied, "I understand the course of your thoughts. But one must not forget that the men-

tality of an island race is different to ours. Their history
and their traditions are different. They are determined by
the historical laws which their insular position has imposed
upon them, and as a consequence of which they are a
colonial power. Theirs is the insular way of life, ours the
Continental, and as a consequence of that we are now a
Continental power. It is very hard to reconcile the two
and quite different national characters that have resulted
from these differences. The English are tenacious, unemotional, and relentless; it is not for nothing that they bear
the name 'John Bull.' A war like this, once it starts, is like
an avalanche. And who would try to calculate the course
of an avalanche?"

"My dear fellow," replied Hitler, "let that be my worry.
One thing more," he said after a pause, "have you been in
touch with Ribbentrop about the Dutch note concerning
the officer who died of wounds?" Then he turned to
Heydrich and began to laugh. "These Dutch really are too
stupid. If I were in their place I would have kept quiet.
Instead they play right into my hands with this note. And
when the time comes, I'll pay them back. They admit the
man was an officer of their General Staff, which proves
that they and not we were the first to violate neutrality."

I said that so far I had not spoken to Ribbentrop.
Another pause followed. Then Hitler said to Himmler,
"There are still several things I have to discuss with you."
He rose abruptly, made a bow to the others at the table,
and then turned to Heydrich and me. "I would like you to
stay too."

We went into the next room where large easy chairs
were arranged comfortably round the fireplace. On the
way Himmler said to me, "You certainly are terribly
pigheaded. But apparently the Fuehrer was amused." And
Heydrich added, "My dear fellow, I had not realized you
were such an Anglophile. Is that the result of your contact
with Best and Stevens?" I realized that it would be wise to
restrain myself and that I had gone about as far as I
could.

For the next hour Hitler talked only to Himmler. He
stood most of the time, rocking back and forth on his
heels as he spoke while Himmler close beside him inclined
his face toward Hitler with an expression of rapt attention. I heard one of the SS adjutants whisper to another,

"Look at Heini—he'll crawl into the old man's ear in a minute."

Hitler was drinking peppermint tea, but for his guests he had ordered champagne. After he had finished his conversation with Himmler, which had been carried on so softly that no one else could follow, Hitler turned again to the rest of the company. He spoke of the Luftwaffe, praising the work Goering was doing, and especially the fact that he availed himself of the experience of the veteran fighter pilots of the First World War. Then anti-aircraft defenses, war production, and other questions of warfare were discussed. I reached home very late and completely exhausted.

The next day, at Hitler's orders, I attended a meeting between Heydrich and Mueller. The latter still looked very pale and overworked. He told us that during the night and morning three doctors, specialists in the psychiatric field, had worked on Elser and were still doing so. He had been given strong injections of pervitin, but had not changed his testimony under the drug's influence.

Mueller had also placed an entire carpenter's shop at Elser's disposal. There he had worked for the last few days and had almost completed a reconstruction of his bomb. He had also made a wooden pillar identical with the one in the Beer Cellar, and was demonstrating his method of concealing the bomb. Heydrich was extremely interested, so we went upstairs to the rooms where Elser was imprisoned.

It was the first time I had seen him. He was a small, pale man, with clear bright eyes and long black hair. He had a high forehead, and strong sensitive hands. He looked a typical highly skilled artisan, and indeed the work he was doing was in its way a masterpiece. At first he was very shy and reserved and seemed rather frightened. He answered our questions unwillingly, speaking with a strong Swabian accent, and with the fewest possible words. It was only when we began to ask him about his work, to praise its ingenuity and precision, that he came out of his shell. Then he really came to life and went into long and enthusiastic explanations of the problems involved in the construction of the bomb and how he had solved them. Listening to him was so interesting that I completely forgot the grim purpose to which he had put all this ingenuity.

When he was asked about his two anonymous accomplices he gave the same answers as before: he had not known who they were and did not know now. Heydrich pointed out that conversations about explosives and fuses with complete strangers might be a dangerous business—hadn't he realized that? Elser replied quite unemotionally, almost lethargically, in fact, that certainly there was danger, but he had taken that into account. From the day on which he had made the decision to kill Hitler he had known that his own life would be ended too. He had been certain he would succeed in the attempt because of his technical ability. The preparations had taken him a year and a half.

We looked at each other. Mueller was quite excited, but Heydrich had a small derisive smile on his lips. Then we left.

The next day four of the best hypnotists in Germany attempted to hypnotize Elser. Only one of them succeeded, but even under hypnosis Elser gave exactly the same testimony as before.

One of these hypnotists made, to my way of thinking, the best analysis of Elser's character and motivation. He said that the assassin was a typical warped fanatic who went his own way alone. He had psychotic compulsions, related especially to technical matters, which sprang from an urge to achieve something really noteworthy. This was due to an abnormal need for recognition and acknowledgment which was reinforced by a thirst for vengeance for the alleged injustice which had been done to his brother. In killing the leader of the Third Reich he would satisfy all these compulsions because he would become famous himself, and he would have felt morally justified by freeing Germany from a great evil. Such urges, combined with the desire to suffer and sacrifice oneself, were typical of religious and sectarian fanaticism. Upon checking back, similar psychotic disorders were found to have occurred in Elser's family.

Himmler was most dissatisfied with our achievements. Before going to report to Hitler he said to me, almost as though imploring my aid, "Schellenberg, this is not really our problem. What we have to do is find the people behind this thing. The Fuehrer simply will not believe that Elser did it alone, and again and again he insists on having a great propaganda trial."

It was a problem that continued to occupy Himmler for the next three months, and during that period I had the greatest difficulty in preventing Best and Stevens from being involved in the trial.

9. SOME OBSERVATIONS ON HITLER

Hitler's personality—His belief in his own "mission"—His agnosticism—Causes of his breakdown in health—The basis of his anti-Semitism—Influence of Plaischinger and others on Hitler's racial theories—His concept of Western supremacy

I KNEW Hitler personally, I worked with him, and I am familiar with numerous details of his daily life, his methods, and his political and sociological conceptions. I ought, therefore, to be in a position to formulate a complete picture of his personality, but though I have often tried to do so, both in my own mind and in writing, I must confess that I have never really succeeded.

Hitler's knowledge was on the one hand sound and on the other completely superficial and dilettante. He had highly developed political instincts which were combined with a complete lack of moral scruples; he was governed by the most inexplicable hallucinatory conceptions and *petit-bourgeois* inhibitions. But his one dominant and dominating characteristic was that he felt himself appointed by providence to do great things for the German people. This was his historic "mission," in which he believed completely.

It was his intense manner and the suggestive power of his personality that created the impression of an intellect and a range of knowledge far above the average. In addition, there was his extraordinary dialectical ability, which enabled him to outargue even the most expert authorities in any field of discussion, often with most harmful results. He threw them so off balance that they did not think of the appropriate replies until afterward.

He had an insatiable craving for recognition and power, combined with a cultivated ruthlessness which reinforced his lightning reactions, his energy, and his determination. While fortune smiled on him these qualities enabled him to dominate Germany and to gain the startled attention of the whole world.

Hitler did not believe in a personal god. He believed only in the bond of blood between succeeding generations and in a vague conception of fate or providence. Nor did he believe in a life after death. In this connection he often quoted a sentence from the *Edda*, that remarkable collection of ancient Icelandic literature, which to him represented the profoundest Nordic wisdom: "All things will pass away, nothing will remain but death and the glory of deeds."

In the end, Hitler's faith in his "mission" increased to such an extent that it can only be described as mania. But this idea of himself as the German Messiah was the source of his personal power. It enabled him to become the ruler of eighty million people—and in the space of twelve short years to leave his ineradicable mark on history.

It was only when the German people failed to fulfill their Fuehrer's expectations at Stalingrad and in North Africa that, with the dawning possibility of defeat, Hitler's powers of intuition and his personal magnetism began to fade. Moreover, from the end of 1943 he showed progressive symptoms of Parkinson's disease. Dr. de Crinis, as well as two of Hitler's personal physicans, Dr. Brandt and Dr. Stumpfegger, agreed that a chronic degeneration of the nervous system had set in.

Heydrich was informed about the smallest detail of Hitler's private life. He saw every diagnosis made by Hitler's doctors and knew of all his strange and abnormal pathological inclinations. I saw some of these reports myself when they were transferred to Himmler's office after Heydrich's death. They showed that Hitler was so ruled by the demonic forces driving him that he ceased to have thoughts of normal cohabitation with a woman. The ecstasies of power in every form were sufficient for him. During his speeches he fell, or, rather, worked himself into such orgiastic frenzies that he achieved through them complete emotional satisfaction. But the inroads thus made upon his nervous system—and perhaps his own awareness of the disquieting strangeness of such a condition—drove him to seek medical advice from his friend, Dr. Morell, and also from Dr. Brandt. Dr. Morell's diagnosis and treatment, however, did not lead to an alleviation of this condition; on the contrary intensified it. For Morell believed that these symptoms were inseparably bound up with Hitler's power of mass suggestion, that it was this intensity which worked upon his audience as a magnet works upon iron filing. It was in this period of mental and physical breakdown that Hitler reached his decision to destroy the Jews.

Hitler's racial mania was one of his characteristic features. I discussed this several times with Dr. Gutbarlett, a Munich physician who belonged to the intimate circle round Hitler. Gutbarlett believed in the "sidereal pendulum," an astrological contraption, and claimed that this had given him the power to sense at once the presence of any Jews or persons of partial Jewish ancestry, and to pick them out in any group of people. Hitler availed himself of Gutbarlett's mystic power and had many discussions with him on racial questions.

Hitler's hatred of the Jews was the obverse side of his theory of the supremacy of the Germanic race. During his stay in Vienna he had come under the influence of the Schoenerer Movement—Schoenerer was the chief exponent of Austrian anti-Semitism, which was a considerable political force there in the early decades of this century. During that time Hitler read a great deal, covering the most diverse fields of study. But his chief interest had been the prehistory of the Germanic tribes, the origins of Nordic culture, and the historic role of the Aryan race. These he made the foundations of his racial theories, and from them developed his antagonism toward Judaism. But the emotional force that reinforced these theories lay deep in his own character.

Another man who exercised a great influence over him was the Austrian engineer, Plaischinger. It was from him that Hitler took the idea of modeling the structure and the leadership of the Nazi party on the organization of the Order of the Jesuits. One sentence which constantly recurred in Hitler's speeches was taken from Plaischinger, the Nazi philosopher: "The Jews are the microbes of pure decomposition. They are only capable of thinking analytically and are incapable of creative thought."

After the year 1943 his hatred of the Jews was intensified to a pathological degree. It was international Jewry that was chiefly responsible for the defeat of Germany. It was they who made Roosevelt and Churchill formulate the demand for "Unconditional Surrender" at Casablanca. Churchill and Roosevelt were agents of the Jews.

All this indicates the influence these prejudices, formulated as pseudo-scientific theories and believed in with pathological intensity, had on the decision of the man who was absolute ruler over eighty million Germans. All his realistic thinking, no matter how well founded in political and historical experience, was distorted by these conceptions. The British were a component part of the Germanic race, and therefore as precious as the Germans themselves. Hitler's final aim was to achieve a fusion of all the Germanic elements in Europe and then lead them against the Communist hordes.

Here, too, his racial theories had a decisive effect. No matter how many Secret Service reports he received to the contrary, Hitler refused to relinquish the insane notion that since 1920 Stalin had been systematically pursuing a secret policy aimed at the intermixing of all the racial components within the Soviet Union. The aim of this program was to bring about the predominance of the Mongol element over all others.

In this connection I recall a conversation with Himmler. It was 1942, and I had just reported on our attempts to negotiate a peace in the East between Japan and China. We were both standing beside a huge globe. Himmler swept his hand across the entire breadth of the Russian continent, then he pointed to tiny Germany and said, "If we lose this time there can be no salvation." Then turning the globe he swept his hand across China, and continued, "And what would happen if one day Russia should unite with China? I can only repeat what the Fuehrer said in this connection the other day—'God punish England!' "

Hitler's original conception had been to create, with the help of Britain, a so-called "Eurafrican Space," which was to be built up as the center of resistance against the East. Finally, after 1940, recognizing Britain's refusal to reach a compromise, he transformed this conception into that of the so-called "Eurasian Space." Relying solely on his own strength, he would achieve the domination of Europe and integrate all the forces of the conquered peoples in this great endeavor. He would win the East as a new colonial space for this united Europe, from which Britain would be excluded.

10. OPERATION "SEALION"

*A setback for the Wehrmacht—Security arrangements for
the invasion of Denmark and Norway—Reporting on the
Venlo incident—Spies in France's heavy industries—
Hitler's hesitation after Dunkirk—Preparations ordered
for the invasion of England—These plans canceled*

THE BEGINNING of the year 1940 found
me overburdened with work. My chief task was the reorganization of the Counter-Espionage Department, which
was to occupy me for the rest of that year. In addition,
through continually receiving orders to carry out special
assignments I sometimes found myself working for as long
as seventeen hours a day. Even the early morning rides,
which were my sole form of relaxation, were now combined with my work. Every day I went riding with Admiral Canaris, chief of Military Intelligence, and as we rode
we discussed problems of mutual interest with a view to
co-ordinating the work of our respective agencies.

At the beginning of the year the German High Command met with a very embarrassing setback. Two
Wehrmacht officers on their way to Cologne were invited
to break their journey at Munster to visit an old friend.
One of these officers was a special courier carrying highly
important secret documents, namely the plans for the
attack on Holland and Belgium.

At Munster the reunion proved so enjoyable that the
two officers missed the train for Cologne. So their friend,
who was a major in the Luftwaffe, offered to fly them
there, and they agreed. But in poor visibility the major
lost his way and they made a forced landing near Malines
in Belgium. The officers at once decided to burn their
documents, but found they had no matches, and before
they could think of another method of destroying them,
they were arrested by the Belgian authorities. At the
police station while they were alone in a waiting room
they made another attempt to destroy their papers by

thrusting them into a stove, but the papers would not catch fire. They were only slightly singed, and the Belgians had no difficulty in saving them and then deciphering them.

When Hitler heard what had happened he raved. He at once suspected that premeditated treason was involved and wanted to have the two officers shot out of hand. Further investigations revealed, however, that at the very worst they were guilty only of criminal negligence.

The Western Powers were, of course, shocked and alarmed when at first they saw the plans for the attack. However, they finally decided that the documents had been placed in their hands by the Germans purposely in order to mislead them. They probably could not imagine that we had been guilty of such a crass blunder.

Shortly after this incident Himmler called me late at night. He told me that he had been unable to reach Heydrich and that I should prepare the draft of an order on secrecy regulations for the Wehrmacht. The order was also to apply to all other branches of the administration and Hitler wanted to issue it that very night.

Himmler was so excited and so confused that I found it impossible to understand just what Hitler did want. Each time I tried to get him to explain a little more clearly he became impatient and irritable and finally ordered me to have the draft ready within two hours.

I sat at my desk for at least half an hour just staring in front of me. Finally I managed to sketch out what seemed to be the main points, but when Himmler placed this draft before Hitler two hours later the Fuehrer was not satisfied with it. He therefore dictated the order himself, calling it *Order No. 1 to all Wehrmacht and Civilian Authorities.*

The main point of Hitler's version was that all matters dealing with the conduct of the war should only be made known to and discussed with persons immediately concerned. This, of course, was nothing new as far as Himmler's and Heydrich's organizations were concerned, where the separation of planning and administration had been an established principle for a long time, and even went so far that the heads of departments hardly ever informed each other of what they were doing. It was found, however, that excessive secrecy not only began to hamper co-operation, but led to a duplication of work and enabled many people to cover up their failures and deficiencies.

At the beginning of March 1940, Hitler issued the code word *"Weseruebung"* to cover all operations leading to the German occupation of Denmark and Norway. In this connection the following task was assigned to me: To activate all Secret Service contacts with Norway, which my organization had established from Hamburg; these were mainly among the personnel of German-Norwegian shipping lines and the large fishing and fish processing firms. (The Norwegian branch offices of these companies were staffed by our agents.) Their most important task now was to provide weather information on which the German Fleet, responsible for the great troop transports, would depend. It would also be of the greatest importance, of course, for Luftwaffe operations. The data, disguised as sales prices, offers, and tonnage reports on fishing, was transmitted by telephone and wireless and proved satisfactory.

Hitler's decision to occupy Denmark and Norway resulted from our Secret Service reports warning him that the British were concentrating their fleet for an attack on Norway, and it now became my tasks to insure the secrecy of our own preparations—transport and concentration of troops and so forth—for the invasion.

But the rapidity with which the fleet, the army, and the air force had to be mobilized made the maintenance of secrecy extremely difficult. I concentrated on the strictest possible control of the ports of embarkation, and all harbor areas, hotels, arterial roads, and passenger trains were placed under the strictest surveillance. In Stettin, however, the security situation was extremely precarious. The whole city was like a great circus when the tents are going up. There were continual comings and goings of large bodies of troops. Soldiers were searching for their units and NCO's and officers cursing and running about excitedly as their forces prepared for embarkation. The soldiers were mostly Alpine troops from Austria, with the broad humor and easygoing attitude that is characteristic of their sort. It was very difficult to impress them with the seriousness of the security measures, and to this day I cannot understand how these troop movements could possibly have escaped the attention of the enemy intelligence services. It would have been quite easy for them to learn the destination of the transports.

Among other inquiries that I received was one from

Ribbentrop, who wanted to know whether I had enough special agents to insure the safety of the Danish Royal Family in case fighting developed in their country. When the time came, however, operations in Denmark proceeded according to plan, swiftly and without bloodshed.

When Hitler decided to occupy Denmark and Norway he did not know of the draft resolution passed by the Allied Supreme Council on March 28, 1940. This resolution dealt with the laying of minefields along the coasts of Norway, Denmark, and Sweden, in spite of the fact that this would violate the neutrality of those countries. Had Hitler known of this, it would have saved him a lot of rationalizing to justify their occupation.

But we only received the full text of the Allied resolution several days later, when one of my agents got access to Paul Reynaud's private switchboard. This version of the resolution also dealt with the bombing of Russian oilfields in the Caucasus and measures to prevent us from receiving Rumanian oil.

Just at this time I received orders from Hitler to collaborate with Ribbentrop in producing as quickly as possible an analysis of the Venlo negotiations and the subsequent investigations of Major Best and Captain Stevens. When I went to see Ribbentrop he was standing behind his desk with his arms folded. He examined me coolly, then with a wooden gesture indicated a chair beside his desk. "What have you to report?" he asked. I thought to myself: Surely you must know that already. With a feeling of some resentment I began dryly and curtly to tell him. I did not go out of my way to impress him and Ribbentrop must have noticed this, for presently he said quite affably, "Can't we be a bit more comfortable while we talk? Let's sit down, it'll be easier for you to handle your documents."

From that point on he assumed his most pleasant manner. He displayed great interest, several times interjecting questions and nodding approvingly. After I had finished he said, "The Fuehrer is enormously interested in your work. He is firmly convinced that with this Venlo material we can prove beyond doubt that Holland has violated her neutrality in favor of Britain. He has ordered us to draw up a complete report together, with the purpose of establishing the fact."

He then called in his chief legal adviser, Undersecretary Gauss, to help us prepare the report. There was hardly an important document that was not drafted by Gauss, and if he had any doubts or objections he always stated them to Ribbentrop in a discreet and objective manner. But invariably he left open a line of retreat for himself by saying, "However, if the Foreign Minister feels that we should choose this course, then we will have to proceed in the following manner . . ." Gauss, who had the square, massive head of a scholar, was probably the greatest German authority on international law. He had served all regimes with the same loyalty and conscientiousness, the Social Democratic government of Scheidemann, the governments of Stresemann and Bruening, and now he served the Nazi. (At Nuremberg he finally appeared as a witness for the prosecution against his own colleagues and testified against me concerning the Venlo incident.) Early in 1940 Gauss had many consultations with me and at that time had not the slightest doubt or hesitation in using his great knowledge to establish that Holland had committed a breach of her neutrality.

On May 1, 1940, I received an order from Heydrich to complete my final report within four hours, and the moment it was finished he took it to Hitler.

The next day I reported to Ribbentrop at the Foreign Office where memoranda, based on my report, were being prepared for transmission to the Dutch and Belgian governments advising them of the imminent occupation of their countries. Those working at this task were not allowed to leave the building.

During the pauses in our work Ribbentrop made long speeches about his experiences with the British Secret Service. He had quite a phobia about British espionage and maintained that every single Englishman who traveled or lived abroad was given assignments by the Secret Service. His deep hatred of all things English was noticeable in everything he said. "This will teach that arrogant British mob a lesson" were his last words on this subject.

We finished the report late at night. I still had to show Himmler the final version of it. He received me at his lodgings and read it through very carefully. The next morning, May 8, I drove in a fast car to Upper Bavaria where Dr. Frick, Minister of the Interior, was staying in a villa on the Starnberger Lake. Our report had to be signed by him, as well as the Foreign Minister, to give it the necessary weight.

It was a beautiful sunny day and I enjoyed the drive immensely. Even the briefest escape from the witches' cauldron of Berlin was a great relief. I arrived toward noon and was received at once. Frick read the report while I gave a brief explanation, and he then signed it with a firm hand. An hour later I was on my way back to Berlin, where I arrived at about nine o'clock that night.

I reported to Ribbentrop, who patted me on the back and asked me to stay and help with the technical task of preparing the various copies of the memorandum. Working with four secretaries, this was accomplished in two hours.

The memoranda went out early in the morning of May 9. On the morning of the 10th the German armies began their offensive in the west.

Military operations in the west proceeded according to schedule and, strangely enough, in spite of the fiasco at Malines, when Field Marshal von Manstein's plans of attack had fallen into Belgian hands, these same plans were in fact carried out. The General Staff wanted to alter them, but Hitler and von Manstein, relying on a double bluff, insisted on their retention. The German units to the south and west of the frontier remained on the defensive while our troops attacked at the junction of the Maginot Line and the Belgian fortifications, where there was a gap covered only by weak defenses.

The Secret Service had done excellent preparatory work. Our agents, who had found employment in the cement factories in Nancy, Saargemuend, and Metz, furnished us with precise information about the fortifications of the Maginot Line. Contact men in the great Schneider-Creuzot armaments factories informed us about the equipment of the French artillery and armored units, and we even managed to secure photostatic copies of secret orders and operational plans from the central office of the *Deuxième Bureau*. Specially trained units attached to the Military Secret Service were employed in the operations against the strongest fortress of the Belgian defense system, the Fort Eben Emael. The plans had been prepared, studied, and carefully rehearsed well before these units went into action. Fort Eben Emael was captured by commando tactics by the Lehrregiment Brandenburg, Z.B.V. 800 supported by specially trained units of paratroops. It was the first time that such a large-scale drop by parachute troops had been attempted and was also the first time use had been made of massed gliders, which landed within the area of the fortress itself. In a similar action the bridge across the River Scheldt was preserved from destruction by our parachute units, and our advancing ground forces were able to establish contact with the airborne units in a relatively short time.

I was given a special assignment. Working with experts of the Propaganda Ministry, I devised radio broadcasts and propaganda for other media designed to create the greatest possible confusion among our enemies, especially the French. Dr. Adolf Raskin, then director of Radio Saarbruecken, and a close friend of mine, was the man chiefly responsible for the great successes we achieved. Working with three transmitters specially equipped with a very powerful signal, he sent a continual stream of news reports in French, purporting to be of official French origin but which were in fact his own imaginative inventions. These false news items were the chief cause of the fatal panic and confusion among the French civilian population. Streams of refugees blocked all the highways of France and made troop movements behind the French lines almost impossible. Meanwhile in spite of the difficulties created by the military situation, our agents in France continued to collect information, which was transmitted to us by a special network of frontier-crossing couriers and by telephone, a cable having been laid across the Maginot Line to Saaralben.

Another device which did great damage was a small and apparently innocuous pamphlet which was distributed in great numbers by our agents and also dropped from aircraft. Printed in French and described as being the prophecies of Nostradamus—many of whose prophecies were actually included—the pamphlet predicted terrifying destruction from "flying fire machines," stressing all the time that southeastern France would be preserved from this horror. While preparing these brochures, I had never imagined that they would have such a tremendous effect. All the efforts of the civilian and military authorities to divert the great streams of refugees from attempting to reach southeastern France proved useless.

There followed the advance of Guderian's armored column toward Amiens and the capture of Abbeville, the capitulation of the Belgian Army, and finally the failure of the Anglo-French forces to break out of the German encirclement at Arras. At this point the whole campaign was virtually won.

The subsequent events, the failure of the German armies to exploit their tremendous victories on the traditional battlegrounds of Flanders and France and proceed with the invasion of England, find their final explanation in the personality of Adolf Hitler. Outside commentators have put forward the explanation that at this moment Hitler's nerve failed, and that he lacked the courage to make the bold move which would have brought certain success. Even among the German General Staff there were those who held this opinion. But the real reason lay in his conviction that France was a dying nation and the British were a Germanic brother-people worthy of preservation. Great Britain woud finally see reason and join Germany. It is true that he gave an order for the preparation of the invasion, but because of his underlying feelings and preoccupations he proceeded very hesitantly. Then he was beset by disagreements among members of the General Staff, and contrary to his usual decisive intervention as Supreme Military Commander, Hitler allowed these difficulties and personal prejudices to delay the decision until in the end the whole thing came to naught. This can be seen clearly in all the orders issued by Keitel at the time.

In spite of this, all the organs of the political and military leadership worked on the preparation of Operation "Sealion" at top speed and with typical Prussian thoroughness. For example, at the end of June 1940, I was ordered to prepare a small handbook for the invading troops and the political and administrative units that would accompany them, describing briefly the most important political, administrative, and economic institutions of Great Britain and the leading public figures. It was also to contain instructions on the necessary measures to be taken in occupying the premises of the Foreign Office, the War Office, the Home Office, and the various departments of the Secret Service and Special Branch. This task occupied a great deal of my time, involving the collection and assembly of material from various sources by a selected staff of my own people. When it was finished an edition of twenty thousand copies was printed, and stored in a room next to my office. They were burned in 1943 in a fire started in one of the air raids, an ending that is symbolic of the ultimate failure of the German opportunity in the west.

11. A PLOT TO KIDNAP
THE DUKE OF WINDSOR

Ribbentrop on the Duke's position—Hitler's views—
Outline of the plan—The order given—I proceed to Por-
tugal—Contact with the German Ambassador—The situa-
tion in Spain—Counteracting British influence—Attitude
of Portuguese officials—Impossibility of my mission—
Creating suspense—My report to Berlin—Return from
Lisbon—Hitler approves my conduct of the affair

ONE MORNING in July 1940, I received a
call from one of my friends at the Foreign Office, warning
me to expect a call from the "old man"—meaning Ribbentrop—as soon as he was "ready for action." My friend
did not know what it was all about, but it seemed to be
something terribly urgent.

At noon Ribbentrop's sonorous voice came over the
telephone: "Tell me, my dear fellow, could you come over
to my office at once? You have time, haven't you?"
"Certainly," I replied, "but could you tell me what it's
about? There may be some material that I should bring
along." "No, no," said Ribbentrop, "come at once. It's not
a matter I can discuss over the telephone."

I called Heydrich immediately and reported the conversation, for I knew his pathological jealousy. Heydrich said
at once, "I see; the gentleman no longer wishes to consult
me—old idiot! Well, go over there and give him my best
regards." I promised Heydrich that I would give him a
detailed report of what Ribbentrop wanted.

As usual Ribbentrop received me standing behind his
desk with folded arms and a serious expression on his
face. He asked me to be seated and, after a few polite
remarks, came to the point. He had heard that I had
various connections in Spain and Portugal and had even
achieved a measure of co-operation with the police of
these countries. I did not know where these remarks were
leading, and answered very cautiously. Dissatisfied with

my evasive replies, he shook his head. "Mmm," he said, then he was silent. Suddenly he said, "You remember the Duke of Windsor, of course? Were you introduced to him during his last visit?" I said that I had not been. "Have you any material on him?" Ribbentrop asked. "I really cannot say at the moment," I replied. "Well, what do you think of him personally? How do you evaluate him as a political figure, for instance?" I admitted honestly that these questions had taken me by surprise and that at the moment my knowledge was not sufficient to give a proper answer. I had seen the Duke at the time of his last visit to Germany and, of course, knew what was generally known about the reasons for his abdication. It seemed that the English had handled the whole problem very sensibly; that in the end tradition and responsibility had had to take precedence over human feelings and personal emotions. It seemed difficult to decide whether the matter should be adjudged a sign of weakness or of strength in the English Royal Family. It seemed that in the lengthy conferences on the subject the members of the government had shown understanding of the human and political problems involved. When I had finished I thought that Ribbentrop's eyes would pop out of his head, so astonished was he at the uninhibited manner in which I expressed these opinions. He lost no time in putting me right.

The Duke of Windsor was one of the most socially aware and right-thinking Englishmen he had ever met. It was this which had displeased the governing clique; the marriage issue had been a welcome pretext to remove this honest and faithful friend of Germany. All the questions of tradition and ceremonial that were raised were completely secondary.

Here I tried to object, but was silenced by an abrupt gesture. "My dear Schellenberg, you have a completely wrong view of these things—also of the real reasons behind the Duke's abdication. The Fuehrer and I already recognized the facts of the situation in 1936. The crux of the matter is that, since his abdication, the Duke has been under strict surveillance by the British Secret Service. We know what his feelings are: it's almost as if he were their prisoner. Every attempt that he's made to free himself, however discreet he may have been, has failed. And we know from our reports that he still entertains the same sympathetic feelings toward Germany, and that given the right circumstances he wouldn't be averse to escaping from his present environment—the whole thing's getting on his nerves. We've had word that he has even spoken about living in Spain and that if he did go there he'd be ready to be friends with Germany again as he was before. The Fuehrer thinks this attitude is extremely important, and we thought that you with your Western outlook might be the most suitable person to make some sort of exploratory contact with the Duke—as the representative, of course, of the head of the German State. The Fuehrer feels that if the atmosphere seemed propitious you might perhaps make the Duke some material offer. Now, we should be prepared to deposit in Switzerland for his own use a sum of fifty million Swiss francs—if he were ready to make some official gesture dissociating himself from the maneuvers of the British Royal Family. The Fuehrer would, of course, prefer him to live in Switzerland, though any other neutral country would do so long as it's not outside the economic or the political or military influence of the German Reich.

"If the British Secret Service should try to frustrate the Duke in some such arrangement, then the Fuehrer orders that you are to circumvent the British plans, even at the risk of your life, and, if need be, by the use of force. Whatever happens, the Duke of Windsor must be brought safely to the country of his choice. Hitler attaches the greatest importance to this operation, and he has come to the conclusion after serious consideration that if the Duke should prove hesitant, he himself would have no objection to your helping the Duke to reach the right decision by coercion—even by threats or force if the circumstances make it advisable. But it will also be your responsibility to make sure at the same time that the Duke and his wife are not exposed to any personal danger.

"Now, in the near future the Duke expects to have an invitation to hunt with some Spanish friends. This hunt should offer an excellent opportunity for you to establish contact with him. From that point he can be immediately be brought into another country. All the necessary means for you to carry out this assignment will be at your disposal. Last night I discussed the whole matter again thoroughly with the Fuehrer, and we have agreed to give you a completely free hand. But he demands that you let him see daily reports on the progress of the affair. Herewith, in the name of the Fuehrer, I give you the order to carry out this assignment at once. You are ready, of course, to carry it out?"

For a moment I sat stunned. I really couldn't grasp the whole thing so quickly. So to gain time I said, "Herr Reichsminister, may I ask a few questions—to clarify my understanding of the matter?" "Be quick about it," Ribbentrop answered. "You spoke of the Duke's sympathy for Germany," I said. "Is it sympathy for the German way of life, for the German people, or does it also include the present form of government?" I saw at once that I had gone too far. Brusquely he said, "When we speak of Germany today, it is the Germany in which you also live." "May I ask," I went on, "just how reliable is this secret information of yours?" "It comes," he said, "from the most reliable circles of Spanish society. The details of these reports need not concern you now. Any details which are of importance you can discuss with our Ambassador in Madrid." I asked one further question: "Do I understand that if the Duke of Windsor should resist, I am to bring him into this 'other country' that you speak of by force? It seems to me there's a contradiction in that. Surely the whole action must depend on the voluntary co-operation of the Duke?" "Well," answered Ribbentrop, "the Fuehrer feels that force should be used primarily against the British Secret Service—against the Duke only insofar as his hesitation might be based on a fear psychosis which forceful action on our part would help him to overcome. Once he's a free man and able to move about without surveillance by British Intelligence, he'll be grateful to us. As far as the money to be placed at his disposal is concerned, fifty million Swiss francs by no means represents the absolute maximum. The Fuehrer is quite ready to go to a higher figure. For the rest—well, don't worry too much. Have confidence in yourself and do your best. I will report to the Fuehrer that you have accepted the assignment."

I nodded, rose, and was about to say good-by, when Ribbentrop said, "One moment—" and, taking up the telephone, asked for Hitler. He handed me the second earpiece, so that I could listen in, and when Hitler's peculiar hollow voice came on the line Ribbentrop briefly reported our conversation. I could tell from Hitler's voice that he was not too happy about the whole thing. His replies were curt: "Yes—certainly—agreed." Finally he said, "Schellenberg should particularly bear in mind the importance of the Duchess's attitude and try as hard as possible to get her support. She has great influence over the Duke." "Very well then," said Ribbentrop, "Schellenberg will fly by special plane to Madrid as quickly as possible." "Good," Hitler answered. "He has all the authorization he needs. Tell him from me that I am relying on him." Ribbentrop rose, made a bow toward the telephone, and said, "Thank you, my Fuehrer, that is all."

I asked Ribbentrop about the transmission of my reports, which were to be sent through diplomatic channels, and our conversation ended with a brief discussion of technical questions about currency, passports, and so forth.

I went at once to Heydrich, who received me somewhat coolly. "Ribbentrop always wants to use our people when he gets ideas like this. You are really much too valuable to me to waste on this affair. I don't like the whole plan. Still, once the Fuehrer gets hold of such a notion it's very difficult to talk him out of it, and Ribbentrop is the worst possible adviser. You have to realize that you will be making front-line contact with our opponents, so I don't want you to travel alone. Take two reliable and experienced men with you who can speak the language. At least you will have some protection. Certainly if I were head of the British Secret Service, I would settle your hash for you."

The next day was taken up with preparations for the journey. I gathered all available information, selected the most suitable assistants for Madrid and Lisbon, and left instructions regarding the work to be carried out in my department during my absence.

Soon afterward Ribbentrop called me again and said curtly, "Please come over to my office right away." When I arrived there all he wanted was to ask whether I was satisfied with my preparations and if I had enough money. He also asked whether I had worked out a plan. I said not yet. He then said that of course everything concerning the affair had to be kept entirely secret and that the Fuehrer would personally punish the slightest violation of secrecy—the Fuehrer had wanted him to tell me that. It was typical of Ribbentrop's methods that he mentioned this only now. I reassured him, and finally was able to take my leave.

The next morning I flew by way of Lyons and Marseilles to Barcelona, whence we flew on to Madrid. A stifling heat lay over the land. The bare brown rocks of the Spanish mountains made me think of a lunar landscape. The pilots, who always worked as special couriers of the Secret Service, were friends of mine, and one of them invited me onto the flight deck to get some fresh air. Presently we swung in a great curve over the old city of Madrid and made a gentle landing.

I went first to a hostel for German state employees, then to a hotel where I registered officially, and finally to a private house where I was actually to live. After I had changed and freshened myself up, I went by a roundabout way to the German Embassy and requested an interview with von Stohrer, the German Ambassador.

I told him briefly about my assignment. It seemed that he had not been given a very clear picture of it. It also transpired that the information on which the authorities in Berlin had based their decision had come in the first place from him. He had social connections which led, through members of the Spanish aristocracy, to the Duke of Windsor. Several Spanish and Portuguese nobles were very close friends of the Duke, and one evening he had told them at a party how annoying the continual surveillance of his movements had become and had expressed dissatisfaction with his whole situation. He seemed also to be unhappy about his appointment as Governor of Bermuda. During various conversations he had often said that he would be pleased to pay a long visit to Spain so that he could get away from it all and live undisturbed with his wife. Thereupon an invitation to a hunt had been sent to him and he had accepted it. The date had not yet been settled.

Von Stohrer said he would soon be able to give me more details about where the hunt would take place and at what time, and would also introduce me into Spanish society so as to give me the opportunity to form my own opinions for the further conduct of the matter. The place that the Duke was to visit was near the Spanish-Portuguese frontier. To allay British suspicions of a planned flight into Spain it might be best to name a locality on the border itself, then during one of the hunting excursions a removal "by mistake" into the Spanish interior would be possible.

The conversation with von Stohrer did not contribute anything very new, so we decided to wait until the Duke of Windsor's plans took more definite shape.

Madrid was one of the most strongly developed centers of the German Secret Service. Apart from active espionage and counter-espionage, its military sector included between seventy and a hundred employees who lived and worked in one of the extra-territorial buildings of the German Embassy. There we had one of our most important short-wave listening posts and decoding stations; also a meteorological station with substations in Portugal, the Canary Islands, and North and South Africa. This station was of decisive importance to our Luftwaffe and U-boat operations off the Bay of Biscay and in the western Mediterranean area, while the center at Madrid also supervised the surveillance of the Straits of Gibraltar.

Later, this most important center was to be a source of great trouble to me, for, as the position of Germany grew worse, Allied pressure forced back German influence in Spain step by step. Still, we managed to maintain our full staff there until the beginning of 1945. In our diplomatic exchange with the Spaniards we used to good effect full lists of the American and British Informaton Service personnel in Spain which we had assembled and with which we justified our own activities.

One evening soon after my arrival I went over to the Embassy, taking my two bodyguards with me, to see the Police Attaché. He was said to be a very able and experienced man and besides his chief function, which was to maintain a liaison with the Spanish police, he carried out Secret Service missions. After he had informed me about our relations with the Spanish and Portuguese police and with other Spanish authorities, such as the passport and customs officials, I decided to reveal the nature of my mission to him, and after a long discussion of the problems involved we settled on the best contacts for our work. As long as we could assure them that we would not violate Spanish interests we could count on their full support, and even active intervention if difficulties should arise. But we decided that we could not reveal to them the nature of my mission.

I then went to call on von Stohrer again and we talked

until late into the night. He told me all the details of the present relationship between Germany and Spain, and we also discussed the war situation. Among other things, he complained about the frequently incorrect information collected by the Auslandsorganisation, the organization of the Nazi party abroad. He felt that it was necessary to unify the now completely uncontrolled and chaotic political intelligence services. We discussed the personal differences between the various heads of the Nazi organizations, between Heydrich and Canaris and between Heydrich and Bohle, head of the Auslandsorganisation. I pointed out to him the growing differences between Himmler and Ribbentrop, who had fallen out over policy in Rumania.

Von Stohrer than explained to me his opinions on policy in Spain and begged me to present these to the Foreign Minister upon my return. The continual pressure from Berlin, especially since the end of the campaign in France, to bring Spain into the war on our side was understandable, but Berlin saw things too much from the viewpoint of their own interests. They showed too little understanding of the Spanish mentality and of the situation in Spain at the present time. He knew that in Berlin they complained about his "soft" attitude, but nothing could change the facts. He had a more comprehensive view of the Spanish attitude and of the great difficulties in bringing about any change. Spain had received the greatest support from Germany in the Civil War, and the country, and especially General Franco, was truly grateful. The chief problem in Spain was the economic condition of the country resulting from the great social upheaval caused by the Civil War. Von Stohrer felt certain that the Spanish leaders were sincerely friendly toward Germany, but friction had been created by Ribbentrop's continual pressure for the formation of a European bloc and the attempts to force Spain into it. Seen from Berlin, this might seem a necessary part of our program, whereas Spain, because of her geographical position and historical development, was more in the nature of a bridge to Africa and was unwilling to surrender this position. Moreover, if Germany was able to offer enough material aid to satisfy Spain's needs, Franco's chief argument against joining the war would be removed. People were greatly impressed by Germany's military successes, but the opinion among well-informed circles was that the war might go on longer than the military and political leaders of Germany wanted to believe. Germany still had not succeeded in destroying Great Britain—which was the prerequisite for final victory. The attempt initiated by Hitler to isolate England politically so far rested only on the points of our bayonets. Real diplomatic success had eluded us, nor had we been able to win over the people of the conquered countries. The construction of a new Europe remained an illusion.

Von Stohrer's purpose in this long conversation was quite clear. He wanted to use me to warn Berlin against any undue optimism as far as Spain's entry into the war was concerned.

We talked briefly about my mission. I had decided to let the whole thing depend upon the Duke of Windsor's attitude. I was against the use of force except to counteract any movements that the British Secret Service might make.

The next day I had lunch with a Spanish friend who was in a position to assure me that he would remove any difficulties I might have at the frontier.

In the meantime there had been no further news from Lisbon. It seemed that the Duke of Windsor was in no great hurry about the hunting excursion. The more I thought about it, the more likely it seemed to be that the whole thing was based merely on an impulsive remark, the result of a passing mood perhaps, and that the seriousness which had been attributed to it was entirely due to wishful thinking. I decided the best thing for me to do would be to go at once to Lisbon where I could form my own opinion on the spot.

In order to be ready for action, I had arranged for an American car to be bought and sent to Lisbon, as well as a fast car belonging to the Secret Service. A highly placed Portuguese official who was a friend of mine had arranged for me to stay with a family of Dutch-Jewish emigrants in Lisbon. First, however, I went to visit my Japanese friend, whom I had met when I stopped at Lisbon on my mission to Dakar. We had a warm and happy reunion. I asked him to procure for me precise information about the Duke of Windsor's present residence in Estoril, how many entrances the house had, what floors were occupied, and all possible details about the servants and the measures taken to guard the Duke. My friend showed not the slightest reaction to this request—except for his usual polite and obliging smile. Nor did he show any curiosity or ask any questions. He merely made a deep bow and said, "For my friend no task is too much trouble."

In the evening I took a short walk through the town, and then climbed up the steep hill to the German Embassy. From its windows one had a marvelous view of the mouth of the Tagus and the harbor. The Ambassador, von Huene, had been informed of my visit, and welcomed me cordially. He was somewhat surprised at the authority I had been given, but said repeatedly that he was completely at my disposal. I told him about my mission right away, and added that in all honesty I had come to the conclusion that it could not be carried out successfully. However, I had got to try and do the best I could, for once Hitler had made up his mind about a thing like this that was the end of any argument. I asked von Huene to help me, especially in securing information, so that I could get a clear picture of what the Duke of Windsor's attitude really was. Von Huene said that he had indeed heard that the Duke had expressed dissatisfaction about his situation, but thought the whole thing had been grossly exaggerated by gossipmongers.

After I had made arrangements for communication with the central office in Berlin, we discussed general problems in Portugal. British influence in the country was considerable, but on the other hand there was great fear that one day England and America might decide to use Portugal as a bridgehead for an invasion of the Mediterranean area, particularly of Africa. Unrest in the country was still widespread, though Salazar was taking very energetic and intelligent measures to balance the economy. Soviet influence in the larger towns, and especially in Lisbon, was not to be underestimated. Portugal's military strength had increased, but still could not be considered an important factor, except perhaps for the coastal defenses, which had received a great deal of attention. The Portuguese security police worked systematically and had a large net of informants. There was a contest between us and the British to gain the greater influence with the Portuguese police.

When von Huene felt he had sufficient confidence in me, he expressed his relief that I did not intend to strain relations between Portugal and Germany by my actions.

We then talked about the Venlo incident and he told me that he had received interesting information about it from the most reliable sources. Great Britain and France had really believed in the existence of a strong conspiracy in the German Army and this had influenced their policy more decisively than they were willing to admit. This was true of France especially, where the government had drawn the ridiculous conclusion that Germany was internally so weak because of the opposition of the army to the Nazis that she could no longer be considered a dangerous enemy.

The next day I again visited my Japanese friend. He and his organization had done excellent work. He gave me a detailed sketch plan of the house, the number of servants, and an account of the guards furnished by the Portuguese police, and of the British security forces. He had also prepared a detailed description of the daily life of the household.

In the evening I had a long conversation with my Portuguese friend. I knew that he was in financial difficulties, so I immediately offered him a sum of money in return for a complete picture of the situation among the Portuguese state officials. Within an hour I had this information. British influence, based on long tradition and experience, was certainly stronger than ours; on the other hand, it was astonishing how much ground Germany had gained recently. With this information, and by spending quite lavishly, I was able to organize considerable undercover activity.

Within two days I had drawn a close net of informants round the Duke's residence. I had even managed to replace the Portuguese police guard with my own people. I was also able to place informants among the servants, so that within five days I knew of every incident that took place in the house and every word spoken at the dinner table. My Japanese friend was also working in his quiet but very effective manner to get me supplementary information. Portuguese society provided a third valuable source and unwitting remarks and gossip at the various soirées and functions were passed on to me.

Within six days I had a full picture: the Duke of Windsor no longer intended to accept the hunting invitation; he was most annoyed by the close surveillance of the British Secret Service; he did not like his appointment to

Bermuda and would have much preferred to remain in Europe. But he obviously had no intention whatever of going to live either in a neutral or an enemy country. According to my reports the furthest he ever went in this direction was once to have said in his circle of Portuguese friends that he would rather live in any European country than go to Bermuda.

However, all my informants felt that it might be possible to influence the Duke, especially if one could increase his already strong aversion to his secret guards. I therefore arranged for a high Portuguese police official to tell the Duke that the Portuguese guard would have to be strengthened because they had information that the Duke was being watched, whether by his own intelligence service or that of the enemy, they could not tell, but it would be better to make certain. That same night I staged an incident in the garden of the Duke's villa; stones were thrown at the windows, and as a result an intensive search of the whole house was made by the Portuguese guard which caused a considerable disturbance. I then started rumors among the servants at the villa that the British Secret Service had been behind the incident. They had orders to make the Duke's stay as uncomfortable as possible and thus make him readier to leave for Bermuda. Four days later a bouquet was delivered at the house with a note which said: "Beware of the machinations of the British Secret Service—a Portuguese friend who has your interests at heart."

These things were, of course, fairly unimportant, but they were discussed and created a certain amount of suspicion and ill-feeling. In any case, I had to take some form of action because Berlin was continually demanding reports of progress, and these moves, somewhat dramatized, served as material for my reports. I even considered getting my friends to arrange for me to meet the Duke, but the possibility of anything useful resulting from this seemed so remote that I did nothing.

A week later my Japanese friend warned me to be very careful. He was convinced that the British Secret Service had become suspicious. Once, indeed, I suspected that two British agents were shadowing me. I tried everything I knew to shake them off, altering my route suddenly, changing from bus to taxi and back again, but I could not get rid of them. Finally, after a two-hour chase, I managed to do so by driving to the Fatima Church near my house and leaving it by a side door. (When I was interrogated by the British Secret Service in 1945, I realized that they knew nothing about my plans at that time and did not even know that I was in Portugal.)

Replies from Berlin to my reports had grown cooler and cooler. Then suddenly after about a fortnight I received a telegram from Ribbentrop: "The Fuehrer orders that an abduction is to be organized at once." This was an unexpected blow. Since the Duke was so little in sympathy with our plans, an abduction would be madness. But what could I do? I was quite certain that it was Ribbentrop alone who was behind this order. He had made a completely wrong evaluation of the situation, and had probably distorted my reports in order to persuade Hitler to sanction this ultimate folly.

The Ambassador was as worried as I was, though I assured him at once that I had no intention of carrying out my orders. In the evening I discussed the matter with my Japanese friend. I thought I discerned mild contempt in his eyes. He remained silent for a long time. Finally he said, "An order is an order. It has to be carried out. After all, the thing should not be so difficult. You will have all the help and support you need, and the element of surprise will be on your side." After another pause he said, "Your Fuehrer certainly knows why he wants the Duke of Windsor in his hands. But what do you really wish to discuss with me? How to carry out this order, or how to evade it?" I was somewhat hurt that he had thought it necessary to remind me of my duty. I tried to explain to him that Hitler had reached this decision on the basis of false information.

Finally he said, making a small motion with his hand, "How you will justify yourself to your Fuehrer is not my affair. Let us not lose any more time, but discuss how you can circumvent the order. You have to save face—that means you have to arrange things so that action becomes completely impossible. There I cannot help you, for I have no influence with those responsible for the Duke's security guards, but these guards will have to be strengthened to such an extent that any attempt at force would be out of the question. You can blame a Portuguese police official whom you can say you suspect to be working with the British. You could even go so far as to arrange a bit of shooting—which, of course, would come to nothing. And perhaps, if you are lucky, the Duke will lose his nerve as a result of all this and blame his own people for it."

Slowly I left the house. We had nothing more to say to each other. It was a lovely night, clear and starry. But I could find no peace. My situation was extremely difficult. All the more so as I could not fathom the attitude of the two companions Heydrich had sent with me.

That evening I had supper with my Portuguese friend in a small restaurant. I felt tired and beaten and really did not want to discuss the matter any more. But in order to test his reactions I said, "Tomorrow I have to bring the Duke of Windsor across the Spanish frontier by force. The plan has to be worked out tonight." My friend awoke from his usual lethargy as I went on, "How many of you people—who will have to leave the country afterward—can I count on? And what will the whole thing cost?"

My friend looked terrified. "I can't be responsible for a thing like that," he said. "People might get killed. It would be very difficult—not only here, but at the border." Nervously he drew geometric figures on the tablecloth with his knife. After a pause he gave his final answer. "No, I can't help you, and I really don't see what use the Duke of Windsor can be to you if you abduct him by force. Inevitably it would become known, and I don't think the prestige of your country would grow by it. And then the order contains no mention of his wife. But it was Hitler who pointed out her decisive importance in the Duke's life. You are right, it must be Ribbentrop who is behind it. Let's be realistic though; if you feel you must carry out this order, I shan't place any difficulties in your way, but I won't be able to help you any further."

I now told him that I was completely of his opinion. His relief was obvious, and with great enthusiasm he discussed with me how we could circumvent the order. Next morning he arranged for twenty additional Portuguese police to be assigned to the Duke's guard. This was followed by an immediate intensification of security measures by the British. These two facts I conveyed to Berlin in a long report, and asked for further instructions.

For two anxious days they kept me waiting. Finally the laconic answer came: "You are responsible for measures suitable to the situation." Not a very friendly message, but it showed that, as I had hoped, Berlin was taking a more sober view of the affair.

Meanwhile the date of the Duke's departure from Lisbon drew near. Sir Walter Monckton, obviously a high official of the British Secret Service (as he appeared to me then) arrived from London to make sure that the Duke left on time.

To preserve face I reported to Berlin that the following information had been obtained through a police official who, we knew, was working for the British: that considerable tension had arisen between the Duke and the British Secret Service during the last few days; that the Duke was determined to remain in Europe, but that he was being placed under great pressure not to do so; that the British Secret Service planned to demonstrate to him the danger he was running from enemy secret services by themselves planting a time bomb on the ship which was to explode a few hours before his departure for Bermuda—taking great care, of course, that the Duke would not be harmed.

What with real as well as false alarms, the Portuguese police were in a state of feverish activity and excitement. The ship was searched several times from top to bottom. Security measures were doubled, then redoubled; everything helped to confirm my reports to Berlin on the impossibility of carrying out the abduction.

On the day of the Duke's departure I was in the tower room of the German Embassy, watching the ship through field glasses. It appeared so close that I seemed almost able to touch it. The Duke and the Duchess went on board punctually, and I recognized Monckton too. There was some excitement about the hand luggage. The Portuguese police in their zeal insisted upon searching that too. Finally the ship cast off, and moved away down the broad mouth of the Tagus. Slowly I returned to my house. The chapter was closed.

There remained only the question of my reception in Berlin. If I could make my report to Hitler personally, I was sure that everything would be all right. But if Ribbentrop made the report, I would probably be in for trouble. I spent the rest of the day drawing up my last telegram to Berlin.

The next day, after bidding my friends good-by, I drove from Lisbon to Madrid, and from there flew to Berlin. I reported at once to Ribbentrop. He received me rather coolly, his expression distant, his handshake perfunctory. It was obvious that he was dissatisfied. He said curtly, "Please report." I remained calm and spoke quietly, my verbal report following very closely the written reports I had sent from Lisbon. When I had finished he stared in front of him for quite a while, then said in a monotonous and tired voice, "The Fuehrer has studied your last telegram thoroughly and asks me to tell you that in spite of his disappointment at the outcome of the whole affair, he agrees with your decisions and expresses his approval of the manner in which you proceeded."

I was extremely relieved to hear this and I must confess that I felt great respect and gratitude for Hitler's reaction. Ribbentrop, who was obviously acting under instructions, now changed the subject, and for another hour and a half we discussed in a rather casual fashion the general situation in Spain and Portugal. Cautiously I sought to convey Ambassador von Stohrer's line of thought, but Ribbentrop interrupted me at once, saying angrily, "It's a pity you didn't put a little pressure on von Stohrer to rouse him from his lethargy. We know ourselves that the situation is not simple, but that's what he's down there for, to change it."

I tried to parry this. "Quite right, but it is extremely difficult to change a man's attitude in a discussion and to influence him psychologically when this attitude is based on the structural development of the country." But Ribbentrop would not agree, and I noticed that he was again trying to cut short the discussion on this point.

Ribbentrop was a most peculiar type. I had an especially strong impression that day that everything about him was studied and unnatural, without the slightest spontaneity. The rigidity of his expression, the visible effort it cost him to smile, the artificiality of his gestures, all this gave the impression of a man who had put on a mask, and I wondered what really went on behind it. It was completely impossible to move him or to convince him by logical discussion. If one attempted it, one soon had the feeling that he was not listening at all. Perhaps this sprang from a feeling of insecurity—a fear that he would not be able to maintain his position and his own viewpoint. I knew that I would never be able to establish any real contact with this man.

In the afternoon I reported to Heydrich. He listened

quietly, nodded several times, and finally said, "A rather disjointed affair. Please don't get yourself involved too closely with Ribbentrop. I feel that you should not have accepted this assignment in the first place. Obviously you realized from the beginning how it would probably end. I must say that you carried it off rather shrewdly."

12. A JAPANESE-POLISH CONSPIRACY

A lead from Warsaw—Spies on the Berlin-Warsaw express—Narrowing the field of suspects—Positive identification—Round-up of a spy ring—Analysis of captured information—Japanese aid to the Polish resistance—Double-dealing by a Japanese Ambassador—Partial release of the ring

HERE I would like to relate an extremely interesting case that we dealt with in the summer of 1940. At that time I received the following message from our Counter-Espionage office in Warsaw: "Y-3, a reliable informant, well known to us, reports that today or tomorrow an important courier of the Polish resistance movement is leaving Warsaw for Berlin, probably on the night express. Name and description of the courier cannot be discovered, neither his destination nor address, nor the nature of the messages he is carrying."

This seemed precious little to go on. If the courier were to leave Warsaw that evening, there would hardly be sufficient time to take any action. However, I instructed Warsaw to try to get further information through Y-3, but to proceed very cautiously so that the suspect should not be forewarned and said that I personally would take charge of operations in Berlin. I then called one of the commanders of our special "flying squads" to my office to discuss the problem. First, we had to sift all suspicious persons aboard the Warsaw-Berlin express. From experience we knew that theoretically the number could hardly exceed eight. At the key points along the route, and especially in Berlin, special agents had to be placed in readiness to take each of these persons under observation. A full surveillance would have to be carried out on each of them, whether it led to any results or not. In such an action luck plays as great a part as ability. But the flying squad chief was an extremely able man. That very night he and his men sifted six suspects aboard the express who might possibly be couriers. He managed to forward the information to the observation squads awaiting the train in Berlin, who in turn succeeded in establishing surveillance over all six—a masterly achievement, in view of the short notice that we had had.

The chief of the flying squad now brought me the report of the check on the passports of all the passengers— these were approximately five hundred—which his men had carried out at the frontier. There was one person who had aroused their special interest, a certain Neb——, whose papers did not seem to be quite in order. The man claimed to be a Polish national, but the linguist expert of the flying squad thought he discerned a White Russian accent. Neb——'s manner was a little hesitant, just enough, in fact, to arouse the suspicion of these experienced criminologists. When questioned about his destination, he first said Frankfurt on the Oder, then Berlin. The purpose of his journey, he explained, was to have business discussions with the Berlin office of the Japanese Mitsui Company—one of the largest Japanese firms. They took him out of the compartment for a body search, but this revealed nothing. There was nothing of interest among his private papers, nor did inspection of them with infrared light reveal any invisible ink.

Neb—— shared the compartment with a traveling companion, K——, who was much calmer and more self-assured and whose papers were all in order. He, too, said that discussions with the Japanese firm were the purpose of his trip. His briefcase contained nothing but business correspondence, and as there was nothing about him that was in any way suspicious, he was not submitted to a body search.

The leader of the flying squad advised us to keep these two under special observation. "Trust my experience," he said. "There is something fishy about Neb——, and K—— is connected with him. I've checked every other person on the train, and always come back to these two."

At noon I received the first reports. Neb—— had separated from his companion and had gone to a hotel near the Stettiner Station. K—— had gone to Berlin-Steglitz, where he had entered a small three-room apartment.

By the evening of that day the other four suspects were cleared. Their background had been investigated and was found to be above suspicion. Just to be on the safe side, however, we kept them under observation for a further three days.

Meanwhile, investigations in Warsaw disclosed that the Warsaw addresses given by Neb—— and K—— were false. Nor was the apartment in Berlin-Steglitz rented in K——'s name. Cautious investigation carried out through an insurance company disclosed a most interesting piece of information: the apartment was rented by a member of the Manchoukuoan Embassy in Berlin.

The surveillance was intensified. Neb—— and K—— could not make a single move or telephone conversation without my knowledge. It soon transpired that K—— was using Neb—— as his contact with the outside world. He was extremely cautious, probably all the more so because of the difficulties he had encountered at the frontier. He did not leave the apartment, and had only one telephone conversation with Neb——, in which he asked him to come to the house. This was on the third day of the surveillance.

Neb—— stayed at K——'s apartment for only half an hour, then returned to his hotel. From there he called the Manchoukuoan Embassy and asked whether he could come along. "Better if you and your friend would go for a walk," he was told, "at the rendezvous in the Tiergarten the day after tomorrow. He can have a conversation with Nicol on a bench."

The next morning Neb—— went back to K——'s apartment obviously to inform him of the appointment. K—— still did not leave the apartment, nor did he receive any visitors. He kept himself shut in like a mole.

That evening a well-dressed woman visited Neb—— at his hotel. I had a report on her the next morning: she was a cook at the Manchoukuoan Embassy, a Polish subject, but with a Manchoukuoan passport. We obtained this information from a caretaker's assistant at the Embassy, a Berlin lad whom my agents used as an informant. He told us that there were six Poles in the Manchoukuoan Embassy, and that they all had Manchoukuoan passports. From our Foreign Office and the Alien Office of the police we ascertained that three of these Poles were entitled to claim diplomatic privilege. We could not find out anything about anyone named Nicol, which was no doubt a pseudonym.

I now had to decide whether to make an arrest at this point or to continue the surveillance. It was an extremely delicate question. The arrest would, of course, have to be made at the rendezvous in the Tiergarten. But who would meet Neb—— and K—— at this rendezvous? A Pole with a Manchoukuoan passport—even one of the three who were allowed diplomatic immunity? Or perhaps a real Manchoukuoan? Or a Japanese?

I could not get any further information from Warsaw. Neb——'s and K——'s names were completely unknown there and no connections of any kind could be established.

One thing seemed certain: the Secret Service of the Polish resistance movement was working in collaboration with the Manchoukuoan Embassy, which was the same thing as saying the Japanese Embassy. In other words, they were obviously working with the Japanese Secret Service.

I spent most of the night trying to reach a decision. Finally I arrived at the following conclusions: Y-3 had reported the journey of a courier. We had got on the track of two suspicious persons, though which of these was the courier remained to be seen. But Y-3 had mentioned only one man, and our observation had shown that Neb—— had all the time played a subsidiary role. It was thus quite certain that K—— was the courier. A courier could transmit information either verbally or in writing. If K—— were to transmit written material at the rendezvous in the Tiergarten, then the arrest had to be made at the moment in which he handed it over, so that we could get our hands on it. The body search of a person with diplomatic immunity would be a difficult undertaking. If he passed on the information verbally, then our agents must try to overhear as much of it as possible.

The same night I contacted the Parks Department of the City of Berlin and the caretaker of the Tiergarten. The next morning my agents were at work in the Tiergarten—dressed in working clothes and equipped with suitable gardening tools. The disguise was well chosen—no one took the slightest notice of them. They had been instructed to arrest all those involved the moment any written material was handed over. If the information was transmitted verbally, they should try to overhear as much as they could. They should decide whether to make an arrest or not on the basis of what they overheard.

Punctually at ten o'clock K—— arrived in a taxi. While he was paying his fare, he took a quick look at the locality, then strolled casually down one of the walks in the park for about two hundred yards and came back. After he had done this a second time another man joined him, and after a short greeting K—— took a small package wrapped in a white paper from his trouser pocket and gave it to the other man. In a moment they were both arrested by my agents. Twenty minutes later Neb—— had also been arrested, and two hours later, the cook of the Manchoukuoan Embassy. By seven o'clock that eveing we had arrested all the Poles working in the Manchoukuoan Embassy. I had decided to disregard their diplomatic rights. We could always explain later that a mistake had been made. However, I at once informed Undersecretary Luther, of the Foreign Office.

We decided that the center of the espionage ring must be in Warsaw. Berlin was only the contact point. Our task in the subsequent interrogations was to try to find out as much as we could about the Warsaw organization.

We had been quite right in supposing that Neb—— was a figure of secondary importance. It was not difficult to break him down in interrogation. However, his evidence was not very informative as he did not know a great deal. His main function had been to act as a courier between one of the chief agents of the Polish resistance in Warsaw, and a Ukrainian group—he spoke Russian better than Polish—which was officially supposed to be sympathetic to us. It was the so-called Melnik Group.

K——, however, was quite a different type. One hundred per cent Polish, he had the stolid calm of the Slav which nothing could shake. He was a fanatical nationalist and my interrogators could get nowhere with him.

The information contained in the package—once we discovered it—was startling: the package itself consisted of a medium-sized clothes brush, almost new, with a silver back, and an unopened tube of toothpaste. The back of the brush, however, was removable, and in it, concealed in a hollow, we found a small aluminum tube containing strips of microfilm. We opened the tube of toothpaste, too, with the greatest care, and found that it also contained an aluminum tube with microfilm in it.

In all there were ten strips of microfilm, which when enlarged revealed three complete files of information. The first dealt with the general political situation in Poland, both in the territories occupied by us and those occupied by the Russians who, incidentally, came off much worse than we did. The report was written party in French and partly in English, but most of it was in Polish and this part, which analyzed the psychological and practical mistakes of the two occupying powers, was extremely well written and the contents excellently arranged. The viewpoint was quite objective, and not narrowly nationalistic. The report could only have been assembled by a well-organized information service, and showed the extent of the subversive activities of the Polish resistance movement, and also the conspiratorial talents of the Polish people.

The report went on to tell of the methods of work of the Polish resistance and their plans for further organization. This was obviously written with the purpose of securing financial support from the intelligence services of other countries. And, from the circumstances in which the material had come into our hands, it was plain that the Japanese were availing themselves of this organization and the extensive information network that was being built up there.

The second part of the report strengthened the impression gained from the first. It dealt with the strength and locations of the German occupation forces. It contained the most exact numerical data. When I showed the report to officers in the OKW—the Supreme Command of the German Armed Forces—they were amazed at the accuracy of the figures, which were correct even to the most precise details, such as the strength of every battalion. It also described plans and measures not yet put into effect, which could not have been gained by observation but only from German officers. The Polish women must have done excellent work among them.

On the second day of the investigation my chief interrogator reported, "I am getting nowhere with K——; he is terribly stubborn. Give me a free hand to be a little rougher with him."

"Out of the question, my dear fellow," I replied. "It just shows that your technique of interrogation is deficient. Rough treatment will not make him talk. Leave those methods to Herr Mueller and his crowd, I don't want them introduced here. I'll talk to K—— myself. Let me have an interpreter whom he has never seen before, so that he won't be inhibited. I will let you see the results of my interrogation later."

I must confess that the man K—— interested me greatly. We had enough evidence to convict and execute him, but that would hardly improve the situation in Poland. Presently he was brought into my room. He was tall, well built, and had a handsome face. His every movement proclaimed the Polish officer. He knew with whom he was talking, and treated me with great respect, but also with reserve. His attitude toward me was subtly different from that he showed toward his interrogators. I treated him as a fellow-officer. I explained my situation to him and begged him to place himself in my position: my subordinates were making no progress with his interrogation. I had forbidden them to use violence. I wanted to treat him as a fellow-officer and hoped that he appreciated that. "You must be aware of your own situation," I said. "The evidence against you is quite sufficient to convict you and, as we are at war, to execute you as a spy. I am certain that you counted on that possibility from the very beginning. I would like you to tell me as much about your organization as you can without endangering your comrades. I admit that if you choose to maintain silence, we will not be able to get much further. I suppose, as a courier, you must already be several days overdue. That in itself would serve as sufficient warning, so that the part of the resistance movement that would be endangered will already have taken the necessary protective measures."

He admitted dryly that everything I had said was correct. Especially the last point. He was four days overdue now, and the protective counter-measures would have gone into effect automatically in Warsaw after two days.

At this point I was ready to dismiss him, but he asked if he could talk to me for another ten minutes. In fact, these ten minutes became many hours.

I spoke of the fate of his country, of the ideal of a European community, but all this made no impression on him. He confessed that his basic attitude inclined toward skepticism and pessimism, and at first persisted in his refusal to reveal anything about the Warsaw resistance center. But after a while he began to talk more and more openly, and in the end gave me an insight into many things. I must confess that this complete change of attitude was incomprehensible to me. Later, when I asked him about it, he said, "There is a common bond between us. Perhaps it is because we have the same profession."

At the end of our conversation I assured him that I would do everything I possibly could to help him. While K—— hated the Germans as the oppressors of his people, he hated the Russians even more, and declared that he was ready to work for us against the Soviet Union. I was able to arrange for him to do so, and thus saved his life. He worked for us in Russia until 1945. I do not know what happened to him after that.

From the conversations with K—— and other information resulting from this investigation, the following picture emerged: the Japanese Secret Service had taken notice of the organization and methods of the Polish resistance from a very early point of its development. At first the resistance consisted not so much of fighting units of officers and soldiers, but of loosely organized resistance centers with an extensive information service. The Japanese decided to provide this movement with financial aid, as it could be of use to their own intelligence organization. The Japanese almost always availed themselves of the services of nationals in those countries in which they were operating. Poland was an especially interesting field for them, as it could be used for intelligence work in two directions, against the Germans and against the Russians. They supplied the Poles with financial support, technical equipment and specially trained couriers, and even went so far as to naturalize their Polish agents and supply them with diplomatic passports.

The General Staff of the resistance movement had organized the center of their Political and Military Secret Service in Warsaw, and had equipped it with an excellent technical laboratory, the head of which was Professor Piodevska, a member of the Warsaw Technical High School. When K—— had been two days overdue this center was reorganized and removed to another place. All traces were so thoroughly obliterated that we were never able to find Piodevska. Probably the Japanese enabled him to escape to Sweden or South America. The Japanese Secret Service had extensively equipped centers in Belgrade, Vichy, and Stockholm, but it was Berlin that served as a rendezvous for their couriers. K—— had already made four or five trips between Berlin and Warsaw, and admitted that the material he had transmitted on these other occasions had been even more voluminous.

At the end of 1943, the Japanese Military Attaché, General Komatu, told me that the Japanese had always wondered why, after uncovering the extremely interesting case of K——, we had not sought to work together with them. Collaboration in the construction of a Secret Service net against Russia should have been especially attractive to us. We must have realized that, in spite of all difficulties, the Japanese could have been of great assistance to us against the Soviet Union—always using, of course, the nationals of other countries, such as Poland, Bulgaria, Hungary, Rumania, and Finland. I explained to Komatu that I had indeed entertained such possibilities, but that political shortsightedness in high places made it difficult. On the other hand, at that time the Japanese had not been as eager as they were in 1943.

But to return to the espionage activities revealed by the case of K——, two copies of the material he had brought were prepared in Berlin. One went to Rome, the other to Stockholm. In Rome the material was transmitted by the Japanese Embassy to a trusted agent of the General of the Jesuit Order, Ledochovski. We could not ascertain the nature of the collaboration with the Jesuits, but it must have been a systematic arrangement.

The material transmitted to Stockholm went to a former Polish officer, who was also in the employment of the Japanese Embassy there. We had been suspicious of this man Piotr before. In our files he was described as employed by the Soviet Secret Service. Twice previously he had traveled through Germany on a Manchoukuoan passport. We had great difficulty in keeping him under observation in Stockholm. All we could find out was that he was a frequent visitor to both the Japanese and Soviet Embassies.

The Japanese Ambassador in Stockholm, Onodera, was one of the key figures of the Japanese Secret Service in Europe. He received secret information from Vichy, Rome, Belgrade, and Berlin for transmission to Tokio and also gathered other material himself. Much of this information—though only what was absolutely reliable—he used for a sort of barter trade, and he expected the same standard of integrity from those with whom he did business. If one gave him bad material once only, he would from then on refuse to engage in any further dealings with that informant. Piotr was in a sense his chief liaison with the Russians.

Because of this affair I went to Stockholm. While I was there I also wanted to initiate measures to counteract the increasing amount of sabotage against our shipping and aircraft instigated by the Russians through their agents in western Europe. I was especially interested in the German Communist, Pietsch, who had worked with Best and Stevens in Holland, had headed a sabotage group in Denmark, and from there had been sent to Sweden.

I found out that Onodera made the material collected by K—— available to both the British and the Soviet Secret Services. Later I succeeded in insinuating one of my agents into Onodera's barter trade. He posed as a representative of the Italian Secret Service, a disguise which he was able to maintain until the end of 1944. It was a really fascinating game requiring the highest intelligence and skill. The material which we traded in Stockholm was prepared by me personally, usually late at night. It was a very careful blend of false, even misleading, material and valid information, the latter mostly of a less important nature.

In this trade the British showed themselves somewhat slow and clumsy, while the Russians were extremely quick and active. I must confess that the material they collected and offered for trade was excellent. That on Great Britain, for instance, showed that they must have had agents in the highest circles of the government. Through them we even got material that came directly from the British War Office. The Russians were already working with the Secret Service of the Chinese Communists and used the Chinese very skilfully, especially in diplomatic circles in London. So important was some of their material that I did not submit it to our British section, but worked on it myself, not wishing to spread the knowledge among too wide a circle.

One other thing about Onodera was that he showed great skill in making every party with whom he traded feel that they were the only ones with whom he shared his secrets. That we knew better was solely due to K——.

It was not until six weeks after their arrest that the Manchoukuoan Embassy asked us about the whereabouts of their nationals. In order to avoid difficulties we freed all those who were protected by diplomatic immunity. They all disappeared in the Balkans and were never again used in any important intelligence activities by the Japanese.

13. COUNTERACTING SOVIET INTELLIGENCE

Hitler decides to test Russia's intentions—Molotov visits Berlin—Surveillance of his entourage—Russia questions our attitude to her problems—I am ordered to rest—Return to Berlin—Disappearance of two SD officials—Anti-Soviet intelligence work—Escape of a Soviet agent

IN THE autumn of 1940 a decisive turning point was approaching in Hitler's strategy. He still entertained the idea of solving the problem of Gibraltar by force, and—against Spain's wishes—of occupying Portugal, so as to secure it against Allied invasion; of establishing air and U-boat bases on the Canary Islands; and then of intensively colonizing North, West, and Central Africa in collaboration with the Italians. It is worth mentioning that, as late as the spring of 1944, General Jodl claimed that if the Spaniards had attacked Gibraltar, Rommel would have been able to secure control of all North Africa, in which case England would have been forced eventually to cooperate and Europe would have been "saved."

But Hitler's attention was now being directed (largely by Himmler) to the danger in the east—the unreliability of Russia as an "ally" and the incalculable problem this presented. Russia's sharp reaction to the sending of special German troops into Rumania was also disquieting. Therefore, in October 1940, Hitler decided to make a final test of Russia's intentions. On his instructions Ribbentrop wrote a letter to Stalin in which he discussed the whole international situation and implied that Russia's participation in a Three-Power Pact with the Axis would be welcomed. Stalin's reply was polite, but showed considerable hesitation. He said in substance that a discussion of various individual problems would first be necessary. This led to an invitation to Molotov to visit Berlin and on November 13 he arrived with the newly appointed Ambassador to Germany, Dekanozov,[1] a friend and countryman of Stalin's. Security measures for Molotov's visit were my special responsibility west of the Polish demarcation line. The Russians wanted precise information about the measures we were taking, and in such things were extremely bureaucratic. I was not particularly worried about protection in Berlin, but the securing of the railway line through Poland presented a ticklish problem. One always had to be prepared for unpleasant surprises with the Poles, and it was obvious that they had as little love for the Russians as they had for us. The Russians announced that they expected specially strong precautions along this route, so we did everything in our power. Along its entire length this part of the route was secured by double guard posts at intervals of 150 yards, while special squads patrolled the railway lines. A strict control of the frontiers and a check of all transport and all hotels throughout Germany were introduced at the same time.

Besides these protective measures we set up an indirect surveillance of Molotov's whole entourage. It might not be the first time that the Russians had used an official occasion to smuggle important members of their Secret Service into a country. Our task turned out to be a difficult one. Dekanozov brought along his own Secret Service agents for his personal protection, and there were at least three persons in his entourage whom we could not identify at all, though they all turned out to be persons who established frequent contacts with Berlin. At one point one of our surveillance men had been ready to make an arrest, but the Russian succeeded in reaching his Embassy in a Russian car and disappeared behind the curtain of diplomatic immunity. After Molotov's visit, Dekanozov and several of his companions remained in Berlin, and it was quite clear that this heralded an unwelcome intensification of Russian Secret Service activity in Germany and the territories occupied by us.

Molotov returned to Moscow after four days. On November 27 the German Ambassador was handed a note

---

[1] In May 1953 Dekanozov became Minister of the Interior of the Soviet Republic of Georgia. But two months later, after the fall of Beria, he was removed from office and was executed at the end of December 1953 as one of Beria's accomplices.

from the Soviet Foreign Office containing the main outlines of the Russian position and asked for clarification of Germany's views on the following points:

What was our attitude toward Soviet policy in Finland?

Russia wished to establish garrisons in Bulgaria and to negotiate the same sort of agreement there as we had with Rumania; for this purpose bases should be established in the Dardanelles; if Turkey refused agreement to this, Russia, Germany and Italy should take measures to enforce the demand.

Spheres of interest in the areas south of Baku and Batum.

That Germany should seek to influence Japan to settle her differences with the Soviet Union regarding the island of Sakhalin.

If satisfactory assurances were given on all these points, Russia would be ready to join a Three-Power Pact.

The conversations between Molotov and Hitler had been rather cool. To these further proposals Hitler did not even reply. Already in September 1940 Hitler had strengthened the eastern front by twenty divisions, and the General Staff had submitted draft plans of a possible offensive against the Soviet Union in the summer of that year. This was followed by large-scale maneuvers under General von Paulus.

Hitler must have arrived at his vital decision by the middle of December. This came to my knowledge in the following way: Admiral Canaris had become worried about my health and had arranged for me to be thoroughly examined by Professor Zahler, Goering's personal physician. Zahler having discussed the results of this check-up with Heydrich, I had been ordered to go to Karlsbad for a rest cure. This was shortly after Molotov's visit to Berlin. Before leaving, I discussed with Heydrich the work to be carried on in my absence, and during our conversation he said, "It may interest you to know that recently the Fuehrer has been concerned almost solely with information concerning the Soviet Union. He doesn't speak any more about the great possibilities of exploitation in the 'Eurafrican Spaces.' He's turned his attention to the 'Eurasian Spaces' instead. His whole strategic concept seems to have shifted, and apparently there'll be quite a lot to do next spring. We must be ready for some surprises, too. So you must get yourself back in working order as soon as possible."

On December 18, 1940 Hitler signed the order: *"Wehrmachtsbefehl Nr 21—Operation Barbarossa"*—the attack on the Soviet Union. It provided for an offensive by a strength of about one hundred infantry divisions, twenty-five armored, and thirty fully motorized divisions. On February 3, 1941, Hitler approved the strategic plan for the offensive which the Supreme Commander of the army, Field Marshal von Brauchitsch, placed before him.

After two months in Karlsbad I returned to Berlin. It was very hard to adjust myself again to the hectic atmosphere of the capital. The chief task now was counter-espionage work against the Soviet Union. The centers of interest here were the border countries, Rumania, Hungary, Poland, and Finland. The Western sectors of our security network had to be weakened in order to strengthen the Eastern ones. A special problem was created by the thousands of Russian émigrés, White Russians, Ukrainians, Georgians, etc., living in Germany. We knew that Russian Intelligence used a number of them as their agents, so I created a net of informants among them, using the Russian system of groups of three—each member of the group had to inform on the others without their being aware of it. At the moment, securing information about them seemed more important than the possibility of using them later on for occupation work in their own countries. We had sufficient Russian émigrés already actively working for our Secret Service.

The Russian Secret Service in Germany was becoming increasingly active and we were able to observe the growth of this extensive network. It was very difficult to decide how long to continue the surveillance and when to end it by making arrests. Merely to observe what objectives interested the enemy sometimes enabled us to draw valuable conclusions. But waiting too long could lead to very damaging results. Once, by delaying longer than I should have done, I spoiled a very important case. My assistants had warned me, but I had not listened to them.

The head of our Counter-Espionage in Breslau was a very able official, a specialist in Eastern European matters, with an excellent knowledge of Russian and Polish. He had been active in this area for many years, and his work showed quite good result. His opposite number in Military Intelligence had a similar background.

After I had been head of Counter-Espionage for some time, I began to feel dissatisfied with the work of these two men, and to suspect that in many instances they were purposely misleading us. I discussed this with the chief of their department and ordered a thorough investigation. We found that Russian was spoken regularly in their homes and that both families had developed an unusually high standard of living. A check of their expense accounts, and particularly of the confidential funds for their agents, showed that these could not have been the source of their increased wealth. They received an unusually large number of visitors in their homes, and we discovered that these were mostly people who did not live in Breslau.

Then one of them reported to us that his car had been broken into while it was parked in the street, and a brief case full of important documents had been stolen. I decided to continue the surveillance and not make an arrest yet. Two days later both men had vanished, having taken with them all the most important documents from their offices.

The wife of the Military Intelligence man died soon afterward from an unknown cause. The wife of the Counter-Espionage man was arrested and interrogated. She maintained from the very beginning that her husband had told her he had become involved with Russian Intelligence, thinking that thereby he might be able to make a valuable coup for us. The woman's testimony was not convincing. The house was thoroughly searched and in a small suitcase were found some fragments of a letter which we were able to put together well enough to read the last sentence—"and you will come and join me." It was obviously a letter of farewell which her husband had written her, but she denied having ever seen it, and said that it was not her husband's handwriting. Our graphologists said, however, that it could well have been his handwriting, though the writer might have been under the influence of alcohol or drugs.

The case was never cleared up. Though I initiated the most intensive and widespread search, not the slightest trace of the two men was found. Nor could we ever determine with certainty whether they were traitors, or whether they had been abducted, or perhaps killed. All the evidence, as well as the testimony of the wife, pointed toward the conclusion that they were traitors. However, I did not take any action against the wife, and arranged to have a small grant paid for the support of the child which the man had left behind. As a result of the affair, we had completely to reorganize the security system of the Silesian war industries, for the material that disappeared with the two men contained a comprehensive account of its organization.

Heydrich was lenient about this error of mine. He even tried to console me, saying that this kind of affair was the sort of "tuition fee" that everyone had to pay, and there was no reason why I should be spared such embarrassments.

The next day I was at his hunting lodge. During the course of our conversation, in which he stressed again the importance of strengthening the counter-espionage work against the Russians, and said that the Fuehrer was watching this work very closely, he finally began to talk about Admiral Canaris. He was very critical of Canaris' work as head of Military Intelligence. He felt certain, in fact, that Canaris had betrayed the date of the attack in the west—May 10, 1940—to the Allies, but nevertheless he did not want to proceed against him just yet. He would wait and gather more evidence. The day would come, however, when Canaris would be punished for all the damage he had caused to the regime.

Heydrich then went on to speak of the problem of the whole intelligence network. He was still very much preoccupied with certain setbacks he had had recently, and saw their cause in the organizational weakness of the various Intelligence Services, especially the SD Ausland, the Foreign Intelligence Branch of the Main Security Office, usually called AMT VI. Until now they had been allowed to function under the loosest control, but if anything went wrong, it was he, Heydrich, who would receive the blame. He realized the great difficulty of integrating a foreign intelligence service into an internal security organization, particularly in wartime, but the whole level of the work of this department was unsatisfactory, the training and experience of the younger people inadequate, and the direction they received from their superiors bad.

I had been aware of these problems for a long time and had come to very similar conclusions. I had therefore been expecting this conversation and was very careful to advance no criticism of my own, but simply to maintain an attitude of attention to what Heydrich was saying. He knew that from the very beginning it had been my aim to work in Foreign Intelligence. Now he said, "Do you think it is possible, in the middle of the war, more or less to reconstruct an organization such as AMT VI?"

I told him that it had to be possible, though there would be great technical difficulties which would call for an immediate reduction in the amount of work. The main weakness was lack of tradition and experience, which could only be acquired over a long period. To attempt to force such a development almost overnight would need the investment of practically unlimited resources and the employment of the best personnel in the whole organization. Much would depend on the co-operation of other government departments and the support given by Hitler and Himmler. But the deficiency of intelligence was a problem that had to be solved, and the sooner the better.

Heydrich wanted me to devote more thought to the problem and added, "I believe that in the near future you will have to undertake this task. But you will have to gain sufficient confidence among the leadership for them to allow you to work quite free of any control—except, of course, mine. In the meantime, please don't speak to anyone about this. Go ahead with your present work of strengthening the Counter-Espionage Department. One more question: Do you think Canaris will use the period of reorganization to extend his influence at the expense of ours?"

I replied that that was a problem which would have to be dealt with at another level, a problem of the relative political influence of Heydrich and Canaris. But, on the whole, it seemed to me that Canaris had enough to do with his own problems, and that if any encroachment was to be feared, it was Ribbentrop rather than Canaris that I would worry about. Heydrich agreed with this. Thus the evening became one of the turning points of my career.

Meanwhile, the work against the Russian Secret Service was proceeding satisfactorily. We had uncovered numerous networks of agents, courier routes, and secret transmitters. Until now I had confined our tactics mainly to surveillance and the insinuation of false information. One had to be particularly careful about using the wave lengths of their secret transmitters because the transmissions were checked most carefully by the Russians and the slightest divergence from the pattern of the signal would warn them that the messages were not valid. We were rather lucky in this work and were able to "play" material to the Russians, in many cases without their becoming aware of the deception. The chief value of this activity lay not only in deceiving them, but in discovering what they wanted to know. We also learned much about their methods and the relationship between the various groups of agents working for them.

The Russians had recognized much earlier than had our leaders the importance of having a secret service that functioned efficiently, and the effectiveness of their methods and organization won the highest praise from our specialists.

There was one case in which we were not very fortunate. One of their agents, whom we thought we had converted to our use, was a most important courier between Berlin and Stockholm. On one occasion he was carrying authentic material of the highest value, dealing with a special welding process of vital importance in aircraft production. He was to show this to a representative of the Soviet Embassy at their first meeting, and then, before he actually turned the documents over to the Russians, misleading material was to be substituted. Our agents were watching him every minute, but he managed to warn his people through an employee at his hotel, who was also in the service of the Russians. Then, on his way to the bathroom, he succeeded, again with the aid of the hotel employee, in slipping out by a back entrance and fleeing to the Soviet Embassy. We never saw him again, and could only assume that he had left immediately for Moscow with a diplomatic passport.

The courier had, of course, warned his superiors, and thus, as a further consequence, our secret radio contact with the Russians was broken off.

However, we had already gained much valuable information about the network of Soviet Foreign Intelligence outposts, and about tensions between the Intelligence Service of the MVD (then NKVD)—the intelligence organization of the Secret Police of the Soviet Communist party—and the Soviet Military Secret Service.

14. THE VIETINGHOFF BROTHERS

A suspicious trio—Enlistment of a new agent—Watching a Russian rendezvous—Tightening the net—Abduction of a suspect—Plans for a new Russian spy center—An agent under observation—Hitler intervenes in the case—Fate of the Vietinghoffs

IN THE autumn of 1940, one of the most interesting cases in our work against the Soviet Secret Service was that of the Vietinghoff brothers. After the occupation of the Baltic States by Russia the Baltic Germans began to stream back to Germany. One of these refugees, a young woman, reported at a frontier post that three people whom she was with seemed suspicious. Two were brothers named Vietinghoff, and the third was the wife of the elder brother. Our official thought at first that the girl's complaint was one of the usual denunciations based on personal resentment; nevertheless the young woman was held for more thorough questioning.

She admitted she had had an affair with the younger brother, who was unmarried, but this liaison had been broken up by the wife of the elder one, who was actually living with both of them. Frau Vietinghoff must have been a remarkably strong and energetic personality. Both men were completely under her influence. Although the younger brother had wanted to start a new life in Germany, however hard he tried he had not the strength of character to disengage himself from this unconventional triangle and always succumbed to the influence of his sister-in-law. During the turbulent days of their emigration he had begun an affair with the young Baltic German woman, and violent scenes of jealousy took place between the two women during the journey.

Such was the young woman's story, which at first seemed clearly motivated by jealousy and of no interest to us. However, it became more interesting when, upon their arrival in Berlin, the two brothers and the wife disappeared completely.

I do not wish to reveal the name of the young woman who brought this case to our attention. Later she became an agent of the German Secret Service under the code name of R-17. She combined considerable charm with intelligence, a talent for the work, and a thorough knowledge of Slavonic languages, as well as of French and German. I used her first on a Secret Service assignment involving members of the Japanese Embassy, and she proved very successful. Being a blonde, she was of a type which the Japanese usually prefer. Later she returned to Riga and did excellent work for us against the Russians.

At the time when she first brought the Vietinghoff brothers to our notice, she admitted frankly that her denunciation was motivated by a desire for revenge. The younger Vietinghoff had broken his promise to her, and she found herself deserted, betrayed, and alone in Berlin, without funds or anyone to whom she could turn. She believed that the young man had been honest in his intentions toward her, but had succumbed to the influence of his sister-in-law. Her fiancé, as she still called him, had told her that his brother was working for the Russian Secret Service, and that he was carrying out an assignment for them which would earn them all a lot of money. The younger brother was also helping in this, and once the mission was accomplished they would escape abroad, he would marry her, and the two of them would be able to live the rest of their lives in comfort.

This and a detailed description of the trio was all the information the young woman could give us. For three weeks we searched diligently for the trio, but without any result, and finally the file was placed before me so that I might close the case.

But I was still not satisfied. The young woman had made a good impression on me, and I felt that her story must be more than just the product of a vivid imagination. So the next day I called in the specialist in charge and told him I did not want to close the case and was convinced that the three Vietinghoffs had taken another name and gone to earth in Berlin or in some other large city, and were probably already at work there. My instinct told me that we should concentrate on Berlin first. If they were engaged on an important mission—and the young woman felt that they were and that it must be very important—it would take them some time to establish themselves. They would have to receive directives and get in touch with some center of the Russian Secret Service, since it seemed extremely unlikely that they would be working in direct contact with Moscow. We knew which were the chief centers of the Russian Secret Service in Berlin. Leaving out Intourist, which I wanted to exclude for the time being, there were the Soviet Embassy and the Russian Trade Commission.

As I talked I could see perplexity growing on the specialist's face, as though he were dubious about what was coming. For some time I had had a plan, and the Vietinghoff case gave me the opportunity to try it out. I wanted to rent two sets of rooms, preferably on the first floor, one diagonally across the street from the Soviet Embassy, and the other from the Trading Commission. They would, of course, be leased through a third party and we would spare no expense. Secrecy, of course, was absolutely essential. I asked my specialist whether he understood, and although he said he did, I saw that he still did not quite see what I was driving at.

"For about three or four months," I said, "we will collect a picture album of all the visitors to these two establishments. We shall take photographs of every single person who goes in or out. Perhaps if we're lucky we shall catch the Vietinghoffs. Anyway, apart from them, we're certain to collect a lot of interesting people. It may seem a bit cumbersome, but it will be thorough and methodical, and it'll give you an amusing game to play in the evenings. You can compare the photos with descriptions of people we're looking for. I think it's really a very promising idea."

Supplied with exact descriptions of the Vietinghoffs, and of various other people whom we were on the lookout for, specially trained members of our search department working in shifts would have to be on duty the whole time, because we could not fix a telephone line with the central office. We had tried once before to lay cables near the Soviet Embassy, but the Russians were much too shrewd and had smelled a rat at once. So this time our people would have to work with field glasses and telescopic lenses.

Within four days our arrangements were completed,

and after only ten days we found a Soviet agent for whom we had been looking for a long time. On the twelfth day, at three o'clock in the afternoon, the younger of the Vietinghoff brothers was caught by our camera. The photographs were excellent and the posture and expression of the young man most interesting. Going into the Embassy his whole attitude betrayed haste and anxiety. Leaving the building, he seemed more relaxed, although embarrassed and uncertain, and had paused for a moment in the doorway, undecided as to which way to go.

I showed the pictures to R-17. She glanced at them briefly, and said, "Yes, that's him all right." She was staring fixedly at me with an expression that was quite alarming. Her deep-set eyes glowed above the broad Slav cheekbones, her teeth were bared, and her whole face revealed abysmal hate.

I said to her coldly, "With this, my dear R-17, your connection with the Vietinghoff case is ended. In future it will be of no interest to you whatever. That's an order. If you do not obey it, I might be forced to break off our working relationship. And after the training you have had, you know what that would mean."

For a moment she was silent. Then she said quietly, "I shall carry out my work obediently and obey your commands, whatever happens."

I have always respected this woman for the courage she displayed. She never broke her promise, but worked for us in Russia until 1945, and remained at her post, even when ours was clearly a lost cause, until the final breakdown, well aware of what was in store for her. I do not know what happened to her.

Now that we had picked up the trail of the Vietinghoffs the chase began. Of course, we had not been able to start shadowing the younger brother right away; we had to wait for him to visit the Embassy a second time. This he did five days later. A special squad followed him without difficulty and the trail led them to a cheap three-room furnished flat where all three Vietinghoffs were living. They had changed their names and now had new passports. The elder brother went by the name of Egon Altmann and was no longer described as being married. The younger one was called Wilhelm Oberreiter, and the woman Maria Schultze.

I felt quite proud of what we had achieved, though of

course luck had played its part. We later found out, incidentally, that shortly before we had seen him, the younger brother had been ordered not to visit the Embassy again under any circumstances, and we had picked up the trail on his last visit.

The old game of tightening the net now began. We noticed that, in spite of their outward poverty, the trio lived very well. Though Maria Schultze lived quietly and rarely went out, she provided the best of everything for her two men; the rent was always paid punctually, and all the neighbors spoke with warm praise of the poor refugees from the East who had set to work so energetically to build up a new existence for themselves. The two brothers worked as representatives of a firm that supplied equipment to hotels and restaurants. Both of them traveled a great deal, but their turnover was not large and obviously their income was too small to provide for their present mode of life. They must therefore have been drawing funds from some other source.

We discovered that the brothers were having some sort of dealings with estate agents, and here something seemed to be brewing with one particular firm whose representative they took out to dinner. Having checked on him very carefully, we decided to take this man into our confidence. He turned out to be trustworthy and was very grateful to us for having warned him about his clients. We learned from him that Egon Altmann, the elder brother, had said he was a refugee who had had a stroke of luck; a large inheritance had come his way six months earlier. He wanted to invest the money in property that would provide a solid income and was interested in acquiring a small hotel, preferably in the neighborhood of one of the large railway stations in the city, the Stettiner, for instance, or the Schlesischer Bahnhof. They had already discussed one particular place, for which there was to be a cash payment of 200,000 marks, with a further 300,000 to be paid off as a mortgage. Repairs and improvements were to be arranged by the purchaser. The Russian Secret Service was certainly not being niggardly in the affair.

It was too early, however, to make an arrest. We still had no inkling of what the Russians intended. They moved slowly and very cautiously, and for two weeks nothing more seemed to happen. Then one night toward twelve o'clock I received a call from the leader of the surveillance squad. He reported that Maria Schultze had received a letter that afternoon. "It was brought by a small boy who was approached by a stranger near the house, who gave him a tip and asked him to deliver it. There's nothing suspect about the boy himself though. After she got the letter Maria left the house—that was at nine o'clock—and got a taxi. One of our cars followed it."

I asked for an immediate report as soon as there was any new development. Twenty minutes later I received another call.

"This is Criminal Inspector Werner. I followed Maria in car No. 3, going toward Bellevue Station. We stopped at the station about fifty yards behind her. She left the cab quickly—she must have paid her fare on the way—and got into a dark limousine which was driving slowly by. It looked like a Ford, but we couldn't read the number. We managed to follow it, though, toward the Avus Racetrack, and from there toward Wannsee. It crossed the Wannsee Bridge, then it drew off so fast that after about six kilometers we dropped behind. They turned off the main street in the direction of Gatow and we lost them completely. We waited for about three hours in case they came back, then we went back to the house. Maria returned to the flat on foot about ten minutes ago."

"You've had bad luck," I said. "Next time take a more powerful car." The case was beginning to annoy me, especially as I needed my men urgently for other work.

I could find no solution that night, but the next morning on the way to work I hit upon an idea: how would it be if I could split up the trio? The weakest link in the chain was obviously the younger brother, Wilhelm Oberreiter. Should I invent a story involving R-17 in order to break him down? If I were also to promise him a happy life abroad with her, might this not be enough to counteract the influence of the other two and his fear of his Russian employer?

I called my specialist and instructed him to bring Wilhelm in for interrogation as soon as he could do so without the other two being aware of it.

The opportunity came the next day. A car with some of my men in it pulled up alongside where Wilhelm was standing in the street, and the driver, pretending to be deaf, asked to be directed to an address. The man sitting in the back then opened the door and apologized for his driver. He asked Wilhelm to speak a bit louder, and as he leaned into the car to do so there was a quick jerk, and the car moved off with Wilhelm sitting in the back.

I saw at a glance that Wilhelm's nerves were all to pieces and I decided that I would not need to use R-17. I let him remain standing at first and spoke to him roughly on purpose. "Well, you German traitor, what have you to say for yourself? If you tell me the complete truth, perhaps I'll be merciful. But lie to me about one single detail and—well, you know very well that as a spy in wartime you'll be a dead man within four days."

He began to cry bitterly. It was all Maria's fault, he said, she had driven them all into disaster. She had already worked with the Russian Secret Service before her marriage to his brother, she was a *femme fatale,* and so on. He went on like this for about half an hour. I did not interrupt him, but just let him talk.

The Russian Secret Service had an especially high opinion of Maria, and had entrusted her with a very important mission. Her husband, Wilhelm's brother, was completely under her thumb and did whatever she wanted. He himself had only begun to work actively with them since their arrival in Germany. He had made many attempts to break with them, but Maria had always managed to hold him: here he admitted his own guilt regarding his sister-in-law, and in this connection mentioned the name of R-17. He admitted that he had obeyed the orders of the Russian Secret Service just as readily as the others, and eventually he blurted out everything he knew, recounting quite a few details of considerable importance. Although he was almost incoherent with fright, toward the end he grew a little calmer.

The change of name—to which the Russians had agreed—had been Maria's idea, partly as a protective measure against R-17. Their assignment was to purchase a hotel in Berlin which would really operate as an intelligence center where messages could be received and some preliminary evaluation made of the material that came in. Most of the work was to cover military matters. The Russians planned to introduce at least four or five of their officers among the personnel of the establishment.

Wilhelm himself had had to go through a technical course in Berlin lasting about ten hours. It was concerned with the development of films, secret inks, and other similar tasks. Maria's work was to be the organization and maintenance of the courier system, for the hotel was to serve as a courier station and rendezvous for agents arriving from Russia. Her husband was to be responsible for the management of the hotel, and to appear as the official owner, while Wilhelm and Maria were to act as his employees. The Russians had conceived this plan because they feared that their official offices would be under too close a surveillance by the Germans, and they planned to increase the extent of their work and to form new cadres of the German Communist party.

Maria spoke Russian perfectly and was a staunch adherent to the Soviet ideal. She was so fanatical, Wilhelm said, that if he or his brother were to betray the cause, she would stop at nothing to bring about their punishment by the Russians.

The Russians were very generous with funds, but any error or neglect of duty was punished ruthlessly. They were most painstaking in their security and precautionary measures, suspicion being the chief principle on which they worked. Maria had made a small error about their ration cards, and they had questioned her about it for hours. To Wilhelm it was a mystery how they managed to learn about such petty details, and he always felt as though he were being watched.

The money for the purchase of the hotel was to be delivered in two weeks' time, but they did not know how, or from whom they were to receive it. They were not to go to or to telephone any of the official Russian establishments, no matter what happened, nor were they to make any sort of contact with German Communist circles, but on the contrary were to join their local groups of the Nazi party, Winter Relief, and Civil Defense.

When Wilhelm had finished I said to him, "I can't quite understand how you got into this thing, and I'd like to help you. But I don't quite see how it can be done. You're not a particularly tough character and this woman has obviously got you under her thumb. Besides, the Russians are keeping a very close eye on you. If they found out you were working for me, I wouldn't give very much for your chances. It's happened before. We'd find your body in a wrecked motorcar. The Russians are experts at road accidents. You'd certainly be no worse off in a German court."

Beads of sweat were glistening on his forehead by this time. I decided that I could afford to be gentler.

"All right then," I said, "I'll do what I can if you'll do your best for me. It's no good feeling sorry for yourself— and feeling sorry for the other two will be even less profitable. I'm going to give you a chance to work for us and to save your own skin. That's my offer, and it's a pretty realistic one."

I let him think it over for several minutes, then stretched out my hand. He grasped it, and agreed to the bargain. The game had begun.

First we discussed how he could leave without being seen, and how he could explain to his brother and sister-in-law the three hours he had spent with me. Having warned him not to let them notice the slightest change in his behavior, but to go on just as before, we arranged a method of contact for the future, so that he could make his reports and receive his instructions without attracting their attention.

I knew I was taking a big risk. I therefore took my time, once more going quietly and thoroughly over all the details with him, and finally said, in order to strengthen his morale as much as possible, "If at any time you feel that you are losing your nerve and can't carry this thing through, come and tell me and place yourself under my protection. It won't affect my promise to you—unless, of course, you try to mislead me."

As a further assurance, and for his own protection, I had him placed under continual observation, while those watching Maria and his brother were removed for the time being.

After four days Wilhelm reported that Maria had received a typed letter, written on white paper and with no signature. It ordered her to travel alone to Leipzig on the following day, and gave the time of the train she was to go by. In Leipzig she would have two hours in which to dine; the name and address of the restaurant she was to go to were also given.

In the afternoon she was to visit the Voelkerschlachtdenkmal [Memorial to the Battle of Nations at Leipzig]. There she was to examine the wall near the main entrance closely, and in the third buttress on the right of the entrance she would see a crack; in it she would find a small parcel wrapped in old newspaper. She was not to remove the parcel until after nightfall, when visitors to the Memorial and the caretaker would be gone, and then to do it quite unobtrusively. After finding the parcel, she was to return on foot, walking for at least an hour, and only after that time had elapsed she was to take a taxi or travel by any other means. Further instructions would be found inside the parcel. No matter what happened, she was to return to Berlin that same night. Obviously these very detailed instructions had been given so that her movements could be checked all the time.

I sent two of our officials ahead to Leipzig to organize a thorough and comprehensive watch. The night before Maria's arrival the crack in the wall at the Memorial was examined and the parcel seen and left in position.

Watching Maria's movements on the following day brought no startling results; apparently the Russians' surveillance was conducted only on the train and at the restaurant. Maria carried out her assignment very skillfully and returned to her lodgings in Berlin without incident.

We wondered what other instructions were in the parcel and whether she would be allowed to discuss them with her accomplices. Wilhelm called me the next evening and told me that the old newspaper contained 400,000 marks wrapped in sailcloth. Nothing else was in the package, which had apparently been lying in its hiding place for at least a year. The next day, however, Maria received another letter, instructing her to use the 400,000 marks for the purchase of the hotel. 250,000 marks were to have come from the "inheritance," and the rest was to go toward a mortgage arranged with a private loan company, for which the documents were enclosed and only needed to be signed by Egon Altmann. In this manner the Russians arranged the whole business so perfectly that no legal difficulties could possibly arise. Maria would have another opportunity of speaking with her superior in about eight days' time and she would receive notice of the time and place.

I at once got into touch with the estate agent, the owner of the hotel, and the lawyer, and to their great consternation ordered them to proceed with the sale.

In the meantime the case had been brought to the notice of Heydrich and Himmler. They agreed that the affair should be allowed to develop, at least until Maria's next meeting with her superior, whose identity we were anxious to establish. I had repeatedly questioned Wilhelm about this man, but he had insisted that Maria knew nothing about him except that he was a Russian who could scarcely speak German.

After six days Maria was ordered to go to a particular platform at the Tiergarten Station. She was there on time, but after an hour's wait with no developments she returned home. The three took counsel together as they were very perturbed, and discussed whether they should not call the Soviet Trade Commission or send Wilhelm there. However, they decided to wait another two or three days.

At this point my own plans were completely ruined. Himmler mentioned the case to Hitler, who became very excited indeed and proceeded to rail against Molotov and Dekanozov, and then ordered the affair be brought to a conclusion at once. "I want to show the Russians that I know all about their increased espionage and subversive activities. An arrest now will fit in very well with my over-all plans." This was at the end of November 1940 shortly after Molotov's visit to Berlin.

All my representations to Himmler were of no avail. He declared that Hitler's decisions could not be changed, and that he too felt the time was ripe for bringing the matter to a conclusion. Another attempt of mine to gain time failed too, and even Heydrich, who inclined toward my view, could achieve nothing with Himmler.

The next day Maria and her husband were quietly arrested in the street. I instructed Wilhelm that he should remain where he was and carry on. In case their employers asked about Maria's whereabouts, he should say she had been taken to the Robert Koch Hospital with acute appendicitis. For Wilhelm's protection, three of my men were placed in the apartment.

After making arrangements with two doctors who were in our confidence, R-17 was placed as a patient in the Robert Koch Hospital, to impersonate Maria. However, the Chief Medical Officer's permission was necessary before an order of secrecy could be imposed on the staff assisting at the bogus operation to be performed on R-17, and so he was informed of what was taking place. (Later we learned that this doctor was a collaborator with the Russian Secret Service and told them at once about the whole thing.) We noticed that the Russians seemed to have become suspicious. They made no attempt to get in touch with Wilhelm, and in the end I forced him to go to the Soviet Trade Commission. There he spoke with the man who had previously given him his instructions. The Russian was very solicitous, and told him that when Maria had returned home he would hear from them. From that moment I knew that the case was closed.

After the arrest, Egon, the husband, had a complete nervous breakdown. Maria, however, denied everything, refused to speak a single word during her interrogation, remaining stubborn and hostile to the very end. Thus we could learn nothing about her previous life or about the eight years during which she worked for the Russian Secret Service. She was sentenced to death by the People's Court on a charge of proven espionage in the service of the Soviet Union, and executed. Egon was also sentenced to death, but was pardoned later.

I kept my promise to Wilhelm. He built himself a new and decent existence and for two more years I kept him under my protection. The Russians made only one attempt upon him, seeking to get at him by means of an organized street brawl, but he managed to get away. I arranged for him to change his residence frequently, both in Germany and the occupied territories, in order to cover his trail, and apparently the Russians finally lost track of him. I used a part of the 400,000 marks that we had won from the Russians to finance his new existence. Some of the money went for bonuses to the most capable of my assistants, but the bulk of it I gave to the German Red Cross.

15. THE CASE OF RICHARD SORGE

Investigation of Sorge's past—Conditions for his employment by DNB—Chief Inspector Meisinger—Suspicions of Sorge aroused in Japan—Growing importance of his material—His arrest by the Japanese—Revelations of his duplicity—The German Ambassador involved—His activities on Russia's behalf

ANOTHER case of Russian espionage which first came to my attention in 1940 was that of Richard Sorge. Herr von Ritgen, head of DNB, the official German News Service, had talked to me about him. At that time Sorge was working indirectly for DNB, and at times also for the *Frankfurter Zeitung*. He maintained a personal correspondence with von Ritgen which, though it was conducted in the form of letters, was in reality a comprehensive rapportage.

At that time the Nazi party, and above all the foreign organization of the Party, were creating difficulties for Sorge because of his political past. Von Ritgen wanted me to look at Sorge's files in Department III (SD-Inland) and Department IV (Gestapo) and see whether we could find some solution of these difficulties, for he felt that he could dispense with Sorge's reports. Sorge had a profound understanding of the Far East and had made a particular study of the political tensions which existed between Japan, China, and Russia on the one hand, and the United States and England on the other, and in von Ritgen's opinion had always judged them correctly.

I looked up the files, and the picture they revealed did not look too good for Sorge. If it did not prove him to be a member of the German Communist party, one could not help coming to the conclusion that he was at least a sympathizer. He had certainly been in close contact with a large number of people who were known to our Intelligence Service as Comintern agents, but he had close ties with people in influential circles and had always been protected against rumors of this sort. In the years between 1923 and 1928 he had been in touch with German Nationalist and extreme Right Wing circles, and also with the National Socialists. Thus the picture presented by the files was somewhat complicated.

I could not agree at once with von Ritgen. In spite of Sorge's wide knowledge of China and Japan, and in spite of his collaboration with Professor Haushofer, the geopolitician, and the excellent articles he had published about internal affairs in Japan—von Ritgen thought them the best things that had been written about the social tensions in that country—there were some very suspicious factors against the man. For instance, his relations with Stennes, a high SA leader who had fled from Germany in 1934, and who had been in close contact with Gregor and Otto Strasser and other factions in the Party who were now considered pro-Russian. At this time Stennes was living in China and was one of the military advisers to Chiang Kai-shek.

Von Ritgen finally concluded that even if we assumed that Sorge had connections with the Russian Secret Service, we must, after safeguarding our own interests, find ways of profiting by his profound knowledge. In the end, we agreed that I should protect Sorge from attacks by the Party, but only on condition that he included in his reports intelligence material on the Soviet Union, China, and Japan. Officially he would work in this direction only with von Ritgen.

I reported this plan to Heydrich, who agreed with it on condition that Sorge should be placed under the closest surveillance and that his information should not go through normal channels, but should be subjected to a special scrutiny, for we had to assume that at the decisive moment he would try to introduce misleading material. I was instructed also to discuss the whole matter with Jahnke.

Heydrich's first point, about surveillance, was extremely difficult to put into practice. Our agents in Japan were very young and for the most part quite inexperienced. I could not give them written instructions, so I delayed doing anything—which was certainly very careless of me—until after Sorge had already begun to work for us.

As Heydrich had suggested, I mentioned Sorge to Jahnke, but he evaded the question, pretending that he knew nothing about him. (I knew from von Ritgen that this was not so, but I did not try to force the issue.)

I also spoke to Chief Inspector Meisinger about Sorge on the eve of his departure for Japan. Meisinger was one of the most evil creatures among Heydrich's bunch of thugs and he carried out the vilest of his orders. He had played a sinister role in the events of June 30, 1934, and also in the cases of the Generals von Blomberg and Fritsch. The Special Department for "Jewish Property," which became increasingly important after 1938, was also under Meisinger. On the surface he was a bosom friend of Mueller, the Gestapo chief, both men having started their careers in the Bavarian Police. Secretly, however, he was Mueller's greatest enemy, and was only waiting for the chance to step into his shoes.

He was a frightening individual, a large, coarse-faced man with a bald head and an incredibly ugly face. However, like many men of his type, he had drive and energy and an unscrupulous sort of cleverness. He always kowtowed to me and treated me with formal politeness, addressing me by my full title. On one occasion, however, he thought he had the advantage of me. I was in an awkward position, having mistakenly sought to protect a man who turned out to be guilty, and Meisinger at once threatened to report me to Heydrich. I defended myself after my own fashion, and then waited for matters to mature, gradually entangling him in my net. I had received an incredible amount of material on Meisinger from Warsaw, and had collected a huge file which proved him to be so unutterably bestial and corrupt as to be practically inhuman. I passed this material on to Mueller, saying that I had come across it in the course of my intelligence work. A painstaking investigation was initiated. which revealed such atrocities that Himmler ordered Meisinger to be court-martialed and shot at once. But at this stage in the proceedings Heydrich intervened: Meisinger knew too much, and Heydrich managed to prevent the trial from taking place and so rescued him, although to this day I do not know how it was done.

In order to get Meisinger out of the way, the unfortunate decision was taken to send him to Tokio as Police Attaché. His only qualifications for the post were an ability to drink incredible quantities of sake and to smoke twenty imported cigars in succession, while carrying on a jovial conversation. It must be admitted, however, that as a result of his long police experience he knew a good deal about the workings and methods of the Comintern. Since 1933 he had been Mueller's right-hand man, and had helped to destroy the various underground organizations of the German Communist party. He also knew about a large number of people and relationships in the international organization.

As he was now going to head our police representatives in Tokio, I had to discuss the case of Richard Sorge with him before his departure. He promised to make a full investigation and to keep us regularly informed by telephone. This he did, usually speaking to Mueller, but the two would converse in such thick Bavarian accents that I could never understand them. It was really quite an effective form of code. As far as I can remember, Meisinger's reports on Sorge were always favorable. He said that Sorge was obviously *persona grata* at the German Embassy, and also had very good connections with the Japanese government.

For the moment I was reassured, especially as the material that Sorge sent to von Ritgen proved very useful and was of such a nature that it could not possibly have been misleading. But in the spring of 1941 I received my first shock. A Japanese police commission was visiting Berlin, and in the course of our conversation, their chief asked me whether Meisinger was placing certain German nationals in Tokio under surveillance. I denied this at once, but the Japanese went on to say, quite casually, that if this were the case, Meisinger would find it advantageous to work with the Japanese police, who could be of great assistance to him.

Meisinger, of course, denied later that he had ever spoken a word about Sorge to the Japanese security organization. But it was clear that he had worked very clumsily, and had drawn the attention of the Japanese police toward Sorge, thereby increasing any suspicions of him which they might have had.

Meanwhile Sorge's intelligence material grew more and more important to us, for in 1941 we were very keen to know more about Japan's plans concerning the United States. Already Sorge predicted that the Three Power Pact would prove of little real—meaning military—value to Germany. And after the beginning of our campaign in

Russia he warned us that in no circumstances would Japan denounce her non-agression pact with the Soviet Union. The pact itself had taken us completely by surprise.

He reported that the Japanese land forces had enough oil and other fuels to last them for the next six months, and that the fleet and its air arm were supplied with even greater quantities. From this Sorge concluded that the emphasis would soon be shifted from land operations on the Asian continent—against China, and, as we hoped, eventually against the Soviet Union—to naval operations in the Pacific.

Sorge was arrested by the Japanese in the summer of 1942. There was no doubt about his having spied for the Russians to an amazing extent. Most important of all, he had revealed to them the exact date of the German invasion (a warning that went unheeded), and the fact that Japan did not seriously contemplate entering the war against Russia. This information had enabled the Russians to shift their Siberian divisions at the crucial moment to meet the German onslaught.

Meisinger reported Sorge's arrest to us as soon as it happened. In the course of the subsequent investigation, the German Ambassador in Tokio, Major General Ott, who had previously been Military Attaché there, was implicated. There was evidence that through sheer carelessness he had helped Sorge, who had been a close friend of his, and Sorge admitted having secured valuable intelligence material through this relationship. Ott's irresponsible behavior had not only heavily damaged the interests of Germany, but had also been detrimental to the Imperial Japanese government, and advantageous to the Soviet Union. Ott was therefore declared *persona non grata*.

In a long and uncomfortable session with Himmler, I had to justify our collaboration with Sorge. (After Heydrich's death I had no longer been able to use his information because Himmler refused to be responsible for it to Hitler.) Himmler had difficulty in reaching a decision. On the one hand, he wanted to protect me, but on the other he considered it necessary from his own point of view to inform Hitler of the whole business.

In course of time, the evidence collected by the Japanese became more and more conclusive. Osaki, the former private secretary of Prince Konoye, gave astonishing details of the espionage work he and Sorge had carried out together. In November 1944, two and a half years after their arrest, Sorge and Osaki were supposed to have been hanged by the Japanese, and although in 1947 the Japanese insisted that the execution had taken place, rumor still has it that Sorge is alive in the Soviet Union. The final picture of Sorge assembled by the Japanese was a logical continuation and conclusion of the material in our own files. Sorge was a man who went his own way and worked alone. Because of his origins—his mother was Russian and his father had lived in Russia for many years—he hoped for a reconciliation between Germany and Russia, his motherland, so to speak, which he saw as a country of unlimited possibilities, believing that the new form of society developing there would lead to the betterment of mankind. Basically, he hated both National Socialism and Fascism, and worked against these two forms of government whenever he could.

It seemed that his whole character was influenced by the insecurity of his childhood and his disappointment in the German people after the First World War. He was left in an intellectual vacuum, from which he slowly drifted into an attitude of spiritual nihilism until at last he found a new belief and a mission in life by working and living for the Soviet Union.

It has always remained inexplicable to me why the Russian Secret Service allowed him such extensive personal freedom, in contrast to their usual practice of keeping their agents under the most rigid supervision. Perhaps he had influential protectors in the IVth Division of the MVD, or perhaps they were sufficiently realistic and, estimating his character correctly, came to the conclusion that he would be more effective if they granted him the individual freedom which both he and they despised. They forgave him his various misadventures, as for instance with women, or on drunken escapades, or through indulging in careless talk, and at the decisive moment always came quietly to his aid and steered him back on to a useful course.

Through his espionage activities, Richard Sorge had inflicted inestimable harm on the Japanese. In 1940 alone, for instance, he had sent thirty thousand coded word groups direct to Moscow. His wireless operator was Max Klausen, who had been trained in Moscow for this work. The wireless department of the Japanese counter-espionage

service had been on the track of Sorge's illegal transmitter
for a long time without ever being able to decipher his
code or establish the location of the transmitter—a proof
of the excellent training Klausen had been given by the
Russians. He usually sent his messages from a small sailing
boat which was continually changing its position.

It is interesting that neither in his confession nor during
his long period of imprisonment did Sorge once admit
having also worked for Berlin. This omission can only be
explained by the strong personal bond between him and
von Ritgen, a relationship such as a man of his character
would not wish to divulge to Moscow. I came to this
conclusion after studying the intelligence material he sent
us, for at no time did he attempt to mislead the German
Secret Service.

As far as Ambassador Ott was concerned, Meisinger did
his best to ruin him. After a careful examination of the
evidence, however, it became quite clear that, while Ott
had been thoroughly exploited by Sorge, he had never
been guilty of knowing complicity in espionage activities.
From this point of view I defended him energetically in
front of Himmler and Ribbentrop, who, incidentally, never found out about Sorge's contact with us. Neither
Himmler, nor Hitler informed him about it, nor did I.

In a confidential discussion between Hitler and Himmler, Hitler agreed that no blame could be placed on
the German Secret Service in this affair. However,
Himmler was never able to allay Hitler's deep suspicion of
Ott. Hitler held to the opinion that a man in Ott's position
should never allow trust and friendship to carry him so far
as to reveal confidential political information. It was lucky
for Ott that Hitler took such an objective view of the
matter. He was recalled from his post as Ambassador,
and, although Meisinger received secret instructions to
look out for additional evidence, nothing was ever found
and no further measures were taken against him.

16. THE SEARCH FOR OTTO STRASSER

Hitler's attitude toward Strasser—The mystery of my appointment—An interview with Hitler—Developing a plan —A new lethal substance—Problems of its potency—A difficulty solved—The search proves fruitless—I return to Berlin

ONE DAY in April 1941, Himmler telephoned me. His tone was curt, he sounded displeased— always a bad sign—as he ordered me to be ready to report to Hitler in the afternoon. I was not to bring any documents with me. I sat there wondering gloomily what was coming. As a precaution I called Heydrich and told him of the conversation. He knew about it already. "I know what it's about," he said, "but I don't want to discuss it over the phone. We'll just have to see what happens."

At three o'clock I had a call from Heydrich. "Get ready, we're leaving in ten minutes," he announced. "But come to my office first."

When I entered he was sitting at his desk, bent over some documents. He closed his brief case, which was unusual for him; it was his custom to continue to read while he issued orders. His face was very serious as he explained the situation to me. "For several weeks we have been informed through a very reliable source that Otto Strasser is in Portugal. Hitler hates Otto just as much as he hated his brother Gregor. He considers them both not only betrayers of our cause, but traitors to him personally. He's convinced that Otto is trying to bring about his assassination and that he's working toward it with the British and American Secret Services. There are still some 'Black Front' characters here in Germany, too, working pretty closely with émigré circles from Moscow, but they take the 'National Bolshevism' line. Personally, I'm not quite sure whether Otto isn't really a 'double agent'— whether he isn't actually working under Stalin's orders.

I've set Standartenfuehrer B——, who used to be a member of the 'Black Front' himself, to track down Strasser in Portugal. So far, he has only succeeded in making contact with the 'Black Front' people there. He hasn't been able to get any definite information from them about where Strasser is, but he's quite convinced that he's somewhere in Portugal, and he's managed to build up an organization from the 'Black Front' people to work with him against Strasser. However, the Fuehrer isn't satisfied with the measures we have taken so far; he says Otto has got to be liquidated right away. He and Himmler have agreed that you should be sent to Portugal to work on this, and he wants to talk to you about it. On our way there it might be a good thing if I tell you some of the details about Hitler's relationship with Strasser. . . ."

I felt extremely nervous. I could not understand why they wanted to assign me to this search, I knew very little about the details and background of the matter, and it was bound to lead to violence in some form or other—and on foreign soil too. Standartenfuehrer B——, who enjoyed Heydrich's special confidence, was much more suited to the mission. He had successfully carried out several assignments of this sort and it was hard to understand why he should be replaced now. I could not help feeling that Hitler mistrusted him—he was too well acquainted perhaps with the "Black Front" and the "Black Reichswehr," and with the émigré clique in Moscow.

A quarter of an hour later we were received by Hitler. As we walked along the vast colonnade of the new Chancellery a heavy silence lay over the place. Now and then a muffled voice would be heard, or the click of heels as a guard saluted. The way to Hitler's study seemed endless.

Himmler was there already. Hitler talked with him for a few minutes after Heydrich had announced in military fashion that we were reporting. Hitler and Himmler were bent over a map spread out on a large table. I could not see what the map was, but I thought I recognized the southern Peloponnesus and the island of Crete. Then Hitler suddenly turned and walked toward us. He shook hands with Heydrich and asked, "Have you anything to report on the Strasser affair?"

"No, my Fuehrer," replied Heydrich, "there is nothing new." Hitler looked at the floor for a long time. He seemed to be thinking hard. Then suddenly he raised his head and, giving me a long and penetrating stare, said in his hollow voice, "You, in your service, like every soldier at the front, are under military discipline and must obey unquestionably the commands of your superiors. It makes no difference to which part of the front you are assigned." There was a moment of oppressive silence, then he went on, "The order I am about to give you is given in the strictest secrecy—and is to be carried out, if necessary, at the cost of your life." These words did not require any reply; their meaning was plain.

Hitler stood brooding again, then began a violent tirade against Gregor and Otto Strasser. Gregor was the greater traitor and he had met his just punishment. Otto was not so important, but his present conspiratorial activity could be just as dangerous, especially as he had the support of foreign powers. This, and his intimate knowledge of the international affairs of the Nazi movement, made him a threat. "I have therefore decided," Hitler said, "to extinguish Otto Strasser—it does not matter what means may be necessary to accomplish this end. I hereby give you the order to carry out this assignment."

He looked at me expectantly, and for the first time I spoke: "Yes, my Fuehrer."

With his hands behind his back he marched up and down in front of us, speaking almost as though to himself: "First one must establish his whereabouts, his present residence. Then he must be destroyed by means of a new preparation which cannot be detected. I hereby give you"— he turned to Himmler and Heydrich—"full authority for carrying out this order." Then he turned to me. "You will discuss any further details with the Reichsfuehrer of the SS and with Obergruppenfuehrer Heydrich. I have already pointed out the importance of complete secrecy. No one— and that means *no one*—is to know anything at all about this affair except those who have to be informed so that you can carry out the assignment."

With that he came up to me, stretched out his hand, looked searchingly at me once more, and then, raising his arm, dismissed me. Heydrich left with me, while Himmler remained with Hitler for another five minutes. We waited until he joined us. He seemed very friendly toward me as he said, "Let us hope you will carry the thing off successfully."

"This matter is not so simple," Heydrich said. "Schellenberg's ability to carry out such assignments must not be overestimated." I looked at Heydrich quickly, and Himmler, noticing this, said it would be better to carry on the discussion in his office.

A little later thoughts raced through my mind as we sat there. Why had I received this assignment? Was it only because they suspected B—— that they had chosen me? Or did they want to test me? It seemed to me that Himmler and Heydrich, who usually conducted such matters with keen fanaticism, did not seem to be taking this affair very seriously.

Himmler began by saying that probably I was not yet fully informed about the situation, but that no doubt Heydrich could give me some idea of it. I realized at once that he and Heydrich had already discussed plans fairly thoroughly. Heydrich said it was pretty certain that Otto Strasser would be in Lisbon in about five to ten days' time. They did not know how long he would stay. It could be assumed that he would establish contact with members of foreign missions there and it would be particularly important to find out whether he had done so secretly with Russian diplomatic representatives or any other Russian organizations. My connections with the Portuguese police should enable me to ascertain these facts. Once these points had been clarified it would not be necessary to wait any longer—Strasser must not be allowed to leave Lisbon alive.

Heydrich's voice began to betray such hatred that I stared at him for a moment in astonishment. Why did he hate Strasser so deeply? Was he afraid of him? Did Strasser know something damaging about him? But I was never to know the answer to these questions.

At this moment an adjutant entered to say that a Dr. St——had been waiting for half an hour to report to the Reichsfuehrer SS, and Himmler said he would see him in two minutes. Heydrich turned to me. "Dr. St—— comes from Munich University. He is one of the greatest bacteriologists in the world. At the moment he is working on the defense against bacteriological warfare. He will give you a preparation for the removal of Strasser and will tell you how to use it. But remember—the assignment itself is not to be discussed in his presence."

Dr. St—— was shown in. He was in his early thirties

and was very self-assured. He began speaking at once, calmly and dryly, as though he were giving a lecture. As had been requested, he had bred a bacteriological serum that worked very rapidly. A drop of it would suffice to kill a man with certainty of one thousand to one and would leave no trace to indicate the cause of death. With variations depending on the constitution of the individual, the serum would work within twelve hours. The symptoms were similar to those of typhus, though the bacteria were not of the paratyphus or the typhoid variety. It would work even after drying out. For instance, if a drop of it were left in a glass to dry and later dissolved in water, it would still have the same effectiveness upon coming into contact with the mucous membranes of the mouth or throat. He went on in this way for about ten minutes till my hair stood on end. I had forgotten the assignment and Otto Strasser, as I listened with dread fascination to this representative of science. He continued his explanation enthusiastically, and yet as coolly and calmly as though he were addressing a class on the most ordinary matters. He was a dangerous tool indeed in the hands of such a man as Heydrich. I glanced at Himmler and saw that he and I were following the exposition with equal fascination.

Dr. St—— now took two bottles from his pocket, and placed them on the table in front of us. They appeared to contain about fifty cubic centimeters of a colorless liquid. I looked at the stoppers fearfully. They were similar to those ordinarily used in small medicine bottles and could also be used as a dropper.

Heydrich finally interrupted the doctor's flow of words rather sharply: "Thank you, Dr. St——, you can wait for me outside."

When he had disappeared, Heydrich turned to me. "You had better be careful with this stuff. Now, you can make your own arrangements as soon as you are ready. Standartenfuehrer B—— will be able to give you the details this afternoon." Then, turning to Himmler, he added, "I believe, Reichsfuehrer, that further discussion is unnecessary. We will have to leave the practical part of this assignment to Schellenberg."

We rose, and, carefully placing the bottles so as to keep them upright in my pocket, I excused myself and disappeared.

In my office the first thing I did was to lock the bottles

in my safe. That in itself gave me a certain relief. Then I locked my door, turned off the telephone, and sat down at my desk to try and think. What should I do now? I sat there for a long time, but came to no conclusions—I had my assignment and was stuck with it. Then suddenly the question struck me: why had that horrible fellow given me two bottles, when one drop was enough for what I had to do? Did he want to use me as a guinea pig for his preparation for future bacteriological warfare?

I was restored somewhat by the matter-of-fact tone and the logically constructed recital of Standartenfuehrer B——, who came to report to me about the "Black Front." He was one of Heydrich's special agents, and there was little that he did not know and had not done. I wanted very much to talk to him about my assignment, but then I realized that he knew nothing about it.

After he had left, I began my preparations for the journey, filled with foreboding. This time I was not to travel with a diplomatic passport, but simply under a pseudonym, like the cheapest agent. Then suddenly I thought what would happen if I got into any difficulties at the customs over the little bottles. I could not simply leave them somewhere or throw them away. That would be a crime. So gradually I worked out a plan.

First I had to get an absolutely safe casing for the bottles, which would protect them against any shock or pressure and which could not possibly leak—and then get rid of them. I could either throw them into the sea during my flight, or take them on to Lisbon and throw them into the harbor. I would carry out my assignment by a more conventional method; if necessary, by hiring an assassin to do the job.

To throw the bottles into the sea seemed to me the simplest solution. But I was still worried, for I had no idea what would happen if the bottles should break, and I had not been given an antidote. I wondered whether their contents might not suffice to poison Lisbon's entire water supply. Finally, I consulted the chief of my technical division. I cautiously placed the two bottles on the table before him. He looked at them thoughtfully, then he said, "We can make just what you need, but it will take about thirty-six hours. Still, you'll have then a real masterpiece."

Two days later he brought me two small steel casings. They were made with the utmost precision and could be hermetically sealed. Inside they were lined with a thickness of rubber to protect the bottles against shock, and if, in spite of this, they broke, the rubber, being porous, would absorb the liquid. The casings were also fitted with a safety catch to prevent their opening accidentally. "How long can these casings withstand the corrosion of sea water?" I asked. "Practically forever," he replied. "They are made of the highest grade chrome steel."

After I had enclosed the bottles in their shining casings I felt much better. I then put them in my pocket, for I could think of no better way of carrying them.

Now all the preparations for my journey were complete, and I took off, flying by way of Lyons, Barcelona, and Madrid, without pausing anywhere along the route, to Cintra, the airport of Lisbon. I had ordered one of my agents to meet me there and to stay close to me, so that I could slip him the bottles in case I was searched. Fortunately I had no such difficulties.

I rested for one day and then set to work. The two steel casings with their lethal contents I deposited in the safe of my chief agent. I told only two of my men, whom I could trust completely, of the nature of my mission. At noon I discussed the details of the matter with a trusted Portuguese collaborator, and through him set in motion a widespread search for Otto Strasser. A large number of Portuguese friends helped me, and the quiet and thorough work of my Japanese friend was especially valuable. Strasser's description was circulated clandestinely among at least a thousand people, and addresses of the "Black Front" characters which Heydrich and B—— had given me were subjected to a thorough and intensive surveillance. So extensive was the net I spread for him that, if Strasser were to arrive, or if he was already in hiding in the city, he could not possibly escape it for long. However, the first six days brought no result, and I reported this to Berlin. After twelve days there was still no sign of him, though there had been one false alarm. A Portuguese police official thought he had recognized Strasser, but within three hours we discovered that the man was an American importer and completely harmless.

The expense of maintaining this large search organization was considerable. Every second evening I held a pay day in the home of a Portuguese friend. It was quite amusing to see what ruses our Portuguese collaborators resorted to to get more money out of us. One police official, for instance, had drawn a friend of his into the search. I fully approved of this, for I wanted the search to be as widespread as possible. But when I received a bill for two pairs of shoes for every member of his family— they claimed that they had worn them out combing the streets for Strasser—I thought it was going too far. We were very generous with funds, but one had to draw the line somewhere.

The whole affair would have been a quite pleasant holiday for me, but for the sinister threat in the background. After fourteen days I began to prepare Berlin for the news that Strasser was not in Lisbon and probably would not be during the foreseeable future. Finally I suggested that I should return and let the organization I had built up continue the search without me. I waited for the answer in anxious suspense. Two days later the reply came from Heydrich: "Agree to your proposal." I immediately informed my chief agent, and told him that I was certain Strasser would not show up in Lisbon during the next three weeks, but that he was to continue the search during that period. At the end of it, he was to take a motorboat along the coast and throw the two steel casings into the sea. He gave me his word of honor that he would do so, and speak of it to no one.

If Strasser should turn up, however, he would send me a wireless message, and I would return to Lisbon at once, so that we could discuss further measures.

I went back to Berlin by the quickest route and reported at once to Heydrich. I described the measures I had taken in Lisbon, and said that I had left the bacteriological serum in Lisbon, where we could still use it if the occasion should arise.

At my suggestion the search for Strasser was called off twelve weeks later. By that time Hitler had lost his interest in him, for other matters had arisen to occupy his attention. The Fuehrer was about to embark upon his attack against the Soviet Union, and Hess had flown to Britain.

17. "SOCIETY ESPIONAGE"

Intelligence reports from Yugoslavia—Hitler orders a surveillance of the Military Attaché—Love and duty—A leakage at the Air Ministry—Careless talk—An exchange of loyalties

THROUGH one of our agents, who had managed to gain access to the Yugoslav Foreign Ministry in Belgrade, we received a running report of secret communiqués which the Yugoslav Embassies and Consulates sent in from abroad. Of special interest were the reports which V——, the Yugoslav Military Attaché in Berlin, sent to his General Staff. Their style was admirably clear, both in language and construction, and his knowledge of the political and military plans of the German leadership was amazingly comprehensive and exact.

One of these reports, which was shown to Keitel, contained accurate and authentic figures of German bomber and fighter production, as well as many other technical details. Keitel showed this report to Hitler, who at once started one of his abusive harangues about the carelessness of the Military Command and lack of secrecy in the German war industry. He ordered Keitel to instruct Admiral Canaris to discuss the necessary counter-measures with us at once, and assigned Himmler to the investigation of V——. He also said that he wanted a complete report from me at the earliest possible moment. To this command Heydrich added that I should take whatever steps I considered necessary, without asking for the approval of any higher authorities—and this would include the violation of the Attaché's diplomatic immunity, if I should consider it to be necessary. This decision was a rather serious one, for in view of the strained relations between us and Yugoslavia, such an action might lead to an open breach and to even greater troubles of a most unpleasant political nature.

I discussed the case with my expert on southeast Europe, and also studied all the reports which V—— had sent to Belgrade during the past few months. The biggest puzzle was where he could have secured such a vast amount of accurate and important information. I knew from our recent surveys that the Yugoslav Intelligence Service was extremely active in Germany. They had built up a great number of contacts, especially through their consulates. But this still could not account for V——'s reports, which were obviously gained through connections with the highest circle of the Wehrmacht. I was certain that he must have collaborators—either paid or sympathetic—in these circles.

We began with the usual thorough surveillance of V—— and everyone who was in any way connected with him. At first the results were disappointing. Compared with other diplomats, his social life was rather restricted. He met Wehrmacht officers only at the usual official functions, and the same was true of his relations with other members of the diplomatic corps, especially the military attachés of other countries, who were his friends. These meetings at parties and receptions could not possibly give him the opportunity to engage in any intensive intelligence work. Listening in to his telephone conversations did not seem to reveal much that was of value. We did learn, however, that he was having an affair with a girl named Jutta, daughter of a Berlin restaurant owner. They were obviously very much in love. He gave her every sort of luxury and comfort and went about with her in public, but he also had relationships with two other ladies, both of them in the highest circles of Berlin society, though nothing suspicious was revealed in their conversations. From these we learned only the times and places of their various rendezvous. There was nothing for it but for us to continue our surveillance.

Then one day V—— received a telephone call from a man we did not know. He said that he must speak to V—— most urgently. "Please come to me at once," he said, "at the usual place. I have everything ready, and I think it should be all right now."

We had no idea who this man might be, and we intensified our surveillance, hoping to discover his identity. But the agents who were shadowing V—— had bad luck. They mistook a complete stranger for him and followed this man doggedly for three days. However, after we had discovered the mistake and had again picked up the trail of the genuine V——, we managed to find out the identity of his mysterious telephone caller. Their various scraps of conversation then began to make sense. The man was a high official at the Air Ministry, in charge of deliveries of aircraft and aircraft parts to foreign countries. He was, therefore, in a position to know a great deal about our aircraft construction program, and in fact was probably one of V——'s most important informants.

I next received a report of an interesting telephone conversation between V—— and his girl friend, Jutta. She, it seemed, had sounded angry with him, and he had told her quite brusquely that he needed "the thing this evening," adding, "I positively have to work on it tonight." Jutta did not want to do what he asked, and said, "You won't really be doing any writing tonight, that's just an excuse. You've got a date with some other girl." To this he said very sharply, "I have to have the documents by this evening," and he then hung up.

Our agents watching V——'s house reported that that evening Jutta arrived punctually at seven o'clock, and left fifteen minutes later. V—— did not go out that night. However, at two o'clock in the morning one of his assistants from the Yugoslav Embassy visited him. He also left after fifteen minutes. From this we deduced that V—— had written another report for Belgrade that night, and that the assistant had come to take it to the Embassy. This proved correct, for within four days we had the confirmation from Belgrade in the form of a copy of V——'s latest report. Again it contained information of the greatest importance. Now we were making some progress. Was the beautiful Jutta furnishing him with information? Probably, and the official from the Air Ministry and the two society ladies also. We decided to watch these two ladies a little more closely.

One was the sister of a German general, an elegant woman of independent means. Her acquaintance consisted mainly of industrialists and high-ranking officers of the Wehrmacht. She frequented the best restaurants and bars, and had a circle of admirers with whom she played bridge in the afternoon. An investigation of her finances showed that she could easily afford to lead such a life. She made no attempt to hide her friendship with V——, and neither she nor her friends seemed to think anything of it.

The second lady was the wife of a leading engineer, a man with a very good name both in civilian and army circles. Their marriage was not a particularly happy one. The husband lived only for his work and felt that by providing his wife with a luxurious existence, which indeed she practically demanded, he was doing all that she required of him. He was quite satisfied with the legal possession of a beautiful wife and liked to show himself with her, but, though in public they behaved like a conventional married couple, they lived together more like brother and sister. Both were apparently quite content to maintain this sort of arrangement, and the husband seemed to have no objection to his wife's close friendship with V——.

These facts presented a basis for a typical case of "society espionage." The two women probably did not realize that they were furnishing V—— with important material. The simplest method of blocking these sources of information would be to forbid these women any further association with V——. Of course, if it turned out that conscious betrayal was involved, then legal proceedings would have to be taken against them. But I was quite certain that this was not the case. The trouble was that if either of these steps were taken V—— would be alerted to the fact that we knew of his operations. He would have to be declared *persona non grata* and ordered to leave Germany within two or three days.

I decided not to take this step yet. I did not believe that we knew all of V——'s sources of information—how could he possibly write reports of such accuracy merely on the basis of these informants? I was certain there must be more to it than this, and therefore hesitated to take a step which might prevent our discovering other sources. My chief assistant, however, urged me to act at once. In such a case, he said, it was always best to block off the sources of information immediately—and certainly the continuing betrayal of such important secrets was greatly damaging to us.

Meanwhile, I was much occupied by other work. We were preparing an attack in the Balkans to relieve the awkward situation into which Mussolini had got himself in Greece, and I was preparing a handbook for the armed SS and the police units, dealing with the political situation and the leading personalities in the countries involved. It took a great deal of time and work, and for the moment I lost sight of V——'s case. Then, two days before the beginning of the advance of our troops into Yugoslavia, I received the following report: "V—— has sent Belgrade a complete report on the German plans for the offensive—the strength and composition of the attacking troops, and so forth. He has even warned them of the air bombardment of Belgrade, which Hitler had planned as a surprise attack."

When Hitler heard of this through Keitel he was convulsed with rage and began to shout, blaming the whole situation on me. Why hadn't I arrested that confounded fellow long ago? I had to act quickly, for I knew what this sort of tirade could mean. Two hours later I reported that I had arrested V—— and all the more important members of the Yugoslav Secret Service in Germany and in the occupied territories.

V——'s interrogation took about six days. He knew that with the opening of hostilities between Germany and his country he had lost the protection of diplomatic immunity, and without further hesitation he told us all he knew. His only concern was to protect Jutta, and he took all the blame upon himself. Again and again he pleaded that the girl never intended to harm Germany's interests. She had not known for what purposes he was using the information she brought him and never suspected that her actions would be detrimental to the country.

I talked to him as much as possible, for he interested me greatly. He tried to satisfy my curiosity as far as he could and described in great detail his methods of work. By checking his statements with the reports we had from the central office in Belgrade, and with the testimony of the others involved in the case, I was able to assure myself that he had told the complete truth.

I had arrested Jutta, and at the same time the two society ladies and the official from the Air Ministry. They were also interrogated very thoroughly. The ladies were filled with consternation at the idea that they might have committed treason. They had simply been friends of V——'s and had not had the slightest notion that anything like that might be involved. They said repeatedly that they had only discussed with V—— those subjects which were common topics of conversation in the circles in which they moved—what all their friends knew and generally spoke about.

V—— admitted that, at his behest, Jutta had secured
information from her father. At his restaurant he had
talked with several officers of the armed SS, who had
been on leave and were on their way back to the SS
center at the Berlin suburb of Lichterfelde-Ost. During the
conversation, at which other members of the armed forces
had also been present, it had come out that army units
were being prepared for a new large-scale action. Remarks made by other visitors to the restaurant supported
this. The information filled Jutta's father with excitement
and anxiety. At lunch the next day he had said to her, full
of anger, "that those in power, the high-ups, had not yet
had enough; they were insatiable. But it was time they
finally stopped—the war had already cost enough lives on
all sides." Repeatedly he had exclaimed to Jutta, "The
blood of our fine young men will be shed again!"

The conversation had made a great impression on her,
and that afternoon she had been very depressed. V——
had noticed that something was troubling her, and
presently she told him everything. "What do you think of
all this?" she said finally. "Do you really think it will begin
again?"

Of course, as she told it the information was very
confused, but all the same V—— had realized that it
concerned something of great importance. Consequently
he had asked her to talk to her father again and try to get
all the facts clearly and write them down for him. Then,
he said, by relating the facts to his knowledge of the
general situation he would be able to tell her what was
really going on. He also stressed that the main task to
which he devoted himself was to prevent an extension of
the war, and especially to prevent an open conflict between his country and Germany. Jutta was so much in
love with him that she believed everything he said and was
completely unsuspicious. Still, the idea of writing down
what her father said disturbed her, and she refused to do
it. Instead, she talked to her father, and, after memorizing
his remarks as precisely as she could, repeated them to
V—— that evening. It was their discussion about whether
she should do this or not that we had overheard on the
telephone.

V—— had also got information from the other two
women whom we had arrested. In his most skilful manner he managed to draw out of them everything of im-

portance that they had heard among their friends. He did this so cleverly during their tête-à-têtes that they never had the slightest suspicion of him.

From that V—— told me I could reconstruct a typical scene: "You know, Vera, I've been thinking about what your husband told you the other day—it's all nonsense." And then he would give his reasons for saying so. The lady would argue in defense of her point, and V—— would finally say, "You must have misunderstood your husband. I cannot imagine he would be such a complete ass as to say a thing like that." At this the lady would become irritated. She had perhaps agreed with V—— that her husband was an ass in certain respects, but he was recognized as one of the leading men in his profession, and as his wife she was duly proud of him. She would react just as V—— had expected: "I will prove to you that it's you who are being stupid. I'll ask Juergen again just exactly what he said, and you will see that he's right, that I didn't misunderstand him."

This little conversation gains interest when one realizes that the subject under discussion could easily have been the precise figure of our monthly production of Tiger tanks.

V—— kept a complete file of all military, political, and technical information. He had worked out his own system of evaluation, according to which he would award each piece of information a number of points, and would only forward those which got more than fifty. In this way, he scientifically analyzed all the odds and ends of Berlin gossip that flowed in to him, and by putting it all together arrived at an astonishingly accurate picture.

He was able to do this because of the expert knowledge he brought to his work as a trained officer of his country's General Staff, which he increased continually by his systematic work. But he never let others suspect his knowledge, and thus at social gatherings could ask seemingly harmless questions of the various officials of the military and political leadership.

Of the surprise bombing attack on Belgrade which Hitler had ordered, he heard in the following way. He had been at the Air Ministry to see about the delivery of spare parts for Junkers aircraft which were operating in Yugoslavia, when a test pilot who was there said to his friend in a voice full of spite, glancing toward V—— as he spoke,

"In a few days those fellows will get it good and proper, right on their fat heads—." The pilot had said it too loudly and V—— had overheard it.

The next evening, very disturbed, he asked Vera, one of his two ladies, what was going on, and she told him that people were saying that Adolf would now have to come to Benito's aid in Greece. Her husband thought that this would not be particularly difficult, for now the Luftwaffe was so strong that it could break any resistance. At these words she embraced him still more closely. "I am so happy," she said, "that you are here with me, and not down there in your country, where everything's in such a mess." She went on to tell further details of a bridge party where the wife of a Luftwaffe general had said that her husband had been assigned to Vienna.

These details were enough for V—— to form the conclusion that German operations against Yugoslavia would be initiated by heavy air attacks. Actually, at this point his report could not change the course of events; it was too late for that, but he felt it his personal responsibility to warn Belgrade, whose air defenses were totally unprepared for the impending attack.

These espionage activities had not cost V—— a penny, except for the presents he gave to Jutta, which were really motivated more by his personal feelings. He was in love with her, and admitted that the relationships with the other women were only for the sake of his work. He admitted, too, that he had planned his work in this matter from the very beginning.

The high official in the Air Ministry was quite a harmless and naïve fellow. His only trouble was that he ate and drank too much and had a greatly inflated sense of his own importance. He considered it necessary to maintain social relations in the course of conducting trade with Yugoslavia for the German aircraft industry, and when we finally made it clear to him in a graphic manner what his charming breakfasts with V—— had produced, he was truly horrified.

These, then, were the main facts in the case of V——. Himmler waited for a favorable moment, then gave Hitler an oral report of the result of our investigation. He managed to secure a free hand to deal as he saw fit with those involved in the case. Thus, as V—— was now willing to work for us, I was able to employ him and Jutta in our service. He operated chiefly in Italy—he spoke Italian fluently—and did excellent work.

Later, to investigate the amount of loose talk which was going on in high military and social circles, I instructed the two society ladies and the official from the Air Ministry to chat with me and pass on what they had heard, just as if I were V——. The amount of highly secret and vitally important information that was bandied about in these circles was really incredible; and so, too, was the extensive harm such careless and stupid gossip could do. The guilty ones were all highly intelligent people, leading engineers, architects, officials, and officers of the German Reich.

18. THE MYSTERY OF RUDOLF HESS

Hitler's reactions to Hess's flight—Vengeance wreaked on his entourage—Astrological influences on Hess's conduct—Hitler's attitude toward astrology—Suspected motives for Hess's decision—Correspondence with his wife

AFTER THE flight of Rudolf Hess to Scotland on May 10, 1941, Hitler was momentarily filled with such consternation that he was hardly capable of any reaction. It was now that Martin Bormann, until then Reichsleiter [National Organizer] of the Party, made those advances which gained him a decisive position in the Fuehrer's confidence. It was he who invented the theory that Hess had "become insane," and persuaded Hitler to include this phrase in the first official communiqué on the matter. From the point of view of political leadership this was an error that could never be remedied, for the people asked how a man could be kept in such an important post as Hitler's deputy for such a long time if it were known that he was insane.

Here, too Hitler's "executive measures" ran riot. Mueller was in his element and without hesitation made unlimited use of his powers, for which this occasion gave him a full opportunity. All Hess's staff, from chauffeurs to personal adjutants, were arrested. Mueller would probably have liked to arrest the entire airport personnel too, as well as the chief designers at Messerschmitts', who were responsible for the production of the plane Hess used. Though only a narrow circle was directly involved, many who never would have imagined that they could have been implicated were affected by these "executive actions." For instance, the reports of the internal SD revealed that Hess had been a "silent adherent" of Rudolf Steiner and the anthroposophists, therefore a large number of arrests were made in these circles. He had made his flight in accordance with astrological advice and, as subsequent interrogations and SD reports revealed, had had close associations with astrologers, seers, mediums, nature therapists, and so forth; consequently a series of collective arrests was also made among the ranks of these mystics. In point of fact, the great mistakes he had displayed in this direction had been known for a long time.

From the day of his flight, so Himmler told me, the great interest Hitler had previously shown in astrology changed to an uncompromising antipathy. In my first conversations with Himmler about the Hess affair, in May 1941, I said that I considered the German people much too intelligent for the story about his "mental illness." Himmler replied quickly, "That was Bormann's influence." After looking at me for a long time he added, "It is too late to do anything about it now."

I can still remember how upset Himmler was by the measures taken against the astrologists. And it was with satanic glee that Heydrich, in Himmler's presence, explained to Mueller in detail Hitler's orders concerning them. Heydrich, of course, knew of this weakness of Himmler's, and would often say to me, complaining about Himmler's indecisiveness, that the Reichsfuehrer had been looking too deeply into his horoscope again. Once during a telephone conversation with Himmler I heard Heydrich say, ". . . one is worried about the stars on the epaulettes, the other about the stars in the heavens. It's a question of who is the more difficult to work with." At the same time Heydrich made a gesture to me, as though to ask whether he had not gone too far. He had taken care to say it as though he were speaking only of Hess, but Himmler understood only too well that it applied to him too.

It was after this telephone conversation that I received the order to complete a report which I was preparing for Hitler. In it I said that our secret information showed that for some years Hess had been influenced by agents of the British Secret Service and their German collaborators, and that they had played a large part in bringing about his decision to fly to Scotland. This was true more particularly of the decisive influence of a Professor G——, a gland specialist in Upper Bavaria.

At one of the conferences at that time, at which both Himmler and Heydrich were present, there was a general discussion of the Hess case. When I was asked my opinion, I said that though pathological causes might offer an explanation, for psychiatrists had described Hess's condition as pathological, the influences of British circles which had been exerted over a number of years should also be taken into account, though neither gave a really satisfactory explanation, and further investigation would probably be needed to clarify the matter. I was convinced, I said, that, because of his fanatical devotion, Hess would never betray the details of our strategic planning to the enemy, though certainly he was in a position to do so. Nor was his intellect so deranged that he would be incapable of giving a clear account of our plans. The precision with which he had prepared his flight, and the purposeful manner in which he had carried it through, were a clear indication of this.

As far as the imminent Russian campaign was concerned, I said I thought that it might be wiser to consider that the whole incident in its context could act as a warning to the Russians. However, it seemed to me very doubtful whether the English would be prepared to send a specific warning to the Russian leaders as a result of the first interrogation of Hess.

For the rest, I believed that Hess, having been the Fuehrer's most intimate friend, was, perhaps without even realizing it, strongly under Hitler's suggestive influence. Thus, following Hitler's original conceptions and his attitude toward England, he had considered it his Messianic task to reconcile the two peoples. This would follow Hitler's conceptions about Britain as expressed to me in 1939, and which Hess kept repeating in his intimate circle —that the English were a brother people and the bonds of race made it obligatory to preserve them. One must not forget that, as a German born abroad, Hess had been subjected to British influences during his youth and education, a fact he never sought to hide or deny, especially when discussing collaboration with the Russians along the lines conceived by the former Reichswehr chief, General von Seeckt.

While I was saying all this Heydrich kicked me several times under the table and shook his head disapprovingly. He did not like my frankness, and afterward said to me, "You still have a great deal to learn. And I don't believe the Reichsfuehrer understood what you really meant." But Heydrich was honest enough to admit to me that my analysis had been correct. As far as my report was concerned, he took up the point about the influence of the

British Secret Service, and said several times that we had to try to go further in that direction for, if the information proved correct, these circles would be able to inflict additional damage on us. He felt that the British were capable of formulating and carrying out that sort of plan, and he would be surprised if we did not have some similar experiences in the future. Then he added an interesting remark: "Well, the Russians are no less clever."

In view of my knowledge of the Hess affair and of the investigations in the Abwehr, I can say definitely that it is quite impossible that Hitler ordered Hess to fly to Britain to make a last offer of peace. I only mention this because the lively fantasy of journalists raises it again and again. The only truth in this notion is that Hess, when he decided to take such action, felt that he was carrying out Hitler's original ideas as far as Britain was concerned, and the time selected for this attempt was determined by Hitler's decision to attack Russia. As I have already pointed out, his character, his mysticism, his racial ideas and Messianic complex, all played their part in his decision. Without being conscious of it, he was led to take this action through the influence of astrological circles and by intimate advisers, such as Professor G—— and Haushofer. Our investigation has never made clear whether negotiations in Switzerland by Haushofer or by Hess himself preceded the flight. Haushofer has always denied it. However, even if this had been the case, the basic psychological motivation still remains, together with the fact that Hess received no express authorization from Hitler for his flight to England.

I was sincerely sorry about the fate of Hess's first adjutant, von L——, a man of honest and open character. He was the victim of Hitler's rage and of the continual intrigues of Bormann. In spite of Heydrich's skillful counter-moves, von L—— was placed in a concentration camp, where he remained until the end of the war, and as if this were not enough, was afterward treated as an antagonist by the Allies.

To a great extent this was Mueller's doing. While acting in an apparently friendly manner toward von L——, he was in fact carrying out Bormann's instructions. Mueller realized that Bormann would become Hess's successor, and that he was a personality of much greater dynamic force. Privately Mueller established good relations with

Bormann, while pretending to oppose him strongly as far as Himmler and Heydrich were concerned. It still seems strange to me that Heydrich did not see through the double game that Mueller was playing, a game which was later to become of considerable importance.

Subsequently the great events of the war pushed the Hess case into the background. But I still had to deal with it, and was ordered to gather further information about Hess, his behavior, and his mental state. I also had to organize a means for him and his wife to write to each other. After a time, the British allowed him to correspond, within limits, by way of the International Red Cross in Switzerland, and it fell to me to supervise this arrangement, since it was carried out without Hitler's knowledge. Himmler, however, was definitely in favor of it, and Bormann was clever enough not to oppose it openly at that time. He therefore agreed with Himmler to permit the sending of the first letters.

After that Hess's replies began to come in regularly. The greater part of the correspondence was of an entirely private nature, and dealt exclusively with his wife and son, for whom he displayed the deepest love and attachment. The rest, which was involved and difficult to understand, was couched in terms of private allusions to previous conversations with his wife or other persons. Sometimes I wondered why the British censors let all this go through— but perhaps, having already examined Hess, they had realized that his mystical and manic notions were matters for a psychiatrist rather than a political censor.

It was astonishing how Hess, with the complete assurance of a fanatic or a madman, believed in old prophecies and visionary revelations. He would recite whole passages out of books of prophecies, such as Nostradamus and others that I cannot remember, and also referred to old horoscopes concerning his own fate, as well as that of his family and of Germany. At times there were signs of uncertainty which must have represented a change to a depressive state. All this he expounded time and again in the most elaborate manner to his wife. She seemed to accept these notions of his and expressed her agreement with them, but whether this actually represented her personal beliefs, or whether she did so out of consideration for him, I cannot say.

19. AT WAR WITH RUSSIA

Differences with Admiral Canaris—The General Staff's estimate of Russia's war potential—Heydrich reports the Fuehrer's views on the war situation—Problems of collaboration between the SD and the Wehrmacht—A solution worked out—Fear of United States active intervention—A report on the subversive activities of the Comintern—Hitler's proclamation of war—I am promoted—Canaris sounds a warning against overoptimism—Complications of the mutual withdrawal of diplomatic staff

THE COMING of spring in 1941 was hardly noticeable in the witches' cauldron that was Berlin. I was restless and nervous and felt an underlying sensation of insecurity, without being able to distinguish the real reason for it. Somehow I seemed to sense that events were drawing near which were too great to be shaped by personal influence.

During the rides that Admiral Canaris and I used to have early in the morning we usually discussed the information that was coming in to our respective organizations, between which there was unfortunately a great deal of wasteful overlapping. Various differences existed between us about Russia, and we argued over these for many months. First, there was the question of production figures of Russian heavy industry. I rated their tank production much higher than Canaris did, and was convinced that they had new models in production that were better than ours, but this Canaris refused to believe. I had come to this conclusion as the result of a peculiar order that Hitler, wishing to impress the Russians, had given in March 1941; we were to show the Soviet Military Mission our most advanced tank factories and tank corps training schools, and all secrecy measures as far as they were concerned were to be dropped. (Nevertheless, we did not obey the Fuehrer's orders and hid our newest models.) It was the attitude of the Russians on this occasion, and the questions they asked, that led me to conclude that they possessed better models than anything we had. The appearance in large masses of T-34 tanks on the Russian front in the summer of 1941 proved that my assumption had been correct.

Another point of disagreement arose because Canaris claimed he had documentary proof that the industrial centers round Moscow, and in the northeast, the south, and near the Urals, as well as their chief centers of raw materials, were linked only by single-track railways. My department had received different information. However, Canaris claimed that his had been verified, while we possessed no means of checking the accuracy of ours.

The army's intelligence departments Fremde Heere Ost and Sud-Ost ["Foreign Armies East" and "Southeast"] were doing excellent work in the correlation and objective evaluation of information, and we ourselves had achieved very good teamwork in our own Intelligence Service. But this difference between Canaris and myself shows how difficult it was for the military leaders who were responsible for planning to make a correct assessment of the information submitted to them. Consequently, if the material did not fit into their basic concepts, they simply ignored it. As far as the top leadership was concerned, things were even worse. Until late in 1944 Hitler rejected all unwelcome information, even when it was based on fact and reason.

The evaluation department of Fremde Heere West never achieved an efficiency equal to ours, because continual changes of personnel led to considerable uncertainty which was reflected in their work. The staff of the evaluation department of the Luftwaffe suffered from the same difficulty; while a sense of insecurity was caused by the Gestapo's arrest of key workers in the department as members of the Russian *Rote Kapelle* [Red Chapel] espionage group. As a result, confidence was never restored in the department.

In spite of Canaris' inclination to underestimate Russia's technical progress, later conversations with him were dominated by fears that we would now become involved in a two-front war, with all its inherent dangers. The General Staff's opinion was that our superiority in troops, technical equipment, and military leadership was so great that a concentrated campaign against Russia could be concluded within ten weeks. Heydrich's own theory, which Himmler and Hitler shared, was that military defeat would so weaken the Soviet system that a subsequent infiltration of political agents would completely shatter it. Both Canaris and I agreed that the optimism of the military leadership was ludicrous, and Canaris also considered Heydrich's political theories extremely doubtful. Indeed, Canaris' estimate of the political strength of the Russian leadership was quite the opposite of Heydrich's. He confided to me, however, that he had been powerless to persuade Keitel, his superior officer, to take this point of view. Keitel had insisted that the measures planned by Hitler were so striking and so forceful that the Soviet system, no matter how firmly it was established, would not be able to withstand them.

Recalling the false estimates that the Western Allies had made of Hitler's strength at the outbreak of the war, I felt convinced that here our leaders were committing a similar error. I tried to point this out to Heydrich, saying that perhaps it would be wiser to base our planning on the probability that Stalin might be able to reinforce the framework of his party and his government, and that for him a war imposed on Russia would become a source of strength rather than of weakness. Heydrich stopped this line of discussion immediately, saying coolly, "If Hitler orders this campaign, a different set of problems will arise." Another time he said to me, "It's curious—Canaris mentioned the same sort of idea to me just a few days ago. You two seem to be developing some remarkedly negative notions on your morning rides together."

I made one more attempt to discuss the matter in May, pointing out to Heydrich that, even supposing him to be one hundred per cent right, it would still be better, just as a precaution, to examine other possibilities and prepare for other eventualities. Again I was abruptly put in my place. "Stop your hypocritical, small-minded, and defeatist objections," he said. "You have no right to talk like that."

I have often wondered since whether the a priori rejection of all such possibilities sprang from the Nazi leaders' fanatical belief in the success of Hitler's plans, or whether many of them did not entertain doubts in secret, while denying them in discussion, fearing that thereby they might endanger their positions. The fact that so many of them made no provision at all for their personal security in case of a debacle suggests that the former was true, and that they had, in fact, a blind faith in Hitler's leadership. However, I am convinced now, as I was then, that Heydrich's intellect was too coldly calculating for him not to have thought out all the possibilities. Yet one never knew what was really in his mind. Thus, one day in the summer of 1941, when we were together at his hunting lodge, he remarked to me, apropos of the direction the war was taking, "The way things are being handled by us, there must be a sticky end. Also it's sheer madness to have created this Jewish question." The meaning of this reference to the problem of the Jews became clear to me only when Canaris told me after Heydrich's death that he possessed proof of Heydrich's Jewish ancestry.

Canaris' great nervousness at this time about a two-front war seemed to be an expression of his deep pessimism. In our conversations he jumped erratically from one subject to another—for instance, in the middle of a discussion on American bomber production, he would suddenly start talking about political problems in the Balkans. Sometimes his remarks were so elusive, so vaguely and obscurely couched, that only those who knew him well could understand what he was driving at. This was especially true of his telephone conversations. Once I jokingly remarked over the telephone that I thought I really ought to tell Heydrich and Mueller about this "pessimistic" line of talk. "Oh dear," said Canaris, "I forgot we were talking on the telephone."

Toward the end of April 1941, Heydrich telephoned me at my office. He made several vague allusions to the approaching campaign against Russia, but, noticing that I did not really understand what he was talking about, he said, "Let's have lunch together, then we can talk this over quietly."

We met at one-thirty in Himmler's dining room. I had just come in when Himmler entered surrounded by a swarm of his personal staff. He greeted me benevolently, then took me on one side. "You will have a great deal of work during the next few weeks," he said. I answered, rather dryly, "That would not be anything new, Herr Reichsfuehrer." Himmler laughed. "Well, Heydrich has a lot of things planned for you."

At dinner Heydrich discussed various problems in the Balkans, among them the question of liaison with various army commands, and asked me to discuss the matter with the proper Wehrmacht authorities. Then he began to talk of the Russian campaign. As I recall it, what he said was something like this:

"You were right—the Fuehrer has not been able to deal satisfactorily with the military and political problem of Britain. He now believes, as our air offensive has been a more or less complete failure, that Britain, given America's aid, might be able to speed up her rearmament. Therefore he's accelerating the buildup of our U-boat fleet. He aims to make our undersea arm so strong that the Americans will be discouraged from ever actively coming into the war, because he realizes the danger of the USA co-operating closely with Great Britain.

"However, he calculates that, although Franco has refused to support us actively, we completely dominate the Continent, and you can rule out for a year and a half at least any attempt by the Western Allies to bring about decisive military action by an invasion. It's of the greatest importance that we make use of this period, and it seems to the Fuehrer that we can now attack Russia without the risk of our getting involved in a two-front war. But if this time is not made good use of, then one has to count on the certainty of invasion from the West, and in the meantime Russia would have grown so strong that we wouldn't be able to defend ourselves if she attacked us. Russia's preparations are so tremendous that at any moment Stalin could exploit any commitment of our forces that we may make in Africa or in the West; which means he'd be able to forestall any future action we may be planning against him. So the time for taking decisive action is now.

"The Fuehrer is convinced that the assembled power of the Wehrmacht is so enormous that the battle against Russia can be won and Russia conquered in the time we now have. But Germany will have to rely solely on her own resources, because the Fuehrer's convinced that the British, with their petty shopkeepers' souls, haven't a broad enough vision to recognize the Russian danger. Russia's demands on Finland and Bulgaria and Rumania, and their latest political intrigues in Yugoslavia, show that they'll soon be ready to bring matters to a head—in other words, that Stalin will soon be ready to join battle with us.

"For anyone hoping to safeguard the new Europe, a conflict with the Soviet Union is inevitable; it will come sooner or later. Therefore, it's better to stave off the danger now, while we still can trust in our own strength. The General Staff is full of confidence. In their opinion we shall be striking at the adversary while he's still getting ready for action. The element of surprise will be so great that the campaign should be successfully ended by Christmas 1941 at the latest.

"The Fuehrer is well aware of the magnitude and weight of this decision, and it's because of that that he does not want to leave the smallest element of our strength idle. In fact, not only has he allowed, he has insisted that all fighting units of the Security and Civil Police are to be used. These units will be assigned to the commander of the army. They'll be used chiefly in support areas, but also in the front line as well. The Fuehrer wants this because he wants the Security Police and the Security Service (SD) employed on protecting us against sabotage and against espionage, and also for guarding important personalities and archives—in fact, on general security of the rear areas. He is thinking particularly of the so-called 'Rollbahnen.'" [These were the specially built motor roads designed to carry the heavy long-distance traffic of the supply columns moving across the vast, scantily populated Russian plains.] "Operations are expected to develop pretty quickly because of the large number of motorized units, which means the fighting units of the Security Police will have to be motorized too, so that they can be active in the operational areas as well as in the fighting zone. All this has been thoroughly discussed with the Fuehrer, and he has given his personal orders for these plans to be carried out. It's an unusual sort of operation, so the technical aspects must be discussed in detail with the Quartermaster General. The Fuehrer has had a further thought, too, which also occurred to me; this is the first time these special units will have been engaged at the front; every one of their members will have the opportunity to prove himself and to earn a decoration. This should finally dispel the false impression that the staff of the executive departments are cowards who have got themselves safe posts out of the fighting line. This is extremely important, because it will strengthen our position in relation to the Wehrmacht, and also it'll have a favorable effect on questions of personnel and finance.

"Discussions with the army have been going on since

March, and I have had Mueller conduct the negotiations with the OKW" [Supreme Command of the Armed Forces]. "He has already had conversations with Quartermaster General Wagner and his staff. But Mueller's terribly clumsy over this sort of thing. He's incapable of finding the right words, and with that typically thickheaded Bavarian manner of his, he gets very stubborn about unimportant details. In the end, he simply treats the other fellow as a Prussian swine. This is impossible, of course. Wagner was quite right when he complained to me about Mueller. So I've told Mueller already that he's to be withdrawn from the negotiations. He'll send you all the relevant documents this afternoon. Now, I have also spoken to Wagner about you and have told him that although you are a very young man, I am quite certain he will find your manner of conducting negotiations more conducive to favorable results. He'll receive you in person tomorrow and begin working through the whole thing with you."

I interrupted Heydrich here for the first time and asked him what were the chief interests that I was to safeguard.

He replied by outlining the problem which, reduced to its simplest terms, was the old story of jealousy and antagonism between the army and the SS. My job was to work out a compromise with General Wagner on the channels and relationships of command, civil and military authority, the problems of transport, fuel supplies, and other necessary details. In short to arrive at a working solution which would be satisfactory to both parties.

In due course this result was achieved, and Heydrich seemed quite pleased.

Events now began to move with precipitous speed. The preparation of such a campaign, the mobilization of such a large number of men and such quantities of material required incredible energy from all those concerned with the work of organization and planning. Anyone who has not himself lived through days such as those cannot imagine how much was demanded of each one of us. This was especially true of my task as chief of the Counter-Espionage Department. For us the war with Russia had already begun, and engagements were being fought on the Secret Service front. One of the principles of our work was to keep the espionage rings we discovered under close observation as long as possible, so that we could infiltrate them before fighting actually started. The vital thing for us was to keep the feverish activities of our mobilization from being observed by foreign intelligence. I gave my staff orders to take preventative action by making wholesale arrests of suspects. These measures were taken in collaboration with the Abwehr of Canaris and other Wehrmacht offices, and special attention was paid to highly "sensitive" localities such as railway marshaling yards and frontier posts.

Where specially important Russian espionage rings were concerned, I had put off making arrests, but these could not be deferred any longer. It was now absolutely vital to shut off all channels of information. However, one or two of these rings were still being used to feed to the Russians misleading material prepared by the Wehrmacht. We managed to pass into their hands faked material about renewed preparations for "Operation Sealion"—the invasion of Britain. It was very important that the Kremlin should have a mistaken evaluation of the political situation and our measures certainly contributed to their unawareness. For instance, in the fortress of Brest-Litovsk Russian infantry battalions were still parading with their bands on the afternoon of June 21.

Canaris was growing increasingly nervous. Both he and Heydrich were being continually pressed by Hitler for more material on the state of Russian defenses and the Soviet armed forces. Hitler studied their reports in great detail. At various times he complained to Himmler about Canaris. "The Abwehr always send me a batch of individual, undigested reports. Of course, they are all of great importance and come from the most reliable sources, but it is left to me to sift the material. This is not right, and I want you to instruct your staff to carry out their work quite differently."

This was said to me many times, until late in 1944, when at last Himmler told me that Hitler was quite satisfied with our system of work.

In spite of all that was going on, Canaris and I still went out riding together at least two or three mornings a week. Though we had agreed not to talk shop, we could not help turning to topics connected with our work. Canaris was terribly worried about the approaching campaign. He criticized in the strongest terms the Wehrmacht leaders who, despite their expert knowledge, were irresponsible and foolish enough to support the views of a man like

Hitler in his assumption that we should be able to conclude the Russian campaign within three months. He
would not be a party to this, and could not understand
how the generals, von Brauchitsch, Halder, Keitel, and
Jodl, could be so complacent, so unrealistic, and so optimistic. But any attempt at opposition was useless; he had
already made himself unpopular by his repeated warnings.
Only a few days earlier Keitel had said to him, "My dear
Canaris, you may have some understanding of the
Abwehr, but you belong to the navy; you really should not
try to give us lessons in strategic and political planning."
When Canaris repeated such remarks he would usually
rein in his horse, look at me with wide eyes, and say quite
seriously, "Wouldn't you find all this quite comic—if it
weren't so desperately serious?"

A continually recurring subject was the attitude of the
United States and her industrial capacity, especially for
aircraft production and shipbuilding. This question was
likely to be decisive, because it would determine the length
of time allowed us before we should have to reckon on
the threat of a two-front war. Canaris and I agreed that if
the full productive strength of America were behind Great
Britain there would undoubtedly be an invasion of the
Continent. Landing operations would certainly be preceded by a mighty air offensive which, if the situation of the
eastern front were strained at the time, would heavily
damage our industrial capacity. Therefore the Luftwaffe
leaders' lack of clarity in their planning was of the
greatest concern. Goering and his staff did not share our
views on this matter, and there was great confusion in the
production schedules of bomber and fighter aircraft.

As an example of the sort of difficulties we met with in
getting a fair hearing from the leaders when one had some
realistic information to impart the following incident is
significant: at the beginning of 1942, on my instructions, a
comprehensive report was prepared, based on our secret
information about American war production, especially
the total steel production and the buildup of the United
States Air Force. The report had taken almost two
months to prepare, and leading economists and trade
specialists had worked out the details. The information
was comprehensive and came from the most reliable
sources and the report was drafted with painstaking ob-
jectivity. Heydrich was astonished by it, and I shall never

forget his surprise when, glancing through it, he came across such figures as "a total steel production of eighty-five to ninety million tons." He took the report to Goering and Hitler, both of whom studied it thoroughly and discussed it together.

The conversation with Goering later on was most unpleasant and I was embarrassed for Heydrich's sake. The Reichsmarschal did not shout—he spoke in short, pregnant phrases. Looking me up and down contemptuously, he pressed the report back into my hand and said, "Everything you have written is utter nonsense. You should have a psychiatrist to examine your mental condition."

That was the end of the interview as far as I was concerned. Heydrich remained with Goering a while longer, and was rather bitter when he finally came out of the room. But he never held this embarrassing incident against me. I heard from Himmler several months later that under Goering's influence Hitler had grown very angry about the report. He criticized it as being too clever by half, written solely to bolster up the author's self-importance, and said that he did not believe a word of it.

Later, at the Nuremberg Trials, for two weeks I occupied a cell across the hall from Goering's. I saw him every day and was able to speak a few words with him. Not until then did I receive any commendation from him. Speaking from his cell in a loud voice he said to me, "Well, it has certainly turned out that you were not talking nonsense after all." I knew immediately what he meant.

One day I received a call from Heydrich, asking me to be ready to report to Himmler on the question of counter-espionage against Russia. When we got there Himmler began by saying that he had had a long conversation with the Fuehrer that day, and had covered a whole series of problems connected with the coming campaign. "For you, Heydrich, there are a number of things that I wish to discuss alone. For you, Schellenberg, I have two special problems. First, the Fuehrer proposes to announce the commencement of the attack in a proclamation to the German people. A report of the OKW" [Supreme Command of the Wehrmacht] "and perhaps also of the Foreign Office is to be appended to the proclamation, and just as at the beginning of the campaign against the West, a report was included from the Minister of the Interior, the Fuehrer now desires a similar report from me, as chief of the German Police. The report in the previous case proved extremely impressive, and he wishes to have a report in the same form on the subversive activities of the Comintern. Unfortunately we only have twenty-four hours. I realize, Schellenberg, that you are not a magician, but try to do your utmost. Heydrich will see to it that whatever you need will be provided with the greatest speed. So don't lose any time."

That was the first assignment.

"The second point: in his proclamation the Fuehrer wishes to mention the Horia Sima affair in Rumania.[1] You know"—he turned to Heydrich—"that is rather dangerous ground for us. Shall I try to dissuade the Fuehrer or not?"

Heydrich said that he considered it quite unnecessary to mention Horia Sima. "What is the sense of it?" he asked; "what does the Fuehrer think he will achieve against Russia by that?"

They looked at each other in silence, then turned to me for my opinion. "At this moment," I said, "with our Rumanian allies about to go into action on our southern flank, the Fuehrer probably wishes to assure Marshal Antonescu that such attempts against his government won't be repeated. He probably wants to remove this dark page in our relations, and no doubt the whole thing will be

---

[1] *Publisher's note*: Horia Sima was the leader of the notorious Fascist Iron Guard organization in Rumania. In 1940 Heydrich helped him to engineer a plot against Marshal Antonescu, the Rumanian dictator. The plot failed and Sima was arrested and, as an act of grace on Antonescu's part, was handed over to the German authorities for internment in Germany. This dubious situation caused considerable embarrassment to Hitler, for the projected invasion of the Soviet Union called for a strengthening of the bonds between Germany and Rumania under Antonescu. This embarrassment, and Hitler's consequent resentment against Himmler and Heydrich, whom he held responsible for it, was revived and intensified when, toward the end of 1942, Sima managed to escape to Italy and the Gestapo was unable for some time to trace his escape route or his whereabouts. To make matters worse, the Gestapo, hoping shortly to recapture Sima, did not report his escape to Hitler until a fortnight after it had happened. This confirmed Hitler's suspicions, and from Schellenberg's point of view had a decisive influence on his own project to overthrow Ribbentrop with the help of Himmler and thus pave the way for his "appeasement" projects.

attributed to a Soviet intrigue. Still, the affair must be well known to the Rumanian public. I don't remember whether Communist forces actually took part in it or not, but the Fuehrer's suggestion can only be effective if it's actually proved that they did."

Himmler left the matter in abeyance and I was excused. As I left, I began to consider how I could best approach my assignment. My own department had most of the evidence I would need, but I decided also to approach Mueller, who, when I did so, ordered all his departmental chiefs to let me have whatever documents I might need.

It was late in the afternoon when I returned to my office. I gave the necessary orders, and within half an hour the files and documents began pouring onto my desk. I sat in front of the immense pile of papers, and it was a little while before I could muster the courage to begin. But by late evening I had selected the most important material, which I then took home with me so that I could work on it in peace and quiet.

During the night both Himmler and Heydrich called me several times. (Both of them always knew exactly at what time I had left my office and where I could be reached at any moment.) Himmler made me nervous. As soon as Hitler asked him a question or said something to him, he would run to the telephone and bombard me with questions and advice: "Schellenberg, the Fuehrer wants to have this put that way . . . and don't go into too great detail, just describe the methods of the Russian Secret Service . . ." and so forth. (I only mention this to show to what extremes the centralization of a totalitarian system could go.)

Fortunately I was well acquainted with most of the material. Thus I was able to complete this task within the short time allotted to me. The report was accepted without any further changes and Hitler's proclamation to the German people was published on June 22, 1941, ending with the fateful words:

"People of Germany, at this very moment military movements are in motion that in extent and volume surpass anything the world has so far witnessed."

Great difficulties arose about disguising our mobilization from the Russians. Not the least of these difficulties was the continuing controversy between the offices of Mueller and Canaris over the activities in Polish-Russian frontier areas of the Ukranian nationalist leaders, Melnik and Bandera. The Military Secret Service naturally wanted to use the services of the Ukrainian minority groups, but Mueller objected that these nationalist leaders were pursuing their own political ends in an unwarranted manner, and that this was causing widespread unrest amongst large sections of the Polish population. I tried to hold myself aloof from this controversy, especially as the meetings dealing with it were extremely long and acrimonious.

Just at this time inexcusable conditions in the Foreign Political Information Service (AMT VI) were brought to light. As the result of measures ordered by Heydrich, many members were disciplined, and there was even talk of criminal charges against some of them. A ruthless purge ensued which showed me what to expect from them should the occasion ever arise for action against me.

The professional failings of the department's members were even more serious than their personal irregularities, but the harshest punitive measures could hardly improve results here. I was more than ever convinced that only a complete reconstruction of the department would be effective. But that this would have to be done in the middle of war and, so to speak, under the very eyes of the enemy services, by leaders who had no understanding of the needs of a secret service, would certainly not make things easier.

It was interesting that at this time Mueller made his first open attempt against the very existence of the organization. He urged Heydrich to dissolve AMT VI completely, to forego a secret service abroad operating as a separate unit, and to concentrate instead on an "Enemy Surveillance Service" within the framework of AMT IV, which was Mueller's own department.

That evening Heydrich ordered me to report to him. He repeated the plan Mueller had suggested and added sarcastically, "He is nothing more than a petty police official, after all." He begged me to consider the whole matter very thoroughly, and then went on, "I have now arrived at a definite decision: after the Russian campaign has begun, I am going to appoint you deputy chief of AMT VI, and then, after two weeks, will make you the chief. This is a new assignment for you—perhaps the most difficult one that has yet come your way. So I'll give you time to consider the matter very carefully, and when you've done so we'll spend an evening at my hunting lodge so that we can discuss the whole thing quietly and thoroughly."

He rose and with great solemnity gave me his hand. I left the room with a beating heart. On the one hand, I was very happy to have received finally the assignment for which I had waited so long. On the other, I was somewhat oppressed that it had been brought about by such a sad failure. From the very beginning I felt the tremendous responsibility that had been placed upon me. I was fully prepared to shoulder it, however, and it is understandable perhaps that, in spite of my being overburdened with work, the new task excited me and I found my thoughts already beginning to turn toward my new field of work.

On June 21, 1941, Canaris invited Heydrich, Mueller, and me to a lunch at Horcher's, one of the most fashionable Berlin restaurants. I knew the reason for this—he wanted to make a last attempt to warn Heydrich and Mueller against overoptimistic ideas about a Russian campaign. It was typical of Canaris to choose a seemingly casual luncheon date as an occasion for giving his opinions on a problem that was of exceptional importance to him. He wanted to enlist Heydrich's support against the optimistic attitude of the Wehrmacht High Command, for it would be extremely helpful for him to be able to say "Heydrich too is not so optimistic in his estimate of the situation."

But Heydrich was not worried. He said, "Yesterday at dinner Hitler was in a very serious mood. Bormann tried to relieve him. He said to him, 'You are burdened with great worries just now—the successful conclusion of this great campaign depends on you alone. Providence has appointed you as her instrument for deciding the future of the whole world. No one knows better than I do that you have devoted the whole of yourself to this task, that you've studied every conceivable detail of the problem. I am convinced that you have planned everything thoroughly, and that your great mission will surely succeed.' The Fuehrer listened to all this, and then said that one could only hope he would be proved right in everything, and that in such a great enterprise one could never know with certainty whether all eventualities had been foreseen. One could only hope so, and pray to providence that the

German people would triumph. All this," Heydrich went on, "was reported to me by Himmler on the telephone this morning, and it proves that the Fuehrer is not so optimistic as his military advisers."

At the end of Heydrich's remarks Canaris concluded the conversation by saying that Hitler's attitude was very noteworthy, and in a way revealing.

At dawn the next day, June 22, 1941, the Wehrmacht began the offensive on all sectors of the front, from the Black Sea to the northern regions of Finland. In General Halder's diary is the following entry:

"I have just described the plan for the Russian campaign to the Fuehrer; the Russian armies will be destroyed in six weeks. . . ."

That afternoon I received a telephone call from the Foreign Office. They wanted me to take part in the negotiations on the exchange of diplomatic personnel. At exactly the same time as the Russian Ambassador, Dekanozov, with his entire staff and consular personnel, left Berlin, the German Ambassador, Count Schulenburg, and his entire staff were to leave Moscow. The two special trains were to meet at Svielengrad on the Turkish-Bulgarian frontier, where the actual exchange was to take place. The Fuehrer demanded a close surveillance of the chief Russian personalities, and also of the staffs of the Intourist Travel Agency and the Soviet Trade Delegation.

After several days the Foreign Office had completed their preparations and our agents reported nothing out of the ordinary, except for repeated reports that the Soviet agencies were burning a great number of documents. Then one afternoon an excited telephone call came in from the Foreign Office: Dekanozov had just informed them that the exchange could not take place and that he refused to leave Berlin because two important members of the Soviet Consulate in Danzig had vanished. He had learned from a completely reliable source that they had been arrested by the Gestapo, and until the two officials had been returned he would not even consider leaving Berlin.

A complication of this sort was all I needed. I sent a message to Danzig at once, asking for an explanation. In my own department all we knew was that the two consular officials were really the heads of an extensive spy ring. Then Danzig came through with additional details. The two Russians had been taken to East Prussia after their arrest and were being held there. Twenty-five Germans and Poles had already been arrested in connection with the case. The ring extended into an army supply office in Berlin, and therefore the Abwehr were working on the matter too. The ring had been sending material to Moscow by wireless, chiefly concerning troop movements and locations. During the last few weeks they had sent out some vital information about troop concentrations in East Prussia, and also about the movements of our Baltic Fleet. Their transmitter must have been working in the Danzig area, but our people had been unable to determine its exact position, nor had they been able to decipher the code that was being used.

Knowledge of the spy ring had been gained chiefly from the testimony of the arrested suspects, and before the investigation was concluded as many as fifty people might be involved. The arrest of the two Soviet officials was completely justified, the case against them being quite conclusive, as it seemed certain they had operated the transmitter. In spite of this I asked to have them released at once.

The next morning at eleven o'clock our chief investigator in Danzig reported to me in person. He was pale, tired, and nervous. He went over all the details of the case and concluded by saying that he was unable to produce the two Russians and because of this asked that disciplinary proceedings should be taken against himself.

I could not quite understand his behavior, or what he was driving at. Rather worried, and afraid the two were no longer alive, I asked what he meant. It turned out that one of the Russians had a black eye as the result of an interrogator losing his temper over the man's persistent denial of proven facts. Fortunately my informant had intervened in time and nothing serious had happened.

I called the Foreign Office at once and told them that the two Russians were available, but that, instead of boarding Dekanozov's special train in Berlin, they would have to go by plane to Sofia or Svielengrad and join the rest of the Russian diplomats there. Our department would provide an aircraft for the purpose. Dekanozov could leave Berlin completely assured that the two men would join his party before they crossed the Turkish-Bulgarian frontier. However, if they failed to appear, he would still be able to refuse to go through with the exchange. After long negotiations, Dekanozov accepted this proposal.

I had the two men brought by plane from Danzig, and one of our Russian linguists, who was to accompany them on the journey, looked after them for a whole day in Berlin. The next evening he reported to me that neither of the Russians had complained, but, on the contrary, one had said repeatedly that he was sorry he had not spoken the truth from the beginning as this would have spared him quite a bit of unpleasantness. The other said that to continue to deny everything would not, in any case, have been possible in the long run, as the evidence against them was conclusive. However, all that was a closed chapter. What they did not like was being flown by special plane, which might make a most unfavorable impression on Dekanozov.

I had them brought before me the next morning because I wanted to get a personal impression of them. They were intelligent men, well trained and physically fit. As the diplomatic train was already waiting for them at Svielengrad, my assistant now decided to hire a car for the rest of the journey. The heat, the dust, the bad roads, and tires that burst every few miles were bad enough; but the greatest problem of all was his two charges. They had seemed quite content at the beginning of the journey, but the nearer they got to Svielengrad, the more restless they became. They were afraid of Dekanozov and of the reception they would get from the central office and feared they might be punished for their failure, for having been arrested, and for having betrayed their mission. My assistant had to use all his skill to dissuade them from committing an act of folly and pointed out to them the uselessness of flight. He was greatly relieved when he delivered them safely at Svielengrad.

The exchange should have proceeded without any further hitch, but the train bringing the German diplomats from Moscow had not arrived. It was being detained in Russian territory until the Soviet government had been assured that the two consular officials had actually reached Svielengrad and were under Dekanozov's care. Consequently it took three more days before the exchange could be carried through as planned.

20. TOWARD A UNIFIED INTELLIGENCE SERVICE

*Responsibilities of my new office—Problems and plans—
Discussions with Dr. Mehlhorn—Reorganizing the department—A commission of inspection appointed—Surprise at
Iceland's occupation—Heydrich proposes the SD's fusion
with the Gestapo—This move countered—My own office*

ON JUNE 22, 1941, the day our armies
marched into Russia, after a conversation with Heydrich
lasting hardly more than three minutes, I went to the
building which housed AMT VI in order to take over my
post as acting chief. Rumors of my appointment had been
circulating for several days and some willing and responsible members of the staff greeted it wholeheartedly, but the
feelings of the great majority ranged from open resentment to silent and watchful anticipation.

First I devoted myself to the very difficult problem of
staff changes, which I had been considering during the
previous weeks. My first days were so crowded with new
and unaccustomed duties that every night I sank into bed
dead tired. I now had to organize a new routine for
myself. I realized during these first momentous days that
though I had achieved the goal toward which I had been
working for many years, I was faced with the tremendous
task of reconstructing our foreign intelligence system at
the height of a two-front war. I was weighed down and
confused by the burden of my responsibilities and at times
I really did not know where to begin. I decided first to
feel my way into the routine work of the organization,
then gradually to approach the larger problems. I had
been considering these for a long time, of course, and
theoretically had worked out clear solutions, but these
were not quite so easy to put into practice.

I felt that I must think the whole thing over quietly, so
I decided to leave Berlin for a few days and visit my
friend Dr. Mehlhorn. He was a man of great experience in

such matters—at that time he was building up the administrative organization of the Eastern Territories—and I knew I could discuss my problems with him and ask for his advice. He was living in Posen, and together we went to visit the estate of a Polish landowner with whom I was acquainted. For the first three days I resolutely put aside all problems of work and devoted myself entirely to hunting, riding, and fishing. The countryside, with its great areas of open space, and the loveliness of its sunrises and sunsets, gave me the tranquillity I needed. One could almost feel the earth breathing and could inhale its manifold scents, sweet and strong, under the clear eastern stars and the wide-spreading night sky. But the loveliness of the summer, and the rhythms of natural growth, were disturbed by swarms of aircraft heading toward the front, reminding me of the harsh and destructive reality of the times. Otherwise I was undisturbed and could pursue my thoughts in peace.

The problems that faced me were many and complex. There was, for one thing, no German tradition in the Secret Service as there is in England, and consequently there was little appreciation or understanding of the difficult but vital role which this service plays. Another serious drawback was the absence of a unified intelligence system. In its place were many overlapping bureaus and agencies which resulted in duplication, waste, inefficiency, and inevitable personal and professional jealousies. Finally, there was a drastic shortage of specially trained personnel.

In discussing these problems and my plans for meeting them with Dr. Mehlhorn, he pointed out that in his opinion I had badly misjudged Himmler's and Heydrich's motives. With them the only consideration was power politics. He was convinced that they would drop me ruthlessly at the first sign of failure. This possibility was not reassuring, but I was determined to try my best and I felt confident that I could do the job and at the same time stay out of any trap.

Refreshed by my stay with Mehlhorn and stimulated by our discussions, I returned to Berlin to begin my task. It soon became apparent that Mehlhorn's analysis was correct.

Heydrich, always extremely suspicious and with a personal aversion toward me, closely checked every phase of my work—and put every difficulty in my way. I realized now to what depths of hatred, envy, and malicious intrigue men are capable of descending. There were times when I felt more like a hunted beast than the head of a department. The only thing that gave me the strength to carry on was the pleasure and satisfaction that I gained from the work itself.

When I took over AMT VI, serious irregularities were revealed in the handling of currencies and in the general accounts. Certain members of the department, including the former heads, were involved. I made this the opportunity to request a general inspection of the department's finances. I wanted a complete audit to be made, so that I would not later be held responsible for the errors of my predecessors.

A commission of inspection appeared, consisting of eight high officials headed by a Ministerialrat [Ministerial Counselor.] Naturally I wanted the commission to confine their investigation to questions of finance and bookkeeping, but wherever payment had exceeded a certain sum I declared my readiness to give the commission a verbal report on the Secret Service purposes for which the money had been spent—but only where this would not endanger the security of our work.

Heydrich used this safeguard to generate suspicion against me. He instructed the Ministerialrat to take note of all cases in which I refused to give full information to the commission, insinuating, of course, that these were probably attempts to disguise abuses. I parried this move by collecting the data on all such cases myself and sending it to Heydrich personally. It was typical of the relationship between us that although I saw him on many occasions at this time, neither he nor I once mentioned the matter. Only by sending back the accounts initialed by himself did he indicate that he had understood my counter-move.

One can imagine how difficult it was under these circumstances to keep to my program, or to try to win the support of a man like Heydrich. Therefore I remained silent about my long-range objectives. However, so many problems arose in connection with the work itself—the collecting of secret information—that those measures which were of immediate urgency in my program could be carried through without Heydrich becoming fully aware of their import. He himself desperately needed information material in order to place himself in a favorable light with

Hitler, Himmler, Goering, and the other chiefs. When he presented the Secret Service reports to them in person he was so eager for results that I succeeded in obtaining executive powers from him which he would otherwise never have delegated. Thus I was able to establish liaison offices in the various Ministries, and secured for myself the right to contact the Ministers in person whenever I had to discuss questions that necessitated collaboration. This was an important step and it was up to me to exploit it as skillfully as possible.

In the meantime I had suffered the first reverses in my work. The worst and most dangerous of these took place when the Americans occupied Iceland in the summer of 1941. Canaris had not provided any advance information at all about this. I had forwarded one Danish report, which, however, could not be considered particularly reliable. It had remained on Himmler's desk, and Hitler first heard of the matter from foreign press reports, and this only belatedly, for the press report service of the Propaganda Ministry was not functioning properly. The result was that I was ordered to organize a special news service in the neutral countries. This was by no means easy, and necessitated the formation of a publishing firm which in turn established relations with publishers in Switzerland, Portugal, and other neutral countries. The Lufthansa and the Central European Travel Bureau served as a channel of communication and special couriers were provided for exceptional occasions.

After about six months I was able to integrate this work, which represented a senseless duplication of effort, with the responsible departments of the Foreign Office and the Propaganda Ministry, thereby easing the drain on my supplies of foreign currency. It was also a proof that collaboration could be achieved in the Third Reich as long as no questions of departmental prestige were involved.

Two months after I had assumed office I prepared a memorandum on the tasks of the Political Secret Service abroad. It showed, on the one hand, every possible connection between Germany and the occupied territories, and on the other, neutral or enemy countries in the spheres of politics, banking, industry, agriculture, science, art, literature, or music. The service was interested in people in these spheres establishing contacts abroad and reporting back.

This memorandum was to serve as basis for a general order by Himmler, as Reichsfuehrer SS and Minister of the Interior, to the various SS Commands and the administrative cadres of his Ministry. Himmler had said that in principle he was in agreement with the memorandum and was even ready to address the highest leadership corps of the SS and the Party about it, thus acting as a propagandist for my ideas. In addition, Himmler's order was to go to the other Ministries so that their interest in this kind of collaboration would be officially requested for the first time.

I was sitting working on this one evening when Heydrich telephoned and asked me to report to him. I was annoyed by the interruption, but gathered the necessary documents and drove to the Wilhelmstrasse. In those days Berlin was still a beautiful city. As I drove through it, taking a long way round, I had soon forgotten most of my worries. I turned off at Kurfuerstendamm toward the Tiergarten and stopped for coffee at Kranzler's in Unter den Linden, where I sat and tried to clear my mind for the struggle that I knew lay ahead.

The main adjutants' office at the Wilhelmstrasse was usually a beehive of activity. I was very surprised, therefore, to see only a few overtired adjutants working on the usual stacks of dispatches; otherwise all was quiet. My relations with the adjutants were always friendly, and now one of them whispered to me, "The chief is not in the mood for work tonight." I foresaw a social evening and thought I could enter the lion's den with an untroubled mind. However, I soon found that I was mistaken.

As I entered I noticed the studied casualness of Heydrich's manner as he continued working on some papers. When he saw that I was watching him he reacted with a typical nervous shrug; finally he pushed the papers aside. "Anything of special importance?" he asked in his rather high, nasal voice. "No, nothing special," I replied. "Have you time to dine with me?" he said. It was practically a command.

We went to the Eden bar and there dined in silence, for I had made it a practice always to let Heydrich start the conversation. A lady whom I knew was sitting at a nearby table, and now and then we exchanged friendly glances. Heydrich, who did not know her, was annoyed by this, but his inordinate curiosity drove him to ask who she was, where I had met her, and how long I had known her. Then suddenly he changed the subject and began to talk about the matter on which he had wanted to see me.

It proved to be a long and unpleasant talk about transferring some of my department's most delicate and important functions to Mueller's AMT IV. Heydrich was applying his old principle of *divide et impera*. My answer was to agree with everything he said, and then patiently and quietly to point out the danger of turning over crucial matters to clumsy and untrained hands. He appreciated my sarcasm, and he was also impressed with my facts. He told me to settle it with Mueller. With that the matter was settled. A detailed discussion followed about the operation of my department in the occupied territories, which ended with a very satisfactory compromise, leaving me a more or less free hand.

When this was over, I had to accompany Heydrich to various night clubs and pretend to enjoy myself, while he engaged in stupid conversation with barkeepers, barmaids, and bartenders—all of whom knew and feared him, while pretending great devotion. Finally, at five o'clock in the morning I was allowed to go home.

The next day I had to confront Mueller with Heydrich's decision and it took me all of two hours to make it clear to him that I had thwarted his attack. At the same time I had to be careful not to let my rejection lead to an open breach between us, for relations were already strained. And Mueller was an opponent who would not recoil from any depths of treachery and would use any means of warfare at his disposal with the utmost ruthlessness.

Then he became quite warm and friendly, and began speaking of the importance of collaboration and mutual confidence. But at the next meeting of the SD department chiefs he suddenly attacked me without warning and accused various agents of mine of negligence and dishonesty. One example he cited had, in fact, been a bad blunder on our part. In Paris the Gestapo had arrested a Corsican who had been supplied with false identity papers by one of my offices in Bordeaux. They had not checked on him carefully enough and a complicated assignment had been given to a member of the Paris underworld who was wanted by the police!

Unexpectedly, Heydrich came to my defense, obviously because the whole matter bored him. Ironically he said,

"I'm sure misadventures of this sort have also happened in your department, Mueller. For instance, when an important witness is given the opportunity to throw himself out of a fourth-floor window—not only because your investigators are asleep on the job, but because they haven't mastered even the ABC of police procedure."

This time Mueller had really burned his fingers, and for three or four weeks I was left in peace.

It might interest the reader at this stage to take a look into the office I occupied as head of the Foreign Department of the German Secret Service.

Entering the room, large, well furnished, and covered with a deep, luxurious carpet, the visitor would be faced by my big mahogany writing desk. The most precious piece of furniture in the room was a big old-fashioned cupboard containing my personal reference library. To the left of the desk was a trolley table covered with telephones and microphones connected directly with Hitler's Chancellery and other places of importance, one telephone providing a direct line to my home in Berlin, as well as to my country house in Herzberg. Microphones were hidden everywhere, in the walls, under the desk, even in one of the lamps, so that every conversation and every sound was automatically recorded. The windows of the room were covered with a wire mesh. This was an electrically charged safety device which was switched on at night and formed part of a system of photoelectric cells which sounded an alarm if anyone approached the windows, doors, safe, or, in fact, tried to get too close to any part of my offices. Within thirty seconds a squadron of armed guards would have surrounded the entire area.

My desk was like a small fortress. Two automatic guns were built into it which could spray the whole room with bullets. These guns pointed at the visitor and followed his or her progress toward my desk. All I had to do in an emergency was to press a button and both guns would fire simultaneously. At the same time I could press another button and a siren would summon the guards to surround the building and block every exit.

My car was fitted with a short-wave transmitter which enabled me to talk with my office from anywhere within twenty-five miles, and to dictate to my secretary.

Whenever I was on missions abroad I was under standing orders to have an artificial tooth inserted which con-

tained enough poison to kill me within thirty seconds if I
were captured by an enemy. To make doubly sure, I wore
a signet ring in which, under a large blue stone, a gold
capsule was hidden containing cyanide.

21. A VISIT TO OSLO

Heydrich appointed von Neurath's deputy—My presence in Prague requested—The invitation shelved—A visit to Oslo—British use of the Norwegian resistance—The story of a woman agent

ON SEPTEMBER of 1941 Heydrich was appointed acting Reich Protector of Bohemia-Moravia under the purely nominal authority of von Neurath. He considered the appointment an important promotion and was very pleased but he expressed the desire to have me go with him to Prague as his assistant. This suggestion filled me with consternation, and it was obvious that I had to scotch this notion before it became a command. It took all my powers to persuasion to convince him that it was to his best interests, as his deputy, that I stay in Berlin and reconstruct the Secret Service. At last he reluctantly agreed.

Originally I had planned to fly to Madrid in September 1941, to inspect our new organization there and look into various problems. This plan had to be postponed, however. Heydrich suddenly conceived the idea of flying with me to Norway. He wanted to clarify a number of points of conflict between himself and Terboven, who was Reichskommissar there. He also had another purpose—he wanted to fly several missions secretly as a member of the Luftwaffe with the Stavanger fighter squadron, so that he would have enough combat missions to his credit to qualify for the Iron Cross, 1st Class, and so would receive the Golden Cross from Goering.

As usual, we traveled in his special plane. During the flight he sat working at his desk and kept his adjutants on the run, chiefly with instructions about our itinerary in Oslo. Meanwhile, he had so far extended the program of his visit that he would barely be able to carry out half of it.

I had decided to give two lectures before a selected

audience of agents. I also wanted to look into the work of the British Secret Service in Norway, and the position of the double agents—Norwegians who had joined the resistance but were, in fact, working for Germany. I was also interested in the chances of using for our service certain Norwegian shipping companies which still maintained overseas connections.

Immediately after our arrival at Oslo we were received by the Reichskommissar. According to protocol, Heydrich, as acting Reich Protector, had to be treated as though he were of ministerial rank, and at first Terboven made every effort to do this. But the two were bitter enemies and I was curious to see how their meeting would develop.

After lunch they had their first discussion. The real point of conflict between them was the relative authority claimed by both over the higher SS and Norwegian police leaders. Was the authority of Terboven, as Reichskommissar, to take precedence over the strongly centralized authority of the chief of the Security Police and the SD in the central office in Berlin? Terboven considered himself complete master of Norway, with unlimited authority to rule as he saw fit. The German police forces were to carry out his orders only. Directives from the central authority in Berlin were ignored or scoffed at; he alone was responsible to the Fuehrer for Norway. Himmler and Heydrich were of interest to him only as personal acquaintances. He could afford to act in this vainglorious and autocratic manner, since he had a very close relationship with Goering which went back to the time when Terboven was Gauleiter in the Ruhr—they had both had a hand in certain questionable transactions in which shares in the German steel industry were confiscated, ostensibly in the national interest.

The discussion quickly reached a deadlock and I was then invited to give my views, which I did, in spite of Terboven's latent—and later open—hostility. However, some progress was made and the meeting ended with Terboven declaring that he thought we could reach a mutually satisfactory solution.

In the evening there was an official dinner. Terboven saw to it that nothing was lacking, for in all things he aped his great patron, Goering. As we had foreseen, the party degenerated into a drinking bout. Terboven drank an incredible amount and forced all those around to keep pace with him. This was a favorite pastime of his. I felt so much out of place that I twice attempted to withdraw quietly, but did not succeed. Finally Terboven forced his two secretaries to ride about the room on bicycles, which was greeted with yowls by the drunken group. I remarked rather loudly, "Quite a circus!"

Terboven must have heard me and had obviously been waiting for an opportunity to make a scene. He suddenly rose, came toward me, and said, standing very stiffly in front of me, "Here, take this glass of beer—" He held out a two-pint mug. "Drink that down at once—you are malingering."

I said that I was sorry, but because of my health I must decline. I had not even finished the sentence before Terboven tried to pour the beer over my face. But Heydrich intervened quickly and held him back, for which I thanked him. I remained for another five minutes, then left without a word.

Early next morning one of Terboven's women secretaries called on me and asked me to come over early as the Reichskommissar wanted us to have breakfast with him. I talked for a while with the secretary, who gave me various interesting details about the curious life and customs at the "Court of King Terboven." I felt quite sorry for her.

At first Terboven clumsily tried to apologize for the incident at the party. "It seems there was a terrible amount of boozing last night—but you see, Schellenberg, the trouble was that you were much too sober."

After breakfast there was another conference in which we all took part, including Mueller, who attended at Heydrich's request. Terboven gave in all along the line. That afternoon everyone went sailing in Oslo Fjord.

The following day I was able to accomplish in peace the work I had planned to do. I was very impressed by the activity of the British Secret Service, which naturally found great support among the freedom-loving Norwegians. They had used the Norwegian resistance movement very methodically for political and military intelligence, as well as for sabotage. In several cases it had been possible to infiltrate double agents, but no really valuable information was to be gained, though I tried everything I could think of to stimulate and encourage their operations.

Several cases of betrayal had cost us valuable help, as well as fishing cutters, short-wave sets, and so on.

At that time the navy and the Luftwaffe were pressing strongly for a short-wave meteorological station on Greenland—the task of setting it up really belonged to the Military Secret Service, and I had been warned to take preventative measures against surveillance by the Norwegian resistance movement. I suggested that those Norwegians who had to maintain our communications and supply lines should be arrested as unreliable elements and brought to Germany. This would be the best way of preventing the Norwegian resistance from becoming suspicious of them. But this idea was thought to be overcautious. Unfortunately I was proved right. Two attempts to install the short-wave station failed and much valuable time was lost. Finally a third attempt succeeded and the short-wave transmitter worked quite well for a while, until British direction-finders managed to locate it and its men were taken prisoner.

At one of the evening receptions I met a very good-looking Norwegian girl. She spoke Swedish, English, and French, but hardly any German. I talked to her for about half an hour and then turned to one of my women agents and paid no further attention to the other girl! Yet I somehow felt she was interested in me, and, sure enough, the next day she telephoned and suggested we should meet.

When we did so I could see that she was much troubled about something and after we had talked for a while she said, "You see, I have been given a special assignment to carry out—against you. Although I have known you only a short while, I know you are not at all the man they described to me. Please help me. I don't want to betray either side, but I don't want to harm you either."

This was a most odd revelation, and naturally, being eternally suspicious, I thought at once: Well, this is certainly a new approach. I could not make up my mind about her. I studied her face closely and saw that she was not really in control of herself. Her eyes were red and she was upset—but she did not give one the impression of hysteria or of play-acting. It's possible, I thought, that she really is suffering from some inner conflict which she is not able to resolve. I asked her whether her people knew where she was at this moment.

"I don't think so," she said. "I came by a roundabout way, and I gave a false name to the reception clerk—besides, I am not known here." I warned her that she should be careful all the same, and tell them she had been here but had failed to carry out her mission. I asked whether she had any relatives in Denmark or Sweden. She said she had some in Sweden.

"Couldn't you go to Sweden for a short visit without attracting the attention of the Germans or arousing your own people's suspicions?" After hesitating a long while she said that she thought she could. So I arranged that she should be contacted by telephone at her address in Upsala and told how to get in touch with me at a cover address in Stockholm. "And if something should happen?" she asked, cautiously. "I shall arrange to have my agent telephone you every two weeks—she will call herself Selma. If there is anything you wish to let me know, you can tell her."

Later I met the girl again in Stockholm and arranged for her to live with one of our honorary collaborators. I had been quite mistaken in my first suspicions of her. It was one of those peculiar accidents of life that for no apparent reason this girl had become fond of me, and, because of the slanders that she had heard about me, had reacted against those who had given her the assignment, and now she hated them. She confessed to me that she had been working against us for a long time. If I was the sort of man she thought I was, I must understand how much she had hated a man like Terboven and those around him.

When she was ordered to act against me, she resented it, and was angry when they tried to force her hand and brought pressure on her to do so. These things had worked a change of heart within her, and out of this grew an increasingly real and passionate feeling for me which I could never reciprocate. Thus, although she could not serve me personally, she did the next best thing by working for me professionally, and very ably too. Once she even went to England on behalf of the Norwegian resistance and spent two months there. But she could not supply me with any important material because her freedom of movement was very strictly controlled. Another time she was more successful. She went alone to Lisbon and returned on a Portuguese freighter with some very valuable information about the RAF. Afterward she worked in various countries, generally concentrating on social espionage. She liked to travel, and was at my disposal for all sorts of special assignments. However, in course of time her work began to decline. She admitted it quite openly and said that she was no longer satisfied to lead this sort of life. We had a long talk, for I wanted to make it possible for her to return to a normal existence. But she seemed skeptical about it. She had made money and had got a certain satisfaction out of her work, but she realized she would never achieve her real ambition; it was that that had kept her going all this time.

For her own protection I had her placed under observation. She went to Paris where she lived quite withdrawn, lost apparently in a dream world. Later my agents reported that she had begun to take drugs. What happened to her after that I never knew. There was a rumor that she had committed suicide in May 1945, and it was also said that she had gone downhill completely and under another name and with a Finnish passport was working for the Russian Secret Service.

22. EXPANDING OUR SWEDISH NETWORK

Reasons for visiting Stockholm—The Communist party in Sweden—An assessment of Germany's situation—Support for a subversive group—A report on Russia's plans—Revelations of our Secret Service in Madrid—A narrow escape—Himmler and the Japanese—An argument with Heydrich—Our Eastern offensive halted

NOT LONG after my trip to Norway I had to go to Sweden. This time my trip was not for the benefit of the Secret Service, but at Himmler's express wish, in order to encourage the dissemination of Hitler's racial ideology. The whole thing was really quite unimportant in itself, and I would not have wasted five minutes over it if Himmler's interest in it had not necessitated my showing the greatest concern. He had a highly romantic idea of Secret Service work and continually gave me advice about how to proceed. Indeed, sometimes I was barely able to keep a straight face at his utterly hopeless suggestions.

Although my main mission was trivial and unnecessary, I intended to use this opportunity to try to penetrate the Soviet intelligence network in Sweden. My aim was not so much to combat the Russians there as to infiltrate my own agents into the ranks of their service, so that I might determine the extent and efficiency of its activities. Of course, the higher the positions achieved by my agents, the more effective they would be. Thus I would not only be kept informed of the aims and results of the Russians' operations against us, but would also benefit by the results of Russian intelligence activities against other countries.

The Swedish Communist party was not sufficiently strong to play a politically decisive role, though it had a large number of adherents. Their chief task was to furnish money, to run courier depots, and to give assistance to agents working against Central and Western Europe. They would therefore serve my purposes. I knew that some years earlier a Swede named Nils Flyg had left the Communist party, his political ideas having changed toward Fascism and National Socialism. He had formed a political party of his own, which was quite efficiently organized, and published a newspaper called *Volkets Dagblad*. In time he had gained a small following, numbering about a thousand, among the working class.

Knowing that Flyg was in financial difficulties, I decided to try to use him for my purpose, though I did not want to do so until I had seen him. My training had taught me to be suspicious of everybody, and I assumed that, in line with normal Soviet tactics, he had left the Communist party with the knowledge and consent of the Russian Secret Service, having been given an assignment of the same sort as I had in mind, namely, to infiltrate our service. I knew from experience that such Trojan Horse tactics were very popular with the Russians, and that they gave their collaborators plenty of time to develop their plans.

I had worked very carefully, for I did not want to embarrass the friends I had made in Sweden. So I had to make it clear that my measures were not directed against Swedish interests. The fact that such a man as Flyg might constitute a liability to the Swedish government was, of course, no concern of mine; that was an internal problem of the Swedes, I decided not to travel incognito, but to appear in Stockholm quite openly. I therefore had several routine questions referred to me by the IKPW [the International Commission of the Criminal Police] which would give me a legitimate pretext for contacting the offices of the Swedish Secret Police. The disadvantage of traveling openly in this manner was that I would be closely watched by enemy secret services, but I made living arrangements which I hoped would enable me, when necessary, to shake off anyone who was on my trail.

As I knew Stockholm well, and liked it, I spent my first two days there taking a brief holiday, free from the tensions and stresses of the last few months. For the first time I realized how much my personal struggle against the machine of the totalitarian state had affected me. At its controls were men who had no consideration for the shortcomings or failures of individuals. The roar of the machine running at full speed was to them an assertion of their power and security, and they were quite unaware, in

the intoxication of that power, of how far they had drifted
into evil.

I was worried not only about Germany but about myself. It was not that I felt any doubts about Germany's
victory, or that I would cease doing everything I could to
bring this about. But it was in Stockholm that the first
warning signal flickered in my subconscious mind. For the
first time I saw clearly the necessity of using all my
personal resources, and those of the service entrusted to
me, to maintain some form of contact with the enemy.
Faced with a war to which there appeared to be no end
except total victory—or total defeat—I decided to direct
the Secret Service, with its manifold and intricate underground channels, not only to the acquisition of secret
information, but also toward the building of bridges between the warring powers, which might one day lead to a
peaceful solution and spare us final disaster. In talking
with acquaintances in Sweden about the war with Russia,
I admitted quite openly that the struggle was an extremely
bitter one, but said that I believed in Germany's final
victory.

My first working days were spent in consultation with
my agents on problems of organization and personnel, and
also in dealing with my main assignment—the secret
financing of the Swedish Nazi group. I felt that I was
being watched very closely by the various intelligence
services, and at one time almost decided to give up my
plan of meeting Flyg. However, a meeting between us was
arranged, and my impression of him was not unfavorable,
although physically he seemed a wreck. But I thought that
he could still do good work for another two or three
years. I started off by giving him a large sum to finance
his work, thus instilling in him confidence and enthusiasm
for the task. I told him that I wanted a general report
from him every fourteen days on what people in various
professions thought about the political problems of the
day. If anything of exceptional interest arose, he should
send an interim report. Every eight days I would give him
special assignments. The main thing would be for him to
build up a reliable and efficient network of informants
within the shortest possible time. He could also use this
network for his newspaper *Volkets Dagblad* and I would
take care of the cost. His chief activity would be to gather
information about the Swedish Communist party, and to

find out in what way its members and the work they did was being used by the Russian Secret Service. Here one could only achieve results by working systematically to fit together the whole picture like a mosaic, from many small pieces. Only then could one draw specific conclusions about personalities, courier routes, and the Party's methods of work against Central Europe.

Flyg was somewhat taken aback, especially when I explained to him that at least ten of his best followers would officially have to break with his group, and return to the Communist party. There they would have to work very actively against him and his newspaper in order to regain the trust of the Russians. He would have to talk to each one of them separately and, unknown to the others, inform them precisely of their duties and insure their loyalty. And I gave him some hints about the security measures necessary to prevent his agents from really going over to the Communists.

If they succeeded in establishing connections with the Russians, communication with them would have to be handled with the utmost care and a good deal of time would have to be allowed before they were given specific assignments. To proceed hastily would be the greatest mistake. In selecting his agents he should take great care to choose only those who were of strong character and completely loyal to him.

Flyg finally understood what I was aiming at and declared his readiness to do all I asked, though he said repeatedly that he would not do anything to harm the interests of his country. But I did not want a binding agreement from him right away, and asked him to think everything over most carefully. When he left, he seemed a more determined and energetic man; the task seemed to have won his interest.

After he had left, I sat for a while thoughtfully in the smoke-filled room. I needed a few minutes to overcome my suspicions. For who can really look into the heart of another human being? The only thing to do was to wait and see. The results of a man's work were the best tests of whether one's suspicions were justified or not.

When it came to financing the operation, great care would have to be taken in transferring the currency not to arouse the suspicions of the Swedish tax authorities. Everything would have to be done in such a way that they would not question the fact that Flyg had acquired a large amount of money. But my efforts in time and money paid surprisingly good dividends. Flyg reported that he had direct information from Russian circles that Stalin was preparing a decisive counter-blow for the winter. The report was precise even to the pinpointing of the area around Moscow as the place for the attack against the wedge which the Germans had driven into the capital at the peak of their offensive. But it was not known for certain whether the troops involved would consist of divisions withdrawn from Siberia or whether they would be newly mobilized units from the region behind the central front. Flyg estimated that there would be between fifty and sixty-five divisions equipped for winter warfare, of which at least twenty would be fully motorized armored units.

I was especially interested by this report, for since the middle of November I had been receiving information from my agents in Russia about the organization of new units in the central area. The evaluation sector of the German General Staff also reported, on the basis of front-line intelligence and prisoner-of-war interrogations, that in the middle of December new troops had begun to appear. Important and detailed information originated from an intimate conversation between high-ranking members of the Russian Embassy, who could not possibly have known that they were being overheard. The informants were themselves members of the Swedish Communist party, who had close personal contacts with various members of the Russian Embassy.

Immediately after this I had a conversation with a Japanese colleague. He was not able to add anything decisive to this information, but he assured me that the Japanese knew the Russians were relying completely on their pledge of neutrality, and were therefore basing their strategy on the assumption that they would remain undisturbed in the east while they continued their struggle with Germany.

This news was so important that I cut short my visit in order to work on the report and present it in person. Consequently I could not meet Flyg for a final conversation, as I had planned.

The first thing I dealt with on the day I returned to my desk in Berlin was a report of a special emissary who had been taking a look at my people in Madrid, as I had not had a chance to talk to them yet. This report made my hair stand on end. The details were really horrifying. Only one of my chief agents was described favorably, a serious and resourceful worker who had organized an effective net of informants. His only difficulties were in his relations with the German Embassy, but even there he had finally managed to establish a working relationship. This was the one bright spot in the whole report. The rest was simply incredible. But I shall not seek, out of false pride, to disguise our mistakes. The main secret wireless transmitter was set up in the back room of a restaurant. Important members of the service had made this place their headquarters, which served also as a rendezvous for the agents, and after each payday there were drinking bouts here with the agents. They had made the owner of the restaurant a co-worker too, and he had become the treasurer of our currency fund. The cash register had become the treasury of our Secret Service, and all our funds and receipts were kept there. The local police were fully informed about everything that went on, and they too joined in the drinking bouts. Some of the police were even counter-agents, who reported everything that happened to other intelligence services. It was obvious that not only the Spanish police, but also the enemy services, knew the code used by this main transmitter and were reading all the messages sent out from the back room. It was very lucky for me that, in keeping with this state of affairs, all that had been sent out on our transmitter was complete nonsense. For a little while I played with the idea of simply letting them go on as they were, so as to mislead our opponents while I built up a new group somewhere else. Finally I put the report aside. It was a frightening thought that information based on such work had actually been passed on to the top leaders.

Meanwhile a number of people were waiting outside my office. One of them was the specialist on Bulgaria from the evaluation section. His report was brief and precise and showed a high level of understanding.

The next interview was a more awkward one. It concerned a problem that affected our whole policy in the Near East—the reaction to the attempted revolt of El-Galiani in Iraq, which had miscarried and had cost us a great deal of goodwill in Arab circles. We had to win the

Arabs back to a favorable attitude toward Germany, and I asked for a written report, for I had to take the matter up with the Foreign Office and with the Supreme Command of the Wehrmacht.

Next followed conferences on technical problems, and finally I was able to turn again to the great stack of documents on my desk.

Toward two o'clock in the morning I began to feel so fuzzy that I could no longer take in what I was reading, so I went home. The whole house lay in deep sleep. I glanced quickly into the nursery, and then with a heavy sigh sank wearily into my bed. My wife had woken up and she looked at me, deeply worried. "You cannot keep up this kind of a life," she said. But I was too tired to reply.

The next thing I heard was her voice coming through my sleep as though from a great distance—"Walter, Walter! Air raid! We must get dressed and take the boy down to the cellar." "It's only the first warning," I said. "If it's really an attack we'll have plenty of time to go down."

I lived just off the Kurfuerstendamm, and there was an antiaircraft battery nearby. We were on the fifth floor, and when they fired our whole apartment shook. The guns were growing louder by this time, and distant bombs were shaking the ground. I went to the window, still undecided what to do, and suddenly I saw a huge bomber caught in the intersecting beams of the searchlights. It tried to escape the lights as flak rose toward it, but it could not do so. "We had better go down," I said. I had just turned away from the window when I heard the whine of a falling bomb. I called to my wife to lie down, but she was making for the nursery and as she got to the door there was a tremendous crash. She fell to the floor and I flew through the air and hit the opposite wall. I heard the tinkle of glass and the crash of masonry, and then— complete silence. In a moment cries for help rang through the night. There were shouts of command and the tramping of many feet. I heard the voice of my wife asking hoarsely, "Are you all right?" I didn't know, I was still stunned. She recovered more quickly than I, and raced over shattered glass and debris to the nursery. I followed, rather ashamed to note how quickly women react under such circumstances. She wrenched open the twisted door and there, under a coverlet gray with dust but undisturbed, the boy was beaming up at his mother with a happy smile. Not a window, not a piece of furniture was left whole in the room, and just above the bed a jagged bomb splinter had buried itself into the wall. My wife and I knelt down by the bed, and for a moment our eyes met.

We were both so excited that we had not heard the shouting from below—"Fifth floor—are you cuckoo up there? Turn off that arc light of yours—can't you hear them still flying around?" We quickly turned out the lights and went down into the cellar. Then I went outside to see what had happened. It was an incredible sight. Within a radius of two hundred yards a stick of five bombs had come down. One of them had hit our house at pavement level and torn away the whole of the left side. It was lucky that there was no shelter there or our fate would certainly have been sealed.

After the "all clear" my wife and I set about clearing up the worst of the debris. I made some coffee and then we sat together until it was time for me to go out. I was meeting Canaris for a ride, and when I told him about the night's happenings he became very excited, which was unusual for him, and scolded me severely for not going down to the cellar right away. We did not ride very well that morning.

Not until breakfast did we speak of service matters. We discussed at length the Japanese war potential. and Canaris asked me to send him the documents I had on the subject for his own evaluation. He also asked me whether Heydrich had submitted any material to the Fuehrer which would strengthen his pro-Japanese attitude.

"No," I replied, "not as far as I know. I do know that Himmler is very interested in Japan, and he has quite a good knowledge of Japanese history. In fact, before the Russian campaign he ordered that certain SS cadets were to learn Japanese. His idea was to send forty of them to serve in the Japanese Army, and we were to have forty Japanese cadets serving with us. Later on he was going to send twenty of our lot, the best ones, on some Secret Service job in the Far East. He wanted me to study Japanese history and religion, and the structure of the state, and the influence of the Catholic Church in the Japanese universities."

Canaris looked at me with wide eyes. "Have you been able to do all this already?" he asked. I admitted that I had not. "This interest in the Japanese way of life stops short when it comes to the so-called racial principles," I added ironically.

"How do you mean?" Canaris asked.

"Well, there was a Japanese on the staff of the Embassy here who wanted to marry a German girl. Himmler was against it, so was Hitler of course; Ribbentrop was for it. They wrangled about it for months. The racial experts had to write reams on it, and in the end they found a loophole in the racial laws and let them get married."

Canaris, with assumed innocence, suddenly asked, "What did you talk about with your Japanese friend in Stockholm?" I became a little annoyed and said that I had discussed nothing whatsoever with a Japanese. Even if I had, he knew very well that I would deny it. He must have understood that I did not want to discuss the subject, yet he acted as though he were pained by my refusal to talk about it. "But you have an excellent confidential agent working for the Japanese there, you must have talked with him——"

This was true. I had a co-worker in Stockholm, a very well-educated Italian, who had a good entree to the Japanese Embassy, where he worked for many years as a translator. He had won their confidence, and, because of his intelligence, experience, and linguistic ability, often got hold of valuable information without really trying to do so. Actually I had raised his pay during my visit to Stockholm, though I had not spoken to him personally. But what was behind Canaris' persistent curiosity?

I was to find this out very soon, during the dinner to which Heydrich had invited me the day before.

Before dinner I reported to him briefly about my work. He was especially interested in the agents who had failed me so miserably in Spain, but I convinced him that punishment beyond dismissal would create psychological difficulties for me in the internal relations with my staff. Then I told him for the first time about the problems that had arisen with my co-workers because of my speedy but necessary reorganization of the department. If anyone deserved punishment, I felt it was my predecessor. This was a thrust which Heydrich understood. He knew that I did not approve of the consideration with which he continued to treat this man, no matter what his private reasons were. He changed the subject at once.

"There are a great many things which we have to

discuss this evening," he said. "It's best if we do so while we eat, then we shan't be disturbed." It was the usual meal, a Bavarian soup, a meat course with vegetables and potatoes, followed by a Bavarian dessert—a speciality of Heydrich's Bavarian cook.

Heydrich was extremely cordial and, knowing him, I was afraid this might mean that he would now announce my transfer to the eastern front, in punishment for a favorable report I had written on Dr. Best, formerly of the SD. As though he had read my thoughts, he said at once, "I cannot dispense with your help here in Berlin, and I've dropped my idea of assigning you temporarily to the eastern front. You may be interested to know, as a matter of fact, that I've already spoken to Himmler, and he's very strongly against the idea. You seem to be rather a protégé of his. He says that any change of assignment for you must have his approval. I'd like to know, my dear Schellenberg, how you've managed it. Still, I wouldn't count on the situation if I were you."

After I had told him briefly about my trip to Sweden, he took out a small notebook and jotted down several points arising out of other matters which we discussed. As far as I can remember them, they were as follows:

First he told me all about Rosenberg's job of building up a government ministry for the East—Ostministerium— the principles of which had been established at a conference on July 16, 1941, where the German occupation policy toward Russia was laid down. Present at the conference were Goering, Keitel, Rosenberg, and Bormann. Hitler's plan was to divide and govern Russia as a colony, ignoring the desire for autonomy among the heterogeneous peoples of the Soviet Union. But, of course, the intelligent handling of this enormous human force was a prerequisite for the effective exploitation of this huge area.

Heydrich's remarks revealed the insanity of Hitler's policy of subjection of the "subhuman Russians." "Hitler," he said, "wants all the formations of the RFSF[1] to be used ruthlessly. He wants a well-planned information system built up as quickly as possible, a system that even the NKVD couldn't improve on—exact, relentless, and working all the time, so that nobody—no leader like Stalin—

---

[1] A Nazi-sponsored Russian anti-Communist liberation movement.

could ever emerge again under the cover of an underground movement—never again in any part of Russia.
Such a character, if he ever did appear, would have to
be recognized in time, and destroyed in time. The mass of
the Russian people were never dangerous on their own
account. They're dangerous only because of the power in
them of creating and developing such personalities."

I looked at Heydrich thoughtfully. He could read my
opinion in my glance, and he gave a shrug. Did he believe
this nonsense? At such times he was unfathomable. I said
quietly, "A people of two hundred millions is hardly likely
to be inhibited by foreign police methods—especially if
those nationalities who already hate the Soviet system, and
would be favorably inclined toward us, are denied any
form of autonomy. In the end, they'll probably be driven
into some sort of imperialistic Pan-Slav movement. My
own idea was that we ought to establish a number of
autonomous states and encourage the national heroes of
these various peoples. Then we could play them off against
each other. Think of the Ukranians, for instance, think of
the Georgians, the White Russians, think of personalities
like Melnik and Bandera—"

Perplexed and annoyed, Heydrich remained silent. Then
he said, "You don't understand these things at all. A
general mix-up of these different races, if its purposefully
carried out for a few decades, will have exactly the same
result, and it'll prove the Fuehrer was right."

I was doubtful. I pointed out to Heydrich that at a
dinner a few nights ago, he himself had heard of the
scientific studies which de Crinis had made; that the
greatest German musicians, philosophers, and scientists
had come from those areas where there had been the
most racial fusion. Heydrich dismissed de Crinis' ideas.
"That fellow has thought up all sorts of nonsense. A very
nice fellow, certainly, but not to be taken seriously as a
scientist." He then closed the discussion with a curt order:
"Your task is to strengthen the Secret Service against
Russia. The Fuehrer has expressed his great concern to
me over this. He considers any information about Stalin's
internal measures of the greatest importance—especially
those dealing with guerilla warfare, and with collaboration
between the Party and the army."

Meanwhile the atmosphere in Berlin had grown darker.
The eastern offensive had come to a halt. Troops equipped

for a summer campaign had been surprised by the biting Russian winter. For this the responsibility must fall equally on the leaders of the Wehrmacht and on Hitler. Both had been living in the same Utopia, and had refused to listen to any criticism. In vain did returning field officers warn headquarters of the approaching disaster.

Stalin's calculations, of which I had received warning, had begun to justify themselves within only six months. My original report of the transfer of Siberian troops to Europe had been acknowledged with interest, but my figures had been considered greatly exaggerated and nothing was done, although front-line intelligence and prisoner-of-war interrogations continued to confirm my report.

On December 19, 1941, Hitler, having removed Field Marshal von Brauchitsch from the post of Supreme Commander, assumed that office himself. This was the final climax of the totalitarian regime and meant its absolute extension to the armed forces. Then came the great Russian winter offensive, and the desperate rearguard action of the withdrawing German formations. The fact that the German armies, ill-equipped, frozen, and utterly exhausted as they were, did not completely disintegrate is perhaps the greatest of our military achievements in World War II.

23. BACKGROUND TO PEARL HARBOR

Hitler snubbed by Japan—Probing Japanese intentions—Seeking Jahnke's reinstatement—His views on Japan's strategy—Critical assessment of material on Japan—Hitler presses Japan to enter the war—His reaction to Sino-American discussions—News of Japanese preparations—Hitler skeptical of SD reports—Japan attacks

IN THE early autumn of 1941, relations with Japan were somewhat obscure, especially as to the negotiations between Japan and the United States. The Foreign Minister and the Deputy Foreign Minister had refused at the beginning of September to give the German Ambassador in Tokio any information about the state of these negotiations. Hitler was rightly displeased about this insulting behavior by a member of the Three Power Pact. In spite of all the pressure Ribbentrop had brought to bear, they had made no response to the suggestions that they should enter the war against the Soviet Union. Nor was it clear whether Japan planned an attack in the South Pacific or whether they would content themselves with continuing their campaign in China. The Fuehrer had therefore ordered Canaris and Heydrich to use every means to secure information about this matter. But the assignment had been given in such general terms that it was left to me to think out and explore ways of approaching the problem.

I suddenly realized why Canaris had been so inquisitive about my conversation with the Japanese in Stockholm. When I told Heydrich about this he said, "The old fox—he just wanted to find out whether we had been given the assignment too." He asked what arrangements I could make, and emphasized that money was not to be spared. I mentioned the already strained currency situation, but he merely said, "Go and talk to the people concerned." I immediately took advantage of this and asked his permission to organize my own currency administration, independent of the RSHA, which would be under my personal control. He agreed immediately. This was an unexpected success, putting me a step further on the road toward the realization of my aims.

Shortly after this I had to fly to Madrid to see how my new organization was working there. While I was there my Japanese friend in Lisbon telephoned and urged me to go and see him. But I had no time to do so, and was therefore extremely surprised the next day to find that he had traveled to Madrid in order to see me.

He seemed very nervous, and spoke in a mixture of languages, mostly German and French. He told me that the negotiations between Japan and America had now practically broken down; it was certain that Japan would attack in the immediate future, and that the blow would be in the form of an amphibious operation toward the south.

The chief reason for his anxiety was that he had personally assured Tokio that Germany would stand by Japan, but now he was having second thoughts about this. His fears were based on Japan's previous passive attitude toward Russia, when Germany had continually been demanding action. He wanted an assurance from me that Japan would not now be left on her own against America.

Answering his questions very carefully, I managed to put his mind at rest. I said that Hitler and Ribbentrop would probably make an immediate declaration of war, especially as the atmosphere between Germany and the United States was very strained. As far as getting information about Japan's intentions was concerned, I suggested that directives should go out immediately to all our agencies which had anything to do with the Japanese—in Ankara, Belgrade, Berlin, Buenos Aires, Lisbon, Rome, Shanghai, Stockholm, Tokio, and Vichy. Vichy seemed to me to be specially important at the moment because the Japanese were engaged in an exchange of ideas with the Pétain government about the occupation of Indo-China. A French agent had brought me excellent material from behind the scenes on both sides, which supplemented the official material in Ribbentrop's possession. I wanted to go through this information at once and draft a report for the Fuehrer.

I asked Heydrich to get in touch with General Fellgiebel, of the Army Technical Information Service, and also with the Forschungsamt, the Research Bureau, so that all decoding sections and short-wave listening posts could concentrate on Vichy and Belgrade. I suspected that out of the various incoming short-wave transmissions we would be able to pick up some interesting bits and pieces. The same would hold true, of course, for the communications between Berlin and Tokio. Heydrich called Fellgiebel right away and spoke to him in my presence, asking him to contact me directly about any further questions.

It was remarkable. The world seemed to be turned upside down. Here was I giving Heydrich assignments! I asked him next to speak at once to Frau von Dirksen. She had a sort of political salon in Berlin, and at the time was basking in the sun of Hitler's favor. I knew that two Japanese who frequented her *salon* carried on lively conversations with two society ladies. I had often got good information from this source, but in this case I wanted Heydrich to talk to her himself; I did not want to be responsible for divulging the assignment to Frau von Dirksen, who was a somewhat talkative lady.

Though I knew it would involve a ticklish discussion, I thought this might be a suitable moment to broach a question to do with staff which had been on my mind for a long time. It was about the re-employment of Jahnke, the Pomeranian landowner. Both Himmler and Heydrich mistrusted him and had a great aversion toward him. They had fought him ruthlessly—for their own purposes—and had almost brought about his downfall. Jahnke had maintained a very cautious and informal relationship with me, however. One day, to my great surprise, all his files covering the years 1933-38 had been confiscated. While I was still in Counter-Espionage I had read them all and had decided to approach him, but I had refrained from doing so because Heydrich expressly warned me not to. Apparently Jahnke was *persona non grata* with Hitler, who suspected him of being a British agent in disguise and of being partly responsible for the flight of Hess. All this was really Heydrich's own opinion, but he had managed to persuade Hitler to the same point of view. So broaching the subject of Jahnke was like picking up a red-hot iron. I mentioned his past, his experience of more than twenty-five years in the German Secret Service, his undeniable achievements during the First World War, and suggested that it was time for the old controversies about him to be forgotten. In any case, it would be my responsibility to keep him under strict control. If it were true that he was an enemy agent, I could handle him very carefully, and in the end this would do us more good than harm.

Heydrich knew immediately what I wanted. He was even better acquainted with Jahnke's past than I was. His Far Eastern contacts were especially important in relation to the task that now faced us. Apart from having been accepted into the family of Sun Yat-sen, Jahnke had been in close contact with General von Seeckt and General von Falkenhausen, who had both been military advisers to the Chinese Army. From 1935 onward he had been Hess's expert on intelligence matters. He was utterly fearless—except in one respect: "Heydrich is probably the only man in this world whom I fear—I can't think of anyone more ruthless or more dangerous," he once told me. "He has more brains than all the rest of them put together. But if he continues to exploit you and work you to death, it'll be the end of him."

For Jahnke to say a thing like that meant he had not only thought it over once, but ten times, for he was very sparing with words. And when he actually talked to Heydrich later in my presence, he repeated to his face exactly what he had said to me. Heydrich blanched, but said nothing.

I said to Heydrich that I could think of no one better suited for the Japanese assignment. I knew of channels through which Jahnke had excellent connections with Japan. One was a former Czarist Russian colonel, now a naturalized Chilean, who lived partly in Berlin and partly in Paris. The other was a German Jew, a member of a well-known family, whose brother had a position of some importance in British banking circles. Jahnke and I had been fighting for years to protect this man from the German racial laws, while Mueller, Jahnke's greatest enemy, had been looking for the opportunity to trip us up. Through his vindictiveness and treachery he had almost succeeded and it was with the greatest difficulty that we managed to save the man and his family from Mueller's vengeance. Finally, we helped him to escape to Switzerland with a Honduran passport.

I wanted to send Jahnke to Switzerland, for he could use his Chinese connections there to gather information, and in the negotiations between America and Japan, China was the central problem. After some persuasion Heydrich agreed to meet Jahnke the next day.

The discussion when they met was relatively friendly. Whenever it threatened to become heated I managed to smooth things over, and from that time on Jahnke worked with me as my closest adviser. He operated quite independently, with only one young assistant, as the "Bureau Jahnke."

Having secured his co-operation, my next step was to send off detailed assignments by short-wave, teletype, and couriers to the various posts abroad. The chiefs in the foreign countries were told of the urgency of the situation and given a deadline for the dispatch of their information. The next day I discussed the whole problem again with Jahnke. In his view my approach was basically wrong: I had laid emphasis on secret information coming from Japanese sources; but American sources were, perhaps, just as important, and might be more readily accessible. I agreed with him, and changed my plan accordingly.

"It is a big mistake," Jahnke said, "to insist on Japan's entry into the war against the Soviet Union. Japan's ruling class has always followed the principle of keeping Japan's rear protected. Their strategy is to confine themselves to the East Asian area, while the European nations bleed themselves white. Their slogan is 'Asia for the Asians,' and they see themselves as the natural leaders in this area. Ribbentrop is incapable of understanding these ideas and is therefore incapable of advising Hitler."

As a result of his intimate discussions with the Japanese, Jahnke had realized that in order to assert her leadership in the Far East, Japan was most likely to mount an advance toward the south. This checked with reports I had received from other sources. The Japanese knew that this policy might lead to war with America, but they hoped in the meantime to gain as much as possible by negotiation. The Japanese Secret Service believed that Roosevelt's main aim would be to help Britain; Roosevelt believed that neither Britain alone, nor Britain allied with Russia, would be able to defeat Germany. For Japan the problem of China was also a decisive one. The Japanese Army was fully committed, and military circles there were unwilling to move an inch from their general objectives. One had to conclude, therefore, that we could not count on Japan's entry into the war against Russia, but should expect a Japanese advance into the South Asian area, provided no satisfactory result could be achieved by negotiations with America.

There was a third problem which it appeared was not being considered either by Hitler or Ribbentrop. A Japanese advance into southeast Asia would constitute a threat to British, French, Dutch, and Portuguese possessions in this area. Europe, and therefore Germany, would lose vital sources of raw materials which would upset their economy. "Might that not be a reason," Jahnke asked, "for pursuing a really long-term European policy?— instead of conducting an occupation policy with the brutal and shortsighted methods of Herr Mueller?" I knew from the way he said this that he would have liked to substitute Hitler's name for Mueller's.

The day after this discussion with Jahnke I gave out the additional assignments suggested by him. All my posts abroad were now working under high pressure and I awaited the results very anxiously. This was one of those occasions when the need for patience was an essential in our work. But the leaders had little understanding of this.

After about eight days the first reports began to come in and the evaluation department went systematically to work. Even the most unimportant messages were studied critically and checked for reliability of source and for the validity of their contents. I refused to pass on any reports to the leaders before the careful work of my evaluators was complete. We could at last follow the ebb and flow of divergent and contradictory influences within Japanese politics and their effect on the shaping of her foreign policy toward the United States, toward her partners in the Three Power Pact, and especially toward the Soviet Union. During the two weeks that were spent in checking and rechecking, the pressure from above had become more and more intensive. But the first report was passed on only after I had been able to document it fully from many diverse sources and could present it with a good conscience.

Hitler's nervousness had increased considerably, especially since the fall of Matsuoko in July 1941. Everything centered on the question of whether Japan would remain loyal to the Axis, in spite of the neutrality pact she had signed with Russia on April 13, 1941; or whether, in order to secure the safety of her rear, she would give way still

further to the wishes of the United States government. If
she were to do this, the Three Power Pact might become
no more than an empty shell. Driven by a sense of
urgency, Hitler began to apply pressure; cost what it
might, he wanted to see Japan involved in active war in
order to secure relief for Germany.

To reinforce this pressure, a series of optimistic press
releases were given out by Dietrich, the Chief Press
Officer of the Reich. Von Ritgen, head of the DNB—the
German News Service—and a close friend of Jahnke's,
telephoned me to find out what all these incredible stories
were supposed to mean, in which the war was being
described as practically won and the bulk of the Russian
armies destroyed and no longer capable of preventing our
victory. "Look, Schellenberg," he said, "will you tell me
what is going on? I'm beginning to feel as though I were
in a madhouse. I've just talked to that Bavarian yokel"—
this referred to a certain Sudermann, of the Government
press office—"and he quacked at me in his dialect, telling
me all the things he was going to write about this final
victory in the *Voelkischer Beobachter*. My people will
want to know what it all means and I don't know what to
say to them."

I tried to calm him. "There's no doubt that the
Wehrmacht have had some outstanding victories in Russia," I said. "But whether Dietrich's conclusions are justified is very doubtful, I would say. Hitler has two ideas:
first, he wants to show the world and the German people
what the Wehrmacht has achieved; and secondly, he's
trying to put pressure on Japan. He wants to make them
feel that if they hesitate any longer they'll be too late to
join in the carve-up, and that if they want to get a part of
Siberia, they'll have to move quickly. I've no idea whether
this will work—after all, we are not dealing with Europe-
ans, we're dealing with the unfathomable Japanese. We've
tried to point all this out to Himmler and Heydrich in our
reports, but whether they'll take any notice is another
matter."

When Hitler had read my reports on the American-
Japanese conference and the Japanese aspirations in
southeast Asia, he fell into a paroxysm of rage, and
contemptuously shrugged off the warnings that these reports contained. He completely ignored the fact that, in
July 1941, the United States had replied to the Japanese

occupation of southern Indo-China by freezing all Japanese assets, a measure in which they were immediately joined by the British Commonwealth and the Netherlands. This financial embargo hit the strained Japanese economy at its nerve center by stopping the supply of raw materials and in particular of oil. When, therefore, in August 1941, Premier Konoye suggested a meeting with Roosevelt, Hitler considered this a personal insult. He tried all possible means of disrupting the Japanese-American negotiations, but his attempts proved entirely ineffectual. Himmler and Heydrich reproached me bitterly on this account, but I was able to meet their attack by pointing to Ribbentrop's complete failure in the same field.

Von Ritgen listened to these explanations with great interest. We decided to lunch together, and during the meal I picked up valuable information bearing out what we already knew or suspected. Through information that came by way of Cairo and Istanbul, Dr. Reichert, one of von Ritgen's most capable collaborators, had secured a report which proved both reliable and decisive: during the summer large-scale maneuvers had been held in the Bay of Gago, off China, by special units of the Japanese Air Force. Both air force and fleet units had proved brilliantly effective in combined operations, and the Japanese Army and Navy had agreed to start a war in the not too distant future. Their strategic planning, however, envisaged an advance into the South Pacific area, but nothing more. It was essential to their plans that Russia should remain occupied with Germany, and with this end in view the Japanese diplomats sought to secure a reassurance of neutrality from Russia. The army was fully engaged in China and Indo-China and was not prepared to shoulder any additional commitments.

These reports, together with one from the DNB representative in Tokio, Sorge, were to be discussed by Heydrich with Hitler, Himmler, Ribbentrop, Keitel, and Jodl. Before Heydrich left for the meeting I was able to give him also a number of individual reports from Buenos Aires and Lisbon which again confirmed our conclusions. As further confirmation, Tokio had reported that the island of Kiushu had been closed to all foreigners, including diplomats, since the middle of August.

At the end of October 1941, Jahnke brought a report from the Japanese Secret Service, which he had been able to confirm through Chinese contacts. Hideki Tojo, it said, the new Premier and Minister of War, believed that Roosevelt and Cordell Hull would never yield in negotiations. As a last attempt to come to terms, and chiefly for reasons of internal policy, he had sent Kurusu, the former Ambassador to Berlin, who was married to an American, to Washington to support Admiral Nomura in the negotiations. At any rate, this step must have been taken with an alternative in mind, and it must be assumed with some degree of certainty that the decision to strike at America had already been taken by the middle of October.

Hitler at first remained skeptical about our reports until at last, in the middle of November, at his wish I sent a message through Jahnke to the Japanese Secret Service, saying that Germany was anxious to secure Japanese participation in the war, no matter what its nature or direction. This message was sent after Hitler had decided that after all it was immaterial where Japan entered the war as long as she definitely did so.

I believe that this encouragement helped to influence Japanese policy, for immediately after its receipt, and without having received any official guarantees, the Japanese completed their mobilization, and at the end of November ordered their entire fleet to sail to the South Pacific on amphibious operations.

Himmler, faithful servant of his master, wanted to inform his Fuehrer at once. However, he received a severe rebuke before he could even come out with his information. Hitler cut him off, shouting out, "At this time I do not want to know anything at all—I want to retain complete freedom of action!"

This was followed immediately by an inquiry by Tokio, whether, in case of war between Japan and the Anglo-Saxon powers, Germany would commit herself not to conclude peace without Japan. Faced with this clear-cut request, Hitler instructed the Foreign Office in the very first days of December to answer in the affirmative.

On December 7, 1941, Japan launched her attack on Pearl Harbor. The next day Hitler declared war on the United States of America.

24. RIVALRY WITH RIBBENTROP

Herr Luther—Draft agreement on rights of the Political Secret Service—Ribbentrop's private network—A device to discredit it—Ribbentrop's hostility to the SD—His influence over Hitler

BESIDES MY daily work, which continued to increase, I had taken up the important problem of liaison with the various government departments. The most important was the Foreign Office. I had already established good relations with the Undersecretary, Herr Luther, when I was head of Counter-Espionage. He was chief of the Deutschland Department, and was a close confidant of Ribbentrop, who would always ask his opinion before reaching any important personal or professional decision. The real reason for this close relationship remained a mystery.

Heydrich had told me to keep in touch with Luther, this being the best way to reach Ribbentrop. According to Heydrich, Luther was a cold unemotional man, smart rather than intelligent, and interested only in power. Ribbentrop, however, trusted him completely. He was perhaps the only man whom he did trust. He had been town councillor for Zehlendorf, a suburb of Berlin, and had been involved in an embezzlement scandal, but through Ribbentrop's and Himmler's joint influence his name had been cleared. Luther was very much opposed to the SS, and Heydrich and Himmler knew that it was he who continually stirred up Ribbentrop's suspicions against the organization, because, so they suspected, he was afraid too much was known about him. Ribbentrop had given him the job of completely reorganizing the Foreign Office.

Heydrich warned me, "You will have a difficult time with Luther. Be careful, he is capable of using your own words against you. Keep me in touch all the time, so that I can help you. He hates me, so it's possible he may hate you too. In any case, he'll probably try to use you against me. As you know yourself, you're inclined to be pretty independent in your work, and I wouldn't want you to fall into any of Luther's traps."

I had made contact with Luther through working on some of the Counter-Espionage Department's problems, such as the work of police attachés abroad and similar matters. Through my working with him in this way he had developed a certain confidence in me which I carefully nurtured by helping to clear up various incidents arising from his dealings with the SS abroad. I made precise notes on each conversation with him, which went to Heydrich and thence to Himmler.

Luther was quite unfitted to be a government official. He would have been much more at home in commerce. He was energetic, very quick to grasp a point, and not ungifted as an organizer. He had an impressive head, but his face was a little too fleshy. He wore thick horn-rimmed glasses, and his eyes were permanently swollen because of a sinus infection. It required a considerable amount of self-control not to resent his aggressiveness. His changes of thought were sudden and rapid and he was capable of saying or doing anything. He was governed solely by the calculations of the business man, and if one knew this and took it into account, one could get along with him, although it was not easy to do so.

How were the permanent officials to deal with such a chief? He condemned their consideration for others, and their careful arguments and doubts as signs of weakness, and called them calcified old fossils. With his glib Berlinese he ran rings round them and most of the time confronted them with *faits accomplis*. He was, in truth, the "Gray Eminence" of those days, as was Baron Holstein in the Foreign Office under the Kaiser, but he was hardly the Baron's equal as a professional diplomat. He was colder and more ruthless, a dangerous figure such as only a totalitarian system could produce.

The strength of my position with him was that he regarded me as a bridge by which to get at his greatest opponents, Himmler and Heydrich. I was some sort of protection for him against their frightening organization, for which in reality he had a great weakness—in a moment of candor he confessed to me that he would have liked very much to become a member of the SS—and I managed on one occasion to defend him from an attack by Heydrich and Himmler. I now made it quite clear to him that our relationship would have to be free of any personal bias, and to do him justice he acceded to many of my service requests, furthering them honestly and skillfully with Ribbentrop. Thus I got results through him which I would never have got through the other officials in Ribbentrop's office.

During the next few weeks I drew up the draft of an agreement with the Foreign Office which, under Luther's guidance, Ribbentrop finally signed. It provided for the inalienable rights for the Political Secret Service.

When I think back on these negotiations, I still wonder at the almost frivolous lack of preparation with which Germany entered the greatest war of her history. According to Luther, there were no clear or binding agreements between the Foreign Office and Military Intelligence.

These negotiations, and the written agreement that resulted from them, were the basis of my continued collaboration with the Foreign Office.

It is rather difficult to assess the value of this collaboration. At times it was exemplary; at others, however, it not only broke down, but there was actual conflict. In most cases this was due to Ribbentrop's personal failings. His ideas and the directives he issued were unacceptable and his personal attitude intolerable. I finally decided to have it out with him, not because of personal animosity, but because he had succeeded in making enemies of everyone.

In order to show Ribbentrop how false were his ideas about a Secret Service, I first showed Luther, Heydrich, and Himmler reports—70 per cent of them faked—which I had prepared about the Polish government-in-exile in London. These I had passed into the hands of the Intelligence Service of the Foreign Office through agents abroad. Fourteen days later Ribbentrop presented these reports to Hitler as especially valuable information. Hitler then had a heart-to-heart talk with Ribbentrop for more than an hour. The Foreign Minister did not say anything about the results of this conversation, but for two days running he dined with Himmler and talked with him about the general difficulties of running a secret service.

Finally, the day came when I was ordered to report to Ribbentrop. I was there punctually and was admitted at once. At that time his office was in a wing of the former Presidential Palace, though the offices of his Ministry remained at the Wilhelmstrasse. The place was furnished in exact imitation of the style of Hitler's new Chancellery. The study, with its huge desk and large windows, was heavily overfurnished with thick carpets, valuable tapestries, and ornate chairs covered with silk. Ribbentrop stood as usual behind his desk with folded arms. He received me very formally and it was obvious that he was out to impress me. He spoke slowly and with emphasis, as though he were receiving me for the first time. After a few words, he came from behind his desk, solemnly gave me his hand, and begged me to be seated. Then he sat down opposite me and said, "Please begin at once. I am already familiar with the subject that you have come to discuss."

During the first half hour his face remained completely unmoved. He listened to me with concentration. But when I came to speak of the organization of various liaison offices with other Ministries, he interrupted me abruptly: "You don't mean that you are going to build up secret services for the other departments too?" With this question he showed clearly that he simply had not understood what I had been talking about. I began again from the beginning and explained to him carefully and slowly that these liaison offices would be indispensable, and that if he thought the matter over, he would realize how much the Foreign Office, and he personally, would profit by them, because, apart from questions of control and authority, the contact of these offices, and of myself personally, with other government departments could be used to deal with all sorts of questions of paramount interest to the Foreign Office. And they would all be handled on neutral ground, so to speak, as matters of importance to the Secret Service alone, not to the conflicting interests of various departments. If the Secret Service could work in close collaboration with the Foreign Office, both would benefit, for the power of the Reichsfuehrer SS would be behind this arrangement, and so it would be unnecessary for me to consult him, Ribbentrop, about every detail. In order to remove Ribbentrop's suspicions that this represented a maneuver by the SS to penetrate the Foreign Office, I suggested that whoever was the chief of the Secret Service should be taken onto the staff of the Foreign Office.

Ribbentrop looked at me completely confused. He still did not understand, and the further my explanation went, the more remote he grew. I therefore decided to change my tactics. I became aggressive. I even went so far as to tell him about the occasions when we had purposely supplied him with false information. I reminded him of his conversation with the Fuehrer, and finally said plainly that the Secret Service was now so strong that he was no longer in a position to attack it. If he was not for it, then I must conclude that he was against it.

At this he grew excited and angry. He would not stand for being personally attacked, he said. He had always tried to create a reasonable working relationship, but now he was forced to realize that we refused to regard the Foreign Office as an independent government department. Thereupon I made a formal apology. I said that I felt the turn the conversation had taken had led to certain misunderstandings, and if he attached any value to it, I was ready to place my plan before him in writing. With an expression of contempt he said, "Thank you, I can do without it."

I then tried to get him to talk, saying that of course it would be very interesting to hear his ideas on the organization and the methods of a secret service. Immediately he began to relax and leaned back in his chair with an expansive gesture. I could see that I had handled the interview in the wrong way. I should not have begun with a dissertation of my own, but should have asked him to explain his ideas first. Unconsciously I had wounded his vanity.

His ideas on the subject were completely different from mine. In his opinion, there should not be more than ten or twenty picked agents working abroad. They should be equipped with vast financial means and should collect their information chiefly according to their own judgment. It would be quite sufficient to be regularly supplied with information by these twenty people. Matters of detail were of no importance in the broader questions of foreign policy; all that mattered were certain basic questions, and these one had to be able to foresee in time.

He had the greatest faith in me personally, he said—I almost fell off my chair at this—and as far as I was concerned, he was ready to do anything he could to make my position secure. Indeed, he was ready at any time to take me into the Foreign Service. There, apart from occupying myself with the study of general questions, I could take over the organization of a small secret service such as he had in mind. I explained to him once again that personalities had nothing to do with this matter, which did not concern me personally, and that I could not agree with his ideas. I felt that questions of detail were most decisive for a secret service, and that only through scientific and methodical evaluation of the material that came to one's net could the real bases for policy be established. This could not be done through accidentally acquired information, or through the minds of ten or twenty people, no matter how able they were.

At this point Ribbentrop suddenly began to look tired, and the conversation faded out. I noticed that one half of his face and one eye grew completely slack. Some days later I reported this to Dr. de Crinis, who had previously been called in more than once for consultations about Ribbentrop. In his opinion there was some serious functional disorder, probably connected with a disease of the kidneys. One kidney had already been removed and the hormone production was probably disturbed.

We said good-by briefly and formally. All my illusions had left me. I knew that I could not agree with this man, not in any way on any issue. He would never show any understanding of the needs or even the existence of the Secret Service.

What Hitler saw in Ribbentrop was inexplicable to me. Probably it was just that, like everyone else around him, Ribbentrop accepted directives with bureaucratic exactness and carried them out correctly. Thus it came to be that the foreign policy conducted by him was degraded to a sort of appendage to his own struggle for power. His behavior seemed to be governed by an inner feeling of his own inadequacy—though how much this was a basic weakness, or how much it had developed in him—or why—I never knew. This might explain a great deal about his attitudes and his actions. How else, for instance, could one explain his hatred of Britain? How else explain his garrulous and overbearing manner?

His vanity and narrowness of mind really shocked me. They showed clearly the reasons for the limitations of our foreign policy, and also for its basic stupidity. Between them, he and Hitler were obviously prepared to go to any lengths, up to the ruthless sacrifice, if necessary, of the German people. At the time of this first long interview with Ribbentrop I did not understand this clearly, though the basis of this policy must already have existed. But I felt something of the sort instinctively, and both he and I knew that we were worlds apart.

On the other hand, he did not altogether dismiss me from his mind. I heard from members of his entourage that again and again he asked about details of my earlier career, and would sometimes say something to the effect that "the Fuehrer is right—Schellenberg is nothing but a decadent lawyer, and one day we shall have to deal with him." He even gave Luther orders to report every detail of our collaboration, and to note especially whether I made any derogatory remarks about him or the conduct of foreign policy. One will never be able to understand how Hitler, in 1939, saw fit to proclaim that Ribbentrop was the greatest master of foreign policy Germany had had since Bismarck.

25. JAPAN AND CHINA

Hitler talks with S. Chandra Bose—Japanese hopes of a Russo-German peace—A strange visit to Goering—Tokio peace feelers thwarted by Ribbentrop—Chinese Secret Service offers collaboration—Their proposal rejected—An alarming report on Jahnke—Japanese demands on China—An equivocal reply—Japan breaks off negotiations

ONE DAY in March 1942 Jahnke came to see me on his return from a trip to Switzerland.

S. Chandra Bose, one of the leaders of the Indian Nationalist movement, who at that time wielded considerable influence in India, was staying in Berlin. The Japanese were trying to ingratiate themselves with Bose, so of course I was interested in getting Jahnke's opinion on the situation. So far, primarily on Hitler's suggestion, the Far East office of AMT VI had relied for its information about India mainly on Sidi Khan, the leader of a small faction within the Indian liberation movement. But between Bose and Sidi Khan, who at the time was in Rome, there existed a state of uncompromising rivalry.

Bose's outstanding intelligence and his mastery of modern propaganda methods had made a deep impression on Himmler, and we were therefore considering whether we should not shift our support to him. One of Bose's favorite ideas was the setting up of an Indian Legion within the German Army. So we arranged an audience for Bose with Hitler, who agreed in principle to the establishment of such a legion. But Bose was deeply disappointed, for Hitler had emphasized that at the moment he was not particularly interested in India and would prefer to leave it to Japan to keep an eye on that country politically and strategically. If his luck should hold, however, if southern Russia and the Caucasus were to be conquered and German armor to reach Persia, then—but only then—he would be prepared to confer with Bose on India's future.

When I mentioned Bose's name to Jahnke he at once

gave me a warning. He said he knew that Bose had lived and studied in Moscow for a considerable time and that he had established close relations with the Cominform. In my own dealings with Bose I had time and time again come across indications of the influence of Moscow's teachings in the way questions and answers were developed dialectically within a set of rules.

At the request of the Japanese, Bose was taken to Japan in 1943 by a German U-boat. After he had left Berlin I did not fail to disclose my misgivings about him to the Japanese there; they insisted, however, that they could make good use of a man of his caliber in Japan.

From Bose our talk turned to the affairs of my own department. Jahnke advised me to drop front-line infiltration tactics and intelligence work in the combat areas, which I could leave to the various army groups, and instead to penetrate as deeply as possible into the Russian hinterland, where much more valuable information was to be found. I pointed out this would require a large number of fast transport planes, either for dropping agents by parachute or to land them in uninhabited areas, and the very few aircraft which the Luftwaffe allowed us would be a serious handicap. At this point Jahnke changed the subject. We were about to discuss the relationship between Japan and Russia when he suddenly broke off. "There's no peace in this place. Why don't you shut everything up and come away for a week end and twiddle your thumbs?"

The idea appealed to me, and so I went out to his estate on the Pomeranian coastal plain. Here were wonderful forests and lakes full of fish. After a wonderful meal, we sat over a bottle of good red wine until late in the night and discussed the problems of our work. It was not for my health that Jahnke had suggested this week end, but to insure the utmost privacy to discuss the information he had got from the East.

Jahnke had learned that the Japanese were intending to try to bring about a compromise peace between Germany and the Soviet Union. The Japanese Cabinet had received extensive and shattering information from their Secret Service on the real strength of Russia's war potential. It was certain that the Russian armies would soon be strong enough not only to halt the German offensive, but to drive us back along the whole front. By the winter of 1942-43 Russian industry would be geared to an overwhelming production of armaments. Guerilla warfare in the German rear areas would be greatly intensified, tying down a large number of German troops and seriously disrupting our long supply lines.

The Japanese feared that in the end Germany would have expended all her military strength in a hopeless campaign. Because of the Western Allies' hesitation about actively supporting Russia by opening a second front, a compromise peace with Stalin was still a real possibility. According to Jahnke, the Japanese leaders were unanimous in this view of the situation and an approach to Germany either directly or indirectly was likely.

We discussed the problem for a long time. Jahnke thought the chief opponent of such a solution would be Ribbentrop, whose narrow mind would be unable to understand the situation. Himmler was too much under Hitler's influence to act independently and was very muddled in his thinking. Goering was no longer of importance; his star had set since the failure of the air offensive against Britain. Since then Goering seemed to have lost nearly all interest in the great military events. This was attributed by many to his increasing dependence on morphia, by others to his excessive and increasingly morbid indulgence in a life of luxury.

At this time Himmler sent me to report to Goering at his beautiful country house north of Berlin—named "Karinhalle," after his first wife—on the suggested incorporation of the "Goering Research Establishment" into Department VI. This Establishment had been built up by Goering with the help of naval experts for the supervision of all telephone and wireless surveillance, including monitoring and tapping. Every single telephone communication inside Germany and the German-occupied European territories could be tapped and often yielded a rich crop of valuable information. Hitler's long-distance calls were all monitored and recorded, and if necessary passed on to the appropriate government departments for reference or action. Once, a production figure on German armaments mentioned by Hitler in a conversation with Mussolini caused the greatest confusion because Hitler himself had been misinformed.

When I arrived at "Karinhalle," I had to wait for some time in the entrance hall. It was vast and deeply carpeted and with its dark oak beams and heavy old furniture it reminded me of an ancient church. After I had waited for half an hour, one of the large folding doors was thrown open and the Reichsmarschall made his entrance, holding his marshal's baton and clad as an ancient Roman nobleman, toga, sandals and all. For a second I felt as though I were meeting the Emperor Nero.

Goering smiled amiably and asked me to follow him into the next room. He motioned me into a huge armchair and settled down behind a small table on which stood a cut-glass bowl containing pearls and antique jewelry. While I made my report, he kept fingering the jewelry, as though he were in a trance. When I had finished, all he said was, "Well, I will have a word about it with Himmler."

A week later Himmler still had not heard from him and was furious about this. He raved at me and then against Goering, "that king of the black markets," as he used to call him. (By the end of 1943 Goering had lost every vestige of authority or respect.)

Thus, already in 1942, the only one who seemed likely to take any interest in effecting a compromise peace was Heydrich, whom Jahnke considered to be one of the outstanding minds in this whole circle. But Heydrich was so occupied with the Protectorate that it was doubtful whether he alone would be able to influence Hitler decisively. Jahnke warned me emphatically not to tell Bormann at this stage about the Japanese offer of mediation. In his opinion Bormann was an unknown quantity and a dangerous confidant. Heydrich was sympathetic to the idea, however, and in fact broached the matter tactfully to Hitler, but without any decisive result.

Four weeks later, in April 1942, Ribbentrop informed Hitler of a Japanese attempt to establish contact with us through the German Naval Attaché in Tokio. Heydrich warned me by telephone that Hitler might even want to talk to Jahnke, whom he knew personally. But at the end of May, Heydrich told me that Ribbentrop had won after all, and the feelers from Tokio had been officially rejected by the German Naval Attaché.

Jahnke insisted that I should make a special effort now to win Himmler's support, so that he would influence the Fuehrer. If Hitler really was a great statesman, he would realize that an honorable peace with Russia was essential, but he must be convinced that no loss of prestige would be involved.

The Japanese, indeed, had not given up the attempt, and in June 1942 they tried again. This time the General Staff of the army contacted the German Military Attaché in Tokio and suggested that a Japanese commission, under the direction of an army general, should fly to Germany in a German long-range aircraft to discuss the co-ordination of political and military policy. Unfortunately they let it be known that the question of a compromise peace with Russia would be discussed. Ribbentrop managed to torpedo this effort very effectively. The Japanese Army were working independently of their government. Ribbentrop suspected this, and immediately informed the Japanese Ambassador. This caused some friction between the government in Tokio and their General Staff. The Japanese Army could only interpret such behavior on the part of the German Foreign Minister as an official rebuff, and indignantly withdrew their offer.

After our defeat at Stalingrad, the Japanese again repeated their offer to mediate without delay—this time through their Foreign Minister, Shigemitsu. Hitler, in his stubborn narrow-mindedness, brusquely rejected the offer.

Later, in 1944, I was to have a long conversation with Rear Admiral Kojima. He had commanded a Japanese battle cruiser in the attack on Singapore, and had been decorated and promoted for exceptional bravery. He told me that he had come to Germany by U-boat in 1943 with the special task of exploring the situation and persuading the Fuehrer to initiate peace negotiations with Russia. This proposal had met with an outright rejection. Of course, when I talked with him at the end of 1944 the opportunity for such a peace had passed.

The second problem I discussed with Jahnke during that week end was his work with the Chinese Secret Service. The centers of the Chinese Secret Service at that time were in Berne, Vichy, London, Stockholm, and Moscow. Jahnke's chief connections were with Berne and Vichy. There was a Chinese diplomat there at that time, an important member of the Chinese Secret Service, who was a very close acquaintance of Jahnke's. He told Jahnke that influential circles around Generalissimo Chiang Kai-shek felt that there were still groups in Germany who were sympathetic toward China and who might be in a position to influence the German leaders toward bringing about a compromise peace between Japan and China. Here was an interesting situation: on the one hand Japan, locked in a struggle with America, was trying to act as peacemaker between Russia and Germany; on the other, the Chinese were trying to persuade Germany to act as peacemaker between themselves and Japan. The Chinese did not wish to discuss details at this point; they wanted first to see whether the Japanese would react favorably toward the idea.

This was the political aspect of the matter. But there was also a Secret Service aspect to it. In return for our mediation, the Chinese were willing to enter into a collaboration with our Secret Service. Of course, this was a very important offer which fascinated me just as much as the political aspect. I knew that the Chinese Secret Service had extensive possibilities, and it must be remembered that they had free access to Downing Street as well as to the Kremlin.

Jahnke and I discussed the offer thoroughly. I feared— and Jahnke agreed with me—that the almost certain rejection of the Japanese offer to mediate between ourselves and Russia would make it extremely difficult to put forward the Chinese plan. I assured Jahnke of my support, and drew up a detailed memorandum which Heydrich placed before Himmler. After this it took Heydrich and Himmler fourteen days to decide on the best way to approach Hitler. They both agreed from the start that Ribbentrop must be kept out of it completely. Himmler himself reported on the situation to Hitler, who gave both matters considerable attention, though his first reaction to the Japanese offer was one of indignant rejection.

The Chinese attempt he considered very interesting. He did not doubt that Chiang Kai-shek was sincere, but he felt doubtful of the Japanese reaction. As he pointed out, it would all depend on the practical proposals and on the detailed conditions. Still, it showed that Hitler was seriously interested when, through Himmler, he ordered me to prepare a report on the proportion of Japan's total war potential tied down in China. Himmler received permission from Hitler to pursue the Chinese proposals independently, for he very cleverly had pointed out that in its present stage this was primarily a matter between the two

Secret Services and should remain so. In this way Himmler managed to exclude Ribbentrop from the affair.

However, eight days later Hitler had changed his mind. The Chinese suggestion and the Japanese offer to mediate with Russia had to be considered as two aspects of the same problem. In both cases, no doubt, the Secret Services should continue to play the main part. But he did not wish to leave Ribbentrop out, and contact with the Foreign Minister had to be maintained. He had already asked Ribbentrop to discuss the Chinese offer with Oshima, the Japanese Ambassador in Berlin, who was a great friend of his.

Meanwhile, the Japanese had already declared their readiness to enter into negotiations on China; however, as had been foreseen, they demanded more definite proposals. For this reason Jahnke again went to Switzerland. He appeared to do so reluctantly, not wishing it to seem that he was involved in the affair at all. He went, therefore, ostensibly for a business trip on behalf of a large Argentine grain firm.

While Jahnke was in Switzerland I received a shattering secret report. It was thirty pages long and was a painstakingly exact compilation of evidence proving that Jahnke was a top-level British agent. The real purpose of his trip to Switzerland was to receive new directives.

I at once gave orders for the most careful surveillance of Jahnke and for a close watch to be kept on his movements in Switzerland. However, nothing out of the ordinary was discovered, nor did his subsequent Secret Service work show even the slightest detail that might be regarded as suspicious. At the time I did not pass on this report to my superiors, for I had decided that even if it were true I would go on employing Jahnke as an agent. Finally, I gave the report to Jahnke himself; while he read it, I studied his attitude and expression very closely. I knew him so well that the smallest reaction of guilt could not possibly have escaped me, but his behavior was completely natural. It could hardly be explained away by saying that he had exceptionally strong nerves.

Jahnke thanked me, I thought, rather enigmatically. "A man in your position is only human after all," he said. "No one can know what is in another man's heart. In your situation you stand alone to face problems that are entirely your own. Your whole life has inclined you toward systematic suspicion, but I think you are big enough to overcome that. What is important is a man's real character—and there you can trust your instinct."

He had returned from Switzerland surprisingly soon, obviously disappointed by the outcome of his mission. The Chinese proposals called for the complete withdrawal of all Japanese troops and the liberation of the Chinese ports. In the ports, however, the Japanese would be accorded certain treaty rights, and I thought these demands went rather far. Even if they were intended as bargaining tactics, I still thought the Chinese had overreached themselves, and we toned down their demands considerably.

The discussions between Ribbentrop and the Japanese hung fire. Jahnke urged speed and I tried to hurry Himmler and Ribbentrop. Finally, in June 1942, the Japanese handed us a series of inquiries for further clarification. A number of these Jahnke, on behalf of the Chinese, was able to answer very quickly; the rest were to be clarified by Chiang Kai-shek himself. As it was too difficult to communicate with China on such complex matters by radio, it was decided to send a special envoy. I succeeded in keeping the interest of the Japanese alive until the middle of September, chiefly by repeating old arguments. The messages which had meanwhile come back from China gave no information about details. Jahnke was certain that a courier from China, who was on the way, would bring further particulars and new authority.

However, in September 1942, in spite of all our efforts to gain more time, the Japanese suddenly declared that they were no longer interested. All our attempts to keep the conversations open were of no avail. The door was closed. I was not clear about the reasons behind this, but I finally came to the conclusion that the Japanese General Staff had intervened, having decided at this point to open a new offensive that would link their territory around Hankow with Indo-China. Before the year was out this offensive had begun.

26. OPERATION "ZEPPELIN"

*Pressure on the SD's services—Its functions and duties—
Russian POW's trained to work for Germany—Theories
of guerilla warfare—A discussion with Russian prisoners—
Plans for attacking Russian heavy industries—Colonel
Vlassov's "Army"—"Druzhina"—The Wannsee Institute—
A report on Russia's situation—Himmler reprimands my
department*

IN SPITE of the impressive successes of
our armies on the eastern front, by the summer of 1942
increasing difficulties were becoming apparent to those
who knew the facts. First, we were greatly astonished by
the quality and even more by the numerical strength of
the Russian armor. Secondly, resistance behind the German lines was no longer the sporadic action of isolated
units, but had developed into well-organized guerilla warfare, tying down security forces that were greatly needed
elsewhere.

Himmler and Heydrich put considerable pressure on
me, demanding more secret information on Russia as the
available material was not enough. Admittedly, the reports
were deficient not only regarding the political situation,
but also regarding Russia's war production. The increasing
pressure of guerilla warfare and the heavy disruption of
communications only called attention to our inability to
retaliate, and this was inevitably brought very forcefully to
the Fuehrer's attention.

There had been several rather heated discussions with
Heydrich, and later with Himmler, for our intelligence
work was not as extensive or as successful as the military
situation required. Himmler wanted to know precisely why
our intelligence reports on the Soviet Union were so
inadequate. Again he reminded me of the Fuehrer's
words: "We have got to finish off the Russians before the
others start." I told him the reason was that I was not
given enough support either in materials or staff. It was

not enough for the personnel officers to say that they had assigned to me so many hundred men. Numbers in themselves meant little in face of the task of training masses of foreign nationals, linguists, and specialists, and the deficiencies in technical equipment were just as serious. How could one possibly expect anything else? There had been nothing like enough preparation and one could not suddenly make up several years' backlog. Our Berlin information network, with its outposts in Sweden, Finland, the Balkans, and Turkey, was running in top gear, but it was not giving us anything like a clear enough picture for long-range planning.

I was asked to make a special point of intelligence work conducted directly across the front lines, but no account was taken of the difficulties which such work would entail. Our staff was inadequate, both in numbers and quality, and the gradual and continuous development of our work was constantly impeded by hasty and contradictory orders from above. On the other hand, we had to reckon with the detailed and relentless counter-espionage of the Russian Secret Police.

The Secret Service work against Russia was split up into three sections. The task of Section I was to gather and co-ordinate all information supplied by our agents working permanently in foreign countries. We sought to secure as much information, both secret and overt, as possible. Overt information included newspapers, official statistics, books, and other publications. This information was chiefly required as a basis for long-range objectives, and the staff that handled it needed high intellectual qualifications. They had to be of all nationalities, and so had to be employed regardless of race, religion, and so forth. To organize this work, information centers in all the capitals of Europe were formed on similar lines to the central office in Berlin.

Through one of the centers—the existence of which was known only to three persons in the central office—we had a direct Secret Service connection with two of Marshal Rokossovsky's General Staff officers. It was interesting that they both expressed doubts about Rokossovsky's loyalty to Stalin. The General, a former Czarist officer, was supposed to have spent some years in Siberia.

Later, when I took over Admiral Canaris' Military Sector, another very important center was added. Its chief was a German Jew, and he conducted its activities in a manner that was unique. His office staff consisted of two persons—everything in the office was mechanized. His information network went through various countries and penetrated every stratum of society. He furnished quick and exact reports from the senior staffs of the Russian Army, which were considered of special significance by the evaluating section of our own Army Supreme Command. The work of this man was really masterly. He was able to report large-scale strategic plans as well as details of troop movements, in some important cases even down to divisional level; his reports usually came in two or three weeks ahead of events, so that our leaders could prepare suitable counter-measures—or, should I say, could have done so if Hitler had paid more attention to the information.

I had to fight like a lion to preserve this valuable assistant from Mueller and from the jealousy and intrigues in my own department and on the Luftwaffe staff. There was a clique hiding behind Kaltenbrunner and Mueller who were determined to remove "the Jew." Not only was this man's Jewish origin used as a pretext for getting rid of him, but his enemies tried to prove in the most treacherous manner that he was engaged in a long-range game of deception for the Russian Intelligence. It was assumed that for a long time they had been deliberately feeding us with accurate reports in order to lead us astray by the substitution of misleading information at a decisive moment.

The second of our sections was responsible for Operation "Zeppelin." The main purpose of this operation was to drop mass formations of Russian prisoners by parachute deep inside Soviet territory. They were allowed the status of German soldiers, wore Wehrmacht uniforms, and were given the best food, clean quarters, lecture films, and trips through Germany. Meanwhile those in charge of their training, aided by informants, were able to find out their real attitude—whether they only wanted to enjoy the advantages offered by this plan; whether they had really turned against the terror of the Stalinist system; or whether, racked by inner conflicts, they were hovering between the two ideologies of Nazism and Stalinism.

Having been trained and equipped, they were sent to the eastern front to gather information and infiltrate the

Russian partisan bands—Operation "Zeppelin's" main task being to counter the effects of guerilla warfare. Because of the vast areas involved, and regardless of the high losses that would be inevitable, special formations were to be trained for certain Secret Service missions, including the establishment of contact with German émigré circles in Russia.

In order to carry out this plan three units, "South," "Central," and "North" were formed. These units, whose tasks were sabotage, political subversion, and the collection of information, were to be flown over the lines by special squadrons of the Luftwaffe along the entire length of the eastern front. A courier system across the front lines and secret wireless transmissions were to be their main means of communication.

Most of the agents were dropped in places where they were able to shelter with friends. Some were equipped with bicycles with wireless batteries and transmitters built into the pedal mechanism, so that regular pedaling would insure inconspicuous and smooth transmission.

On one occasion an agent succeeded in reaching Vladivostok with a Russian troop transport. There he observed and sent back full details of certain troop movements.

The enormous size of Russia's territory enabled our agents to move about without hindrance, sometimes for months on end, although finally most of them were caught by the NKVD who, when the need arose, would mobilize a whole division near the front line, or detachments of guerilla fighters in the rear, in order to track our agents down.

Operation "Zeppelin" was now well under way, but my explanations of the difficulties involved were always met by the stereotyped answer: "That's all very interesting—but your assignment is still as before—to furnish the Fuehrer with information." The overwhelming lack of preparation and of trained staff and special equipment was entirely overlooked.

Hitler wanted precise information on the organization of the Russian guerilla units, their structure and channels of command, and details of their missions. I therefore gave this matter priority, and planned to issue special assignments during my intended visits to Sweden and Norway.

I had worked out certain theories about guerilla war-

fare which I propounded first to Heydrich, then to
Himmler: every guerilla war, every growing and active
resistance movement, must in order to thrive possess an
idea or ideal which binds the guerillas or the members of
the movement together. This idea must be strong enough
to arouse and perpetually renew the energy and determination of the partisans. Training and the highest qualities
of leadership are, of course, necessary for systematic partisan warfare, but the morale of the individual remains
always the decisive factor. I had occupied myself with this
problem during many a night's discussion with Russian
officers, and also with our Russian agents at the Wannsee
Institute. It had become clear to me that Stalin and the
other Russian leaders were systematically developing a
form of warfare through their partisan units which exploited the fierceness with which the struggle was being
conducted on both sides.

The Russians used the harshness with which the Germans were conducting the war as the ideological basis for
their partisan activities. The so-called "*Kommissar-
Befehl*" (order to shoot all Commissars), the German
propaganda about the "subhuman" nature of the Russian
peoples, the mass shootings carried out by the "Einsatzgruppen," the special security units operating with the
army in and behind the combat zone—all constituted
arguments which were psychologically effective in arousing
a ruthless spirit of opposition among the partisans.

My Russian advisers believed that in reality Stalin welcomed these German measures, and reports of whose
validity I was practically certain supported this theory.
One of them stated that the most important aim of the
partisan warfare was ruthlessness in itself, that anything
was justified which would make the population support the
struggle. The brutalities committed must always be
ascribed to the German invaders, so that a hesitant population would be forced, as it were, into active resistance.
If, because of Russian interests, unreliable elements had to
be punished, this must be done in such a way that the
punishment would seem to be imposed by the Germans.
The rest of the population would then be all the more
willing to support the partisans' struggle.

Another report gave special directives to the NKVD on
how it was to support the partisan bands. The NKVD was
to send some of its best and most reliable agents as

advisers and informers into the German Army and administrative offices. Their task, apart from keeping in close touch with the partisan units, either by sending false or accurate information, was to use their wits in influencing and inciting the German occupation authorities to take harsh measures against certain sections of the population, such as Jews and Kulaks. Executions, liquidations, and deportations were, of course, to be presented as brutalities consciously committed by the Germans against the Russian people. It was a truly devilish program which the Russian leaders seemed to have evolved, and its effects were no less brutal than the measures taken by the Germans.

Himmler and Heydrich did not believe the Russian leaders had the time or ability to work out such complicated ideas. I told them that I had based my views on the reports which had come in, and on the professional views of my advisers. Furthermore, I added, the Russian leaders seemed to have a much sounder knowledge of their own people than we had, deceived as we were by our own propaganda creation, the "subhuman" Russian. For making this point I got a serious dressing down, and for a while had to keep my mouth shut.

Later I took up the subject once more, but this time very cautiously. I suggested that it would be necessary to offer the Russian prisoners working for us an ideal worth risking their lives for. National Socialism was not suitable; its ideals were alien to them. The obvious thing would be to hold out the hope of eventual autonomy. But no one was interested. They went on with the old policy of putting Russians in uniforms and giving them better conditions. They gave them medals and lectured them on the high German standard of living and the efficient organization of the German State. With some of them this policy showed results, but the majority needed something better suited to the Russian character, something which would satisfy their eternal longing for independence.

In later conversations I was able to speak to Himmler more openly about these problems. Toward the end of 1942, he showed a much more receptive attitude, but because of his basic prejudices toward all Eastern questions, I could hardly hope to succeed in obtaining his final agreement. He was too much influenced by the ideas with which Hitler had imbued him during the last twenty years.

I had given up discussing this question with Heydrich very early on. He had revealed to me quite openly the way his mind was working when he said, "Be careful you don't get a medal from Stalin one day." This was clearly a warning that he only wanted purely National Socialist conceptions used in propaganda work among the Russian prisoners.

I had some interesting discussions with two members of the Russian Army, one of them a General Staff officer, the other a corporal. Both of them were from Moscow, the one a professional officer, the other in civil life a hydraulic engineer. They had been taken prisoner at Bryansk in August 1941, and had gone through several phases of our training program. Both had proved open-minded, intelligent, and reliable, so they had been co-opted onto a special advisory board of Operation "Zeppelin" in Berlin and sent to live in lodgings as ordinary civilians. Here I visited them with the chief of the section and a Baltic German, a well-educated man who was an excellent interpreter and had already had many discussions with them. Through him, a lively and interesting conversation took place, stimulated by a supply of drink that we had brought with us.

There was a considerable contrast between these two Russians. The officer was a trained dialectician and a convinced Stalinist. The other man was only moderately influenced by the regime and admitted its shortcomings with a healthy realism. Both of them were firmly convinced that Russia would win the war. This conviction did not spring from the influence of the propaganda to which they had been subjected, but was a fundamental belief. Each of them based his conviction on different reasoning. The officer derived his from Stalin's superlative qualities as a leader and from the strength of the Russian Army. The other man, who thought in more primitive terms, said simply, "You Germans will never be able to overcome the Russian people and the vastness of Russia. Even if you managed to give the various Soviet peoples their independence, this would only be a temporary step to the inevitable development of Communism." He also said that a wave of national feeling was sweeping across Russia, and that plays such as *Kutusov, A Life for the Czar*, and *Prince Igor* had been revived in Moscow with great success. In all of them an invader, after great successes to begin with, is finally defeated by the superlative courage of the Russian people and the vast expanse of Russia itself.

The officer spoke of what he had heard discussed by the leaders of the Red Army. According to them, Stalin was ready to sacrifice as many as twenty to thirty million people in order to draw the enemy deeper into the country. This would gradually blunt the force of the Germans' attack and insure that the last decisive battles would be fought in terrain chosen by the Russians and under the iron severity of their winter. The supply lines alone would eat up a great deal of the Germans' material resources, and would be highly vulnerable to partisan warfare. In their retreat the Russians would not let a single factory, machine, or can of gasoline fall into the hands of the enemy. Then, weakened by the forces of nature, their own successes, and the counter-measures of the Russians, the Germans would suddenly be overwhelmed by a new, well-organized counter-offensive.

After this conversation I was decidedly thoughtful. I was much impressed by the simple manner in which the two men presented their opinions, which I had to admit sounded feasible.

I reported these talks to Heydrich, but took care to add that, of course, it was not easy to follow their reasoning. Our military successes had been so tremendous that I could not imagine how the Russian State and people could be capable of such a major reorganization as would be necessary. There was some doubt, of course, whether Stalin possessed the industrial war potential to carry out such a plan, although we must not forget that the Luftwaffe had not yet struck at the industrial regions of the interior west and east of the Urals.

Heydrich discussed the matter with Himmler and asked for a written report to show Hitler. Three weeks later the report was returned to me by Heydrich, who told me that the Fuehrer considered it to be complete nonsense. I said, very cautiously, "I am not quite of the same opinion," but added that for the present we should not risk burning our fingers.

If we had been allowed sufficient aircraft, we would have been able to deal very heavy blows at Russian industry. The preparatory planning for such actions had been completed and we had made tests with a V-1 projectile carried to the target area by a long-range bomber, with a so-called "suicide pilot" to steer it directly onto the target. Many of these pilots were already waiting for their suicide missions. Their attacks were to be launched against the industrial combines in the Kuibishev, Chelyabinsk, and Magnetogorsk areas, and against the Donetz Basin.

These nerve centers had been decided on with the help of experienced technicians who had carefully analyzed each plant according to its nature and location. The operations were to be aimed mainly at central power plants, transformers, and blast furnaces. However, all these well-thought-out plans were frustrated by the inadequacy of the Luftwaffe. We were able to carry out only small-scale raids which blew up some high-tension transformers, important electric pylons, and so on. But, of course, these were mere pinpricks and were without any real effect, except that they tied down a certain number of the NKVD's security forces. But this did not in any way affect the front line strength of the Russian armies.

Other plans included the dropping of battalions of specially trained Russians, commanded by Baltic German SS leaders, in several of the large and more isolated Russian labor camps. The guards were to be overpowered and the inmates, in some cases numbering twenty thousand or more, liberated and helped to make their way back to the settled areas. Apart from the labor force that would have been lost to the Russians, the propaganda effect on the population would have been considerable.

Preparations for one of these actions had been carried to the point of our establishing contact with the inmates of one such labor camp. However, the Luftwaffe failed us again. They were certainly willing, but they were hampered by shortages of material and delays in the aircraft construction program. Later, we employed the men who had been trained for these missions on tasks behind the Russian lines, where they were able to organize the return of seriously wounded soldiers and even of small units that had become isolated.

Valuable psychological support was given us secretly by the so-called "Vlassov Army," which had inscribed on its banner, "The Liberation of Russia from the Soviet Regime." There was a secret agreement between us and General Vlassov, a deserter from the Russian Army, and his staff which gave him the right to build up his own secret service in the Soviet Union, provided that any information he secured was made available to me. This form of co-operation suited me admirably. Certainly our Russian colleagues worked with an entirely different spirit now that they were fighting for their freedom and for a new Russia, without the discouraging effect of German interference in their work.

Hitler's and Himmler's refusal to grant General Vlassov recognition until the bitter end, and not to employ his forces until then, was a fundamental error that sprang from the arrogant determination not to give autonomy even to the smallest group, and from an unholy fear that Vlassov might not be entirely sincere and might open an important sector of the front to a Russian break-through. There was also the fear of organized resistance in Germany, for with such a tremendous number of foreign workers, especially the millions of Soviet Russians employed in the Reich, such a possibility could not be ignored. This situation was Mueller's particular hobby horse. He would point to it as a growing danger and one that made it impossible for him to guarantee industrial peace. The doubts about Vlassov's reliability did not really affect the question, for there was ample opportunity to employ his army in a sector of the front where German units could have been attached to it to guard against any danger of his defection.

As to who should claim authority over him and his army there was an unpleasant conflict that must have made Vlassov laugh. At one time the army claimed jurisdiction, then Rosenberg's Eastern Ministry, then Himmler, and finally, astonishing as it may seem, Ribbentrop put in a claim. The best thing would have been to mount all these gentlemen on Cossack ponies and send them into battle ahead of Vlassov's army. This would have solved the problem once and for all.

After the psychological and ideological preparation of the volunteers, their practical training began, with special attention being given to their instruction in wireless transmission. Because of their large number, and the shortage of teaching staff, their training had to be carried out with military discipline, and as all the volunteers had to use pseudonyms the whole time, considerable confusion resulted.

Of course, the NKVD succeeded in inflicting sizable losses on us. Still worse, they began to send their own people through the front lines to infiltrate Operation "Zeppelin" and undermine it from within.

In order to fly the agents into Russia a combat squadron was put at our disposal, but the military and political sectors of the Secret Service, which at that time were still working separately—and often at cross-purposes—had to share between them the limited number of aircraft and the very limited supplies of fuel. Consequently, the dispatch of the agents on their various missions fell further and further behind schedule. Nothing is more destructive of an agent's nerve and morale than to keep him waiting too long before sending him out. We therefore organized the agents who were waiting into a combat unit called "Druzhina." This organization was to help maintain security behind the lines and, in case of need, to go into action against partisan bands. Their commander was the Russian colonel called Rodjonov, known as Gil, with whom I had already had a conversation.

Now, as a result of further talks with him, I began to feel that his original opposition toward the Stalinist system was beginning to undergo some modification. He considered Germany's treatment of the Russian population, and of her prisoners of war, catastrophic. These were things against which I had protested in vain. On the other hand, I had to defend Himmler's point of view. I told Gil not to forget that the conduct of the war and the methods employed were getting harsher and more ruthless on both sides. When one considered the partisan war, it was very doubtful whether the Russians were not guilty of equal or even greater crimes than the Germans. He reminded me in turn of our propaganda about the "subhuman" Russian people. It was he himself, I said, who had chosen the word propaganda—in wartime it was difficult to draw clear-cut lines of morality. I was convinced that the White Russians, Ukrainians, Georgians, Azerbaijan, Turkmen, and other minorities would understand these slogans for what they were, merely expressions of wartime propaganda.

When we began to suffer reverses in Russia our Secret Service work naturally became more difficult. At the same time certain complications arose about the direction of "Druzhina," and finally, in spite of my repeated warnings, what I had feared would occur actually happened. "Druzhina" had once again been employed in the ruthless "screening" of a partisan village. While guarding a long column of partisan prisoners on their march back to concentration camps behind the lines, Colonel Rodjonov ordered his men to attack the SS detachment accompanying them. Taking the Germans completely by surprise, the Russians massacred every one of them in the most bestial manner. Men who had originally been sincere collaborators had slowly become our most bitter enemies. Rodjonov had made contact with the Central Organization for Partisan Warfare in Moscow and had forced his subordinates to turn against us. After the massacre he took off from a hidden air base of the partisans and flew to Moscow. He was received by Stalin personally and decorated with the Stalin order. This was a serious setback for which, however, I was not personally held responsible, for I had asked Himmler again and again to withdraw Rodjonov from anti-partisan combat.

Besides the arrangements made for recruiting Russian manpower for the Secret Service, a file was established in which the more skilled Russian prisoners were recorded. In the course of time these valuable specialists were taken out of the dull and useless prisoner-of-war life and given an opportunity to work at the jobs for which they were qualified, electrical engineering, chemistry, steel production, and so on. In time their mistrust was overcome, they organized debating societies and study groups, and grew accustomed to lectures by German experts. Through collaboration directed on psychological lines such as these, much valuable material was gained which helped us not only to assess Russia's scientific progress, but also to stimulate our own defense industry. In addition to "mass employment" there were also special assignments. Volunteers who were considered suitable for these were given civilian clothes and properly housed, mostly in private lodgings belonging to the Secret Service.

The third sector in our department was responsible for the work of the "Wannsee Institute," so called because it had been moved from its original home in Breslau to the Berlin suburb of Wannsee. The Institute was a library which contained the largest collection of Russian material in Germany. The special value of this unique collection was that it also included a wealth of scientific literature in the original languages. The head of the Institute was a Georgian, who held both Russian and German professorships, and the staff was selected from librarians, scholars, and Russian language teachers from various universities. They were allowed to travel in occupied parts of Russia, so as to maintain contact with the Russian people, and to be able to gather first-hand material.

The Institute had proved extremely valuable even before the war with Russia, assembling information on Russian roads and railways, on the economic and political basis of the Soviet regime, and on the aims and composition of the Politbureau. The wide experience and scientific thoroughness of its members meant that their work led to important conclusions on problems such as those of nationalities and minorities, the psychology of the Kolkhoz and Sovkhoz—the Collective and State Farms—and on many other questions.

In 1942 the Institute was able to offer the first proofs that the statistical and scientific material made available to the public by the Soviet Union was unreliable. It had been altered or, shall we say, adjusted, so that the outside world would not be able to measure the state of development in any field of production knowledge, or social activity. In time our collecting sector was able to produce additional material to support this hypothesis.

The Russians for their part had set up an institution whose sole task was to check all the material published in the various fields of science, statistics, chemical formulas, and so forth, and falsify them at decisive points. At the same time, this institute rigorously controlled the various fields of research and under special secrecy regulations distributed the correct material only to those Russian scientists and technicians who needed it for their work. Thus, population figures and other demographic data, as well as maps of Soviet Russia, were falsified. Although this could not inflict any great damage on us, it did lead to complications.

As a further example of the work done by the Wannsee Institute, I should like to mention an incident that took place in 1943. The catastrophe of Stalingrad had already occurred and had induced Hitler to declare "total war." The German lines in Russia were still holding, but we had sustained heavy defeats. It seemed as though we should soon lose North Africa, and with it our ability to threaten the British lifeline at Suez, thereby increasing the possibility of an Allied invasion of the Continent. Taken in conjunction, these factors should have led to a change of our general policy, as well as in our military strategy in Russia, not to mention in our occupation policies in the defeated countries.

Having summarized these considerations, I presented them to Himmler. I purposely confined my comments to the Soviet Union because I wanted to give a sound and solid report on Russia's industrial and war potential, which had been analyzed to the smallest detail. We had employed all our secret intelligence sources and had questioned, separately and individually, thousands of Russian prisoners. My aim was to establish the need, or rather the duty, of our leaders to mobilize and make use of all physical, moral, and material resources in the German-occupied areas of Russia. At the end of the report I made some extremely forthright suggestions, armed with a sharp dialectical edge. I intended to give the leaders a serious jolt.

The Reichskommissars in Russia who headed the German political administration should be withdrawn, as well as the Einsatzgruppen—the special units which "cleaned up" behind the German lines. Autonomous states should be created at once, and the German administration of industry and agriculture in them should be completely and simultaneously overhauled.

The result was a report of some fifty pages, with considerable additional data. On the whole, it was a very good piece of work. However, after Hitler had read it he discussed it with Himmler, and then ordered the arrest on a charge of defeatism of all the experts who had helped to compile it. This was a triumph for Kaltenbrunner. Later he and Himmler met and had a heated discussion about my "intellectual" and "out-of-step" attitude. Kaltenbrunner blamed Himmler for my favored treatment and demanded that I should be subject to the same rules and discipline as the other heads of departments in the Reich Security Ministry.

My next interview with Himmler was a very rough one. He castigated all my experts, called the scientists of the Wannsee Institute, and especially their chief, Professor A——, agents of the NKVD. He attacked me too, and said the burdens of my post were obviously becoming too heavy for me and that I was beginning to fall under the defeatist influence of some of my assistants.

I could not suppress a smile at this, whatever it might have cost me. Himmler was so astonished by this reaction that he looked like a scared rabbit: he had never encountered insubordination of this sort before. But I could react in no other way. Psychologically it seemed to be the correct reaction, for it dissipated the dangerous tension. *"Enfant terrible!"* Himmler said, with a shake of his head. And with that I knew I had won.

I then began quietly but forcibly to state my case. After two hours there was no longer any talk of arresting anyone. Instead, a thoughtful Himmler sat before me, chewing his thumbnail. "Well," he said, "it would be terrible if you were right. Still, one cannot let intellectual considerations deflect one into showing weakness, there is too much at stake. If we don't manage to overcome the East this time, we shall disappear from history. I believe we should follow your conclusions only after we've won the war against Russia."

"That's the decisive point," I said, "when to start on this new course. But I must repeat—if we don't start now we may never have a chance to start at all."

In the end, I failed to convince Himmler. Still, I had succeeded in defending my assistants and the political line of my department. Today that may seem unimportant, even academic, especially for those who have never been embroiled in a war of nerves and cannot appreciate the inner excitement and disappointments one suffers. To decide to continue one's own line of policy in these circumstances required some courage, for Hitler's sensitivity and pathological suspicion rose in direct ratio to the deterioration of our general situation.

27. "ROTE KAPELLE"

*Combating Russian espionage—A report on the problem—
Extent of the Russian network—A spy trio arrested—
Discovery and breakdown of a code—The Luftwaffe in-
volved—More arrests—Tracing a Russian transmitter—
The search for "Gilbert"—The enemy grows suspicious—
Profiting from experience*

DEKANOZOV, Russian Ambassador in Ber-
lin until the outbreak of war in 1941, had been the power
behind the Russian Secret Service in Germany. The story
of the Vietinghoff brothers, and many other cases of
Russian espionage, both in Germany itself and the territories occupied by us, had aroused Hitler's intense interest,
and again and again he demanded information about our
counter-espionage work. He believed the Russian Secret
Service to be much more thorough and probably much
more successful than the British or any other secret service. In this case his intuition was to prove correct.

Toward the end of 1941 he had already ordered that
steps must be taken immediately to counter the rapidly
spreading Russian espionage activities in Germany and the
occupied countries. Himmler was asked to supervise the
close collaboration of my Foreign Secret Service Department with Mueller's Security Department of the Gestapo
and the Abwehr of Canaris. This operation, to which we
gave the code name of *Rote Kapelle*—"Red Chapel"—
was co-ordinated by Heydrich. Through our united efforts
we not only discovered the largest Russian spy ring in
Germany and the occupied countries, but also managed to
a very large extent to break it up.

After Heydrich's assassination in May 1942, Himmler
had taken on the job of co-ordinating and supervising
Rote Kapelle. Very soon serious tension arose between
him and Mueller, which worsened to such an extent that
sometimes when Mueller and I were reporting to him
together, Mueller, many years my senior, would be sent

out of the room so that Himmler could discuss matters with me alone. Mueller was intelligent enough to recognize this situation, and whenever he had anything particularly difficult to bring up would ask me to do it for him. Once with an ironical smile, he said to me, "Obviously he likes your face better than my Bavarian mug."

In July 1942, Himmler ordered both of us to appear at Supreme Headquarters in East Prussia with a full report on *Rote Kapelle*.

We had only a few hours in which to get the report ready and when we met Mueller began by telling me how invaluable my reports on *Rote Kapelle* had always been to him, and how very comprehensive my knowledge of Russia's spying activities seemed to be. After a few more obvious flatteries, he asked me to take the report to Himmler for both of us. But I said that as I was responsible for only about 30 per cent of what had been achieved he might as well report on the matter himself. "No," he said, "you'll get the red carpet; I'll probably get the boot."

I was not then aware of Mueller's real reasons for this request. He must already have been planning to pull out from the work against the Russian Secret Service; but I shall refer to this later.

When I arrived at Supreme Headquarters I was surprised to hear that Himmler had ordered Canaris to report to him at the same time. He had planned to discuss the matter with Hitler that evening and wanted to have us all available to answer any questions. Himmler was in a very bad mood that day. He probably realized that Mueller was avoiding a discussion with him. He read the first paragraphs of the report—it was to go to Hitler—and at once began to criticize it in the most disagreeable way. It was obviously biased, he said; the credit due to the Foreign Counter-Intelligence of the Wehrmacht (Canaris' organization) and the Military Wireless Counter-Intelligence were not fairly presented. "Are you responsible for this report or is Mueller?" he asked with a malevolent sneer. I said that he was.

"That is typical of him," he said, "to belittle other people's achievements so as to put himself in the most favorable light. A thoroughly petty attitude, and you can tell him I said so."

To make things worse, he called in Canaris and asked him for details of the Abwehr's collaboration with Military Wireless Security on the case. It became increasingly clear that Mueller had somewhat distorted the truth in his own favor. Himmler became quite unpleasant toward me, forgetting that it was not I who was responsible for the report. In the end he realized this. "I give you the right to repeat this reprimand to Mueller word for word," he said.

The Fuehrer was so upset by this report and by the treachery it revealed that he did not wish to speak to anyone, so neither Canaris nor I was required to report to him that evening.

Rote Kapelle, the Russian espionage network, extended over the whole territory ruled by Germany at that time, as well as over the countries that were still neutral. With its many secret short-wave transmitters, it extended from Norway to the Pyrenees, from the Atlantic to the Oder, from the North Sea to the Mediterranean. As always, luck played an important element in its discovery.

At the beginning of the campaign in the east our Wireless Counter-Intelligence was very active. A few days after the beginning of the campaign, one of our listening posts in the west detected the presence of a transmitter, but was unable to establish its position. Wireless direction-finders indicated that it was the area of Belgium, but it was impossible to pinpoint it more accurately. This unsolved problem led to discussions between General Thiele, the chief of Wireless Security, Mueller, Canaris, and myself.

Wireless Counter-Intelligence later detected a transmitter that was apparently working in the Berlin area, but within a few days of Counter-Intelligence's efforts to pinpoint it the transmitter ceased operating, and did not appear again. Our calculations indicated that the receiver to which this transmitter was beamed must have been in the neighborhood of Moscow, and was probably a large central station. It was obvious that the transmitter was being operated by agents of the Russian Secret Service in a code which we had not broken.

Special branches staffed by Mueller's most able officials were now working hard in Belgium and France, as well as in the Berlin area. The Belgian section of our Counter-Espionage began to get results, and at the end of 1941, after consulting Canaris and me, Mueller decided to make an arrest in a suburb of Brussels. Three members of the Russian Secret Service were taken into custody. One,

Michail Makarov, was the director of a post for collecting information; another, Anton Danilov was a trained wireless operator; while the third, Sofia Poznanska, worked as cipher clerk. This espionage group lived together in a small villa in which the secret transmitter was also situated.

Their interrogation proved extremely difficult, as all three made repeated attempts to commit suicide and refused to give any information at all. The Belgian housekeeper, who had been arrested at the same time, gave us only the vaguest information. Although she was ready to tell all she knew, this was of very little use to our investigation. After a long interrogation we finally managed to get it out of her that the three agents frequently read books which lay about on their table, and she told us several of their titles. As it was often our own practice to use a code based on sentences out of various books, we began to hunt for copies of those that she had seen them reading; there were eleven in all. Bookshops and publishers all over France and Belgium were ransacked for copies.

In the meantime the mathematical department of Wireless Security and the decoding section of the Wehrmacht Supreme Command worked feverishly on a fragment of an already encoded message found in the fireplace of the villa, half of it burned to ashes. The decoding section came to the conclusion that a code based on French books was involved and by mathematical analysis a small fragment of a key sentence was reconstructed. This contained the name "Proktor." Now, having at long last found the eleven books, came the task of searching them for the name "Proktor." The right book was eventually found, the key sentence identified, and the decoding section of OKW then set to work.

In due course they managed to decode the message found in Brussels and others which our monitors had picked up in the meantime. The results were truly astonishing: they revealed the workings of an extensive network of the Russian Secret Service, with links that ran through France, Holland, Denmark, and Sweden to Germany, and from there on to Russia.

One of the chief agents was a man who sent his wireless messages—invariably they contained important secret information—under the code name of "Gilbert." In Germany two chief agents were actively at work under the code names of "Coro" and "Arvid". There was no doubt that their information could only have come from the highest levels of the German government. The chief agent for Belgium, who worked under the code name of "Kent," still remained undiscovered; he had escaped when we made the arrests in Brussels at the end of 1941.

Our entire security organization was now working at full pressure, but time passed and we were still unable to get onto the track of the two agents in Germany. Then once more chance took a hand. Our decoding section came across a wireless message which in itself seemed relatively unimportant. But it revealed that "Kent" had been instructed by Moscow in the autumn of 1941 to go to Berlin and visit three addresses which were given in the message. This was the first real break in the case, for now we had not only the real names of those involved, but also their code names and their addresses.

General Thiele, of Decoding and Wireless Security, Colonel von Bentivegni, of the Military Counter-Intelligence, Canaris and I, immediately initiated a joint surveillance which in Berlin alone involved some sixty people. After about a month we decided to arrest most of these, but to leave a few at liberty so that the spy ring could continue to operate for the Russians.

The situation revealed that a colonel of the Engineers, named Becker, who played a decisive part in the aerotechnical development of our fighters and bombers, was a Communist who passed highly secret information to a central transmitter in the north of Berlin, whence it was sent to Moscow. Further investigations revealed that at least five other persons who had high positions on the General Staff of the Luftwaffe were suspect.

A lieutenant colonel of the General Staff, Schulze Boysen, was also arrested. His was the fanatical driving force of the whole espionage ring in Germany. He not only furnished secret information to the Russians, but was also active as a propagandist. On one occasion, at five o'clock in the morning, wearing Wehrmacht uniform, he threatened a subordinate agent with a pistol in the street because the man had neglected his Communist propaganda work in a certain factory.

Another member of the ring was Oberregierungsrat Harnack, a high civil servant, whose wife was an American Jewess. He was responsible for planning the allocation of raw materials in the Ministry of Economics. Through the information that he continually furnished to the Russians they knew more about our raw materials situation than, for instance, the responsible departmental chief in the Armaments Supply Ministry, to whom such information was not divulged because of red tape and conflicts between various authorities.

Among the large number of those arrested at this time was Legationsrat von Schelia, First Secretary at the Foreign Office, who carried out assignments there for the Russian Secret Service. He worked entirely by means of "society espionage." Not only did he know everything that went on in the Foreign Office, but his apartment became a favorite meeting place in the evenings for the whole diplomatic colony, from whom he collected secret information with cold-blooded skill and in the most methodical manner.

The Russian Secret Service, in fact, had its agents in important positions in every Ministry of the Reich, and was able to send secret information in the quickest way by means of secret wireless transmitters.

Naturally, these circles were centers of resistance against Hitler and his policies, and against National Socialism in general. But resistance to Hitler and his regime was not the primary cause of their treason—nor did money make much appeal, except to some lesser agents. Their basic motive can be explained only in spiritual terms—escape from the ideologically sick Western world into Eastern nihilism.

The arrests continued; new circles of suspects were uncovered and the special units were kept working strenuously and for long hours. In the end, hundreds of people were dragged into the whirlpool caused by our security measures and were prosecuted. Some of them perhaps were only sympathizers, but during the war the harsh principle of "caught together, hung together" applied.

In the meantime a new transmitter had appeared in the vicinity of Marseilles. Wireless Counter-Intelligence suspected that this was the successor to the transmitter which we had uncovered in Brussels. This was deduced from the nature of the signal and the code that was used. At the same time new transmitters appeared in Belgium, Holland, and many other places. The signal they sent out seemed to indicate that they all belonged to the same spy ring. It became increasingly difficult to locate these transmitters, as the Russians had learned from experience and were careful not to make the same mistake twice.

In the course of a large-scale investigation in Paris, Counter-Intelligence accidentally came across a circle of persons who, in their interrogations, gave information about "Kent" which enabled us to establish his identity. He traveled under an alias and with a South American passport. "Gilbert's" name also was discovered in Brussels. He was a German Communist who had been trained for many years in Moscow. On the basis of this small bit of information a general search for "Kent" and "Gilbert" was started throughout the European continent. The quarry turned up under various names: Kaufmann, Vincent Seirs, Trepper, and others. For months the hunt for these people went on. Only after the most painstaking surveillance and tireless work by our agents were we finally able to pick up "Kent's" trail in Brussels. His downfall was brought about by his love for a beautiful Hungarian girl, who had the code name "Blondine" and whose real name was Margerete Marcza. They had a lovely daughter, and "Kent" was extremely attached to this woman and their child. We knew that once we had found the woman, "Kent" would turn up sooner or later. Margerete never betrayed her friend, but involuntarily she led him to us. When we finally interrogated "Kent," his concern for her proved invaluable. He would do anything for this woman— if necessary give up his life for her. Thus, for the first time we were able to establish contact with the central station in Moscow, using "Kent's" transmitter for our own purposes. Over a period of several months we managed to pass misleading information of considerable importance to the Russian Secret Service and caused much confusion there.

After this successful appropriation of "Kent's" transmitter, we managed to do the same with a number of other transmitters, until finally about sixty-four transmitters were sending misleading information to Moscow. Of course, the Russian Secret Service noticed the setbacks their work was now suffering and tried even harder to frustrate our counter-espionage activities.

The search for "Gilbert" and his secret transmitter proved extremely difficult. As soon as our investigations disclosed enough for the direction-finders to begin the process of closing in on him, he would cease transmission, and then start up again in a spot perhaps as much as sixty miles away. Whenever we decided to go in and make a raid we would find nothing; then, as if he were making fools of us on purpose, that same night the transmitter would be sending out its messages from a different town.

But finally our relentless search brought us success. In the course of investigating Communist resistance groups in Belgium, we found a man who had once worked as "Gilbert's" right-hand man. He was a special courier trained in Moscow, a former German Communist who had lived for a long time in Belgium and held an important post with the German authorities. At the time, he was running a short-wave station which served as a liaison between the "Red Marquis" and the Belgian resistance movement. The transmitter was then diverted from this activity, and he received permission from the Russians to take up direct communication with Moscow. In reality, however, he was an agent we had "turned around." This time we furnished him not with false material, but with valid material, for our purpose was to establish contact with "Gilbert," whose headquarters were in Paris. In this way the agent succeeded in reawakening "Gilbert's" interest, and a closer collaboration between them developed. "Gilbert," however, remained extremely careful and suspicious.

First of all we approached his secretary, then our special search unit decided on a sudden raid in which they would be able to grab both the secretary and "Gilbert." But luck was against us, for, when the search unit went to make the arrest, they discovered that "Gilbert" had gone to the dentist. They were unable to find the dentist's address and a wild goose chase through Paris developed. We had got to arrest "Gilbert" before he could be warned. At the last moment we managed to get the name of the dentist from the concierge of a neighboring house, and the moment the dentist had finished his treatment, "Gilbert" was seized by quite a different pair of forceps—those of the German Abwehr. He gave in quite quickly and his well-equipped station was afterward used by us to carry on our work of misleading the Russians.

We now began to notice that the Russians were gradually starting to direct radio messages both from their own transmitters and from those under our control toward a central reception network. Here the information was passed on to a specially trained evaluation group. Obviously they were growing suspicious of the information they were getting. Therefore, for about three months we sent out accurate and valuable information, even though we had considerable misgivings, and gradually we managed to allay their suspicions of the material they were receiving.

Again and again new transmitters appeared. The battle flared up in Brussels, Antwerp, Copenhagen, Stockholm, Berlin, Budapest, Vienna, Belgrade, Athens, Istanbul, Rome, Barcelona, Marseilles—and again and again the direction-finding units went into action. The search was most difficult of all in the neutral countries, where the apparatus, the technicians, and the agents all had to be carefully camouflaged. Naturally the technical discoveries made in the course of this work were of the greatest value to me, for, as chief of the active Intelligence Service, I had to exploit the experience thus gained in order to acquire better and less easily traceable wireless transmitters than the enemy services possessed.

The work on *Rote Kapelle* was to continue right up to the end of the war. The silent struggle became more and more intense, until the conflict was carried on not only in Germany and the countries occupied by her, but throughout the world.

28. THE ASSASSINATION OF HEYDRICH

Heydrich discusses the shortcomings of the army—
Bormann and Himmler jealous of his success in Moravia—
Heydrich's car blown up—Slaughter of Czech partisans—
Heydrich's funeral—Himmler delivers an oration—His in-
terest in my future

IN THE spring of 1942 a series of confer-
ences which I had to attend had been arranged by Heydrich
at the Hradcĭn Palace in Prague. I was just preparing
to return to Berlin by air when he asked me to stay
another night so that I could dine with him. I was overworked and irritable and rather sickened by the prospect
of an evening which would probably end in a drunken
orgy. However, this time I was mistaken and we spent a
most interesting evening discussing the problems that were
foremost in Heydrich's mind. To my surprise, he criticized
Hitler's decision to take over the Supreme Command of
the army. He did not doubt Hitler's ability as a commander, but he feared that he would not be able to cope with
this additional burden. Then he began to revile the generals of the Supreme Command. When they were with
Hitler they said "yes" to everything. They were too slow
and too dumb to remember any difficulty until they had
left the room.

Heydrich was disgusted with the shortages of supplies
for the army. Goebbels' *Bekleidungsaktion*—the drive to
collect civilian winter clothing for the troops—had been
carried out with the usual fanfares but also with a great
deal of genuine enthusiasm. However, this did not remedy
the damage that had been done. Heydrich suggested that
for every hundred German soldiers who froze to death,
someone in the Quartermaster's Department—starting
from the very top—should be shot. It was a crime to have
sent combat troops wearing summer uniforms to face the
Russian winter.

Field Marshal von Brauchitsch (whom Hitler had dismissed) had been used simply as a scapegoat. Certainly he was partly to blame, but those who were directly responsible were still sitting in their cozy offices, slightly sobered, but still flashing around with their gold braid. Hitler was relying more and more on Himmler, who was a good tactician and could exploit his present influence with the Fuehrer. If only he would let himself be advised by me, said Heydrich. He then touched briefly on the problem of France and Belgium. His aim was to increase his own authority and organization by appointing supreme SS and police leaders there, since there was no longer likely to be any opposition from the Wehrmacht leaders.

I did not agree with this idea. The administrative problems would become unnecessarily complicated, and it was already difficult to find suitable men for these important posts. Heydrich concurred absent-mindedly, then suddenly said, "Himmler insists on it, and just at this moment I must show my goodwill. The situation between us is pretty tense just now."

Apparently there had been differences between him and Himmler, who had become jealous. Heydrich's policy in the Protectorate had been a great success, and the Fuehrer was very satisfied with his plans and the measures he had taken. He had begun to confer with Heydrich alone, and although Heydrich was greatly honored by the favors showered on him, he was worried because of the jealousy and antagonism of Bormann and Himmler. He was afraid that Bormann would react by stimulating intrigues; Himmler was more likely to be just mean and bloody-minded.

Things had really become very difficult for Heydrich. So far his successes had served to protect him with the Fuehrer, but he felt by no means secure and could not see how to resist the restraints which the rivalry of Bormann and Himmler imposed upon him. To attack either of them openly was always dangerous, for Hitler felt even more strongly than Himmler about the internal loyalty of the SS. He felt that in any case it was almost too late, for it was only a matter of time—and that time was coming fairly soon—before Hitler succumbed to their promptings, and then he would turn against him.

Heydrich was considering the possibility, he said, of trying to get me attached to Hitler's entourage, but I managed to talk him out of this idea. However, before I left for Berlin he brought the matter up again. It was particularly important that he should have someone looking after his interests "up there." Also he felt it would be a good thing for me to report directly to the fountain-head for a time. Finally we arrived at a compromise: I was to remain in Berlin for another month, and in the meantime he would arrange a six weeks' assignment for me at Hitler's headquarters. However, it was not to be. Shortly afterward I had to go to The Hague to discuss ultra-short-wave transmissions with some technical experts.

It was while I was there, in June 1942, that a teletype message reached me saying that an attempt had been made to assassinate Heydrich and that he was seriously injured. I was instructed to return to Berlin at once.

I wondered who was behind the attempt, and I remembered Heydrich's recent difficulties with Himmler and Bormann. I could well imagine that people who knew Heydrich's methods would be afraid of him, and they both knew that he would shrink from nothing where his own ruthless schemes were involved. His successes in the Protectorate must have been very galling to Himmler and Bormann and the tension between the three of them had obviously been at breaking point, or Heydrich would not have mentioned it every time we talked. It was the practice of Hitler and Himmler to rule by playing their associates off one against the other. But with a man like Heydrich this was impossible. Besides, as head of the Reich Security Office, and also as Acting Reich Protector, he had become too powerful for them.

I suddenly remembered an incident which Heydrich had mentioned to me. During his last meeting with Hitler he had been called on to report about certain economic problems in the Protectorate. He had been waiting for quite a long while outside Hitler's bunker, when he suddenly came out accompanied by Bormann. Heydrich had greeted him in the prescribed manner, and then waited for Hitler to ask for his report. Hitler stared at him for a moment, then an expression of distaste came over his face. With a confident and easy gesture Bormann took the Fuehrer's arm and drew him back into the bunker. Heydrich waited, but Hitler did not return. The next day Bormann told him the Fuehrer was no longer interested in his report. Although Bormann had said this in the most amiable tone, Heydrich sensed his implacable hatred. Hitler's antagonistic attitude on this occasion was obvious, and was probably based on hints and slanders put about by Bormann and Himmler.

It was interesting that in my last conversations with him, Heydrich, although convinced of his own powers, had shown that he was afraid. There was little doubt that he had been filled with foreboding, and his anxiety to place me in Hitler's entourage undoubtedly sprang from this feeling.

The attempt on his life certainly had its effect on the work of the central office in Berlin. Instead of the hum of intensive activity, there was a hush of incredulity, almost of fear. How could such a thing have happened?

Himmler ordered me to fly at once to Prague where the chiefs of AMT IV and V, Mueller and Nebe, were already on the scene. I arranged for a consultation with Mueller, who promised me a short report. Heydrich lay unconscious in the hospital, where the best doctors were attempting to save his life. Bomb splinters had torn his body, forming numerous centers of infection. Part of the material of his uniform had penetrated his wounds and intensified the danger to his injured spleen. On the seventh day, general sepsis set in, which quickly brought about his death. Toward the end he was under the care of Himmler's personal physician, Professor Gebhardt, whose treatment provoked serious criticism by the other specialists. One opinion was that an operation to remove the injured spleen should have been attempted so as to get rid of the main source of infection.

Later I received from Mueller an account of how the assassination occurred. Heydrich was on his way back from his country estate near Prague to the Hradčin. He was sitting beside the driver (who was not his usual chauffeur) in his big Mercedes. On the outskirts of the city there was a sharp bend and the car had had to slow down. Three men were standing at intervals along the roadside, the first about twenty yards before the bend, the next one on the bend itself, and the third about twenty yards beyond it. As the driver slowed down the first man jumped into the road, shooting wildly with his revolver. The car came almost to a stop and at this moment the second man rolled a spherical bomb toward the car which exploded directly underneath it. Although badly wounded, Heydrich shouted to the driver, "Step on it, man!" He then jumped out of the car and fired several shots at the men, who were making their escape on bicycles, and wounded one of them in the leg. Then he collapsed, unconscious. The driver was bleeding profusely and the car, in spite of its heavy armor, was almost demolished.

Had Heydrich's old and experienced chauffeur been at the wheel, he certainly would not have let himself be duped by the assassin who jumped out into the road. The natural reaction of the quick-witted driver would have been to jam his foot on the accelerator so that the car would have leaped ahead, then the effect of the explosion would not have been so devastating.

After a long examination, the specialists of the Kriminaltechnisches Institut [the Institute of Criminal Technology] found that the bomb was of an unusual and clever construction hitherto unknown. Its explosive mechanism could be adjusted according to the distance which it was to be rolled—in this case about eight yards—and it must have worked with extraordinary precision. The explosive itself was alleged to be of English origin, but this gave no indication of the identity of those behind the act, for in our own service we used almost exclusively a certain type of captured English explosive. It could be molded into any shape and was of very high power.

The investigation was conducted with all the resources of modern detective science. The official directive stated that the assassins were members of the Czech resistance movement. Every possible clue was followed up, many suspects were arrested, and all known hide-outs raided. In fact, police action was conducted against the entire Czech resistance movement. The reports read like the script of an exciting film. Finally, four possible theories were evolved, but none led to a solution. The assassins were never captured, not even the one with the injured leg. Through the ruthless action of the Gestapo, 120 members of the Czech resistance movement were finally rounded up in a small church in Prague, where they were besieged. On the day before the church was to be captured, I went, acting on Himmler's orders, to see Mueller. On the telephone Himmler had said to me, "It's rather difficult to keep tract of this investigation." That was all he had to say about his feelings in the matter. I had nothing to do directly with Mueller's investigations in Prague, nor did he speak his mind very openly to me at first, though later he began to talk more freely.

The Reichsfuehrer was gradually driving him crazy, for Himmler had made up his mind that the whole affair was staged by the British Secret Service, and that the three assassins had been dropped by parachute near Prague for this special purpose. Mueller admitted that such a theory was possible—"for after all, the whole Czech underground is financed and directed on one hand by the British, on the other by Moscow. Tomorrow we'll take this church, and that will be the end of the matter. Let's hope that the murderers will be with the ones inside." Mueller looked at me quickly as he said this, then asked, "Have you any inside information? I thought Himmler said that you might have." I was sorry to disappoint him.

After I had left his office, I could not help reflecting that Mueller wasn't altogether happy in this affair. Somewhere something was not quite right. The next day an all-out attack was launched against the church. Of the Czech resistance fighters, none fell into German hands alive.

The secret of who Heydrich's assassins were was thus preserved. Had they been in the church? Were they members of the Czech resistance movement, and, if so, of what part of it? All those inside the church had been killed, though whether this was done on purpose or not remains uncertain. Their fanatical resistance and determination to die was emphasized in the report that was made afterward, but of those 120 members of the underground there was not one who had previously been wounded. Our investigations had come to an impasse, and with it the inquiry into Heydrich's death was brought to a close.

Heydrich's body had been placed on a ceremonial bier in the forecourt of the castle at Prague and a guard of honor was chosen from his closest associates. It was a considerable strain for me to stand in full uniform with a steel helmet for two hours at a stretch with the temperature at one hundred degrees in the shade.

Three days later the body was borne in procession from the castle to the railway station, and thence to Berlin. The citizens of Prague followed these events attentively and many houses had black flags hanging from the windows. No doubt the citizens were using the occasion to show that they were mourning for their own fate under the foreign occupation.

Before the funeral, Heydrich's body had lain in state for two days in the Palais in the Wilhelmstrasse where he had had his beautifully furnished office. On the first morning the chiefs of the departments were called into the office by Himmler. In a short address he paid tribute to Heydrich's accomplishments, to the noble traits of his character, and to the value of his work. No one could ever control the giant machinery of the RSHA as well as Heydrich, who had created it and controlled it. The Fuehrer had agreed that for the time being Himmler himself should take over its direction until Heydrich's successor had been chosen. He called upon the heads of the departments to do their best, and forbade all conflicts arising from jealousy. He warned them not to work against each other, or try to usurp each other's authority. Any such attempts would be sharply punished by Hitler himself.

Pointing to the coffin on its bier and addressing each of the heads in turn, he gave them what was in effect a severe dressing down, speaking with a biting irony that emphasized their characteristics and defects. At the end, it was my turn. I steeled myself for what I was about to hear, expecting the cold shower of his criticism to envelop me as well. Himmler must have noticed my apprehension. A trace of a smile came over his face, which was deathly pale. He looked at me for a while, then, turning more toward the others than to me, he said, "Schellenberg has the most difficult office, and is the youngest of us all. However, the man lying in state here considered him suitable for the position and placed him there. I too consider him capable of undertaking the tasks placed before him. Above all, he is incorruptible. You, gentlemen, know best the sort of difficulties you have been putting in his way. You resent him because of his youth, and because he is not an old member of the National Socialist party. I do not consider there is any justification for your objections, and I wish to make it clear once and for all that the decision in this matter is mine, not yours. He is, so to speak, the Benjamin of our leadership corps, and therefore I shall give him my special support. I have said this openly and in his presence because it accords with the intentions of your murdered chief, and I consider Schellenberg too intelligent to grow conceited because of what I have said. On the contrary, I hope it will be a further incentive to him to work carefully and industriously at the tasks assigned to him. If anyone wishes to say anything further on this matter, or on any other raised on this solemn occasion, he now has opportunity to do so. . . ."

There was an oppressive silence. I had felt relatively calm until this moment, but now I began to blush—the more as Himmler again took up his theme, saying that from now on he wanted me to work closely with him, that he needed my abilities, and wished me to report to him as frequently as possible. Then, rather abruptly, he adjourned the meeting.

In the evening Himmler, accompanied by SS Obergruppenfuehrer Karl Wolff, again gathered all the leaders of the RSHA in Heydrich's office. This time he made a speech in which he dealt with the essential phases in Heydrich's personal development, and pointed out to the SS leaders their obligations to the memory of their dead chief. It should induce them to give the best of themselves in their conduct and their work. He ended with a reference to the increasing importance of our work abroad, hoping that as we developed our shortcomings and the gaps in our tradition would be overcome, for our achievements in this special sector still could not compare with those of the British Secret Service. Therefore, our motto should be: "My Fatherland, right or wrong"—as well as the general motto of our order, the SS: "My Honor is Loyalty."

At the memorial service in the Reich Chancellery which preceded the state funeral, orations were delivered by Hitler and Himmler. It was a most impressive spectacle, which did full justice to Himmler's gift for pageantry and drama. In their orations both Hitler and Himmler spoke of "the man with the iron heart." I could not help thinking that with all the Ministers, Secretaries of State, high party officials, and family mourners, the whole thing was like a Renaissance painting.

After the coffin had disappeared into the earth, I saw, surprisingly enough, that Canaris was weeping, and when we turned to go he said to me in a voice choked with emotion, "After all, he was a great man. I have lost a friend in him."

About two months later Himmler stood with me in front of a death mask of Heydrich. Suddenly he said,

"Yes, as the Fuehrer said at the funeral, he was indeed a man with an iron heart. And at the height of his power fate purposefully took him away." His voice was deadly serious, and I shall not forget the nod of Buddha-like approval that accompanied these words, while the small cold eyes behind the pince-nez were suddenly lit with sparkle like the eyes of a basilisk.

Three months later, going to Himmler's office to make a report, I noticed that the corner in which the mask had been placed was now empty, and I asked him why. He replied cryptically, "Death masks are tolerable only at certain times and on special occasions, either for the sake of memory or example."

In the summer of 1942, Himmler arranged to meet me in Berlin. As usual, he set aside ample time so that he could talk at length. After discussing various matters, I felt that our conversation was about to reach a dramatic climax. As usual, Himmler sat with his head a little to one side so that his glasses reflecting the light made it difficult to see his small, crafty eyes. Rising suddenly, he asked me to sit down with him at another table—always a sign of unusual confidence. He explained to me that it was proving extremely difficult to find a successor to Heydrich, as none of the departmental heads could possibly be considered—with one exception: myself. "I have talked to the Fuehrer about this at various times." He leaned forward, looking at me intently. I was well aware, of course, of the far-reaching implications of what he was saying, and it took all my resolution to look him firmly in the eye. After an almost unbearable silence I finally managed to say in a strained voice, "It would certainly be a very difficult position for me, and I think you might find me a rather awkward assistant."

Again there was a pause.

Then, with a decidedly benevolent change in his tone Himmler said, "You won't be chosen. The Fuehrer thinks that you are too young, although he agrees that you're well qualified. Personally, I think you're too soft for the job. The Fuehrer wants you to concentrate entirely on the Secret Service abroad—he's shown much more interest in it lately—so you'll do that, whoever is appointed chief. The final choice will probably be between three or four of the higher police and SS leaders—the older ones—but I'll tell you more about that later. From now on you must maintain close contact with me the whole time. As far as the outside world is concerned—administratively, that is—you will still function within the framework of the RSHA, but all decisive problems you'll discuss with me personally, and you'll have access to me at any time. Now, this is a special position and it won't make things any easier for you with other members of the department, nor with whoever is appointed chief, still less with other opponents of yours.

"You need this special position, not only for yourself, but for your department; it must be given greater weight in its relations with the Foreign Office and other Ministries. They must realize that you are acting as my direct representative. All the same, you mustn't neglect your health. I'll arrange leave for you whenever you need it, but you must take care to look after yourself: we shall need you later on. Try to live a life of abstinence, to live completely in the interest of your work. If you do this, you ought to be able to increase your output without expending any more energy." (Later on, cases of fruit juices, mineral waters, and all sorts of things to build me up were delivered to me regularly.) "In the future," Himmler went on, "Kersten, my own doctor, who is also a neurologist, will take charge of you. I want him to examine you, and if he considers it advisable, he'll treat you regularly, just as he treats me. He has worked wonders for me, and he certainly ought to do you a great deal of good. He is a Finn, and completely loyal to me personally, so you can trust him. The only thing is that you'll have to be careful—he talks too much. Also, he is very inquisitive. Otherwise he's not a bad fellow—good-natured and extremely helpful."

After the years that have intervened, it is difficult to reproduce the impression that this conversation made upon me at the time. On the one hand, I felt as if I had been hit over the head; on the other, I felt extremely proud at the recognition of my work. But all the time I could not help wondering what would have happened if I had been chosen as Heydrich's successor. To reject the appointment would have been impossible; to accept it would have been fatal. I am sure I would not have fallen in with the methods which Hitler—and therefore Himmler—would have wanted. I left Himmler's study feeling very empty, as one feels, in fact, after some moment of great danger has passed. I was not really myself until several hours later; then I felt as happy as a small boy.

That night I went out to celebrate with my wife and, in spite of Himmler's admonitions, drank a bottle of good wine.

This conversation with Himmler gave me an interesting insight into the manner in which he used to work. He was consciously but very discreetly striving to create a new leadership for the Reich, naturally with Hitler's approval. This policy was to insure that all those who held leading posts in the Reich Ministries, in industry, commerce and trade, in science and culture—in short, in all spheres of the modern state—should be members of the SS. This process was almost completed, and it is easy to see what tremendous power was thus concentrated in the leader of the organization—that is, in Himmler himself.

His aim so far as I was concerned was to build up a position of power for me that would open all doors and provide help in whatever quarter I needed it. It was really a marvelous system, and I felt a little ashamed that it would no longer be through my own achievements that such doors were being opened to me, but through some incalculable, anonymous, and all-pervading influence. Scarcely a week passed without Himmler's assistant arranging for me to call on some leader of importance—a Minister or Secretary of State, an economist, scientist, or military leader. Over all this Himmler maintained a close personal supervision. Years later he told me that the establishment of these relationships with important persons in the state and the Party had been arranged not only for practical reasons of policy, but also as a kind of testing process. Directly or indirectly he had obtained their personal impressions of me.

In considering the working of this secret scheme, I began to realize that the establishment of a secret service such as I envisaged would be impossible without some support of this kind. And still this was only the modest beginning of my idea, the preparatory work within one's own country. Here and there connections somewhat similar, if on a different level, began to be established in political, economic, and military circles abroad. But all these were contacts which neither the other departmental heads nor the agents of the inner circle knew anything about.

29. PLANS FOR PEACE

*"Total Victory" no longer a possibility—Obstacles to a
negotiated peace—Military circles confident of our success
—A rendezvous with Himmler—Dr. Kersten—Himmler
and German peace feelers—My plan discussed—Outlines
of a future Europe—My authority endorsed by Himmler*

MY CONVERSATIONS during the summer
of 1942 with the various heads of government departments, leading economists, and scientific experts, considered in conjunction with the secret information that was
continually coming to me, gave me feelings of considerable uncertainty. What troubled me most was the war
potential of the United States, which had not even been
engaged yet, and the strength of the Red Army, which our
Wehrmacht leaders, confident in their offensive power and
the superiority of their strategic and tactical commands,
still underestimated. The immense area of the Russian
plains and the climatic conditions of the country had not
been sufficiently taken into account. Although much progress had been made in mechanizing Wehrmacht units,
again and again one heard of technical deficiencies. Tank
tracks, for instance, were not wide enough and tanks were
often bogged down in muddy roads; moving parts did not
function properly in the extreme cold; very often the
turrets could not turn, and many other defects cropped up
in other types of armament.

Our main industries, as yet unharmed by the effects of
total war, were working at top speed. At this moment we
still stood on the dizzy heights and the Nazi leaders
believed that victory was in sight. I felt, however, that for
me this was the real turning point. I was forced to the
conclusion that the idea of "total victory," and its later
version, "final victory," could no longer be realized. This
brought me to the problem of how to inform our leaders
of these unpleasant facts, since they rigidly refused even to
consider their possibility.

My work had forced me to realize that our leaders had
no real understanding of conditions abroad. Their actions
were determined entirely by their own narrow political
views. The Foreign Office did nothing to change this
siutation. There may have been people employed in that
department who saw things just as I did, but they played
no part in the formation of the political will. None of them
was willing to advance from recognition of the facts to the
inevitable conclusion—that the idea of final victory was
impossible; still less would they stand up for their opinions
in front of their superiors.

I began to think seriously about the problem and came
to the conclusion that as long as the Reich had the power
to fight, it would also have the power to bargain. There
was, in fact, still time to achieve a compromise with our
enemies, but one would have to calculate coolly like a
broker: it is better to lose 50 per cent than risk complete
bankruptcy and lose everything.

At this time, in August 1942, our evidence showed that
Stalin was dissatisfied with the Western Allies. That this
seemed to offer a realistic basis for doing business was
confirmed by the Japanese for, in spite of the passing
setbacks we had suffered on the eastern front, they still
considered that compromise negotiations with Russia were
possible.

The situation in the year 1942 had developed into a
race for time. Britain was too weak to act alone, and was
waiting for the arrival of American strategic material.
Stalin was waiting not only for the delivery of material, but
for effective relief in the opening of a real second front. So
long as the Western Allies delayed their invasion, no
matter from what motives, there was a good chance of
conducting compromise negotiations. Germany's superiority of power at this time placed her in a good position to
bargain with both sides. It was important therefore to
establish contact with Russia at the same time as we
initiated our negotiations with the West. An increasing
rivalry between the Allied Powers would strengthen our
position. Such a plan had to be launched very carefully,
however, and with regard to Russia we were handicapped
by previous Japanese attempts to act as mediators, for we
could negotiate more freely if we did not have to consider
Japanese interests.

But it was no use considering means of negotiating until

our own leaders had been convinced of the necessity of our doing so. I was well acquainted with the attitude of Hitler and Ribbentrop, and it was the latter who seemed to be the main obstacle. Unfortunately he was so firmly in Hitler's confidence that it was not possible to undermine his position. Goering was already more or less in disgrace. There remained only one man who had sufficient power and influence: that was Himmler. Of course the fact that I had immediate access to him was an important factor, for after Hitler he was—and remained to the very end—the most powerful man in the regime. For these reasons I determined at the first opportunity to exploit the possibilities of my position with him and make an attempt to launch plans for negotiations. But I still had a great amount of routine work.

At the beginning of August 1942, I was called to make my usual report to Himmler at Zhitomir in the Ukraine, near Hitler's headquarters at Vinnitza. Himmler had requisitioned a beautifully situated officers' training college for himself and his staff. Within two days it had been transformed into a completely equipped field command post. Short-wave and telephonic communications had been installed to enable him to be in constant touch with even the most remote localities of the territories occupied by Germany. Everything for his personal needs was also provided: there was even a tennis court. In his heavy command car Himmler was driven every day over the so-called *Rollbahn*. This *Rollbahn* connected Zhitomir with Vinnitza, where Himmler spent several hours every day with Hitler.

One morning he telephoned to me from Vinnitza. First I spoke to his personal assistant, SS Standartenfuehrer Brandt, with whom I was on very good terms. Brandt was a small, plain-looking man, who in his appearance and gestures aped his master. A walking reference library, he was Himmler's living notebook and was the most industrious of all his entourage. I believe he was the only person in whom Himmler had complete confidence.

Brandt would begin work at seven in the morning, no matter what time he had gone to bed the night before. Three or four hours of sleep were sufficient for him. As soon as Himmler had risen in the morning and washed, Brandt would go to him loaded with papers and files, and while Himmler shaved he would read him the most important items of the morning's mail. This was done with the greatest seriousness. If there was bad news, Brandt would preface it by saying, "Pardon, Herr Reichsfuehrer," and thus forewarned, Himmler would temporarily suspend his shaving operations—a precautionary measure to prevent him cutting himself. Brandt was certainly most important. He was the eyes and ears of his master and the manner in which he presented a matter to Himmler was often of decisive importance.

On this particular morning Brandt asked how I was and how my work was going. From the sharp way in which he spoke I knew it would only be a matter of seconds before Himmler took the receiver from him. And so it was. Himmler flooded me with questions on various matters. It was his custom when speaking on the telephone to employ all sorts of private code words and names which he had invented himself and remembered with great accuracy. He could carry on a conversation consisting entirely of such words, which sometimes created difficulties for the person at the other end. He once asked me, "And what is 'Highcollar' doing?" Although by then I was quite familiar with his nomenclature, for a moment I could not think who he meant. Impatiently he explained, "Why, the long cellar, the entrance to the cellar, down in the pit, the mine—" Only then did I remember that "Highcollar" was his code name for Schacht, the president of the Reichsbank, who always wore a high collar—and the other allusions were to his name, which means "shaft." That morning, however, I remembered all the code words, and at the end he ordered me to report at Zhitomir and bring various documents with me.

That same evening I took the Wehrmacht courier train from Berlin to Warsaw. There I was entertained with magnificent hospitality at the royal palace by Governor-General Frank. Frank entertained all the higher Wehrmacht, SS and Party leaders en route to and from the Fuehrer's headquarters in the east. A message from Himmler awaited me. He wanted me to rest for a day in Warsaw so that I should not be too exhausted by my journey and then to take the special courier plane the next day.

At Frank's place I met many higher Wehrmacht officers, divisional commanders of the Waffen SS, higher SS and police leaders, and it interested me to sound the opinions of all these people On the whole, they were completely assured of the fighting power of the German people. On this score they had no doubts whatsoever and all were striving to achieve their utmost and to be one hundred per cent efficient. It made me even more conscious of the difficulty of the task I had set myself. For the confidence and assurance of all these important officers would strengthen and confirm the opinions of the leaders. Another interesting thing was that these circles, perhaps because of their origins, saw everything solely from a military point of view. They had only the haziest notion of the meaning of the Secret Service. Theirs was the prevailing German idea on the subject, which saw the Secret Service as a rather interesting and adventurous enterprise, but had little idea of its importance in the conduct of the war.

The next morning I flew on to Zhitomir in Himmler's special aircraft, which had landed by chance at Warsaw. The flight captain was a Bavarian who had been Himmler's personal pilot for years. A few days later he went alone into a Russian village against Himmler's strictest orders and was murdered in the most horrible manner by the partisans. That morning, however, he had no foreboding of the fate that awaited him.

Gazing over the vastness of the Polish and Russian plains from the flight deck of the four-engined Condor, I saw only occasionally the marks of warfare. They ran like strips burned by lightning across the face of the earth, but for hundreds of miles to the right and left of them the country was completely untouched. Oppressive heat scorched the land and a vaporous haze in the sky arched over us like a great glass dome. There was an uninterrupted view to the horizon and as the engines droned on steadily hour after hour I began to have some understanding of what our troops had had to achieve in order to conquer this enormous area. Here and there one saw peasants at work. All were barefoot, the women with colored kerchiefs around their heads. Very few of them took any notice of the sound of our engines.

Finally we arrived at the airfield, then came a ride to Zhitomir at breakneck speed in a command car. The buildings shaded by tall trees were white and untouched by the war. Everything looked spick and span, as was always the case at any of Himmler's headquarters. He placed the greatest importance upon the best possible treatment being given to his guests. I was shown to my room at once and was able to take a shower, then while I waited I chatted with the various adjutants, experts, and secretaries whom I knew. This I did with a purpose, because it was important to get the feeling of the atmosphere here. I was not to report until late in the afternoon, but when the time came there was another delay. I was then asked most politely how long I could remain away from Berlin. As I wanted to have time for a quiet talk with Himmler, I said one or two days would not make a great deal of difference.

In the evening I was asked to dinner. Until the very last part of the war Himmler was insistent upon his guests appearing in trousers, white shirts, and shoes instead of military boots. He received me with great amiability, and for some little time made small talk, carefully refraining from coming to the point of my visit, as a mark of politeness. This was one of his conversational tactics. He questioned me very closely about my health, told me that Dr. Kersten, who would certainly be happy to treat me, was there too, and asked whether I had had frequent conversations with Langbehn, and so on.

At dinner he talked to me on various scientific questions and told me about an expedition to Tibet. Then he spoke of India and Indian philosophy. This led him to speak of a subject which was a hobbyhorse of his: in a lively manner he described to me the result of researches in German witchcraft trials. He said it was monstrous that thousands of witches had been burned during the Middle Ages. So much good German blood had been stupidly destroyed. From this he began an attack on the Catholic Church, and at the same time on Calvin; before I had caught up with all this he was discussing the Spanish Inquisition and the essential nature of primitive Christianity. Suddenly he said to me, "By the way, what is dear Fraenzchen von Papen doing?" and asked me to include Turkey when I made my report to him.

In this way the dinner went on very harmoniously and pleasantly. Later in the evening I talked with Dr. Kersten. I had met him several months before at Himmler's suggestion. He was an interesting and exciting personality. Through his manual dexterity, and perhaps a certain magnetic gift, he was able to achieve remarkable cures through massaging the nerves. He could feel nerve complexes with his finger tips and through manipulation increase the blood circulation, thus reconditioning the entire nervous system, and could cure headaches and neuralgia within a few minutes. During all the years of the war he was Himmler's shadow, so to speak, for Himmler believed that without Kersten's treatment he would die. Kersten's system must have worked, because in the end Himmler became completely dependent upon him. This, of course, gave the doctor considerable influence over his patient.

So great was Himmler's faith in Kersten's ability that he submitted everyone in the Third Reich whom he regarded as important to a sort of test, which consisted of a physical examination by Kersten; for Kersten claimed that through his manipulations he could feel the nature of the nervous reactions and the nervous energy of an individual, and thereby judge his mental and intellectual capacities. Himmler once told me that Kersten had described me as a very sensitive type, my dominant inclinations being toward intellectual work. I would never be capable of commanding troops in action, for that required an entirely different kind of nervous reaction; but Kersten felt that in my present position I was the right man in the right place, and my intellectual capabilities qualified me for still higher posts.

Kersten had come to Himmler with a great reputation, having been introduced by the director-general of the German Potash Syndicate, Dr. August Diehm. Among his patients were industrialists from all over the world and various people of position, including Queen Wilhelmina of the Netherlands. With such a reputation it was not difficult for Kersten to get himself well in with Himmler.

In appearance he was a fat, jovial man, weighing almost 250 pounds. His massive hands would never have led one to suspect the extreme sensitivity of his finger tips. He had one disturbing feature—an unusual black ring round the iris of his light blue eyes, which at times gave them a strangely piercing and reptilian look. He was a self-taught man who had worked himself up in the world through his singular talents. He was a fanatical bargain hunter. Anything that could be acquired at a knock-down price, such as a dozen watches or cigarette lighters, he would buy. On the whole, he was good-natured and kindly, although he admitted that it was often difficult for him to be so. He

had many enemies, some because he was envied, some he
made through his passion for backstairs intrigue, although
he was unable either to profit by his schemes or to keep
them from becoming entangled. Some people even suspected him of being a British agent. Once I asked
Himmler about this. "Good God!" he replied, "that fat
fellow? He's much too good-natured; he would never want
to harm me. We must let him have his bit of egotism;
everyone suffers from it in some form or other. If you
want to investigate, why, that's your business; but avoid
upsetting him if you can."

Kersten always knew how best to exploit Himmler to
his own advantage. He was able to bounce unharmed out
of all difficulties. What usually happened was that so much
confusion was created around him that you never knew
where you were. But without Himmler's support, Kaltenbrunner and Mueller would have brought about his downfall, and Langbehn's, in 1943 or, at the latest, 1944.

But to return to that night in August 1942: after a long
conversation I was quite sure that Kersten not only agreed
with my ideas regarding a compromise peace, but was
enthusiastic about them. He had completely fallen in with
my plans and agreed to use all his influence with Himmler
to prepare the way for me. He assured me that I could go
a long way with Himmler, who had a very high opinion of
me! Here at last was the first active supporter of my
plans.

Then Kersten began to tell me of his own difficulties.
He needed protection against Mueller's hostility and I
promised him my help. When I went to bed early in the
morning I could not sleep. Again and again my thoughts
returned to the question of how to convince Himmler of
my ideas.

The next morning I was unexpectedly called to report
to Himmler. He was planning to go to Vinnitza in the
afternoon and wanted me to inform him before he went on
the present status of the Sino-Japanese compromise negotiations. This took up the entire morning. I had almost
finished my résumé when Himmler suddenly changed the
subject and said he was happy that I had made good
friends with Kersten, and begged me to improve my
relationship with Langbehn as well.

It seemed to me the time had arrived for me to broach
the subject that was most on my mind. Himmler must

have noticed that I had something to think about, for he said to me suddenly, "You look so serious—are you unwell?"

"On the contrary, Herr Reichsfuehrer," I said, "the treatment I had from Dr. Kersten today has toned me up considerably. I know how great the demands on your time are, but the most important part of my report is not in my brief case—that's almost empty now; it's in my head. But I don't want to begin until I can be sure that you really have got time to listen in peace."

Himmler, suspicious as always, became a little nervous. "Something unpleasant? Something personal?" he said.

"Nothing like that, Herr Reichsfuehrer. It is simply that I want to place before you a matter that involves a most important and difficult decision."

At this point Brandt was called in and Himmler made certain decisions, dictated several directives, and postponed various appointments and conferences. Then he invited me to lunch with his adjutants and secretaries and asked me to be ready to report to him again at four o'clock. In order to keep this appointment he set back his trip to Vinnitza.

During the meal I consciously restrained myself, and noticed how Himmler's curiosity was increasing. Several higher Wehrmacht and SS leaders were present, and Himmler was especially gay and jovial. He had the ability to change his personality as easily as he changed his uniform, from being the cool executive to being an amusing and pleasant host.

After lunch Himmler excused himself and disappeared with his shadow, Brandt. About half an hour later I was called into his study. He came from behind his desk, a thing he very rarely did, and asked me whether I wanted anything to drink, then invited me to sit down with him and lit a cigar—which was also unusual for him. "Well, please begin," he said cheerfully.

I asked his permission to start in a somewhat broader manner than usual because of the extensive nature of the matter I wished to raise. He nodded.

"You know, Herr Reichsfuehrer," I began, "that I did my final preparatory work for the Bar in Düsseldorf. The president of the court there once asked me to prepare a draft judgment; it involved a tremendous amount of work and I kept putting it off until in the end I had to do the

whole job in two or three days. Well, the next morning I
was told to report to the president. The first thing he said
to me was, 'I'm sure you'd like a cigar.' " This remark had
an ironical undertone, for in German it has a double
meaning: "to receive a cigar" is to be given a rebuff.

At this Himmler smiled for the first time, pressed a bell,
and told the orderly to bring me a good cigar. When I
protested, he said with a smile, "Perhaps you prefer the
president's?"

I went on, "The president told me that there were two
good things about my report. One, I had been punctual
with it. The other was that, as I'd quite failed to get any
grip on the matter that I was writing about, he could
take the occasion to give me some advice which he hoped
I'd remember for the rest of my life. He said that going
through the evidence he had noticed three or four points
which could have led to different conclusions, and asked
why I hadn't dealt with these alternatives in my draft.
Also, he said, why did I not give an alternative verdict
instead of keeping rigidly to the same line of argument?
Later in life, he said, I would often have to face very
difficult problems indeed, and would then do well to think
of his words: never forget the alternative solution. 'Make
those words one of the basic principles in your life,' he
said." Looking Himmler firmly in the eye, I went on,
"Well, you see, Herr Reichsfuehrer, I have never been
able to forget this advice given me by a very wise man.
May I be so bold as to ask you this question: In which
drawer of your desk have you got your alternative solution for ending this war?"

The ensuing silence lasted a full minute. Himmler sat
before me quite aghast. He could not have misunderstood
my introductory remarks and must have realized quite
soon what I was driving at. Slowly he came to life. At last
he spoke, softly, then in a voice that grew louder until he
was almost shouting at me. "Have you gone mad? You've
been working too hard. Shall I give you five weeks' leave
right away? Are you losing your nerve? And anyhow, how
dare you talk to me this way?"

I remained completely cool. I waited until his excitement had subsided, then, assuming for the moment a
detached tone, I said, "Herr Reichsfuehrer, I knew you'd
go on like this. In fact, I thought it might be even worse.
But I should like you to consider that even such a great

man as Bismarck at the height of his power always kept
an alternative solution in mind; and such a solution is
possible only as long as one can keep one's freedom of
action. Today Germany still stands at the zenith of her
power. Today we are still in a position to bargain—our
strength makes it worthwhile for our opponents to seek a
compromise with us."

In broad strokes I outlined to him the relationship of
forces in the world as it appeared to me. As I went on he
became noticeably calmer. My own assurance had its
effect upon him. During the course of my remarks he
became more and more interested. Every now and again
he nodded. By the time I had finished, after an hour and a
half, he had interrupted me only a very few times, and I
was able to repeat my question in a different form: "You
see, Herr Reichsfuehrer, that was my motive when I asked
you at the beginning—in which drawer have you got an
alternative solution for the war?"

He got up suddenly and now he was pacing up and
down the room. Presently he stopped and said, "As long
as that idiot Ribbentrop advises the Fuehrer, this cannot
possibly be done."

I said immediately that of course Ribbentrop would
have to go. "He is always fighting with the Reichmarschall"
—meaning Goering—"and as the one wants to be Duke of
Burgundy, let us make Ribbentrop Duke of Brabant."
Himmler understood the jest, and also the serious purpose
behind my words. He went to his desk and opened the
large map of his Brockhaus atlas. For several minutes he
studied it intently. I, too, had risen for the sake of courtesy
and he called me over to his desk.

"How will your ideas work out in practice?" he said. "I
think you overestimate Russia's strength, but I am very
worried about what's going to happen when American war
production really gets going. How—how are we to go
about it? In my present position I might have some chance
of influencing Hitler. I might even get him to drop Ribbentrop if I could be sure of Bormann's support. But we
could never let Bormann know about our plans. He'd
wreck the whole scheme, or else he'd twist it round into a
compromise with Stalin. And we must never let that
happen."

He spoke almost as if to himself, at one moment nib-
bling his thumbnail, then twisting his snake ring round and

round—sure signs that he was really concentrating. He looked at me questioningly, and said, "Would you be able to start the whole thing moving right away—without our enemies interpreting it as a sign of weakness on our part?"

I assured him that I could.

"Very well. But how do you know that the whole business won't act as a boomerang? What if it should strengthen the Western Powers' determination to achieve unity with the East?"

I said, "On the contrary, Herr Reichsfuehrer, if the negotiations are started in the right way, it will prevent just that contingency."

"All right," Himmler said, "then exactly how would you proceed?"

I explained that such operations could never be conducted through the official channels of coventional diplomacy, but should go through the political sector of the Secret Service. Then, in case of misfiring, the persons directly involved could be officially discredited and dropped. On the other hand, it would be essential for the other side to know that the person with whom they would be dealing had real authority behind him. If Himmler were prepared to appoint such a person, and at the same time would promise to get rid of Ribbentrop by Christmas 1942, then I would take up contact with the Western Powers. Ribbentrop's removal would prove to them that a new wind was blowing and that our plan had powerful backing. At the same time, rumors of a new Foreign Minister representing a more conciliatory policy would strengthen my position even more.

Here Himmler interrupted me. "Perhaps it would be a good idea to dig up Fraenzchen again?"—meaning Franz von Papen, at that time our Ambassador to Turkey. Then he shook his head. "No, let's forget that for the moment. I'll have to probe the possibilities more carefully. Do you really think a change of Foreign Minister would be sufficient indication of a change of policy on our part?" I said that I thought it definitely would be.

On the whole Himmler seemed to agree with my plan. He had not said so in so many words, but he kept nodding as if in affirmation. Then he turned round and studied the map of Europe for a while. After a pause he said, "Until now you have only explained the necessity for such an

alternative solution and the way to start it moving. Now
let us talk about the concrete basis on which such a
compromise could be reached."

I answered him cautiously. "Well, that is just what I
supposed you would have in the drawer of your desk, Herr
Reichsfuehrer."

By this time he was in a very amiable mood. He did not
take my remark badly. "Well then, let's start with the
British," he said.

"Well," I said, "from all the information I have it seems
the British would insist on our evacuating at least the north
of France. They would never tolerate German naval batteries mounted on the Calais coast."

"Then you don't believe in a grand alliance with our
brother nation?"

"Not in the immediate future," I said. "The road from
a state of war to a grand alliance by way of a negotiated
peace is a very long one."

Himmler nodded. "Well then, what about Germanic
regions, like Holland and Belgium?"

"They should become objects of the negotiations," I
said. "But I believe we will have to restore these territories to their former status. However, if you want to
slavage something in deference to your racial policies,
those that have been faithful to the creed could be reset-
tled inside German territory."

Himmler was nervously drawing on the map with his
green pencil and had already marked Holland, parts of
Belgium and northern France, as bargaining countries.
"Well—and France?"

"Herr Reichsfuehrer," I replied, "I am thinking of a
solution which aims at the economic integration of German and French interests. France's own political physiog-
nomy must be restored, but inevitably Germany and
France will be drawn together, and France, with her
colonial possessions, will bring Germany tremendous advantages. Therefore, one must not limit one's actions by
doctrinaire preconceptions or political resentment. Take
Alsace, for example—you know I am from Saarbruecken
myself, and I know from experience how wrong it was of
France to try to swallow up the Saar after Versailles."

Himmler raised his head and said disapprovingly, "But
there's a great deal of German blood in Alsace which has
hardly been touched by French culture." I suggested that

this point could remain open as a subject for negotiations, but that if Alsace ever were restored to the French in compensation, there should be closer economic co-operation between the two peoples.

Unwillingly Himmler made a green semicircle round France. Then he looked at me questioningly again. "Do you believe that such a solution would satisfy the British?" I said I could not anticipate the attitude of the British government, but I thought that they might consider such a solution worth discussing. Their chief interest would prob-ably lie in the form which the new Europe was to take.

Himmler interrupted me at this point. "Well, let's leave that—" Then his eyes rested inquiringly upon Switzerland. He poked at it with his green pencil. "Leave Switzerland, sir," I said quickly. "Its constitution can serve as a good model for the new Europe. We shall need Switzerland as a bridge to the West too, and as a European clearing house for trade and currency."

Himmler turned to Italy. He stared in front of him for a long time, then said, "Yes, yes—Mussolini—we cannot relinquish the north Italian industrial area—"

I said that I felt sure that the industries of northern Italy and Germany would compliment each other very well, but that I did not believe Italy could lose any part of her own territory. "She'll have to give up enough of her colonial aspirations in any compromise peace." Again Himmler nodded his head like a Buddha. "Well, I can't say that I'm convinced about northern Italy yet." Then he jumped to Austria and said in a voice full of decision, "But that remains ours." I said, "Yes, I'm sure that no one will have any objections to that."

"Well, and what about Czechoslovakia?"

"The Sudeten territories will remain affiliated to the Reich, politically and administratively. Czechia and Slovakia will each be governed by their autonomous gov-ernments, but economically integrated with the Reich. I believe this ought to apply also to all southeastern Europe, including Croatia, Serbia, Bulgaria, Greece, and Ru-mania."

At first Himmler did not agree, but after a discussion he admitted that these areas could hardly be integrated into the framework of a new Europe in any other way. While I was explaining this he interrupted me. "But in the long run this will develop again into nothing but an economic race with Great Britain and there'll be the same old tensions."

"Herr Reichsfuehrer," I said, "let us not think about the tensions that might perhaps arise in the future. Let us first of all remove the immediate tensions which are preventing the formation of a new Europe; and this means finding a basis for a compromise solution to end the war."

He made a great leap across the map to Poland and said, "But the Polish people have to work for us!" I said, "We have to create a solution in which everybody will collaborate of their own free will. We must all be in the same boat, and anyone who doesn't pull his weight will be drowned."

Himmler went on to the Baltic States. "Here an area of expansion must be created for Finland—but the Finns are intelligent people, and this northern corner won't cause me any headaches." He looked up again. "And what about Russia?"

"We must wait and see," I said.

There was a long pause. Then Himmler said, "If I understand you correctly, your basis for a compromise peace really means the preservation of the Greater German Reich in its approximate territorial extent on September 1, 1939." "Broadly speaking, yes." "Do we have to use all our additional territorial gains to bargain with?" Himmler asked, and again I answered, "Yes."

I went on to say that as the nucleus of a reconstituted Europe, the Greater German Reich would be able to approach social problems with renewed vigor—private initiative combined with direction and planning. "I believe that in order to achieve a new Europe nationalist tendencies will have to be curbed; but the experts will have to investigate all these problems thoroughly. To begin with, Herr Reichsfuehrer, all that matters is that it's well worth our while to seek a compromise while we are still at the height of our power. This compromise peace, if it can be achieved, will create the right basis from which we can face the conflict with the East. At this moment we are already fighting a two-front war, and once the U.S.A. adds its full weight, the scales will be laden pretty heavily against us." I reminded him of Laval's words to the Fuehrer: "Herr Hitler, you are conducting a great war in order to build a new Europe. But you should first build a new Europe in order to conduct your great war."

Himmler had to smile, "Yes, yes, yes," he said, "that Laval, he's too clever by half; whether you read his name forward or backward, it still remains Laval."

By now it was three o'clock in the morning. Himmler noticed that I was rather exhausted and cut the conversation short. "Very well. I am extremely glad to have had this full exchange of views with you. Your plan has my approval—with this condition however: if you make a serious error in your preparations I will drop you like a hot coal. Of course, it remains to be seen whether I shall be able to convince Hitler by Christmas."

It will be difficult for the reader to realize how much this conversation meant to me in August 1942. Himmler had given me full authority to act. But I did not realize at the time that such a decision could later be influenced by factors outside my control, nor that his character was so changeable that these influences could reverse his best intentions. In any case, before I left him that night he had given me his word of honor that by Christmas Ribbentrop would no longer be at his post.

From now on all my thoughts and efforts were to be directed toward extricating Germany from her present situation with a minimum of territorial loss. I was still an idealist and I firmly believed that I would succeed; but, from this point on, the long uneven road of disillusionment started, punctuated again and again by intervals of restored hope. At times I felt certain that the situation was firmly in my grasp. But in the end I was made to realize that I was only a tiny cog in the great machinery of historical development. I could really do nothing but spin in my own fixed orbit.

30. MUELLER

Himmler in financial difficulties—Bormann's influence on Hitler—First suspicions of Mueller's loyalty—His criticism of Party leaders—Reports of his death in Russia

DURING THE summer of 1942, a serious conflict arose between Himmler and Bormann in which Himmler continually made small tactical errors which Bormann always exploited to the full. Himmler's biggest mistake, about which he told me a year afterward, was made during a sort of truce between them in 1943.

Himmler's first marriage had been unhappy, but for his daughter's sake he had not sought a divorce. He now lived with a woman who was not his wife, and they had two very nice children to whom he was completely devoted. He did what he could for these children within the limits of his own income, but although, after Hitler, Himmler had more real power than anyone else in the Third Reich, and through his control of the many economic organizations could have had millions at his disposal, he found it difficult to provide for their needs. He therefore asked Bormann, his greatest opponent within the Party, for a loan of eighty thousand marks out of Party funds—a completely incomprehensible action.

When he told me about this he said that it was for a building loan, and asked whether I thought he had not been taken advantage of over the rate of interest. What could I say? I suggested he should repay the loan immediately and secure a mortgage on his house, which could easily be arranged. But he rejected this with an air of resignation. It was a completely private matter and he wanted to act with meticulous rectitude; under no circumstances did he want to discuss it with the Fuehrer. Obviously he could not afford to pay a high rate of interest, or for that matter make any other payment out of his official income.

At about this time I began seeing a good deal of Bormann. He was a short, stocky man with rounded

313

shoulders and a bull neck. His head was always pushed forward a little and cocked slightly to one side, and he had the face and shifty eyes of a boxer advancing on his opponent. His fingers were short, thick, and squarish and covered with black hair. The contrast between him and Himmler was really grotesque. If I thought of Himmler as a stork in a lily pond, Bormann seemed to me like a pig in a potato field. At later meetings with him I had ample occasion to consider the source of his influence with Hitler.

In Hitler's entourage it was Bormann who, through his constant presence, made himself indispensable simply by habit. In anything which concerned Hitler, Bormann was there. He shared in all large and small decisions, in all the excitements, rages, and fatigues. Indeed, Bormann governed the range of these events in Hitler's daily life. He had developed great skill in finding exactly the right word with which to change unpleasant subjects and to push new interests into the foreground—in short, to dispel the Fuehrer's worries. He also had a cast-iron memory, which was invaluable to Hitler, particularly in the last years, for the more absolute the regime became, the more difficult it was to reconcile the decisions of such a war machine with the Fuehrer's commands. The greater the burden on Hitler's nerves, the more soothing was Bormann's continual presence at all hours of the day and night with his stalwart and unflagging spirit. He had the ability to simplify complicated matters, to present them concisely, and to summarize the essential points in a few clear sentences. So cleverly did he do this that even his briefest reports contained an implicit solution. I saw examples of this several times and was so impressed by his exemplary manner that I decided to adopt similar methods of reporting.

I once discussed Bormann's personality with Himmler, who confirmed my supposition. "The Fuehrer has become so accustomed to Bormann that it's very difficult indeed to lessen his influence. Again and again I have had to come to terms with him, though really it's my duty to get him out. I hope I can succeed in outmaneuvering him without having to get rid of him. He's been responsible for a lot of the Fuehrer's misguided decisions; in fact, he's not only confirmed his uncompromising attitude, he's stiffened it."

In course of time Bormann methodically strengthened his position. Originally he had been the administrator of an estate in Mecklenburg, then a saboteur in the resistance against the French occupation in the Ruhr, and was also a former member of the "Black" or illegal Reichswehr. He had joined the Party at an early date and had made his career under the protection of Hess, whose position he took over and exploited for its political power to an extent which Hess never achieved. In 1945, with a very clear idea of the general situation, as well as of the dangers of his own position, he was one of those who made a determined attempt to move over into the Eastern camp.

Another top leader with a definite leaning toward the Russians was Mueller. My first serious suspicions about the sincerity of his work against Russia were roused by a long conversation I had with him in the spring of 1943, after a conference of foreign-based police attachés. Mueller, with whom I stood more and more on a footing of open enmity, had been especially correct and courteous that evening. I imagined, because it was so late, that he had been drinking when he said he wanted to have a talk with me.

He began talking about *Rote Kapelle*. He had occupied himself a great deal with the motives for these treason cases and with the intellectual background from which they stemmed.

"You will agree with me, I suppose, that from your own experience, the Soviet influence in Western Europe does not exist among the working classes alone—that it's also gained a hold among educated people. I see in this an inevitable historical development of our era, particularly when you consider the spiritual 'anarchy' of our Western culture, by which I mean to include the ideology of the Third Reich. National Socialism is nothing more than a sort of dung on this spiritual desert. In contrast to this, one sees that in Russia a unified and really uncompromising spiritual and biological force is developing. The Communists' global aim of spiritual and material world revolution offers a sort of positive electrical charge to Western negativism."

I sat opposite Mueller that night deep in thought. Here was the man who had conducted the most ruthless and brutal struggle against Communism in all its various forms, the man who, in his investigation of *Rote Kapelle*, had left no stone unturned to uncover the last ramifications of that conspiracy. What a change was here!

Presently he said, "You know, Schellenberg, it's really too stupid, this thing between us. In the beginning I thought we would hit it off very well in our personal and our professional relationship, but it didn't work out. You have many advantages over me. My parents were poor, I'm self-made; I was a police detective; I began on the beat and I learned in the hard school of ordinary police work. Now, you're an educated man; you're a lawyer, you've got a cultural background, and you've traveled. In other words, you're stuck fast in the petrified system of a conservative tradition. Take, for instance, men like those you know from *Rote Kapelle*—Schulze-Boysen or Harnack—you know, they were intellectuals too, but of an entirely different kind. They were pure intellectuals, progressive revolutionaries, always looking for a final solution; they never got bogged down in half measures. And they died still believing in that solution. There are too many compromises in National Socialism for it to offer a faith like that; but spiritual Communism can. It's got a consistent attitude toward life which is lacking among most of our Western intellectuals, excepting perhaps some of the SS. I am not speaking now of the mass of the German people—they're steady and tough and courageous—nor of the heroism of our front-line soldiers: I am speaking of the intellectual élite and wishy-washy forms of their muddled spiritual attitude. National Socialism has never really possessed their kind or transformed them. If we lose this war, it won't be because of any deficiencies in our war potential; it will be because of the spiritual incapacity of our leaders. We haven't got any real leaders—we do have a Leader, the Fuehrer—but that is the beginning and the end of it. Take the mob immediately below him, and what have you got? You've got them all squabbling among themselves night and day, either for the Fuehrer's favors or about their own authority. He must have seen this long ago, and for some reason that's incomprehensible to me he seems to be exploiting this state of affairs in order to rule. That's where his greatest failure lies. His statesmanship shows a grave lack of wisdom there. I can't help it, but I am forced more and more to the conclusion that Stalin does these things better. Just think what his organization has stood up to during the last two years, and the assurance that he's asserted himself with before his people. I see Stalin today in quite a different light. He's immeasurably superior to the leaders of the Western nations, and if I had anything to say in the matter we'd reach an agreement with him as quickly as possible. That would be a blow which the West, with their damned hypocrisy, would never be able to recover from. You see, with the Russians one always knows where one is: either they chop your head off right away, or they hug you. In this Western rubbish heap they're always talking about God and all sorts of other lofty things, but if it seems to their advantage they'll let a whole people die of starvation. Germany would have been much further ahead if the Fuehrer had really got down to it. But with us everything is only half attempted and half done, and if we are not careful it'll finish us. Himmler is only tough when he knows that the Fuehrer stands behind him. Otherwise he wouldn't make up his mind one way or another. Heydrich was far superior to him in that way; the Fuehrer was right when he called him 'the man with the iron heart.' Bormann is a man who knows what he wants, but he's much too small to think in a statesmanlike way. And look at him and Himmler—like a couple of snakes fighting. Himmler will have a tough job to come out on top."

I was amazed to hear Mueller express such opinion. He had always said that Bormann was nothing but a criminal, and now suddenly there was this change of attitude. I grew more and more nervous: what was he driving at? Was he trying to trap me? He was knocking back one brandy after another and in gutter Bavarian he began to revile the decadent West and the leaders—Goering, Goebbels, Ribbentrop, and Ley—till their ears must have burned. But as Mueller was a walking filing system and knew all the most intimate details about every one of them, this had its amusing moments, though for me they were overshadowed by a most uncomfortable feeling of apprehension. What did he want, this man who was so full of bitterness and hatred, suddenly talking like a book? It was something no one had ever heard Mueller do before. Once, to steer the conversation onto a lighter and more jocular course, I said, "All right, Comrade Mueller, let's all start saying 'Heil Stalin!' right now—and our little father Mueller will become head of the NKVD."

He looked at me with a malevolent glint in his eyes. "That would be fine," he said contemptuously in his heaviest Bavarian accent, "and you'd really be for the high jump, you and your die-hard bourgeois friends."

At the end of this strange conversation I still could not work out what Mueller was driving at—but I was enlightened several months later. The conversation had taken place just at the time when Mueller was making his intellectural somersault. He no longer believed in a German victory and thought peace with Russia the only solution. This was completely in accordance with his methods. His conception of the relationship of the state to the individual, as far as this was shown by his actions, had from the beginning been neither German or National Socialist, but in truth Communistic. Who knows how many people he influenced at this time and pulled over into the Eastern camp?

Mueller knew quite well that he had made no impression on me, that the truce which we had made for this one evening was over. His enmity was to cost me dear in nerves and energy—it was a sort of duel in the dark, in which most of the advantages lay on his side, especially after I discovered toward the end of 1943 that he had established contact with the Russian Secret Service, so that quite apart from his personal antagonism I had to reckon with the objective enmity of a fanatic.

In 1945 he joined the Communists, and in 1950 a German officer who had been a prisoner of war in Russia told me that he had seen Mueller in Moscow in 1948 and that he had died shortly afterward.

31. MY HOPES FRUSTRATED

*The case of Horia Sima—Ribbentrop and Undersecretary
Luther—An agreement broken—Luther's arrest—
Himmler's attitude toward peace proposals revised—
Ribbentrop's ban on their further discussion—Talks with
the Swiss Secret Service—Ernest Kaltenbrunner—His ha-
tred of Heydrich—Our working relationship*

AT THE end of 1942 the leader of the
abortive Rumanian Iron Guard *putsch*, Horia Sima, managed to escape from the SD school at Bergenbrueck, near
Bernau. Mueller had organized a big search, but had not
reported Sima's escape to Himmler. Nine days later
Himmler telephoned to me in a terrible state and told me
to go to Mueller immediately and do all I possibly could
to help recapture Sima. I realized at once how dangerous
this situation was for Himmler, and put all the resources of
my organization to work on the case. Within four days I
had got Horia Sima back to Germany.

Meanwhile, Ribbentrop had heard of his flight, and had
also found out that Hitler knew nothing about it. This
brought the bitter struggle between Ribbentrop and
Himmler to a climax. Ribbentrop went straight to Hitler
and told him that Horia Sima was again attempting a
putsch from Italy. Without even ascertaining the facts,
Hitler flew into a terrible rage, for he had given Marshal
Antonescu his word of honor not to release Horia Sima
until they had mutually agreed that he should do so.
Ribbentrop managed to phrase his report so cleverly that
Hitler was firmly convinced that Himmler and I were again
trying to launch a plot in Rumania. He became mad with
rage and for three hours shouted that this was a scandal
and—referring to the black uniform of the SS—that he
would smoke out this "Black Plague" with fire and sul-
phur.

For us the whole thing was an ill-starred business from

the very beginning. And Hitler's attitude was, after all, quite understandable; he simply could not believe that Himmler had not known of Sima's flight.

The atmosphere was extremely tense for about ten days, then very slowly Himmler began to re-establish his position. However, this ridiculous incident had decisive repercussions and enabled Ribbentrop to strenghten and re-establish his own position, while it took Himmler a considerable time to regain Hitler's confidence. Mueller, to justify himself, wrote long reports. I alone was left to hold the baby, for of course Ribbentrop could not now be removed, and my credit was damaged with the Western Powers, to whom we had promised that Ribbentrop would be got rid of. They no longer believed in the seriousness of our intentions and regarded the whole thing as a desperate attempt to upset the unity of the Allies. It is even possible that news of our first abortive peace feelers reached Roosevelt and that this may have decided him to put the "Unconditional Surrender" resolution before Churchill at Casablanca.

My discussions with Himmler at this time about his failure to keep his promise concerning Ribbentrop were stormy. He was deeply depressed and seemed completely to have lost his nerve, and it was only with the greatest effort that I could get him to give further authorization for my plans.

Here I should like to digress for a moment in order to refer to the important and tragic part played in the moves against Ribbentrop by Undersecretary of State Luther, of whom I have already made some mention. In spite of an estrangement that had developed in his relationship with Ribbentrop, Luther, who supported our ideas, had managed to persuade him of the importance of the Secret Service in the conduct of the war. The feelings between the two of them were aggravated by difficulties in their private relationships, particularly those that existed between their wives. Luther no longer felt able to meet the Ribbentrops continual and increasing demands on the large secret Foreign Office funds for which he was responsible. So far he had managed to manipulate them in order to meet his chief's extravagant way of life, but things had got to such a pitch that he began to doubt Ribbentrop's sanity. For instance, the tapestries in the Ribbentrops' house had to be changed four times because their colors were not precisely to Frau Ribbentrop's liking. Luther felt that he could not go on working under such conditions, and though he did not wish to be disloyal to Ribbentrop, whose closest confidant he was, he did not hesitate to tell me how things stood.

In view of what had passed between Himmler and myself at our long conference at Zhitomir in August, I felt that the time was ripe to inform Luther, very judiciously, of my plan for peace negotiations. I also mentioned to him the unfortunate influence which Ribbentrop had on Hitler, and begged him to help me to get material which might enable me to bring about Ribbentrop's downfall. Luther was convinced by my arguments, and indeed was very pleased that Himmler was adopting such a reasonable policy. It would now be much easier for Luther to forget his earlier resentment against the "black corps," as he called it. Mentioning the continual difficulties he had had with the SS leadership, he said, "Some of these gentlemen are utterly unreasonable—they want the earth. They don't understand my difficulties at the Foreign Office, and especially with Ribbentrop. I know they're constantly slandering me to Himmler, so I'm very glad of this opportunity to improve relations with him. I'll certainly give you all the help I can to bring your ideas to success."

Toward the end of the year at a reception given by the Italian Ambassador, Signor Attolico, Luther met Himmler again after a long estrangement. I had told Himmler all about Luther's attitude, so he was well disposed toward him and received him in the most friendly and even jovial manner. Luther in return began to behave like an ill-bred upstart. In spite of the many foreigners present, he buttonholed Himmler as though they were bosom friends and began to talk shop. It was the worst mistake he could have made. Himmler was extremely sensitive about such things, especially when he felt himself in the public eye; but though he was irritated he remained polite and friendly. This only encouraged the unfortunate Luther to further unwelcome intimacies.

The next day they both telephoned me. "You know," said Himmler, "that man Luther really is a common, unpleasant sort of fellow—slimy and uncouth."

I tried to defend Luther as well as I could. I said that he had probably been overflattered by Himmler's attitude and had been tempted to open his heart to him. Eventually

I succeeded in persuading Himmler to forget the incident.

Then Luther's clipped speech, full of Berlin slang, came over the telephone: "I must say, my dear chap, your chief is a real sport—he's a man one can talk to. You know, last night I really got on well with him. My boss can lump it now, as far as I am concerned." He went on for some time, until in the end I suggested that I should call on him the next day so that we could have a talk.

When we met I gave him a good dressing down and warned him that Himmler was a man of the most complex and changeable disposition who needed time to reach difficult decisions. I insisted also that he should make no move against Ribbentrop without telling me, so that I should have a chance to discuss them fully with Himmler beforehand. Luther gave me a solemn promise that he would do this.

Then one day in January 1943, one of his assistants came to me in a state of great excitement. He told me that Luther had compiled a file against Ribbentrop which contained reports on his personal behavior, raised serious doubts about his sanity, and indicated that he was obviously not fit to carry on his duties as Foreign Minister. Confident of Himmler's support, and of mine, he had sent this report to various government departments in the hope of bringing about Ribbentrop's downfall. Those involved were waiting for Himmler to say the word "go" before taking any action. Luther therefore wanted me to induce Himmler to begin his attack without delay, and asked me to arrange for him to see Himmler immediately.

I had to think the situation over quickly—Luther seemed to have acted in defiance of our agreement. I was by no means certain whether Himmler had managed to re-establish and strengthen his position with Hitler sufficiently to be able to launch an all-out attack against Ribbentrop. On the whole, however, I welcomed Luther's move, though it would have been foolish to commit myself prematurely. Consequently, I made everything conditional upon Himmler's approval, which I said I would try to secure that very day.

This conversation took place during the afternoon. It was not until the evening that I telephoned Himmler, who told me to go to him at once. Unfortunately, I had first of all to discuss some urgent Secret Service matters with him, which took a great deal of time because of his lack of decision. I did not know that he had got to appear at an official gathering that evening; however, I did notice that while I was telling him what Luther had done, he became increasingly nervous and impatient, and presently SS Obergruppenfuehrer Wolff looked in to warn him to get ready.

I had to act swiftly, and as soon as Wolff had left the room I began to press Himmler to take immediate action in support of Luther. But he hesitated, twisting this way and that, then was just about to say "yes," when Obergruppenfuehrer Wolff appeared again, carrying Himmler's coat. Himmler rose, and in a few words explained the situation to him, then said, more by the way of a question, "That, I presume, will settle—"

At this dramatic moment Wolff, who had always held Luther in contempt, butted in. "But, Herr Reichsfuehrer, you cannot let SS Obergruppenfuehrer Joachim von Ribbentrop, one of the highest ranking members of our order, be kicked out by this scoundrel Luther. It would be a grave infringement of the rules of the Order. I'm certain you would never get Hitler's approval."

Suddenly all Himmler's old animosity against Luther was revived. I knew only too well that if Luther were dropped now, for reasons of SS etiquette, his fate would be sealed. It occurred to me therefore that it might be more prudent to give up for the moment and return to the matter when circumstances were more favorable. But it seemed as if Luther's destruction was preordained. A nervous restlessness had seized Himmler, and he muttered repeatedly, "Yes, yes, Woelffchen, you are right." I interrupted him: "Herr Reichsfuehrer—I must beg you not to reach a hasty decision in this matter. It is too complex and its effects are too far-reaching."

It was impossible to guess what was going on inside Himmler's mind at this moment; I imagine he was trying to gauge his present position with Hitler and decided what risks he could take. I felt the decision was going against me, but he left without making up his mind.

I was disappointed and at a loss what to do next. I wished that I could have had another talk with Himmler that night, but, knowing his fixed habits, I realized it would be unwise even to try. I turned over a thousand possibilities and still could find no way out. Then at midnight I was aroused from my brooding by a telephone call.

It was Mueller, who told me curtly that Himmler had decided to turn Luther's case over to him for investigation. He asked me to put myself at his disposal and give him information. He then told me to have Luther's assistant in my office the first thing in the morning and get a written statement from him about his conversation with me. This Mueller wanted to use as the principal part of his evidence. I hung up without saying good-by. It was a most unpleasant situation.

The next morning I telephoned Himmler. He could not have been more evasive and indefinite, but eventually he said, "Now, now, calm down. After all, no final decision against Luther has been reached yet. Whatever happens I will have time to think the matter over and I'll give you a chance to discuss it with me once more."

Luther's colleague was cross-examined by Mueller the next day, and then arrested. A succession of Foreign Office officials was then interrogated. Finally, Luther himself was arrested and put through a non-stop interrogation. All of them stood resolutely by their opinions. Ribbentrop was seriously incriminated by their testimonies, and if the country had been run by responsible leaders, they should have been enough for his dishonorable dismissal. But the machinery of the Third Reich worked in a different way; the protocol of the High Order of the SS stood above everything. Specially incriminating facts were removed from the testimony and disappeared into Himmler's desk. I was never clear whether Himmler did this in order to have a reserve of incriminating material should a need arise for it later on, or whether he did it to protect the good name of the SS.

After eight days Ribbentrop received a summary of the files and went at once to see Hitler. Of course, his was an extremely one-sided version of the incident. This affair, he told the Fuehrer, was nothing but an unpleasant attack by a subordinate official on the foreign policy which Hitler himself ordered. Ribbentrop demanded that Luther should be removed from office for insubordination and hanged for defeatism. But this was too much even for Hitler. He must have discussed the case with Himmler too; anyway, he finally ordered that Luther be dismissed and put in a concentration camp for the duration of the war.

When I discussed the matter with Himmler later on, I did not try to conceal my disappointment. I told him frankly that his handling of the affair had been most unfortunate. Himmler silently accepted this reproach. I demanded that he should not carry out the severe sentences which Ribbentrop wanted to impose upon Luther's colleagues. Himmler agreed, and no further punishments were dealt out, except to a few officials who were transferred to front-line duty with the Waffen SS. Hitler had expressly forbidden that I should visit Luther, but I used my influence with Mueller to secure preferential treatment for him. Later I heard that at the end of the war Luther refused to help in building a bridge for the Russians in the Eastern Sector of Berlin, claiming exemption as a concentration camp inmate, and that he had been shot on the spot by a Russian sergeant for refusing to obey orders.

While I should have liked to go ahead as quickly as possible with the plans laid down at Zhitomir, I realized that hasty action would be fatal. I could only employ such Secret Service contacts as I had built up over the past few years, and I did not wish to use the most important of these hastily, but to reserve them for the final negotiations. At the same time, I confess I was a little worried by the fact that I, the youngest member of Himmler's staff, had succeeded in securing such sweeping authority for myself. I had to overcome a feeling of insecurity. Was Himmler's promise honestly and seriously meant? I already suspected a strong element of indecision in his character, and I decided not to rush my fences.

I began carefully by establishing contact with the British Consul General in Zurich, who expressed his readiness to begin preliminary conversations with an authorized German representative. Later he sent word that he had in fact received authorization from Churchill to carry on tain assurances. Finally, he was even ready to come to Germany to pursue these talks at the appropriate Secret such unofficial exploratory conversations, subject to cer- Service level. He was well informed about me and my attitude.

After these preparations were completed I reported to Himmler on the first steps that I had taken under his authority. My object was to secure his agreement before venturing any further, but here I experienced my first disappointment. He discussed the affair with me for hours, and I soon began to notice that his views on the matter were becoming more and more involved and changeable. At first I did not understand why he was behaving in this manner, but then I realized he was scared by his own daring. It is easy to imagine my disgust and disappointment when, in his best schoolmaster's manner, he came out with the suggestion that perhaps it would be best to discuss the whole thing with Ribbentrop first of all.

I pointed out that fundamentally this would be against the general line of policy he had laid down and developed. It would be catastrophic if Ribbentrop agreed to the scheme, for the whole thing depended on his exclusion. Should he reject it—as was most likely—then we should merely have called his attention to our plans. I was at a loss to understand Himmler's motives in wanting to bring him in.

He replied to my argument impatiently, "I am tired of working against the Fuehrer—I want to work with him. That's my final decision, and you'll have to put up with it."

And so the whole matter was placed before Ribbentrop. As far as I could gather, neither of them in discussing it went beyond courteous and meaningless formalities— fencing with their visors closed—and neither of them divulged his real thoughts.

As I had feared, all this put Ribbentrop on his guard; he decided to discuss the affair with Hitler. Himmler watched this development apathetically, showing a cowardly lack of decision and doing nothing, while Ribbentrop, as they say, "cleaned up."

It was obvious that Hitler discussed this matter with Himmler, and later I received a note from Ribbentrop in which occurred a passage that I have never forgotten: "I forbid the political sector of the Secret Service to contact enemy nationals in this way. I regard this as defeatism, which, from now on, will be severely punished. On the other hand, if any Englishman should wish to converse with us, he must first hand us a declaration of surrender"— an echo of Hitler's own words on the subject.

When we next discussed the matter, Himmler was sullen and taciturn, possibly because of a guilty conscience. In an impassioned appeal I declared that things could not possibly go on like this; it indicated a complete misconception of the nature of a secret service. One expected such things from Ribbentrop, but I asked Himmler to show more understanding for my tasks, as well as for me personally, and for the scheme which he himself had approved.

He rambled on evasively, and finally said, "Well, you know, perhaps you did make a mistake after all, but I won't hold it against you. Perhaps it was unwise to contact the British directly. Maybe you should have used a neutral as a buffer."

Of course, this was only an attempt to save his face. But I grasped the opportunity at once and answered casually, "Very well, in the future I shall see to it that these things are handled through neutral channels." I wanted to try to save at least part of the foundations laid at Zhitomir.

Himmler agreed. His reaction was typical; he seemed relieved, freed from the trammels of his own conscience, and therefore generous. I exploited this at once, and said that in future I would continue to work along the lines which we had discussed, but would take all possible precautions. I was careful to add, however, that contact between members of my service and enemy nationals might still occur, since this could not possibly be avoided.

Again Himmler's reaction was true to form: "Well, I don't wish to know all those details—that's your responsibility."

It was then that I decided personally to take up certain secret and long-standing service connections with Switzerland, for no other purpose than to try to bring peace one step closer. I had a personal conversation with Brigadier Masson, then chief of the Swiss Secret Service, and this led to further talks. But the failure to remove Ribbentrop, Himmler's wavering, and the unconditional surrender policy of Casablanca, frustrated any real progress in the matter, despite continual efforts to keep these tenuous contacts in being.

After a short time Himmler succeeded in re-establishing his former position of power and confidence with Hitler, who at length believed his version of the Horia Sima affair. He attributed the whole thing to the fact that Himmler had been overworked because no chief of the Reich Security Center had yet been appointed to replace Heydrich. Thus the whole matter also affected the appointment of the new chief of the RSHA. My own choice

would have been almost anyone except the man whom
Hitler finally selected, Obergruppenfuehrer Ernst Kaltenbrunner. But Hitler was convinced that this countryman of
his—for Kaltenbrunner was an Austrian—had all the
necessary qualifications for the job, of which unconditional obedience and personal loyalty to the Fuehrer were not
the least important.

Incidentally, Himmler, in accordance with one of his
peculiar foibles, had been able to arrange for Dr. Kersten
to examine all the higher SS and police leaders who were
being considered for the post. Thus, even Kaltenbrunner,
having no idea as yet of his impending appointment, was
examined by the "fat fellow" one day. Afterward Kersten
said to me, "I've seldom had such a tough, callous ox to
examine as this fellow Kaltenbrunner. A block of wood
would be more sensitive. He's coarse, hard-bitten, probably only capable of thinking when he's drunk. Naturally
he'll be the right man for Hitler. I gave Himmler a report
on all this, but he still seems to think he's the right man."

Kaltenbrunner was a giant in stature, heavy in his movements—a real lumberjack. It was his square, heavy chin
which expressed the character of the man. The thick neck,
forming a straight line with the back of his head, increased the impression of rough-hewn coarseness. His
small, penetrating, brown eyes were unpleasant; they
looked at one fixedly, like the eyes of a viper seeking to
petrify its prey. When one expected Kaltenbrunner to say
something, his angular, wooden face would remain quite
inexpressive; then, after several seconds of oppressive
silence, he would bang the table and begin to speak. I
always had the feeling that I was looking at the hands of
an old gorilla. They were much too small, and the fingers
were brown and discolored, for Kaltenbrunner smoked up
to one hundred cigarettes a day.

My first proper contact with him was in January 1943,
and from the first moment he made me feel quite sick. He
had very bad teeth and some on them were missing, so
that he spoke very indistinctly—in any case I could understand his strong Austrian accent only with great difficulty—
Himmler also found this extremely unpleasant and eventually ordered him to go to the dentist.

I met Kaltenbrunner during the time of the Anschluss
in Vienna, but had formed no clear or lasting impression of
him then. I tried not to let our working relationship be

affected by my personal feelings, but after only a short time this proved impossible. Perhaps he felt an equal antipathy toward me; anyway there was soon a complete breach between us. Our personalities were too much opposed for us ever to be able to work together harmoniously.

There were various reasons for this, interesting in themselves, which I would analyze thus: first of all Kaltenbrunner was a doctrinaire and fanatical adherent of National Socialism and followed the principle of absolute obedience to Hitler, and also to Himmler. To him I was just a careerist who held his position purely because of professional ability; I had rendered no special service to the movement, and from my opinions and associations it appeared that I was politically unreliable. Kaltenbrunner's ambition had been to become Secretary of State for General Security in Austria. This was very quickly blocked, however, by Heydrich, who appointed him SS and police chief of Vienna. His personal influence was so effectively checked by Heydrich that he did not play any part in the hierarchy of the Third Reich until his appointment in 1943 as chief of the SD. Kaltenbrunner had great personal weaknesses; above all he drank, which in itself was enough to damn him in the eyes of Heydrich, who of course exploited his weakness in his usual effective way.

Kaltenbrunner knew all this, but his hatred of Heydrich induced him to commit one stupidity after another in his dealings with him. This finally brought about in him what one could almost call a "Heydrich complex." When he became chief of the organization which Heydrich had created, he sought to surround himself entirely with Austrians, until Himmler intervened. Whether through the influence of the chiefs of other departments, or through some of the members of my own department, Kaltenbrunner eventually transferred his "Heydrich complex" to me. I suddenly became the object of all the animosity he had previously entertained against him.

Of particular importance to him was the fact that he knew of my aim to separate the Secret Service from the RSHA. The significance of this was reinforced by the fact that, though he was chief of the RSHA, I was the only one of the departmental chiefs under him who had the privilege of direct access to Himmler, who had quite clearly indicated to Kaltenbrunner the nature of my excep-

tional status. On the other hand, Himmler gave Kaltenbrunner the right to take a personal interest in the Secret
Service abroad, and indeed encouraged him actively to
occupy himself with the needs of my department. My
having direct access to Himmler was the worst thorn in
Kaltenbrunner's flesh. My limited interest in nicotine and
alcohol was another thing which infuriated him. On several occasions he tried to force me to exceed my quota of
one or two glasses of wine.

The more desperate the situation became toward the
end of the war, the more Kaltenbrunner drank. I would
find him in his office at eleven o'clock in the morning,
having risen hardly more than half an hour earlier, his
small eyes dull and empty. With the joviality of a drunk-
ard he would reach under his desk, or bellow, "Orderly!"
and pour out a glass of champagne or brandy for me.
Then, when he became too obstreperous, I would take a
nip or two to pacify him and pour the rest onto the
carpet. Usually he did not notice this, but once when he
did, the veins in his face became so swollen with rage that
I thought he was about to have a stroke.

In the last years of the war I was forced to have lunch
with the departmental heads of the RSHA, which we all
had together on Himmler's orders. Kaltenbrunner presided,
and availed himself of the opportunity to attack me in the
most sadistic manner. To put up with this cost me dear. I
complained to Himmler that this half hour took more out
of me in nervous control than ten days' hard work.
Himmler was much concerned and tried to calm me by
telling me not to pay any attention, but, because of
Kaltenbrunner's relationship with Hitler, Himmler considered it important that I should not increase my reputation
for unsociability. Among the top leaders I had few friends
and many enemies, so there was nothing for me to do but
to put up with it. I am not exaggerating when I say that
because of such associations alone those terrible last years
of the war seemed a real torture to me.

32. OPERATION "CICERO"

A mysterious offer from Ankara—British secret documents photographed—"Pierre" interviewed—The truth of "Cicero's" claims questioned—A key to the British Ambassador's safe—"Cicero's" material—Turkey moves toward the Allied camp—Cessation of "Cicero's" activities—Speculation on his motives

ON THE morning of October 28, 1943, I had arrived at my office and was just going over the short-wave messages which had come in during the night, when I got a telephone call from Ribbentrop's right-hand man, Legationsrat H. Wagner. He asked if he could come to see me at once; it was an extremely urgent matter which could not be discussed on the telephone.

When he arrived he told me of a telegram which had just come from von Papen, and of a strange offer from a man who claimed to be the valet to the British Ambassador in Ankara, Sir Hugh Knatchbull-Hughessen. In return for the tremendous sum of twenty thousand pounds sterling, to be paid at once, he offered photographs of the most secret documents of the British Embassy. He would sell further photographs of such documents at a price of fifteen thousand pounds per roll of film. As this offer was a purely Secret Service matter, and a pretty risky one too, Ribbentrop wanted to have my opinion as to whether the offer should be accepted.

At first glance the whole affair seemed quite staggering. However, the information placed before us so far was of much too general a nature to permit a really considered decision. But in the course of my Secret Service work I had frequently faced equally risky decisions and had developed a certain intuitive feeling. The suggestion that payments be made upon the delivery of each set of copies seemed to offer a certain security, but it would be best for a quick inspection of the films to be made before handing over the

money. I was pretty sure this case would be handled in
Ankara by Moyzisch, and I knew him to be intelligent and
experienced.

After weighing up the considerations involved, I suggested that the offer should be accepted. The initial sum,
carried on the account of the Secret Service, should be
dispatched to Ankara at once by special courier. Ribbentrop agreed with me, and informed von Papen by telegram. The next day twenty thousand pounds sterling was
flown to Ankara by courier plane.

I waited in anxious suspense for the first report from
Moyzisch. It reached me three days later. He had established contact with the man, whom for the time being he
called "Pierre," and who had been introduced to him by
the envoy, Jenke, for whom "Pierre" had worked for a
short time as a valet several years earlier. As a diplomat,
Jenke had to take precautions against Secret Service tricks
from the enemy, and therefore did not wish to be involved
with "Pierre." For this reason, as soon as "Pierre"
presented himself at Jenke's house, Jenke asked for
Moyzisch to be sent for, and that night he met "Pierre" for
the first time.

"Pierre" was of medium height, pale, with deep-set dark
eyes and an energetic chin. He said very little, but impressed Moyzisch as being a ruthless and very able man;
his answers to all Moyzisch's questions were definite and
precise. After a rather dramatic conversation with this
strange character, Moyzisch found himself in a difficult
situation. As a Secret Service agent he was, of course,
tremendously tempted to accept. On the other hand, the
sum demanded was extremely high and the business itself
very risky. Furthermore, Moyzisch did not have enough
foreign currency at his disposal.

To complicate matters, "Pierre" set a time limit of
three days for Moyzisch's decision and indicated with an
unequivocal gesture toward the Soviet Embassy that he
had other customers lined up. Moyzisch decided to confide
in von Papen and get a decision as quickly as possible
from the Foreign Office, also, if it were to be needed, the
money with which to pay "Pierre."

When Moyzisch received the first films from "Pierre" he
was able to develop them and give them a brief glance
before handing over the money. The contents of the first
two films were breath-taking and were at once radioed to

Ribbentrop by von Papen. After receipt of the first reports, I was able to look at the copies of the photographs themselves. I could see that we had here highly secret correspondence between the British Embassy in Ankara and the Foreign Office in London. There were also private notes in the Ambassador's own hand, dealing with developments between Britain and Turkey, and Britian and Russia. Of special importance was a complete list of the materials shipped from the United States to the U.S.S.R. under Lease-Lend during the years 1942 and 1943; and there was a provisional report from the Foreign Office on the results of the Conference of Foreign Ministers (Cordell Hull, Eden, and Molotov) held in Moscow in October 1943.

The contents so impressed me that at first I devoted myself entirely to the study of the documents and almost forgot to initiate those measures which must be carried out by the chief of a secret service in such cases. However, I then ordered:

1. The immediate presentation of the reports to Hitler through Himmler.
2. General Thiele (chief of the Wireless Security and Decoding Section of the Wehrmacht Supreme Command) to visit me at once to receive the material, which would enable him to start work on deciphering the British diplomatic code. (The four greatest decoding experts in Germany, two professors of mathematics among them, worked on this material for weeks until finally they were able to "crack" a part of the code. It was a tremendous achievement. Especially revealing were a number of handwritten notes on the margins of the documents, technical data on code messages from London to Ankara. Such things were of the greatest value to our experts.)
3. The experts concerned to compile a list of questions, which, when answered by me, would substantiate the reliability of the material for Hitler. Of course, this was of the greatest importance, for on it would depend whether the material could be used for decisions on policy.
4. The Undersecretary of State, Steengracht, to be informed of the measures I had taken, and that my assistant, Moyzisch, had taken the matter in hand. (As the sums involved were quite considerable I asked him on whose budget they should be carried. Steengracht replied that it would be better if I handled the whole

thing, but if it proved too great a burden on my funds the Foreign Office would participate financially.)

A wireless message that reached me from Istanbul said that Moyzisch had been ordered to go to Berlin to make a personal report to Ribbentrop. I was very annoyed that I had not been consulted, and at once arranged for Moyzisch to speak to me before seeing Ribbentrop. I was not going to give him the opportunity to intervene in the case of "Cicero"—this was the name by which Papen called "Pierre" because his documents spoke so eloquently!

Meanwhile, I met Kaltenbrunner for dinner and during the course of our conversation I complained about Ribbentrop's intervention in the case. While we were talking I suddenly had the idea of using Kaltenbrunner as a spearhead for my plans against Ribbentrop, and as soon as I disclosed the fact that Himmler was backing my scheme for his removal Kaltenbrunner showed great interest. To increase his enthusiasm, I pointed out how different Germany's position would be if only Seyss-Inquart or Dr. Neubacher—two fellow-countrymen of Kaltenbrunner's—were Foreign Minister. Finally I played my trump card and, under the seal of complete secrecy, disclosed to him Dr. de Crinis' opinion that since Ribbentrop's kidney operation a deterioration of his mental faculties had set in. I thus succeeded for once in gaining Kaltenbrunner as an ally, in spite of his personal antagonism toward me and his opposition to all my plans.

I had my first full discussion with Moyzisch the day after he saw Ribbentrop, and we sought to analyze "Cicero's" possible motives. At this time, nothing final could be said about the validity of the photographs, but both Moyzisch and I agreed that the tremendous expenditure had been justified; for even if the material should later prove to have been a deception by the enemy's secret service, such knowledge would have considerable value in itself, for it is most important to know by what means your enemy tries to mislead you. But, as I remarked to Moyzisch at the time, I believed the material to be genuine. It corresponded completely to the general picture of the political situation as I saw it. However, I would devote my attention and energy not only to its evaluation—the second phase of intelligence work—but especially to the third phase, the utilization of the information. Normally a secret service should not have to concern itself with this at all; its work should be completed with the first two phases, but the seriousness of Germany's position required that most of my skill should be devoted to the use made of the material. I told Moyzisch that I still hoped to be able to carry through the peace plans which I had discussed with von Papen, though the difficulties and the resistance to them were overwhelming.

I instructed Moyzisch that all rolls of film brought to him by "Cicero" should be sent on to Berlin at once, so that our technicians could make the required number of copies for distribution to the interested authorities. If he needed technical assistance, we could use the twice-weekly courier planes. A technician, with all the necessary equipment for a modern photographic laboratory, was to be sent to Ankara at once under diplomatic immunity.

Moyzisch and I then discussed some of the more curious personal aspects of "Cicero." "Cicero" had claimed that his father had been living in Constantinople at the time of the First World War, had become involved in an unpleasant quarrel over "Cicero's" sister, and had been shot. In a later account that he gave, he said his father had been shot by an Englishman while hunting in Albania. It was this that made him hate the English and thus motivated his actions. The discrepancy between these two stories gave rise to some doubts about "Cicero's" truthfulness, but the documents spoke for themselves. He also claimed not to speak a word of English, although later this was found to be completely untrue. I considered all this of incidental importance, but it did raise considerable difficulties in my proving to Hitler and Himmler the validity of "Cicero's" material.

Toward the end of December further doubts were thrown upon his veracity, and therefore upon the validity of the documents, for two of his fingers appeared on one of the photographs. "Cicero" always maintained that he worked quite alone and took the photographs without any assistance, having trained himself for two years in the photography of documents. His version of how he worked was as follows: as the Ambassador's valet, he attended him when he retired to bed. The Ambassador usually took sleeping pills, and after he had fallen asleep, "Cicero" would remain in the room in order to clean his master's

suit. On these occasions he was able to take the key, open
the safe, and then, using a strong light and the Leica we
had given him, take the photographs. Within half an hour
all the documents would be back in their proper place,
and his master's trousers cleaned and pressed. But now
suddenly "Cicero's" own fingers appeared on the photographs!

I consulted the photographic experts and technicians of
my department. By trying to reconstruct "Cicero's" actions, we came to the conclusion that it was quite impossible for him to have held the document and operated the
camera at the same time. My experts therefore came to
the conclusion that the man was not working alone after
all.

This merely proved "Cicero's" untruthfulness, but did
not necessarily mean that the material was false. In the
meantime, by using the documents we had been able to
decipher part of the British diplomatic code. One of the
first important pieces of information we found in
"Cicero's" material was that the planned invasion of
France was to carry the code name "Operation Overlord."
After the first appearance of these words in the document,
I immediately conferred with General Thiele. He at once
started operations that would enable us to determine
where and when the code word "Overlord" appeared in
the enemy's short-wave communications.

My experts had suggested that "Cicero" might get an
impression of the key of the safe on a specially prepared
wax which we could send him. The materials were thereupon dispatched to him, with instructions on how to use
them, and a small specially made box in which the wax
impression could be returned to Berlin. Within a remarkably short time the impression of the key was sent to us,
and our locksmith went to work. Three days later a key to
the safe of the British Ambassador in Ankara lay before
me on my desk. It was a masterpiece of German work-
manship.

"Cicero" was overjoyed when he received it. He said
that it functioned better than the original key, and now he
was able to do his work in much greater safety when the
Ambassador was absent.

There is one more incident about Moyzisch I would like
to relate. It was during the trying period of my imprisonment after the collapse of Germany. An English officer

was driving me from Richmond, near London, where I was interned for an interrogation by a special Anglo-American commission on codes and deciphering. On the way, the Englishman asked me, "What did you really think of Herr Moyzisch?" I did not wish to answer the question and shrugged my shoulders. Whereupon he continued, "He was very capable, wasn't he?" Again I replied with the same non-committal gesture. The English officer said, "You know, Moyzisch has told us that he's really Jewish, and that you forced him to join the SS and work for you at pistol point." For the first time since I was interned I laughed. Moyzisch and I had always worked on the very friendliest of terms.

Apart from the drafts of code telegrams made by Sir Hugh Knatchbull-Hughessen on the relations between Turkey and Britain, the material furnished by "Cicero" contained:

1. A report on the conference at Cairo in November 1943, between Roosevelt, Churchill, and Chiang Kai-shek. The most important result of this conference was Roosevelt's promise to return Manchuria to China after the defeat of the Japanese. It was therefore astonishing when, at the end of February 1945, a Polish woman agent working for our Secret Service reported a secret agreement between America and Russia. In this Roosevelt, without having consulted Chiang Kai-shek, agreed to turn over the Trans-Manchurian railway and the naval harbors of Port Arthur and Dairen to the Russian sphere of influence—all this in order to secure from the Russians a promise that they would declare war on Japan three months later. It was difficult to convince our leaders that this change of attitude on the part of the United States had really taken place.

2. Reports on the conference at Teheran (November 28 to December 2, 1943) between Roosevelt, Churchill, and Stalin, and the discussions of the Allied Military Commanders that took place there. On the basis of these reports one could see clearly that while differences, both military and political, existed between the Allies, on the whole these had been resolved at this conference. Our evaluation established with a certainty of 60 per cent that Churchill had not been able to maintain his plan for a second front through an invasion of the Balkans. Obviously Roosevelt's military advisers played a decisive part in this question. The political situation in the Balkans may have seemed

too complex and uncertain; also such strategy would favor British interests in southeastern Europe, and Roosevelt was still continually afraid of a possible Russo-German understanding.

The documents photographed by "Cicero" showed clearly that a special status was provided for Turkey. There were, unfortunately, no indications about Greece. However, it was quite evident that, according to the agreement reached at Teheran, Poland, Hungary, Rumania, and Yugoslavia would come under the "protection" of the Soviet armies. Stalin even demanded that Poland should become Russian territory as far as the Curzon Line and should receive parts of eastern Germany in compensation. With defeat growing ever more imminent, Germany's ultimate fate could clearly be foreseen.

The study of these documents was quite breath-taking. Our evaluating commentaries were simple and straightforward, and there was no mistaking their meaning. Only Ribbentrop tried to read between the lines, and saw there, as always, continuing tension between Russia and the Western Allies—and, of course, found a ready audience in his supreme master.

Hitler reacted as I had expected. He declared that now more than ever before it was necessary to gather all our forces for total war, for total destruction of the enemy by means of ruthless expenditure of all physical resources.

"Cicero's" reports obviously put Himmler into a state of uncertainty. Shortly before Christmas 1943, he asked me to go to see him. I was reporting on various matters when suddenly he interrupted me: "Schellenberg, I realize now that something has to happen. Only everything is so terribly difficult—" I could hardly believe my ears when he went on to say, "For God's sake don't let your contact with Hewitt[1] be broken off. Could you not let him be told that I am ready to have a conversation with him?"

From that point on the blows fell in rapid succession. "Cicero's" documents showed clearly that the continued neutrality of Turkey would be short-lived. Step by step the Turks were going over into the Allied camp. The Turkish diplomats proceeded carefully and according to plan—

---

[1] Mr. Abram Stevens Hewitt, President Roosevelt's special representative in Stockholm.

almost exactly as Knatchbull-Hughessen had described in his dispatches to the Foreign Office. First, there was the continuation of neutrality, but with the concentration of Turkish forces in Thrace to tie down German divisions in Bulgaria. Meanwhile, there were increasing shipments of Allied war material to Turkey, and finally, more and more consultations between the Turkish and Allied General Staffs. According to the documents, this process of wooing the Turks over was to be completed by May 15, 1944, and was in some way connected with "Operation Overlord." Therefore, from that date on we had to count on an all-out effort from the West.

Had Churchill been able to carry through his plan for an invasion of the Balkans at the end of 1943, then, according to my calculations at the time, the war would have been over in the spring of 1944. The Balkans were like an overripe plum, ready to fall at the slightest touch, and this would have torn open the German southeastern flank. Instead, the Western Allies inaugurated the bombing by their strategic air arm of important road and railway junctions and oil installations. The first victim, according to the schedule photographed by "Cicero," was to be Sofia on January 15, 1944. The city was thus forewarned in ample time, though there was nothing much we could do to counter the attack.

About February or March 1944, "Cicero" stopped his activities, and in April Turkey broke off relations with Germany and went over to the camp of the Western Allies.

From the beginning I was convinced that "Cicero" had worked with one or more accomplices. I never discovered his motives—whether greed, hatred, or just love of adventure—but often during my many journeys my thoughts would turn again to his strange case. Again and again I wondered whether perhaps there lay behind "Cicero" the shadow of the Turkish Secret Service. The more I thought about this, the more likely it seemed to me that through his material Turkey had tried to warn Germany and prevent her from continuing on her path to total destruction. At the same time, she would be warning us of the almost inevitable transference of her loyalty to the camp of the Western Allies, and would thus be safeguarding herself against the oppressive menace of Russia.

33. THE DOWNFALL OF ADMIRAL CANARIS

*A blunder by the Abwehr—Heydrich orders a surveillance
of some Abwehr personnel—I sound Canaris on a leakage
of information—A Catholic intrigue—Friction between
Canaris and Heydrich—Administrative defects in the
Abwehr—Canaris' dossier goes to Himmler—His campaign against Canaris—The Admiral's arrest ordered—He
declines an opportunity for suicide—Our last meeting*

BY THE end of February 1942 the posi-
tion of Admiral Canaris was no longer secure. His friends
and subordinates may not have been aware of it, but I
knew that Hitler was seriously considering getting rid of
him. His downfall was precipitated by an incident that assumed considerable importance in the battle of wits between technicians that was joined throughout the war.

Since the middle of 1941 we had put into operation a
new device for defense against enemy aircraft. It had been
developed with great skill by the technical department of
the Luftwaffe and was being employed so extensively that
our anti-aircraft defenses were able to determine exactly
the position and distance of all approaching enemy aircraft. This device, together with our highly developed
automatic aiming devices, enabled us to inflict heavy casu-
alties on the enemy, as all the main airlanes of northern
and western Europe were covered by it.

One of the most important installations from which it
was operated was at Cap d'Antifer, near Le Havre. At
midnight on February 27, 1942, a British Commando unit
made a surprise raid on the installation. They succeeded in
removing important parts of it and took photographs of
other parts that could not be removed. After massacring
the German garrison, they were able to withdraw with
their booty. It can well be imagined that this daring and
successful stratagem aroused no great enthusiasm in Hitler's headquarters. He was in a blind fury, and this time
his anger was justified, for an investigation of the incident
showed serious shortcomings in the army's defensive mea-

sures and more especially in the camouflaging and security protection of the installation.

After brooding over this for several days, Hitler sent for Himmler and demanded a full report on the technical progress of the Western Powers with regard to radio detection. He complained bitterly about Canaris, who had so far given him no real information on this subject.

The technical research department of the Luftwaffe compiled a report based on their own researches and on the analysis of captured equipment. However, this was not what Hitler wanted to see. He demanded that the secret intelligence material which Canaris' organization had collected on this subject be placed before him. As usual, Canaris failed to provide the required information. This finished him with Hitler, and from that moment his fate was sealed.

This was the opportunity for Himmler and Heydrich to make a decisive attack on Canaris, and I was asked by Heydrich whether my AMT VI would be able to provide better ammunition than the Abwehr—the Military Intelligence Department run by Canaris. I said that at the moment I was not in a position to take on any additional responsibilities. This refusal must have contributed to their decision not to follow up their advantage against Canaris for the time being.

Later on, when I discussed the matter with Himmler, he admitted that my reluctance to take over the responsibility had made no difference; it would in any case have been easy to remove Canaris, but the Fuehrer was not prepared to assign the direction and organization of a unified intelligence service to Himmler.

The fact that I could not help liking the Admiral made things more difficult for me. Canaris was a highly intelligent and sensitive man with many likable qualities. He loved his dogs and his horse almost more than any other living creatures. He often said to me, "Schellenberg, always remember the goodness of animals. You see, my dachshund is discreet and will never betray me—I cannot say that of any human being."

He was very good company on the many trips we made together, and his attitude toward me was always kind and paternal. Whether in Spain, Portugal, Hungary, Poland, Finland, or Scandinavia, Canaris always had a fund of knowledge about the peculiarities of the countries, and especially about their cooking and their wines. In the south he always made sure—in spite of the great heat— that I wore a woolen stomacher! And he would ply me with all sorts of medicaments and with pills which he himself constantly took.

He often asked me to attend the various meetings of his organization, and I was thus able to acquaint myself with the weaknesses of the Military Intelligence Service. In this huge overinflated organization, Canaris' methods were far too humane. His subordinates were able to twist him around their little fingers, and when he was eventually forced to take strong measures, he would always try to make up for his severity afterward.

In many ways he was of an almost mystical turn of mind. Though he was a Protestant, he was a great admirer of the Roman Catholic Church, of its organization, and of the strength of its faith. He was greatly influenced by Italy and the Vatican and many of his conspiratorial activities could be traced back to this influence.

His first attempts at peace negotiations dated back to 1939 and were centered on the Vatican. It was for this reason that Heydrich gave the "file Canaris"—dealing with the circle round the Admiral and General Oster, of the Supreme Military Command—the code name *Schwarze Kapelle* (from the Black Chapel in Rome). Heydrich opened this file on Canaris to be able to bring about his downfall at any given moment.

During the last days of May 1940 I became deeply involved in these intrigues, in which, of course, Canaris featured prominently. I was working in my office one evening when Heydrich telephoned me and told me in his high, nasal voice to come to his office. Mueller had also been summoned, and when he and I entered the room, Heydrich motioned us to sit down without saying a word. For almost a minute we sat round the table in silence. Mueller watched the smoke of his cigar thoughtfully and drummed nervously with his fingers. I waited for what was coming.

Heydrich opened the conversation by turning to Mueller and asking, "What about the investigation of those Abwehr men in Munich—Josef Mueller, von Dohnanyi,[1]

---

[1] Hans von Dohnanyi, a judge, was a member of the Oster-Canaris group and was executed in April 1945.

and the others? Isn't it pretty clear that this is the circle which started the peace feelers via the Vatican?" (Later it turned out that through the mediation of the Jesuit Father, Dr. Leiber, in the Vatican, the Pope had attempted to sponsor a peace offer in 1939 which involved a government without Hitler. The British Minister to the Holy See, Sir D'Arcy Osborne, had assured the Pope verbally that His Majesty's government would be in agreement, provided that there was a change of regime in Germany and that no attacks would be launched in the west. He had implied that Austria and the Sudeten territories could remain within the Reich, subject to the agreement of the French government.)

Then Heydrich turned to me. "Tell me, Schellenberg, I seem to remember that this Josef Mueller once had something to do with your service—I believe, in connection with Dr. Knochen. Is that right?"

Not for the first time I marveled at Heydrich's fantastic memory. Dr. Knochen, an SS Sturmbannfuehrer, had reported to me that a man named Josef Mueller had direct access to the highest levels of the Papal hierarchy. According to Knochen, this Josef Mueller was a very clever man and, although one could not quite trust him, his reports were not without interest. I now explained this to Heydrich, who nodded thoughtfully. Then, turning to Mueller, he said, "See to it that this whole circle is closely watched."

He then went on to another matter. "The Fuehrer and the Reichsfuehrer have asked me to investigate one of the most important cases of treason in the whole history of Germany. Some time ago two wireless messages that were sent by the Belgian Minister at the Vatican to his own government were intercepted. In them he gave the exact date and time of our western offensive thirty-six hours before it was officially issued by the Fuehrer. And this information was also passed on to the Dutch government. The Fuehrer's enraged about this. It really is a shocking state of affairs and he's demanding that at all costs the traitors have got to be found. Now this is the point: he's also assigned Canaris to the investigation—about the worst thing he could have done—that really is making the goat your gardener; because if one thing is certain, it is that Canaris' circle will have to be included in *our* investigations. I've already spoken to him on the telephone—and of course I've given him an entirely different line to work on."

Mueller, who had not spoken a word up to this point, said in a dry voice, "Of course Canaris is mixed up in the affair. I suggest that Schellenberg takes over the whole matter and keeps us informed. He's on very good terms with Canaris, so the Admiral will be less suspicious of him than of anyone else. And I don't doubt Schellenberg will deal with the matter with his usual tact and skill." This last remark was, of course, intended sarcastically.

Heydrich looked Mueller up and down for a moment, then turned to me and said, "All right. The best thing would be, Schellenberg, if you would contact Canaris and have a talk with him." With that our meeting ended.

The next day I visited Canaris. As usual we talked about all sorts of things, the weather, riding, and so on—but not about the matter which we both knew had to be discussed. Only when I was about to say good-by did Canaris broach the subject. "Did Heydrich speak to you about this incredible thing, the give-away of our offensive?" "He did," I said, "and I think this might be a good opportunity for us to discuss it."

Canaris then gave me an account of the circumstances, as he knew them, but mentioned not a word about Rome, the Ambassador, the Vatican, or the wireless messages. According to his version of the story, on the evening before the offensive began, a German Embassy official at some function at the Dutch Embassy in Brussels had noticed that the Dutch Ambassador's wife had had a telephone call which had obviously excited her considerably, and immediately afterward she had left the Embassy.

After the capture of Brussels, a note had been found written by a member of the Belgian Foreign Office, which contained a message from the Dutch Ambassador in Berlin giving warning of Germany's offensive. When I discussed this with Heydrich I pointed out that Canaris' version of the story completely ignored the leads to Rome.

In spite of our joint efforts, neither Canaris nor I succeeded in tracing the culprit. Canaris placed Colonel Rohleder, the head of the Foreign Department of the Army Counter-Espionage, in charge of the investigation. He was a most able officer and I discussed the matter with him several times, but it was not until 1944 that any light was thrown on the affair.

After the arrest of Canaris in that year, Rohleder was questioned about the results of his investigation of this case. He confessed that in 1940 he had submitted a report to Canaris, Dohnanyi, and General Oster, in which it was stated quite clearly that the Belgian Ambassador in Rome had received his information from a Jewish journalist named Stern. This man was a Roman Catholic convert who had established connections with Josef Mueller, an Oberleutnant in the Abwehr post in Munich. Stern had testified that Mueller had been his informant. Mueller, however, maintained that this accusation was a malicious slander originating from a certain Benedictine Father who was jealous of his (Mueller's) close relations with the Jesuit Father, Dr. Leiber. In short, it was simply an intrigue calculated to disrupt Mueller's influential connections.

Apparently Canaris believed Mueller and forbade the journalist Stern to engage in any further activities. Nevertheless, Rohleder emphasized in his report to Canaris that Mueller was by no means above suspicion. Canaris, however, ordered Rohleder to say nothing about the matter. A large sum of money was placed at Stern's disposal and he was transferred from Rome to Sweden. By these moves Canaris successfully managed to cover up for Josef Mueller.

As well as on visits between our families, and on our morning rides, Canaris and I used to meet in Heydrich's house, and I was usually present at the talks between him and Canaris. Indeed, they not only tolerated me but seemed glad of my presence. If ever I failed to attend of my own accord, one or the other of them would be sure to call me in. It was curious to see how they would both ply me with questions afterward, though I was far younger than either of them. "What should I have understood by that?" "What do you think was behind this?" "Did I say the right thing?" "Was I too aggressive?" I was a sort of go-between—a *postillion d'amour* for them, whom they both trusted.

Heydrich always had the greatest respect for Canaris, who in 1923 had been in command of the cruiser *Berlin* which had served primarily as a training ship for naval cadets, of whom Heydrich had been one. Though he liked to assert his superiority over his former chief, he always maintained an outward respect for him; and for a man like Heydrich this meant a great deal.

Shortly before his death, Heydrich spoke to me about the continual differences and frictions between him and Canaris. He was no longer willing to give in to Canaris, whatever might be the outcome. "You should not let yourself be lulled to sleep by him," Heydrich warned me. He suggested that I should assert myself more ruthlessly. "Seeing the two of you together, one would take you for bosom friends. You won't get anywhere by handling him with kid gloves." Canaris was fatalistic, said Heydrich, and only firmness would be effective with him. "And you have to be even tougher with his followers—a bunch of talkative highbrows; they interpret courtesy as a sign of weakness."

He suggested that I should think all this over and for the time being should try—and this was an order—to act as a mediator between him and Canaris. But now Canaris would have to come to the mountain—he would have to come to Heydrich.

Soon after this I again went riding with Canaris; in fact, we rode together several times and discussed service problems. But he realized that the chief purpose of these rides was to preserve the last links between him and Heydrich, for their relationship was now on the verge of a complete and final break.

One morning I had to have it out with him on a rather unpleasant subject. On at least six occasions agents of his Abwehr had been arrested by the authorities of neutral countries and had claimed to be members of the Political Secret Service. Two of them had said that they were counter-espionage agents of the Gestapo, but, checking with Mueller, I had found that they were completely unknown to his department.

Canaris' response to this was extremely curious: he suggested that each of us should give orders to our own people that in case of arrest they should claim to belong to the other service, that my agents should say they were working for the Abwehr, and his should claim to be working for me. He thought that would cause great confusion in the enemy counter-espionage services, which in any case were incapable of understanding our complicated departmental relationships.

I noticed now for the first time signs of an inner weariness in Canaris. He was worn out by the continual internecine conflict. Heydrich's ice-cold tactics of the last months were beginning to show their effect. He felt insecure and restless, and, or so I thought, had something like a physical fear of Heydrich. And his pessimism about the war situation was increasing. Repeatedly he said to me, "Haven't we said again and again that things in Russia would not go the way the Fuehrer and his advisers imagine? But they won't even listen to the truth any longer. I know I'm much older than you, but please let us stick together. If those at the top notice that we both hold the same opinions, perhaps they'll take some notice. I insist on returning to a workable relationship with Heydrich, though. Things can't go on this way much longer."

At last the discussion between Heydrich and Canaris, which they had both asked me to arrange, took place. Canaris gave in all along the line and a joint meeting in Prague of the two intelligence services was set for May 1942. A working agreement, the so-called "ten commandments," in their newly formulated version, was to be proclaimed.

After this discussion Canaris admitted that Heydrich's intrigues had greatly upset him. Though a solution had been found for the moment, he could not rid himself, he said in a resigned voice, of the feeling that Heydrich would attack again. The agreement offered no more than breathing space. I had the feeling that Canaris was right. I am convinced that had Heydrich remained alive, Canaris would have had to leave the stage in 1942. Not so much, I believe, because of his conspiratorial activities—for reasons best known to himself, Heydrich always kept these carefully in the background—but because of the failure of the Military Intelligence Service, the Abwehr.

Canaris felt all this, but with an almost Oriental fatalism made no attempt to resist. He believed in his preordained fate and let himself and his organization drift with the stream. Inflated with false hopes, he neglected his own duties and traveled restlessly from one country to another and from one sector of the front to another. From time to time he made real attempts at a far-reaching conspiracy, but drew back at the decisive moment. He was bedeviled by his anxiety about the outcome of the war and the muddle of his own plans.

For me the situation was difficult both from a human standpoint and from that of my work. I took no account of the struggle for power or the tactics of the two irreconcilable opponents, but quite soberly regarded the apparent facts, and here Canaris came off very badly. He was overinflating his organization, indiscriminately enrolling serious workers and dubious riffraff; reforms were feebly attempted and then allowed to peter out. To me his whole organization was a nightmarish oppression, for how was the general situation to develop if no efficient work was done in this important sector of military intelligence? How were we to reach a position from which to influence the leaders and, if need be, change the direction of their policy?

This was 1942, which represented for me the climax, as in the classical structure of a drama. (The year 1943 was the penultimate pause, while 1944 and 1945 were the tragic conclusion.) I explained these lines of thought frankly to my colleagues in innumerable conversations in order to drive them to the greatest possible effort. I wanted them to realize clearly that otherwise we would not achieve the aims set for our work. Our information and data had to be so complete and so well founded that we would be able to convince the leaders of the necessity of an alternative solution—a compromise peace.

Later, in 1943, Canaris had become directly suspect in a matter of serious sabotage in Italy. It was at the time when General Badoglio began to establish contact with the Western Allies with a view to ending the war for his country. General Amé, Head of the Italian Secret Service, tried every possible maneuver, together with Canaris, to conceal Italy's change of front from the German leaders. All the reports received by our Military and Political Intelligence Services pointed clearly to the imminence of such a change. Yet in spite of this, Canaris' reports to his immediate superior, Field Marshal Keitel, were reassuring. Hitler's anxiety and suspicion had been aroused, however, by my reports. But as the only possible preventative measure would have to be of a military nature, the army had the last word. At Keitel's suggestion Canaris was sent to discuss the situation with General Amé—a suggestion which was probably Canaris' own in the first place. For he and Amé were both agreed that Italy's exit from the war should proceed undisturbed by any German measures. This agreement, of course, remained a secret between the two, while officially Amé's reassurances were brought back to Keitel: Long live the Axis—Italy is the most faithful of allies.

Six days later I was able to present Himmler with a dossier which included absolute proof of Canaris' treachery. Nevertheless, Himmler refrained from passing the dossier on to Hitler. The facts of the case came to light in the following manner. One of Canaris' assistants, Colonel Helfferich, was on the staff of the German Military Attaché in Rome, General von Rintelen. The Colonel employed two Italian chauffeurs who were both homosexuals and both in Amé's service. I pointed out the dangers of this arrangement to Canaris, but Helfferich was of such high standing that he pooh-poohed my warning. "Ach, Schellenberg, after one's been in our profession a while one begins to see pink elephants everywhere."

One of these chauffeurs was unwittingly the most valuable source of information for my Political Secret Service, for he repeated all Amé's assignments and conversations to a friend who was in our pay. Thus we were able to piece together a very clear picture of the planned coup, and of how far Canaris was involved in the affair.

I remember adding the following sentence to the dossier which I gave to Himmler: "It would have been better for Admiral Canaris to have concerned himself with his own tasks in Italy, rather than carry on such sessions with Amé."

During the years 1941-42 the greater part of the work of my organization was concerned with silencing treacherous informers in Italy. Until the capitulation of the Afrika Corps in May 1943, there was not a single German tanker, troopship, or aerial transport whose position was not reported to the Western Allies. This is an established fact. It certainly would have been more in the interests of the German soldiers if the Abwehr had honestly carried out their tasks of counter-espionage.

Himmler always held Canaris up to me as a wise and experienced chief of Secret Intelligence from whom I could learn much. His faults and his opposition to the regime were another chapter, with which I need not concern myself. When I presented my reports about his various betrayals, Himmler would nervously tap his thumbnail against his teeth and say, "Leave the dossier here with me. I will bring it to Hitler's attention when the right opportunity arises." Again and again I raised these matters because of their importance to Germany's war effort, but Himmler obviously did not wish to be burdened with the responsibility. Like Heydrich, he seemed to have some inhibitions with regard to the Admiral. I am certain that at some time or other Canaris must have got to know something incriminating against Himmler, for otherwise there is no possible explanation of Himmler's reaction to the material which I placed before him.

During the following years Canaris' work grew continually worse. In spite of his intelligence, his behavior aroused suspicion and many people became convinced that he was involved in treasonable activities. Himmler had decided to employ a sort of snowball tactic against him. He never spontaneously expressed his opinion on Canaris to Hitler, but always waited until the problem of Canaris was raised by Hitler himself. Meanwhile, he saw to it that other leaders, both political and of the Wehrmacht, who for one reason or another were opposed to the Admiral, continually kept the subject of Canaris in the limelight. Himmler regularly furnished this anti-Canaris clique with new material against him, and so added continually to the stiffening opposition.

In the middle of 1943 Canaris' staunch supporter, Keitel, tried to come to his aid by arranging a game of musical chairs in Canaris' departments. He told Hitler that he had taken these steps as chief of the OKW. A fresh wind was to blow in Canaris' service and new heads were appointed to all departments. But this last attempt was in vain because by 1944 Canaris' personal and professional failings had so incriminated him in Hitler's eyes that he had been relieved of his post. The official reason was simply that the conduct of the war now demanded the creation of a unified German Intelligence Service.

The inevitable downfall of Canaris came on a Sunday afternoon at the beginning of August 1944. I was working in a Military Secret Service office with several others, when I received a telephone call from SS Gruppenfuehrer Mueller. He and his chief, Kaltenbrunner, had been assigned to carry out the investigation into the plot of July 20. (Both of them had their suspicions about me and tried to incriminate me with all their cunning.) In a sharp voice Mueller ordered me to drive to Canaris' home and inform him that he was under arrest—this was an official order

from Kaltenbrunner. I was to take Canaris to Fuerstenberg in Mecklenburg, and not to return with him to Berlin
until everything had been cleared up.

I said that I was not an executive officer and would not
dream of carrying out such an assignment, which was
most unwelcome to me. "Furthermore," I said, "I shall
telephone Himmler at once. This is an imposition."

"You know," said Mueller, "that Kaltenbrunner has
been put in charge of the investigation of July 20—not
Himmler! If you refuse to comply with the order, which I
herewith repeat, you will have to suffer the consequences."

I realized at once what their game was. If I refused to
obey they would have an excellent excuse for proceeding
against me. Mueller and Kaltenbrunner, in the abysmal
hatred which they bore me, had already tried in 1943 to
denounce me as a British agent in connection with the
affair of the lawyer, Dr. Langbehn. Therefore I had to be
on my guard. Without another word to Mueller I hung
up. After considering what to do, I finally decided to
comply. I also thought that in this difficult situation I
might be able to be of some help to Canaris. I told SS
Hauptsturmfuehrer Baron von Voelkersam about the situation and ordered him to accompany me. The Baron had
distinguished himself in airborne operations in Belgium in
1940 and in the Caucasus in 1943, and he had also served
under Canaris.

I went to Canaris' house in Berlin-Schlachtensee and he
himself opened the door. In the living room were Baron
Kaulbars and a relation of the Admiral's, Erwin Del-
brueck. Canaris asked them both to leave. Baron von
Voelkersam had been discreet enough to wait in the hall,
so we were alone. Canaris was very calm. His first words
to me were, "Somehow I felt that it would be you. Please
tell me first of all, have they found anything in writing
from that fool Colonel Hansen?" (This officer had been
involved in the affair of July 20.)

Truthfully I answered, "Yes; a notebook in which there
was among other things a list of those who were to be
killed. But there was nothing about you or participation
on your part."

"Those dolts on the General Staff cannot live without
their scribblings," Canaris replied.

I explained the situation to him and told him what my

assignment was. "It's too bad," he said, "that we have to say good-by in this way. But"—and here he made an effort to throw off his apprehension—"we'll get over this. You must promise me faithfully that within the next three days you will get me an opportunity to talk to Himmler personally. All the others—Kaltenbrunner and Mueller— are nothing but filthy butchers, out for my blood."

I promised to do as he asked and then said in a completely official voice, "If the Herr Admiral wishes to make other arrangements, then I beg him to consider me at his disposal. I shall wait in this room for an hour, and during that time you may do whatever you wish. My report will say that you went to your bedroom in order to change."

He understood at once what I meant. "No, dear Schellenberg," he said, "flight is out of the question for me. And I won't kill myself either. I am sure of my case, and I have faith in the promise you have given me."

We discussed quietly whether it would be wise for him to put on his uniform, what things he should take with him, and other details. Then he went upstairs. He returned after about half an hour having washed, changed, and packed a handbag. Again and again he shook his head, saying, "Those devils—they had to draw you into this thing too! But be on your guard—I've known for a long time that they are after you too. When I talk to Himmler I'll tell him about your case as well." He embraced me with tears in his eyes, and said, "Well, then, let us go."

We drove in my open car. After we left the city, the road led through the lovely countryside of Mecklenburg. The sky was slowly darkening. Our conversation grew increasingly monosyllabic, for each of us was pursuing his own thoughts. Canaris assured me several times that he knew very well I had no share in bringing about his dismissal. He hoped that fate would be kinder to me, and that I would not one day be hunted down as he had been.

Presently we arrived at Fuerstenberg, which was a school for the border police, and were received by the director, Brigadefuehrer Trummler, whom I found most unsympathetic. He preserved the forms of military politeness, however, and conducted us to an anteroom where we took off our topcoats. He asked us whether we would like to have supper together, and Canaris begged me to stay with him a little while longer.

We were taken to the mess hall where about twenty generals and high officers—all under house arrest in connection with the assassination—were just finishing their meal. After lively greetings, the Admiral and I withdrew to a small table where we had supper. I suggested to him that I should try to reach Himmler by telephone, and he agreed. But when I rang the Reichsfuehrer, his adjutant told me he was on the way from his special train to Hitler's headquarters. Canaris and I drank a last bottle of red wine together and he gave me a few final instructions on how I was to conduct the conversation with Himmler.

It was about eleven o'clock when I said good-by to him. He accompanied me to the anteroom, and we stood there talking for another five minutes. Once more he reminded me of my promise to arrange an interview with Himmler, and again embraced me with tears in his eyes. "You are my only hope," he said. "Good-by, young friend."

Upon my return to Berlin I sent a curt teletype message to Mueller: "I have carried out the order which you transmitted to me by telephone today. Further details you will hear through the Reichsfuehrer SS. Schellenberg."

The next day I had a long telephone conversation with Himmler. He had known nothing about Kaltenbrunner's move against me. He assured me that he would have an interview with Canaris, and this must have taken place, for there is no other explanation of the fact that Canaris was not sentenced to death until the very last days before the collapse of the Third Reich.

The evidence against him was certainly sufficient to satisfy the People's Court, under its bloodthirsty President Freisler, of his guilt. In July 1944 two dispatch cases containing incriminating documents had been discovered in a safe in one of Canaris' offices outside Berlin. They gave final proof of the guilt of him and his collaborators. In 1944, however, Himmler was still powerful enough to protect Canaris from the death sentence, and instead he was sent to a concentration camp at Flossenberg in Bavaria.

From the middle of 1944 I took over Canaris' Military Intelligence Department, incorporating its various tasks in departments IV and VI of the Counter-Espionage organization.

In March 1945 Hitler and Kaltenbrunner jointly ordered the execution of Canaris.

34. OPERATIONS OF THE SECRET SERVICE

Exchange of information with other departments—Transmission of material from abroad—The uses of wireless—Technical research—"Tapping" Britain's Atlantic cable—The infiltration of resistance movements—"Aktion Bernhard"—Effects of Goebbels' propaganda—Contact with Roosevelt's special envoy—Ribbentrop plans Stalin's assassination—The plot miscarries—Hitler's deterioration

I ALWAYS considered highly efficient and skilled technicians the most important part of a good secret service. The wartime Manpower Act allowed me to draft into my service the most brilliant experts and scientists, from university professors to artisans, until its technical standards were second to none. I was greatly helped in my task by the fact that as well as having the rank of SS Brigadefuehrer, I was accorded the disciplinary powers of a divisional commander of the army—General-major of the Waffen SS.

I spent a great deal of time and effort in winning the trust and co-operation of the heads of the intelligence departments of the various services. Already in 1942, General Fellgiebel and General Thiele, the heads of the Army Technical Information Service, regularly exchanged information with me. Every three weeks or so I gave a dinner party at my home where the technical heads of the three services, Defense Ministry, Post Office, and Research Stations discussed new developments and helped each other with their problems. These meetings were perhaps more than any single factor responsible for the high standard of the scientific and technical side of my service. It was the co-operation and interest which these people showed toward me personally which made most of my successes in Secret Service operations possible.

The problem of transmitting information from foreign or enemy countries is of central importance in the running of an intelligence service. Many secret services communicate their information either verbally or in writing through couriers. But a great deal of time may be lost in this way, so that information becomes of no value by the time it reaches the evaluation department. Verbal transmission, furthermore, is very difficult and unless the courier is highly skilled, is usually the source of serious errors through lapses of memory or lack of understanding of the material itself. Written transmission, except through the diplomatic bag, often has to pass through frontier control stations in several countries, and this process brings with it great dangers. Wireless communication therefore became increasingly important in our Secret Service, as it did in the services of other countries. Naturally, its employment produced counter-activities by our enemies, but modern direction-finders and methods of pinpointing usually proved so successful in locating illegal transmitters that the effort and expenditure of clandestine wireless networks became hardly worthwhile.

In her wireless defense organization Germany scored exceptional successes. We were able to intercept the wireless communications between enemy units at the front, and often intercepted important orders about troop movements and offensives. A technique was developed for "turning round" the illegal transmitters which we captured; that is, we continued working them as though they were still being operated by the enemy, but we transmitted material chosen by us, of which about half was valid and half faked, thereby often misleading the enemy on points of vital importance. Sometimes we carried the game so far as to ask for new agents, codes, arms, money, or explosives so that to the enemy it seemed that he was successfully extending his espionage network, whereas he was really being induced to expend large sums of money and valuable personnel for nothing. We were especially successful with the Russian wireless center in Moscow. At one time we had at least sixty-four "turned-round" stations transmitting to Moscow for us.

One of my chief aims was the complete mechanization of the wireless service, which would make the lengthy training of wireless operators unnecessary. An incident that illustrates the importance of this development concerned an individual closely connected with the Vatican, who felt it his duty, as a German and a western European, to pass on important information about Russia. But he

refused to do so in writing or to communicate with me
through an intermediary, nor could he travel to Germany.
He was afraid to pass his messages through one of my
transmitters in Rome as he had previously had very unfortunate experiences with this means of communication. I
therefore asked my technical staff to develop an apparatus
which he could use for direct wireless communication to
me.

After eighteen months the first apparatus was ready. It
was disguised as a box of cigars and was of about the
same weight, with a genuine layer of cigars concealing the
mechanism, which might equally well have been disguised
as a box of chocolates or built into a small overnight
handbag. On the front of the apparatus was a dial such as
is found on a telephone, and three buttons. To operate it
one merely had to plug it into an ordinary electric socket,
turn the first button, and dial the message (in code) as
one would dial a telephone number. The message would
then be automatically transferred onto a magnetized wire
tape inside the apparatus, on which about two typewritten
pages of code words could be recorded. After completing
his message, the sender would turn the second button and
a "magic eye" would begin to glow. When it reached its
greatest brilliance the sender would know that he was
beamed directly to our receiver somewhere in Germany.
Then by turning the third button the actual transmission
of the message would take place. The apparatus could
transmit the entire contents of the wire tape within three-
fifths of a second. The rapidity of the transmission made it
impossible for any direction-finder to establish the location
of the transmitter. The only inconvenience for an untrained sender was that the apparatus required an antenna
wire between twenty and thirty feet long.

The receiving stations in Germany were briefed as to the
exact times when transmissions would take place, but their
machinery was so intricate that I, being a layman, can give
no detailed information about them. They were enormous
and took up almost three rooms. I used to watch them
spark and hum and crackle, and I marveled to see all the
intricate operations completed within a fraction of a
second and the automatically decoded messages rattled off
as though on a teleprinter. Unfortunately we could never
devise a simple method for an agent in the field to receive

a message, so this startling radio link had to remain a one-sided means of communication.

The amount of equipment required by my organization in the various countries can hardly be imagined. The mass employment of agents in Russia alone required hundreds of sets a month, and getting these manufactured by our already overburdened defense industry involved enormous difficulties, though I managed to relieve the situation to some extent by having the valves manufactured in foreign countries.

After 1942 I set up a special department provided with large funds to carry out research in microfilms, invisible inks, codes, and decoding; and I also set up another department for the forging of identity papers, rubber stamps, and passports.

A curious incident arising out of this occurred during my first interrogation by the Americans in 1945. The interrogating officer got more and more annoyed when I insisted that I had never been to America. Finally he confronted me with an American passport made out in my name, complete with the stamps of embarkation, debarkation, and health authorities, fingerprints, etc. and with my photograph, properly stamped, affixed to it. I was flabbergasted, until I remembered that our technical department had given me this, the first faked passport which they had produced, for my birthday in 1943. At first the Americans refused to believe that it was faked, and maintained that it must be a genuine one, but extensive tests finally proved that I had told the truth.

One of my assistants was a man who had the extraordinary ability of imitating any handwriting within a few minutes, and so accurately as to deceive all the graphological experts. When the "National Committee for a Free Germany" was formed in Moscow in 1942, handwritten statements by General von Seydlitz and others, and letters written to his family by General von Paulus who had commanded the German armies at Stalingrad, were received in Germany. Hitler wanted to know whether the handwriting of these officers could possibly have been falsified in Moscow. With one accord the graphologists and psychologists stated that this was quite impossible. But they were all proven wrong when my own expert wrote long reports in the handwriting of von Paulus, von Seydlitz, and other members of the Free German Committee. He himself, however, believed that the statements we had received from Moscow were genuine. I used the services of this man in certain cases where signatures had to be obtained of people who were absent.

There was a separate department for research into listening and recording devices, which obtained astonishing results by using the newest electronic techniques. We also made great progress in the development of photographic equipment and had special cameras with which one could take photographs without being noticed. Even pictures taken indoors came out clearly. The camera was no larger than a flat matchbox, and the lens was so skilfully disguised that it could appear as a cuff link when the camera was worn under the cuff, or in the form of an insignia as a lapel button. There were special cameras for every sort of assignment. We could reduce a page from a full-sized newspaper to the size of a pin's head, and when it was enlarged it could be read perfectly easily; complete files of documents could be presrved in this way on a strip of film half an inch long. Several times when I was traveling without the protection of diplomatic immunity I carried such films inside a hollow porcelain tooth.

Because of the constant threat of destruction by air attacks that hung over Berlin after 1943, I had all the most important files of my department photographed on microfilm. The films were placed in two steel strongboxes, small enough to fit into a brief case. As a further precaution, a mechanism setting off an explosive was built into the box, so that the contents would be destroyed if anyone who did not know the combination attempted to force the box. Eventually both boxes were destroyed in this way.

Our leading chemist succeeded in preparing secret inks which were completely secure against all chemical and infrared examination. I cannot recall the precise details, but I remember that one of the chief elements was an admixture of hemoglobin from human blood so that, when the ink was required, the agent would simply prick his finger, mix a drop of blood with the prepared solution, and have a red ink which would disappear completely after three minutes. Only those who possessed the secret formula could restore the writing, which would then appear as if written in green ink. The process did not involve purely chemical reactions; it also made use of biological processes.

Through collaboration with experts of the Reich Post Ministry we succeeded in tapping the main cable between England and America. The word "tapping" is used here in a figurative sense. In spite of the insulation of the cable we were able, by the use of short-wave instruments, to record the high-frequency impulses running through it, and by an incredibly complicated process to decipher them. The cable that we "tapped" was used for communication between England and the United States, chiefly concerned with requests for reinforcements and materials such as aircraft, gasoline, guns, and tanks. Through a systematic evaluation of this material we could determine the emphasis in armament production and supply. A great deal of information on convoys and shipping could also be deduced, which was invaluable for our U-boat raids on Allied shipping.

Early in 1944 we hit a bull's eye by tapping a telephone conversation between Roosevelt and Churchill which was overheard and deciphered by the giant German listening post in Holland. Though the conversation was scrambled, we unscrambled it by means of a highly complicated apparatus. It lasted almost five minutes, and disclosed a crescendo of military activity in Britain thereby corroborating the many reports of impending invasion. Had the two statesmen known that the enemy was listening to their conversation, Roosevelt would hardly have been likely to say good-by to Churchill with the words, "Well, we will do our best—now I will go fishing."

Although in the occupied territories our security measures against the British Secret Service were not without considerable success, the gradually increasing resistance among the civil population in Holland, Belgium, France, and Norway made for a struggle that grew ever more bitter between our Counter-Intelligence and the British Secret Service. The British made full use of the resistance in order to gain footholds for their organization, even in the heart of Germany, by infiltrating the swollen ranks of forcibly recruited foreign labor. However, these underground resistance movements in the occupied countries were not only often traced by us, but were infiltrated by our own underground agents. There were even cases where resistance groups were jointly "directed" by the British and ourselves, and we were sometimes able to "order" from England radio equipment required by us, as well as currency and explosives (these, incidentally, were superior to our own) to be dropped by parachute. Sometimes it took no more than ten days for our "order" to be given and the necessary material to be parachuted into occupied territory. The British Secret Service thus became my never-failing currency reserve. The sums collected by me in this way ran into millions, though whenever the British discovered such treachery by their agents in foreign resistance movements they did not hesitate to liquidate them.

The situation in regard to the foreign currency and gold reserves of the Reich was always very strained, and the Secret Service had begun relatively early to forge the pound notes, banknotes, and gold roubles required for its own needs. It took two years to imitate the so-called grease-proof paper needed for English pound notes, and two paper mills, one in the Rhineland and the other in the Sudeten territory, were devoted solely to this task. The highly complicated process of engraving could only be started after the 160 main identifying marks had been determined; then the most skilled engravers in Germany were drafted, sworn to secrecy, and set to work in three shifts. Professors of mathematics worked out, with the help of complicated formulas, the system of British banknote registration numbers, so that our output was always one hundred to two hundred notes ahead of the Bank of England. These forgeries were so accurate that even the most cautious cashier in a bank would not have suspected anything.

A plan had been worked out to send bombers over Britain which, instead of dropping bombs, were to drop forged pound notes by the ton. The country was to be flooded with them. One can imagine what the result would have been. The government would probably have been forced to withdraw all treasury notes from circulation which, apart from the expense involved, would have placed a great burden on the administrative machinery. The population would have been entirely confused, and would have lost confidence in the Bank of England. However, this plan was dropped because the air above Britain was too well defended, and the fuel situation was critical.

We were assured of the technical perfection which our banknote production had achieved when at the end of 1941 one of our men changed a large quantity of five- and ten-pound notes in Switzerland. Boldly he requested to have their validity checked saying that he had acquired them on the black market. The Bank of England withdrew about 10 per cent of the notes as forgeries, but the rest they confirmed as bona fide Bank of England notes. This was the sign for me to change over to mass production.

However, we made only the most sparing use of the notes. Kaltenbrunner, for reasons of his own, sought to use them for purchases in the black market of occupied countries. But this was prevented because it would have threatened our own currency situation by forcing the Reichsbank to buy our forgeries and change them into gold and hard currencies.

I used the notes myself for the financing of enterprises abroad where I knew that I had to deal with cold-blooded and mercenary businessmen. The forged money was also used in the extensive trade of smuggled arms in which the Secret Service was employed. Wherever there was a resistance movement—in Italy, Greece, and also in France—the trade in such arms flourished and we were able to acquire British and American weapons with our forged pound notes. Most of them were automatic hand weapons which we used in combating the partisan groups. It seemed ironical that the partisans should have sold us the very weapons which we used against them.

The operation of producing these forged notes went under the code name "Aktion Bernhard." In 1945, because of "Aktion Bernhard" the Bank of England was forced to start printing a new issue of five-pound notes and had to withdraw all the old ones from circulation.

Unfortunately, more often than not a great deal of money was wasted as a result of the unrealistic fantasies and brain waves of the leaders. Their imaginations became even more erratic and more fantastic as the fortunes of war turned against Germany. But orders were orders, and I was frequently forced to take my most valuable technicians away from their serious tasks to work on some crackpot idea.

Goebbels, as Propaganda Minister, had established a comprehensive monitoring service which served mainly to supply his Ministry with suitable material for propaganda to enemy countries. This service, with its host of foreigners working as monitors, was of course a breeding ground for the enemy's intelligence services, and was therefore under constant and thorough surveillance by the Gestapo. My approach in this matter was cautious and involved a great deal of patient and painstaking work, in which I was given valuable assistance by Naumann, Undersecretary of State in the Propaganda Ministry, who also enjoyed the fullest confidence of Himmler. Naumann, a dynamic personality, identified himself fully with the tasks of the Secret Service, and indeed he was the only one who was able to match and counter the brilliant dialectics of his chief.[1] Time and again he managed to neutralize violent attacks by Goebbels against me personally.

During 1943 Goebbels and I were at loggerheads over the question of the treatment of the churches. I had warned Himmler not to fall in blindly with Goebbels' and Bormann's anti-church campaign, for as Hitler's heir presumptive he would lose any potential confidence abroad once he allowed himself to be involved in these matters. Under the influence of Goebbels a point had been reached in the autumn of 1943 when Hitler was seriously considering the deportation of the Pope into a kind of exile at Avignon. In extensive reports I tried to point out the immense disadvantages that would result from such an action and how it would discredit Germany in the eyes of the entire world. At last Himmler agreed with my views and took the matter up with Hitler, who then gave him a comparatively reasonable answer: "If full churches contribute to the maintenance of unity among the German people, then I cannot object to it, in view of the strains imposed by such a war as this."

The setbacks we had received in rapid succession in the years 1943 and 1944—the capitulation of our armies at Stalingrad, the collapse of our African army in Tunis, the landing of the Allies in Sicily, the fall and arrest of Mussolini, the capitulation of Italy, all in 1943, and finally the invasion of France in 1944—confirmed the analysis of the situation that I had given to Himmler at Zhitomir during August 1942.

In view of this meeting, I had taken up indirect contacts with the Russians through Switzerland and Sweden, and it seemed to me that they were genuinely interested in negoti-

---

[1] Werner Naumann was arrested by the British authorities in January 1953, together with six other Nazi leaders on the grounds that they were trying to seize power in Germany. He was released in July of the same year.

ations which might end the fighting with us. But all my efforts were wrecked by Ribbentrop's shortsighted clumsiness and his incredible conceit and optimism in spite of all reverses. Before agreeing, for instance, to meet the Russians, he demanded proof that their representatives were not of Jewish origin. Of course it may easily have been that the willingness of the Russians to negotiate was simply a maneuver to bring pressure on the Allies to open their second front. But whatever the reason, we were in no position to turn them down.

As soon as I heard from Dr. Kesten that a Mr. Hewitt, an American diplomat, was in Stockholm ready to talk about the possibility of peace negotiations, I took a special plane to Sweden. Mr. Hewitt was Roosevelt's special representative for European affairs. Taking all possible precautions for secrecy, I met him in his suite at one of the largest hotels in Stockholm. Afterward I asked some well-informed Swedish friends to tell me precisely the extent of Hewitt's influence. The references they gave him were excellent. Apparently he had a decisive influence on Roosevelt in all matters concerning Europe. Therefore, on my own responsibility and without reservations, I told him how essential a compromise peace was to Germany. He agreed to arrange official negotiations as soon as I gave my consent. When our talks ended, I flew back to Berlin and worked all night on a report to Himmler.

The next afternoon at three o'clock I saw him and informed him fully about my conversations with Hewitt. He was confused and quite aghast at my independent actions, and kept shaking his head and literally gasping for breath. Then he began to talk and gradually worked himself into a state of rage. Fortunately at its climax he had to take part in some ceremony, but later he called me to his office again to continue our talk. There followed a heated discussion between us. I was lucky not to be arrested, but all my plans were upset. My powers of persuasion, my efforts to present my analysis of the situation of Germany in a form that would be comprehensible to Himmler, were unavailing; nothing could break the spell which Hitler still exercised upon those around him.

When in the summer of 1944 Ribbentrop asked me to go and see him at his summer residence, Schloss Fuschl, I was full of apprehension. I had not heard from him for a few months and felt sure that he must have been brooding over one of his "intuitions," which would solve all problems and win the war in one stroke. I combined the trip with an interview with Himmler, who had set up his headquarters in a special train near Berchtesgaden, Hitler's mountain retreat. I was very overworked at the time for it was just when I was taking over Canaris' military sector of the Secret Service.

Ribbentrop lived at Fuschl in a very beautiful palace with a magnificent park, which the state had placed at his disposal so that he could receive important visitors there and still be near Hitler. Contrary to his usual custom, he received me with great cordiality, asked how my work was going, and emphasized how important my department had become to him. I did not know whether this was plain hypocrisy or whether he had some special motive. Calmly I waited for his flow of words to subside.

After declaring his wholehearted recognition of the importance of the Secret Service, he said he wanted detailed reports about the United States and especially on Roosevelt's chances of re-election. He also wanted me to arrange the passage by U-boat of special agents to work in America on the German minorities there. He visualized a great radio campaign directed toward the various national minorities in the United States to create feeling against Roosevelt's re-election. We discussed details of this plan, and I asked why these minorities should have any special reason to prevent Roosevelt's re-election. He looked at me with astonishment. "They don't have to have any special reasons," he said. "The important thing is for us to find a way of speaking to these minorities by broadcasts from Europe. The reasons will be invented later."

I pointed out that there were certain technical difficulties, among them the great burden borne by our U-boat fleet, which would prevent any of our larger boats being available for such an operation. Suddenly I remembered my former conversation with Ribbentrop, and his strange theories of Secret Service work, and I could not help adding, "You are somewhat late, Herr Minister. After all, a handful of super-agents for the whole world cannot accomplish everything." Ribbentrop stiffened. "My dear Schellenberg," he said, in a pained voice, "that is really unjustified. You should realize that I have done everything in my power to help and encourage the Secret Service."

This was so contrary to the truth that I could find nothing to say. I turned, intending to leave the study, when Ribbentrop rose and, with a very serious expression, drew me into a corner.

"One moment, Schellenberg. I have a matter of considerable gravity to discuss with you. The utmost secrecy is essential—no one knows of this except the Fuehrer, Bormann, and Himmler." Fixing me with a penetrating stare, he went on, "Stalin must be removed." I nodded, not knowing quite what I was supposed to say. He explained that the whole strength of the Russian regime lay in the ability and statesmanship of one man—Stalin. Then he turned away and strode to the window. "I have intimated to the Fuehrer my readiness to sacrifice myself for the sake of Germany. A conference will be arranged with Stalin, and it will be my mission to shoot down the Russian leader."

"Alone?" I queried. Suddenly he turned to me. "That is what the Fuehrer said—one man alone cannot do it. The Fuehrer asked me to name a possible accomplice"—here he stared at me intently—"and I named you." Hitler, he said, had directed him to discuss the matter with me alone, and was sure that I would see the practical aspects of the plan in a realistic light. "And you see," Ribbentrop concluded, "that is the real reason for my sending for you."

I don't know what kind of face I made, but it can hardly have been an intelligent one. I felt utterly at a loss and more than a little confused.

Ribbentrop had thought everything out very carefully, and now began explaining the details to me. Undoubtedly there would be an extremely close security check, and it would scarcely be possible to smuggle a hand grenade or a revolver into the conference room. But he had heard that my technical department had developed a revolver disguised as a fountain pen, from which one could shoot a heavy-caliber bullet with reasonable accuracy at a range of between eighteen and twenty-five feet. He had been told that it was so cleverly made that a superficial inspection would not reveal its real purpose. We should certainly be able to take it, or something like it, into the conference room—then all that would be needed would be a steady hand. . . .

At last he stopped talking. I had been watching him

very closely. He had talked himself into such a state of enthusiasm that he seemed like a boy who had just enjoyed his first thriller. But it was quite clear that I was confronted by a determined fanatic, and all he wanted was to hear me express my agreement with the plan and my immediate readiness to join him in it.

I considered the whole thing as the product, to put it mildly, of a neurotic and overstrained mind. But the situation was not a very comfortable one. I had to assume that every word I said would be reported at once to Hitler. At last, I thought I saw a way to wriggle out of the dilemma. I said that, though I considered the plan technically feasible, the whole project was based on whether we could succeed in bringing Stalin to the conference table. This, I thought, would be extremely difficult, especially after the experience the Russians had had with us at Stockholm. Therefore, I refused to have anything to do with any new attempt at making contact with the Russians, for already I had completely lost face in front of them, and all because of Ribbentrop's attitude on the last occasion. I suggested that he himself should try to establish the necessary basis of his plan and get Stalin to agree to come to a conference. Once he had accomplished this, I would be ready to stand by him both in word and deed.

"I will consider the matter further," Ribbentrop said, "and discuss it again with Hitler. Then I will call on you."

He never mentioned the matter to me again. But Himmler did, and was obviously very pleased about the reply I had given to Ribbentrop. However, after further discussion with Hitler, Himmler himself suggested that something on the same lines as Ribbentrop's plan should be attempted. Accordingly our experts constructed a special device for Stalin's assassination. It consisted of an adhesive charge of explosives which was about the size of the fist and looked like a lump of mud. The idea was for it to be attached to Stalin's car. The charge contained a fuse which was controlled by short wave and was so powerful that very little remained of the car on which we tried it out. The transmitter, which would automatically set off the explosives, was the size of a cigarette box and could send out an ultra-short wave for a distance of about seven miles.

Two members of the Red Army who had previously been exiled for a long time to Siberia, and one of whom was acquainted with a mechanic in Stalin's garage, accepted the assassination assignment. They were flown in a large transport aircraft at night and dropped near the place where our agents had informed us by short wave that Stalin had his headquarters. The two men jumped and, as far as we could ascertain, landed at the correct place; but that was the last we ever heard of them, although they both carried short-wave transmitters. I doubt very much whether they attempted to blow up Stalin. I feel it is more likely that they were either picked up soon after they landed, or that they reported their mission to the NKVD.

Meanwhile the threat of collapse was coming nearer. When Himmler took me with him to report to Hitler in the Fuehrer's headquarters, there was the usual atmosphere of intensive work and excitement. I had not seen Hitler for a long time and was really alarmed by his appearance. His eyes, which before had been so strong and dominating, were listless and tired. His left arm trembled so violently that he was forced to hold it, almost desperately, with his right hand. He tried to hide the ungainliness of his movements. His back was so bent that he appeared hunchbacked. His gait was clumsy and heavy. Only his voice was still as strong and clear as before, but more staccato, his sentences shorter.

He and Himmler were striding up and down the room. They broke off their conversation as soon as I entered, and Hitler sat down for a moment, then turned to Jodl and gave orders concerning the eastern front—the replacement of two divisions in the central sector, and other military matters. Turning to me, he discussed several of my recent intelligence reports: the problems in the Balkans, especially relations between General Mihailovitch and the British, and British relations with Tito. He also wanted to know more about our intelligence activities in the Near East. Then he asked about the elections in the United States, and I reported as briefly and concisely as possible.

Suddenly he rose, looked at me piercingly, and said in a deep voice which vibrated angrily, "I read your reports regularly." There was a long pause, and the words seemed to stand, suspended accusingly in the air of that room. I noticed that Himmler began to show visible signs of uneasiness. Involuntarily I had retreated two steps. But Hitler followed me, and said in the same voice, "Remember this one thing, Schellenberg: in this war there can be no compromise, there can only be victory or destruction. And if the German people cannot wrest victory from the enemy, then they shall be destroyed." I shall never forget his concluding words: "Yes, then they deserve to perish, for the best of Germany's manhood will have fallen in battle. Germany's end will be horrible, and the German people will have deserved it."

I felt that stark insanity stood there in the middle of the room, and any ties which still bound me to the man fell away at that moment, for he was willing to condemn what was dearest to him, his own people. He willed the destruction of all this to satisfy his vengeful spite.

I recall another conversation between Hitler and Himmler at which I was present. Hitler claimed that by the year 2000, no more infantry units would be employed in warfare: there would be only armored units composed of one-man tanks. These would be able to withstand all types of weapons, including chemical ones. Liquid fuel would no longer be needed, and the tanks, which would have an operational radius of more than two thousand kilometers without the need for servicing or supplies, would carry new types of incredibly destructive armament.

Before the launching of the great offensive in the Ardennes in 1944 Hitler summoned his army commanders to his headquarters. He dwelt at length on the "fateful position of Germany as between East and West" and emphasized that this was for Germany a life and death struggle. "If Germany loses, it will have proved itself biologically inferior and will have forfeited its future existence. It is the West that forces us to fight to the last. However, it will transpire that the winner will not be the West, but the East."

35. PEACE FEELERS

Herr Musy's efforts to save Jewish internees—Discussions between Himmler and Herr Musy—Kaltenbrunner frustrates the efforts of the International Red Cross—A message from Count Bernadotte—Himmler consents to a meeting with the Count—Agreement reached on the transference of prisoners—The SS supervise the transfer

WHILE HITLER'S fortunes declined rapidly, I had to make frequent and desperate use of my position with Himmler to insure that at least Swiss neutrality was respected, and I honestly feel that it is largely due to my influence with and through Himmler, which I was never tired of exerting to the utmost that a "preventive" occupation of Switzerland did not take place. Needless to say, these purely negative interventions were inevitably linked with my ceaseless attempts to establish direct or indirect peace feelers. My efforts brought on me the wrath of Kaltenbrunner, Bormann, and Mueller, who were waiting for just such an excuse to bring about my downfall. They almost succeeded.

A radio message about Dr. Langbehn's negotiations with Allied representatives in Switzerland was intercepted, and the fact that Dr. Langbehn had my blessing in this completely unofficial undertaking was mentioned, as well as Dr. Kersten's part in furthering these negotiations. Kaltenbrunner and Mueller immediately arranged for a secret investigation, but Kersten's influence with Himmler saved me from disaster. Later I was able to repay Dr. Kersten by warning him or taking counter-measures whenever Mueller's Gestapo had plans to liquidate him.

It was at this time that my contacts in Switzerland brought me into touch with Herr Musy, a former President of Switzerland. He was an utterly selfless man, highly intelligent and knowledgeable, who had one aim—the saving of as many as possible of the hundreds of thousands of concentration camp inmates. Toward the end of 1944, after weeks of persuasion, I managed to arrange a secret meeting between Musy and Himmler. At first Himmler kept the conversation on general lines, but at length Musy's forceful personality and clever arguments, together with the pressure I managed to exert, made Himmler come to a decision. He let it be understood, however, that he would only agree to a mass evacuation of Jewish concentration camp inmates in return for tractors, cars, medicines, and other things of which we were badly in need. Musy made a counter-suggestion that Himmler should content himself with payments in foreign currency to be credited to the International Red Cross. Himmler could not realize that the freeing of thousands of Jews was important from the point of view of Germany's foreign policy; he seemed only to be concerned with the effect such an action would have on the Party clique and on Hitler. I realized during this talk that he genuinely wanted to free himself from his past record on the Jewish question, but he could never work up enough courage to take the decisive step. This part of the talk ended with a suggestion that Switzerland should be recognized by the United States as a place of transit for Jews who would eventually emigrate there, and Musy promised to discuss the question with certain Jewish organizations in Switzerland.

Just before Musy left for Switzerland I persuaded Himmler to prove his sincerity by conceding one of Musy's special requests: that a number of prominent Jews and Frenchmen should be released. Himmler reluctantly agreed, and asked me to be responsible for seeing that the arrangement was carried out. He also asked me to keep in close contact with Musy and arrange a further meeting between them.

I immediately got in touch with Mueller to get his permission to take care of these prisoners, but he rejected this request, ostensibly because I was not a member of the Gestapo, and therefore he could not reveal its internal affairs to me. However, he did allow me to contact the officials in charge of the various Gestapo establishments, and I was able to find out where the various prisoners were and get them better food and lodging and enable them to receive food packages; in some cases I was also able to get them civilian clothes and lodgings in hotels, and to arrange for their emigration. All this required the unraveling of endless red tape and constant liaison with Gestapo offices.

The second conference between Himmler and Musy was at Wildbad-Schwarzwald in the Black Forest, on January 12, 1945. The following agreement was then reached through my active intervention:

1. Every fourteen days a first-class train would bring about 1,200 Jews to Switzerland.
2. The Jewish organizations with which Herr Musy was working would give active support in solving the Jewish problem according to Himmler's suggestions. At the same time, the beginning of a basic change in the world-wide propaganda against Germany was to be brought about.
3. According to my suggestion, it was agreed that the money should not be paid over directly to the International Red Cross, as had originally been decided, but should be handed to Musy as trustee.

The first transport went through at the beginning of February and everything functioned very well. Musy acknowledged the receipt of the five million Swiss francs, which were paid to him as trustee at the end of February 1945, and also saw to it that the fact was made known to the press, as had been agreed, while an article was published by President von Steiger in Berne, and another appeared in the *New York Times*.

Unfortunately a decoded message referring to these arrangements, which came from one of de Gaulle's centers in Spain, was brought to Hitler's notice. It was alleged in this message that Himmler had negotiated with Musy through his representative, Schellenberg, to secure asylum in Switzerland for 250 "Nazi leaders." This obvious nonsense, cunningly circulated by Kaltenbrunner, had the most uncomfortable consequences for me. Hitler immediately issued two orders: that any German who helped a Jew, or a British, or an American prisoner to escape would be executed instantly; any such attempt was to be reported to him personally.

Musy was desperate and shed tears of rage and bitter disappointment. During his last visit to Berlin we both decided to make a final attempt to see if some sort of plan could be worked out. I suggested to Himmler that a four days' truce on land and in the air be requested from the

Western Allies and that this period should be used to bring all Jews and foreign internees through the front lines in an organized manner, and thus show Germany's goodwill. I brought the chief of the Prisoner of War Administration, Obergruppenfuehrer Berger, into this plan. He accepted my advice not to pass on many of Hitler's orders, and by doing so save the lives of hundreds of people.

Herr Musy and I felt that if such a truce was brought to the Allies through official and responsible channels it would be accepted. Further negotiations might then lead to a general compromise, which would benefit not only those directly involved, but indeed all men. However, Himmler lacked the courage to place this proposal before Hitler. Favoring the plan himself, he turned instead to the leader of the circle around Hitler, to Kaltenbrunner, who himself gave me his answer: "Have you gone off your head?" This was on April 3, 1945.

Musy and I agreed after this that there was only one thing to be done. In view of the continually worsening military situation, Himmler must be made to issue an order to prevent the evacuation of all concentration camps which might be overrun by the Allies. After a long discussion Himmler finally consented (in this matter Dr. Kersten, who was then in Stockholm, exerted considerable influence on Himmler and was of great help to me) and I was able to tell Musy on April 7, 1945, that Himmler had agreed not to evacuate any concentration camp, and especially asked that his decision be conveyed to General Eisenhower as quickly as possible. In spite of being over seventy years of age, Herr Musy left in his car that same night, and three days later informed me that Washington had received the message and had reacted favorably.

He then sent his son back with the car in order to fetch several Jews whose release from Buchenwald had been promised him by Himmler personally. The younger Musy went to the camp commandant and was very badly received. He was horrified to notice that preparations had been made for the evacuation of the camp and at once came to see me in Berlin.

I had been quite certain that Himmler's original order would be carried out. However, after hearing Musy's story, I decided to look into the matter. I found that the numerous intriguers had achieved their aim and Himmler was now completely discredited with Hitler. It was Kaltenbrunner who had given the orders to evacuate all the Gestapo camps. I was still not certain, however, what arrangements were being made about the prisoner-of-war camps.

I telephoned to Himmler at once. He was very embarrassed by my reproaches and annoyed that he had been bypassed and promised me that he would intervene. An hour later I talked with his secretary, Brandt, who assured me that Himmler was doing everything in his power to keep his promise not to evacuate the camps. Himmler, by his energetic intervention—I believe I am right in maintaining this—succeeded in countermanding Kaltenbrunner's orders, and thereby saved the lives of innumerable people.

Through our many negotiations I had by this time established close personal contact with Herr Musy, who confided to me much of the rich experience of his political life, while I was able to explain to him the oppressive worries of my own position. Our discussions were of great help to me, and we determined to work together to prevent as many as possible of the evils that we had to fear.

Herr Musy had suggested that M. Herriot, the famous French statesman, should be set free, for this would be a real service to France and would show a delicate sense of political timing. I discussed the matter with Himmler, but he brusquely rejected my suggestion, obviously having talked it over with Kaltenbrunner.

Because of repeated requests from various friends in Switzerland, I tried also to secure the release of another former French Minister, Paul Reynaud, but this attempt also failed because of Kaltenbrunner's opposition. Finally I tried to secure the release of some of General Giraud's family, and although at first my efforts failed, after six weeks of continual struggling against Kaltenbrunner and Mueller, I succeeded in getting Himmler's permission. Later Giraud thanked me personally in a letter written in his own hand.

Herr Musy had established contact with Dr. Burckhardt, the president of the International Red Cross, who wanted to secure a generous approach from Germany to the question of political prisoners, especially those of French and Polish nationality, and of the Jews. Dr. Burckhardt expressed the wish to meet Himmler and for several

days I sought to secure his agreement, but as usual he
delayed discussing the matter with Kaltenbrunner. Finally,
I asked Kaltenbrunner to approach Hitler, who, of course,
gave a sharp refusal. I then suggested that Kaltenbrunner
should meet Dr. Burckhardt. He covered himself by inform-
ing Ribbentrop, but at length the meeting took place.

Dr. Burckhardt came away very satisfied with the result. At last it seemed that the Red Cross would be able to
intervene in the question of concentration camp inmates as
well as of prisoners of war. Dr. Burckhardt formulated
the results of the conversation in a long letter. But Kaltenbrunner found these results much too concrete. He could
not possibly fulfill Dr. Burckardt's proposals, he said,
but in order to save face he agreed to let the Red
Cross remove most of the Frenchwomen interned in
Ravensbrueck. I tried to put further pressure on Himmler
and pointed out the seriousness of the breach of faith with
regard to the Jewish transports, but I was unable to move
him sufficiently to take energetic action. Thus, this attempt to solve the problem on a humanitarian basis came
to naught.

This, then, was the atmosphere when, in February
1945, while my negotiations with Herr Musy were going
on, a message from the Swedish Ambassador, Amtnan
Thomsen, stated that Count Bernadotte wished to come to
Berlin to talk to Himmler. Ribbentrop sent his personal
adviser, Geheimrat Wagner, to me to ask whether I had
organized this move through my connections with Sweden.
I told Wagner quite truthfully that I knew absolutely
nothing of Count Bernadotte's suggestion, and at once
informed Himmler and Kaltenbrunner. Himmler was very
interested, but was annoyed that the matter had gone
through the Embassy and the Foreign Office. This forced
him to treat the Count's visit officially, which meant
reporting everything to Hitler. As Himmler was at that
time in command of the Army Group Vistula, and had his
headquarters in Prenzlau, he instructed Kaltenbrunner to
talk to Hitler at an opportune moment and to sound the
Fuehrer on his attitude. Kaltenbrunner was present every
day at the main military council in the Reich Chancellery,
and would often be alone with the Fuehrer for hours
afterward. However, in order not to risk a personal rejection, he also requested Gruppenfuehrer Fegelein (whose
wife was Eva Braun's sister) to ask Hitler about the

Count's visit. Fegelein reported Hitler's reaction the next day and repeated his comment: "One cannot accomplish anything with this sort of nonsense in a total war."

In the meantime, Count Bernadotte had already arrived in Berlin. I spoke to Himmler on the telephone and begged him earnestly not to miss this opportunity to receive the Count, and emphasized that various points of political interest would be bound to come up during their discussions. After talking back and forth for a long time, Himmler finally agreed to a suggestion that would still leave a line of retreat open to him: Kaltenbrunner should speak to Ribbentrop, while I at the same time should speak to Wagner. Both of us should try to persuade Ribbentrop to receive Bernadotte, but not to inform Hitler, and Ribbentrop should not be told that Hitler had already expressed objection to the visit. If Ribbentrop agreed, then Kaltenbrunner and I could receive the Count immediately afterward. Himmler would thus have time to see how the affair was developing before committing himself officially. What actually happened, however, was that Count Bernadotte telephoned to me from the Swedish Embassy. First he was received by Kaltenbrunner and myself, and went to see Ribbentrop immediately afterward.

Though I was reserved during this first conversation, I felt that I had established good relations with the Count. In this visit I saw the possibility of pursuing my original plan—to end the war for Germany. Contact with Sweden could be extremely important in this connection, for she would have a special interest in the pacification of northern Europe. Thus my original effort to do something for Denmark and Norway would be in line with the Count's aims. The next step would be to secure Sweden as a mediator for a compromise peace. At the close of our conversation the Count again told Kaltenbrunner that he wished to speak to Himmler, having something which he wanted to say to him personally and alone.

I decided to make a bold move to try to win Kaltenbrunner over, in spite of his personal antagonism. As soon as Bernadotte had left, I praised Kaltenbrunner for the pliant and skillful manner in which he had responded to the Count's questions, and told him that he had handled this delicate situation in the best traditions of the old Austrian school of diplomacy. All this went down beautifully, and I continued by telling him that I had decided to suggest to Himmler that it was now high time to remove Ribbentrop and appoint him, Kaltenbrunner, as Foreign Secretary. The slow-thinking Kaltenbrunner took this bait so eagerly that I could hardly hold him. In the subsequent telephone conversation with Himmler he became the most ardent protagonist of the proposed meeting between Himmler and Bernadotte, in spite of Hitler's orders forbidding it. Himmler declared himself ready to receive the Count, on condition that Kaltenbrunner should not attend the meeting. Disillusioned and embittered by this rebuff, Kaltenbrunner soon returned to his old antagonism toward me.

The meeting between Count Bernadotte and Himmler took place at Hohenlychen two days later. During the drive I was able to offer him some advice about the impending conversation and prepare him for some of Himmler's peculiarities. The Count's original plan had been to transfer all Danish and Norwegian prisoners to Sweden and intern them there for the duration of the war. I knew that this would never be agreed to, and suggested a compromise proposal—that these prisoners should be collected in a central camp in northwest Germany. This was, in fact, the basis of an agreement reached between the Count and Himmler during their meeting.

I had an opportunity of speaking to Himmler immediately after his conversation with the Count. He had been very favorably impressed by him, and intended to maintain close contact with him. He wanted me to supervise the implementation of their agreement, which, as he very well knew, would meet with considerable difficulties from Kaltenbrunner and Mueller, and perhaps from Ribbentrop too. I was to inform Ribbentrop of the essential points of the conversation and of the agreements reached, so that he could present them to the Count officially.

First, I informed Kaltenbrunner of the outcome of the conversation. He began to reproach me at once for having exerted an undue influence on Himmler. Mueller, whom he brought into the discussion, immediately produced insuperable technical difficulties—the whole idea was completely Utopian; he was not in a position to furnish lorries and petrol for all the widely dispersed Danish and Norwegian prisoners, nor would the Camp Neugamme be available (as had been suggested), since it was already full up. It was always the same thing, he grumbled, when the

gentlemen who considered themselves statesmen talked
Himmler into agreeing to one of their ideas. . . .

To his objection about the lorries and the petrol, I
replied that the Swedes could furnish these. The quickness
of my counter-suggestion caught Mueller off his guard and
he agreed to it without perceiving its full implications. But
the next day he raised new objections: all the roads in
Germany were crowded with refugees, and it would be
imposing on the German people to have Red Cross lorries
rolling past them full of prisoners. To this I said that they
could be transported during the night, and I offered to
assign members of my own department to this operation.
Thus, the intervention of my own faithful personnel saved
many lives. They worked in conjunction with the Swedish
Red Cross in transporting Danish, Norwegian, Polish, and
Jewish prisoners, and their combined activities created
such uncertainty among the camp commandants that
many conflicting orders which came in from Kaltenbrunner and others were lost sight of in the general confusion.

36. HIMMLER SHIRKS THE ISSUE

The struggle for Himmler's soul—I try to persuade him to act—His fear of Hitler—His bodyguard degraded— Pressure on Himmler to end the war

AFTER THE meeting with Count Berna-dotte I talked very seriously to Himmler, and told him clearly that the collapse of Germany was inevitable. I begged him to avail himself of the good offices of Sweden and attempt to steer the wrecked German ship of state into the harbor of peace before it capsized. I suggested that he should ask Count Bernadotte to fly to General Eisenhower and transmit to him his offer of capitulation.

I also tried to make it clear that his proper place as the commander of an army group was in Berlin, and not in Prenzlau. He should have realized that it was Hitler's advisers who, for the second time, had succeeded in removing him from the Fuehrer's side. He ought to return to Berlin at once and arrange preparations for peace. If need be, he must use force. It was a very stormy conversation, but Himmler finally gave in and granted me the widest authority for negotiating with Count Bernadotte. But the next day he revoked everything. He would only permit me to retain superficial contact with the Count and perhaps influence him to fly to Eisenhower on his own initiative. From that day on—it was at the beginning of March 1945—there was an almost daily struggle between Himmler and me in which I wrestled for his soul.

I had already told Count Bernadotte about this struggle. In our talks we had agreed that I was to notify him as soon as Himmler finally made up his mind (I had planned to accompany the Count myself on his flight to General Eisenhower) and we also arranged that in case the Reich itself was cut off by the enemy, I would fly with Himmler to south Germany and make contact with Bernadotte by way of the Swedish Ambassador in Switzerland.

Though in the first place Count Bernadotte had undertaken his mission on behalf of the Danes and the Norwegians, he also tried to intervene on behalf of the Jews, and through his intelligent handling of the situation he had already been able to save the Danish Jews. Of special importance were the conversations between Bernadotte and Himmler which started at the end of March, when Himmler had promised the Count not to evacuate the internment camps at the approach of the Allied armies, but to surrender them in good order—especially Bergen-Belsen, Buchenwald, and Theresienstadt, and the camps in southern Germany.

I kept on reminding Himmler how desperate the situation was, and warned him that one day history would hold him responsible for his lack of decision. He replied that the Order of the SS had been built on the principle of loyalty and he could not violate this. If he did, he would threaten the very basis of his own position. I told him that compared to the existence of the whole nation the SS represented only a small minority, and after their long period of suffering the German people would expect a release from their ordeal. They looked to Himmler, for he was a man who had not sought to profit personally from the regime. To this kind of talk he would merely say, "So you want to remove the Fuehrer?" And such was his changeable nature that there were days when it would have cost me my position to have answered, "Yes."

Hitler's appearance as seen in the newsreels confirmed my impression that he showed increasingly obvious symptoms of Parkinson's disease, so I arranged a meeting between Himmler and Professor de Crinis, to which Himmler asked Reich Health Leader Conti, to discuss this. De Crinis told me later that Himmler had listened with great interest and understanding.

Several days later, on April 13, Himmler asked me to go and see him at Wustrow. He took me for a walk in the forest and during it he said, "Schellenberg, I believe that nothing more can be done with Hitler. Do you think that de Crinis is right about him?" I said, "Yes, though I haven't seen the Fuehrer for quite a while—but everything he has done lately seems to indicate that now is the time for you to act."

On this occasion I pointed once again to the necessity of improving the treatment of the Jews, and of his promise to Herr Musy. Then we discussed Kersten's plan to come to Germany in the course of the next few days with Hillel Storch, a representative of the World Jewish Congress of New York, who wanted to talk about the Jewish problem with Himmler personally. As this visit drew nearer, Himmler was still unable to decide on a definite reply. I told him that for Kersten's sake, and even more because of the basic problem, arrangements for this meeting could no longer be put off.

Himmler was well aware that to have a conversation with Herr Storch while Hitler was still alive would be an action of fundamental importance which would have the greatest consequences for his relations with his own associates in the Party and in connection with the Jews. I too felt that such a meeting would be of symbolic importance, and for that very reason urged him most strongly to agree to it. Himmler was afraid that if Kaltenbrunner found out he would immediately report the matter to Hiler, but, as I pointed out, Kaltenbrunner was going to Austria, so the meeting could take place at Kersten's estate without his knowledge. Himmler finally agreed to this, but not without reluctance.

He was very greatly troubled about his rupture with the Fuehrer, which by this time was almost complete. Hitler had even given orders that Himmler's special SS Leibstrandarte (bodyguard) were to have the stripes removed from their sleeves as a mark of dishonor.

Himmler said to me that I was the only one, apart from Brandt, whom he could trust completely. What should he do? He could not shoot Hitler; he could not give him poison; he could not arrest him in the Reich Chancellery, for then the whole military machine would come to a standstill. I told him that all this did not matter; only two possibilities existed for him: either he should go to Hitler and tell him frankly all that had happened during the last years and force him to resign; or else he should remove him by force. Himmler objected that if he spoke to Hitler like that the Fuehrer would fall into a violent rage and shoot him out of hand. I said, "That is just what you must protect yourself against—you still have enough higher SS leaders, and you are still in a strong enough position to arrest him. If there is no other way, then the doctors will have to intervene."

Our talk lasted about an hour and a half, but Himmler was still unable to arrive at a decision. Instead he wanted to confront Bormann with Professor de Crinis, Professor Morell, Hitler's personal physician, and Dr. Stumpfegger, another of Hitler's doctors, who was also an SS leader.

Two days later I asked Professor de Crinis what the decision had been. He was very disappointed. The doctors had refused to commit themselves, and nothing that they permitted themselves to say would have been of any help with Bormann. When I reported this to Himmler he begged me to maintain silence about the whole matter. I then pointed out to him the senselessness of the Wehrwolf organization, which was being forced to carry on the struggle after Germany's defeat. This plan, I said, would bring nothing but suffering to the German people. Opportunities would arise for every sort of crime to be committed, as each individual would take it upon himself to decide what he considered justified in the national interest. Yet these grave measures were being lightly and irresponsibly advocated by the German leaders. They were even announcing over the German radio that they would repudiate the Hague conventions. I ended with the words "criminal and stupid," but Himmler was obviously too exhausted by this spiritual struggle with me. He merely said, "I will try to think of some way to finish this business."

During the first week of April I had established contact with the Reich Minister of Finance, Graf Shwerin von Krosigk. We had a long conversation and von Krosigk agreed with me that the war had to be ended quickly in order to save as much of Germany's resources as possible. I had been talking about this with Himmler too for quite a time. Himmler had gradually become estranged from von Krosigk, and therefore I brought the two of them together again for a discussion, which took place on the afternoon of April 19. Once again Himmler jibbed at the last moment, and it was touch and go whether the meeting would take place. However, when we finally arrived at von Krosigk's office, we found that the Minister of Labor, Seldte, was also there.

Von Krosigk and Himmler carried on their disucssion privately, while I had a conversation with Seldte. Seldte felt that Himmler should seize power himself and force Hitler to read a proclamation to the German people on his birthday, announcing a plebiscite, the formation of a second party, and abolition of the People's Courts. He elaborated this thesis for almost two hours, then asked me what my opinion was of the chances for a defense of the Alpine area (known as the Redoubt). I replied that I saw no chance at all in any further military action, that only by speedy action on the political level could anything be achieved.

In the meantime, the conversation between von Krosigk and Himmler had ended. Von Krosigk was very satisfied, although he knew that it was really much too late and that little chance of success remained. He begged me to continue to influence Himmler so that he might take the decisive step with or without Hitler.

After the meeting Himmler thanked me for bringing it about. I told him that I was convinced that von Krosigk was the only man in Germany who could become Foreign Minister.

After we arrived in Hohenlychen the general report of the military situation made a sad picture. I advised Himmler most emphatically not to drive into Berlin for Hitler's birthday the next day. A message had come that Kersten and Norbert Masur, who had come in Herr Storch's place as representative of the World Jewish Congress, had arrived at Tempelhof airport and had gone on to Kersten's estate at Hartzwalde. As Count Bernadotte was expected in Berlin at the same time, there was a great danger that these two meetings might conflict, especially in view of the difficult military situation. Therefore Himmler begged me to drive to Kersten that night and begin preparatory conversations with Masur, and also arrange a time for Himmler to meet him.

I had dinner at Hohenlychen and tried to persuade Himmler to send Berger to southern Germany. I thought he would be a counterpoise to Kaltenbrunner, whom I deeply mistrusted, so much so indeed that I feared for the safety of my family. But Himmler defended Kaltenbrunner, whom he described as a politically intelligent and farsighted man. In fact, the more clearly he perceived my opposition, the more he praised him.

I excused myself shortly before midnight, just as Himmler, quite contrary to his usual custom, had ordered another bottle of champagne in which to toast Hitler's birthday at twelve o'clock.

It was a bright moonlight night, but we were held up on our drive for a considerable time by aircraft which were dropping flares over Berlin. We arrived at the Hartzwalde estate at two-thirty and I found the whole place fast asleep.

I talked to Kersten until four o'clock in the morning. He was very unhappy about Himmler's hesitation, and doubted whether a successful meeting between him and Masur could still be brought about. But it was very important that Himmler should show his "goodwill." I explained to Kersten how difficult my whole situation had become lately, and how I had tried all possible means to bring this meeting about.

37. NEGOTIATIONS WITH COUNT BERNADOTTE

Himmler gives assurances concerning the Jews—An all-night discussion—Himmler confers with Count Bernadotte—A plan to contact President Roosevelt—The Count is asked to transmit a declaration of surrender—Himmler and the Count confer again—The Allies refuse to negotiate with Himmler—I renew discussions with the Count—Terms agreed for our evacuation of Scandinavia—Kaltenbrunner dismisses me from my posts—Admiral Doenitz nominated to succeed Hitler.

ON THE morning of April 20 I was awakened at nine by the noise of planes overhead, and while I was shaving a bomb dropped about a mile away—an unpleasant surprise for Herr Masur. I breakfasted with him, and immediately afterward we had our first discussion. He insisted that nothing could be accomplished without a meeting with Himmler, but he would have to leave Berlin by Monday at the latest. As I knew that Himmler intended once again to put off meeting him, I had got to get him to keep to the agreed date.

At this point a telephone call came through from Count Bernadotte, who was staying at the Swedish Embassy in Berlin. He told me that he would like to speak to Himmler once more before leaving for Sweden at six o' clock the next morning. Somehow or other I had to get Himmler to see Masur, and arrange for a meeting with Count Bernadotte, who was coming to Hohenlychen for this purpose that same night.

At about nine in the evening I went to Wustrow to wait for Himmler, who was delayed by heavy air attacks. When he eventually arrived, I managed to persuade him to drive with me to meet Herr Masur. Accompanied by a driver and Himmler's secretary, Brandt, we left for Hartzwalde at one-fifteen. On the way Himmler told me what he intended to say to Masur. In essence it was a chronological summary of the past with a clever attempt at justification. I asked him not to speak of the past at all, or to expound his astrological and philosophical theories but to determine precisely what had to be done in the future. Now and then we had to take cover from low-flying aircraft, and we arrived at Hartzwalde around three in the morning.

Masur and Kersten were waiting for us and after a brief greeting their conversation began. It was conducted for the most part by Himmler who wanted to prove that he had tried to solve the Jewish problem in terms of expulsion, but that this could not be done because of the outside world's resistance on the one hand, and, on the other, the opposition within the Nazi party. Masur did not embark on any long discussion on the various points, but said after about three-quarters of an hour that, although Himmler's account had been very interesting, it was not in any way conducive toward changing the situation. That, however, was his main purpose for coming here, and he wanted the following assurances: that no more Jews would be killed; that the remaining Jews—and their numbers were very uncertain—should remain in the camps and under no circumstances be evacuated. He asked for lists of all the camps in which Jews were still being held to be given to him.

On these points agreement was reached, Himmler repeating every time that he had already given such orders. He was, in fact, ready to free the Jewish women in Ravensbrueck camp and turn them over to Masur, for he had received permission from Hitler to free all the Polish women from that camp. Therefore, if there were any questions about it afterward, he could say the Jewish women were Poles.

I then went into another room with Masur in order to decide on other points to be discussed, but when the conversation was resumed it tended to become more and more vague, dealing with completely unimportant side issues. I was anxious to bring it to a conclusion in order to be able to arrive at Hohenlychen with Himmler by six o'clock in the morning, so, after briefly saying good-by, we left Hartzwalde; it was now half-past four. I assured Masur once more as we left that I would do all in my power to arrange for his departure the next day.

We arrived at Hohenlychen punctually at six o'clock—

this was on the morning of the 21st—and had breakfast
with Count Bernadotte. I hoped that the frank conversation between Himmler and the Count, which I had desired
for so long, would now take place. Himmler told the
Count of the possibility of transporting all the Polish
women in Ravensbrueck to Sweden.

In fact, I had made all preparations for this and had
drawn up a list of all the Poles in Ravensbrueck camp.
As they were mostly children or young girls, I was determined to free them at all costs. I impressed most strongly
on Himmler the shamefulness of this situation, and emphasized the high racial qualities of the Polish people by
pointing to my own wife as an example. This impressed
him greatly and he seemed considerably preoccupied with
the question, for he constantly referred to it, although it
was not until much later that he took any action.

Count Bernadotte asked whether it would not be possible to transport the Danish and Norwegian internees to
Sweden, but Himmler was unable to grant permission for
this, though he agreed that should the Allied armies
threaten to overrun the Neugamme camp there would be
no evacuation.

The Count thanked him for his willingness and for the
confidence shown him in previous conversations. The discussion then came to an end and they said good-by.
Himmler, knowing I was to accompany the Count part of
the way, hoped that I would once more beg him to fly to
General Eisenhower and try to arrange for him to have a
conference with the General.

However, at our parting on the road near Waren in
Mecklenburg, Count Bernadotte said to me, "The Reichsfuehrer no longer understands the realities of his own
situation. I cannot help him any more. He should have
taken Germany's affairs into his own hands after my first
visit. I can hold out little chance for him now. And you,
my dear Schellenberg, would be wiser to think of yourself."

I did not know what to reply to this. When we said
good-by, it was as though we would never see each other
again. I was filled with a deep sadness.

I drove back to Hohenlychen, slept for two hours, and
was then called to Himmler at about twelve-thirty. He was
still in bed, the picture of misery, and said that he felt ill.
All I could say was that there was nothing more I could

do for him; it was up to him. He had got to take some action. At lunch we discussed the military situation in Berlin, which was steadily growing worse.

At about four o'clock, having convinced him that it would be unwise to drive to Berlin, we drove toward Wustrow. In Loewenberg we were caught in a traffic jam, troops having become involved with the unending columns of fleeing civilians which blocked all the roads between Berlin and Mecklenburg.

As we drove on, Himmler said to me for the first time, "Schellenberg, I dread what is to come."

I said that this should give him the courage to take action. He did not answer. Just before we got to Wustrow we were attacked by low-flying planes. However, their main target was the column of refugees and troops through which we had passed.

After dinner, when we were alone again, we spoke of various problems, of food supplies, the danger of epidemics, reconstruction, prisoner-of-war administration, and so on. I told him of Kaltenbrunner's blind and unrealistic attitude in insisting on the evacuation at all costs of all the concentration camps. Himmler grew very nervous when I called this a crime, and said brusquely, "Schellenberg, don't you start too. Hitler has been raging for days because Buchenwald and Bergen-Belsen were not completely evacuated."

At that moment Fegelein telephoned to say that Hitler and Goebbels were raging because Berger had not remained in Berlin—he had in fact just left Berlin to fly to southern Germany in Himmler's place. He was needed by Hitler to carry out the sentence passed on Dr. Brandt, Hitler's former personal physician, who had just been condemned to death for smuggling his wife into the hands of the Americans in Thuringia. Apparently this was a complex intrigue among Hitler's entourage involving Hitler's "friend" Eva Braun, and her sister, who was Fegelein's wife. Himmler did everything he could to prevent the doctor's execution and immediately gave instructions over the telephone to the Gestapo chief, Mueller. Dr. Brandt was transferred to Schwerin, which was safer from air attacks, and Fegelein was told that Berger was on his way south by plane. For this reason sentence could not be executed at the moment, unless Bormann and Goebbels wanted to do the job themselves.

When Himmler returned he told me what he would do once he had complete power in Germany, and asked me to think about a name for the new alternative party which I had suggested to him. I suggested National Unity party. After referring once more, though only in the vaguest terms, to Hitler's removal, he dismissed me—it was now about four-thirty—and went to bed.

The next morning—it was Sunday, April 22—it appeared that the military situation had become so much worse overnight that four Waffen SS Divisions, under Obergruppenfuehrer Steiner, had been ordered by Hitler to make a suicide attack on the Russians. Himmler was convinced that this order was necessary, though both his military adjutant and I agreed that it would only mean unnecessary bloodshed.

After breakfast Obergruppenfuehrer Berger came in. He was to drive back with us to Hohenlychen and Wustrow was to be evacuated as it was threatened by the enemy.

We discussed the case of Vanamann, an American Air Force general who had formerly been Military Attaché in Berlin, and was at this time a prisoner of war in Germany. Berger and I suggested that Vanamann, together with another United States Air Force colonel, should be got out of Germany and flown via Switzerland to the United States to contact Roosevelt. He was to try to get better supplies and conditions for the American prisoners of war, and at the same time tell Roosevelt of Himmler's desire for peace with the Western Powers. I had planned this long ago, having in mind the freeing of influential British prisoners of war so that they might work toward an understanding between their country and Germany. Hitler and Himmler, however, had given strict orders against this.

I had had long conversations with Vanamann, and we were in full agreement. As Himmler had refused his permission, I arranged with friends in Switzerland and with the United States Military Attaché in Berne, General Legg, for Vanamann to cross the border illegally. I did this on my own responsibility and arranged for a car to bring him and the Air Force colonel to the frontier near Constance.

As I had no news of them, I asked Berger to attend to

the matter. By this time Himmler was in agreement with the plan.

Toward noon we had to leave Wustrow in great haste as Russian armored spearheads were reported in the vicinity of Oranienburg, as well as in the general direction of Loewenberg and Kremmen. We drove in a northerly direction from Wustrow toward Mecklenburg, and then angled off to the east in order to reach Hohenlychen. For more than an hour and a half we drove past Wehrmacht columns, artillery, and armor on the move, constantly harassed by low-flying light bombers and fighters. Finally we arrived at Hohenlychen.

After a belated lunch Himmler said to me, "I almost believe you are right, Schellenberg—I must take action now. What do you suggest?"

I explained to him that things had gone too far. Certainly there could be no hope from Vanamann's mission, though there might still be a possibility of talking frankly about the whole situation with Count Bernadotte. (Without Himmler's knowledge, I had already informed the Count much more fully about the true situation in Germany.) I did not know whether I could reach the Count in Denmark, but he might still be in Lübeck. Himmler decided that I should go to Lübeck at once. He was prepared now to ask the Count, officially and in his own name, to transmit a declaration of surrender to the Western Powers.

I prepared immediately for my departure, and left for Lübeck at four-thirty in the afternoon, but because of enemy aircraft and the blocked roads I did not arrive there until late at night. I found that Count Bernadotte was in Apenrade in Denmark, and in spite of tremendous difficulties I got through to him on the telephone and asked him to receive me at Flensburg the next day. He agreed to meet me at three o'clock on April 23 at the Swedish Consulate in Flensburg.

It was already morning. I rested for three hours, then telephoned Himmler to inform him of my appointment, and afterward drove on to Flensburg. I arrived at one o'clock, and was received by the Swedish Attaché, Chiron, who took me to lunch with the Consul, Petersen.

Count Bernadotte arrived at three o'clock. After discussing the general situation and Himmler's intentions, the Count said he believed it was no longer necessary to go to

Lübeck to meet Himmler, and that the best solution would be for Himmler simply to set down his proposals in a letter to General Eisenhower announcing unconditional surrender to the Western Powers. As I did not think this would be possible as long as Hitler was still alive, I begged him to drive with me to meet Himmler at Lübeck. After an hour's conversation the Count agreed to do so.

From Flensburg I telephoned to Himmler's special train to ask him to come to Lübeck. Brandt answered, and said that Himmler could not be reached at the moment but promised to call me back. It was very fortunate that in spite of the emergency situation the telephone still functioned so well. Brandt called me back at six o'clock and said that Himmler would be glad to meet Count Bernadotte at Lübeck at ten o'clock that night, and that he wished me to be present.

After a quick meal, the Count and I left Flensburg and drove to Lübeck, arriving at the Swedish Consulate at nine o'clock. I went to the office which had been set up at the Danziger Hof Hotel and got in touch with General Wuenneberg's office, where Himmler planned to stay. At ten o'clock I saw Himmler and told him the essential points of my conversation with the Count and sought to strengthen his decision to make a declaration of capitulation. For a little while Himmler hesitated, but finally he agreed. "Very well, we will drive to see the Count at eleven o'clock," he said. "Please arrange for the meeting at that time."

At eleven I drove with him to the Swedish Consulate, where the meeting took place by candlelight owing to a power cut. After formal greetings had been exchanged, there was an air-raid alarm, followed by a heavy raid on a nearby airfield. We had to go down into the cellar and it was midnight before we were able to resume the conversation.

Himmler made a lengthy exposition of the military and political situation of the Reich before reaching his summing up—it was a comparatively honest one—of the situation: "We Germans have to declare ourselves defeated by the Western Powers; and I beg you to transmit this to General Eisenhower through the Swedish government, so that we all may be spared further unnecessary bloodshed. It is not possible for us Germans, and especially it is not possible for me, to capitulate to the Russians. Against them we will fight on until the front of the Western Powers replaces the German fighting front."

Himmler pointed out that he had the right to make the decision on these matters, for it would only be a question of two or three days before Hitler gave up his life. At least he would have died in the struggle to which he had devoted his existence, the fight against Bolshevism.

Count Bernadotte expressed his readiness to transmit Himmler's declaration. As he pointed out, he, and probably the Swedish government, too, were primarily interested in preserving the Scandinavian area from senseless destruction through a continuation of the war. For him, as a Swede, this was his justification for agreeing to Himmler's request. Himmler said that he fully understood this point. In reply to a further question from the Count, he said he was ready to permit the transport of Danish and Norwegian internees to Sweden.

A great deal of time was taken up in deciding how the declaration of surrender should be transmitted to the Western Powers. The original plan, that Count Bernadotte should fly direct to General Eisenhower, without any diplomatic preliminaries or preparation, was abandoned. Eventually they agreed that Himmler should write a letter to His Excellency Christian Günther, the Foreign Minister of Sweden, begging him to give his kind support to Himmler's communication, handed to him through Count Bernadotte. Himmler briefly discussed the wording of the letter with me and then drafted it himself by candlelight.

The Count expressed his readiness to fly to Stockholm the next day, April 24, to initiate the necessary arrangements. It was agreed that I should drive the Count to Flensburg and remain there to act as liaison over any further questions that might arise. After warm farewells, Himmler and I left the Swedish Consulate at 1:30 P.M.

Both on the way to and from the Consulate, Himmler drove his car—a very heavy one—himself. He drove so badly that I and one of my men, acting as our guide, were in a cold sweat. He was never a good driver to begin with and now was in a state of considerable nervous strain. He repeatedly jumped the curb, and each approaching lorry was a fresh ordeal. When we set off from the Swedish Consulate he started too quickly and drove into a ditch.

All of us, including Count Bernadotte, had to struggle for a quarter of an hour to get the car going again.

I accompanied Himmler back to General Wuenneberg's office and stayed with him for another half hour in order to calm his fears about the steps he had taken. I tried to give him courage, and told him that he had not committed an act of betrayal toward the German people. Then I went to the Danziger Hof, and at five o'clock in the morning returned to the Swedish Consuate to fetch Count Bernadotte and drive to Flensburg.

When we arrived at the German-Danish frontier I said good-by to the Count, who expressed his hope of telephoning good news to me shortly.

It was getting on for midday before I was at last able to try and get some rest at the Swedish Consul's house, but I had scarcely settled down when I was woken again by a heavy air raid and a naval bombardment from warships lying offshore. I hurried down to the cellar, only half dressed, and was rather embarrassed to meet my hostess for the first time.

The next day, April 25, I ordered Standartenfuehrer Bovensiepen to report to me at Flensburg. First I showed him my special authorization signed by Himmler which read: "Acting under special assignment from me, General Schellenberg's orders are to be obeyed without question." I told Bovensiepen that all inmates of Danish and Norwegian concentration camps were to be turned over without fail to Sweden. I said that I intended to go to Copenhagen the next day to discuss the Danish political situation with Dr. Best [Minister Extraordinary and Plenipotentiary in Denmark], and asked him to make arrangements for this meeting. The chief aim was to stop all death sentences and executions.

On April 26 I received an interim report from Count Levenhaupt, of the Swedish Consulate, that the neogtiations were not going very well, and that the Allies refused to negotiate with Himmler. I did not pass this information on to him, however.

During the night I was informed that Count Bernadotte would arrive from Copenhagen at Odense airport the next morning. When I got there I learned that the Count's departure from Copenhagen had been delayed by bad weather, and I waited with increasing anxiety as the weather continued to deteriorate. The airport commandant instructed all observation and anti-aircraft stations to be on the lookout and flares were shot off continually until the plane finally landed at four o'clock in the afternoon.

We then drove to Apenrade where we were able quietly to discuss the negative result of our plans, and the difficult situation which resulted from the Allies' attitude toward Himmler. We then considered what conclusions could be arrived at. Count Bernadotte spoke as a private person, but his chief concern remained the prevention of further fighting in Norway and Denmark and he offered to drive with me to see Himmler in order to discuss this.

Not only had our plans come to nothing, but the Allied press had published an account of the matter. My position with Himmler would therefore be a rather delicate one, and I was very glad to have the Count come to Lübeck with me. We arranged to meet at four the next morning and to drive there together.

I returned to Flensburg and tried to get in touch with Himmler, but was only able to speak to Brandt, who asked very excitedly what the results were. I said that they had been negative, but that the Count wanted to come to Lübeck to discuss the question of the German armies in the Scandinavian area. This proposal was sharply rejected; I was to report to Himmler alone.

This conversation took place just after midnight. I did not wish to awaken the Count at that hour, so I left for Apenrade at three o'clock and at the appointed hour saw the Count and asked him not to accompany me—I was to meet Himmler, I said, to the south of Lübeck and would have to approach too close to the front line. Then I left him and drove to Lübeck. This was on the morning of April 28.

I realized that my position with Himmler would now be so difficult that I should have to face the fact that I might be liquidated. I therefore arranged for an astrologer from Hamburg to accompany me. Himmler knew this man personally, and thought very highly of him. He could never resist having his horoscope read, and I felt this would soften his reaction to the disappointment.

The first part of my talk with Himmler need not be described here. It was not easy, and looking back on it I cannot understand why it turned out so well.

For a long time we discussed the grounds of the Allies' rejection. Himmler was bitterly disappointed, and particularly annoyed that the facts had been published in the world's press. He feared that his letter to the Swedish Foreign Minister would now be published as well. We then discussed the problem of Denmark and Norway. The fact that Himmler held me responsible, as the instigator of his peace move, for its failure, which could have such fatal consequences for his relationship with Hitler, did not seem to offer a very good basis for my plans to save the Scandinavian countries. However, with the aid of the astrological gentleman, I was able to persuade him to accept my view and, after thinking the matter over for an hour, he gave me permission to discuss with Count Bernadotte the ending of the German occupation of Norway and the internment in Sweden of the German occupation forces for the remainder of the war. Himmler stated that he was prepared to arrange a similar solution for Denmark, but that this should be finally decided later on. However, he authorized me to prepare Dr. Best for such a plan. Furthermore, he was prepared to appoint me as his special representative to the Swedish government to negotiate a peaceful solution in the Scandinavian area. At that time he still took for granted that within a day or two he, as Hitler's successor, would be in a position to decide these questions without any difficulty.

I immediately returned to Flensburg, arriving at Apenrade at about noon on the 29th, and lunched with the Count and Ambassador Thomsen at the latter's house. Afterward the Count and I discussed Himmler's agreement concerning the Scandinavian area, and he arranged a meeting for the next day between the representatives of the Swedish government and myself, at which he would also be present. Thomsen drew my attention to a number of special requests involving the prevention of execution and the freeing of Danish policemen, and the following day I was able to deal with these matters to his satisfaction.

That afternoon at about five o'clock we left Apenrade for Copenhagen. The Count drove, and after a smooth journey we arrived at the Danish capital, where we stopped at the Hotel d'Angleterre.

On the morning of April 30, I first drove to Dr. Best to inform him of my authorization concerning the peaceful lifting of the German occupation of the Scandinavian countries and of Himmler's assumed succession to Hitler. As I had foreseen, Dr. Best agreed to everything.

At noon I met Herr von Post, of the Swedish government, and Count Bernadotte. All went very smoothly. The Swedish government asked for the whole plan to be arranged through me, with clear binding proposals on the part of the German government. At the close of the meeting the Swedish Ambassador at Copenhagen, von Dardel, gave a lunch to which Dr. Best was also invited.

Immediately after lunch I drove to Korsor to take the ferry, which had been held up for me for two hours. I arrived at Flensburg at night and there met a member of my organization, Sturmbannfuehrer Dr. Wirsing, who informed me that Kaltenbrunner had dismissed me from all my posts, and had appointed Obersturmbannfuehrer Wanck chief of the Political Sector of the Secret Service, and Oberstumbannfuehrer Skorzeny chief of the Military Sector.

After a short telephone conversation with Himmler, Dr. Wirsing and I drove on to Lübeck, as I wanted him to be able to fly back to the south with Himmler's counterorders in connection with my dismissal. Our journey, which was only thirty miles, took us three and a half hours because the roads were completely blocked by troops streaming back from the Mecklenburg area. We arrived at four o'clock in the morning on May 1, and I was conducted to Himmler's new quarters at Kalkhorst, near Travemuende, by one of his adjutants.

As Himmler had not gone to bed until three o'clock, I went to Brandt, who told me the startling news that Hitler had committed suicide and Admiral Doenitz, not Himmler, had been made his successor.

38. MY LAST MISSION

Count von Krosigk replaces Ribbentrop—Military opposition to the surrender of Scandinavia—a manifesto to the German people prepared—A dangerous journey—Von Krosigk offers to appoint me his assistant—Doenitz remains adamant on the question of evacuation—I am appointed von Krosigk's envoy—Copenhagen on the eve of surrender—Peace discussion in Stockholm—My authority in question—Germany surrenders

HIMMLER AND Admiral Doenitz, the new chief of the German Reich, had met at Ploen and conferred late into the night on the immediate future policy that was to be adopted. Himmler had prevailed upon Doenitz to proclaim, as his first act, the removal of Ribbentrop and the appointment of Count Schwerin von Krosigk as Foreign Minister. But the Admiral and his entourage, consisting wholly of Wehrmacht officers, had shown no understanding of Himmler's political moves toward the Western Powers, and consequently the Reichsfuehrer was in the worst possible mood. He was playing with the idea of resigning, and was even talking of suicide.

I tried to rest for half an hour, and then at nine o'clock Himmler called me to join him for breakfast. I reported to him on my conversations with Herr von Post, Dr. Best, and the Count. He was very nervous and distracted, and told me that he was no longer capable of taking action in the matters I had discussed with them. The only thing he had been able to achieve was to secure the removal of Ribbentrop and the appointment of von Krosigk. Himmler wanted to take me to Doenitz right away, so that I could act as von Krosigk's assistant on questions of foreign policy. It would also be an advantage if I could report to the Doenitz government on my efforts regarding Denmark and Norway. If I could persuade them to agree to the peaceful surrender of the two countries, someone else should be sent to Sweden and I should remain with the government.

At eleven o'clock that morning we set out to drive to Ploen to see Doenitz. We went by way of Lübeck and, after a difficult journey, arrived at two in the afternoon. There was an air of great excitement among the whole staff, and, after paying my respects to Doenitz, Keitel, and Jodl, I got into touch with von Krosigk.

In the afternoon I learned that, although von Krosigk agreed with my view on Scandinavia, Doenitz, Keitel, and Jodl were by no means ready to surrender Norway without a fight.

I had promised Herr von Post to return immediately to Copenhagen with a decision. To continue waiting at Ploen would only mean a loss of time and might make it impossible for me to accept the Swedish offer. General Oberst Boehme, Reichskommissar Terboven, Generaloberst Lindemann, and Dr. Best had, in the meantime, been called to Ploen to discuss the problem with Doenitz. I therefore decided to tell Herr von Post about the new situation, and Himmler agreed to my returning to Copenhagen for this purpose. In the meantime, he and von Krosigk would continue to press for a peaceful solution.

I left Ploen at three in the morning and arrived at Flensburg at seven. I remained there for three hours, working with Dr. Wirsing on a draft which was to represent my first collaboration with the new Foreign Minister. I suggested that the National Socialist party, the Gestapo, and the SD should be dissolved and that this should be proclaimed over the wireless. Dr. Wirsing completed the draft for me and sent it off, for I could no longer fight off my overwhelming need for sleep.

Dr. Wirsing was to fly to southern Germany the next night, so, in view of Kaltenbrunner's action in removing me from my office, I instructed him to tell my staff to submit outwardly to his authority, but to preserve their professional loyalty toward me. In the evening I left for Copenhagen.

From Padborg, in Denmark, Count Bernadotte's personal Red Cross car was placed at my disposal. This was a great advantage, especially in getting past Wehrmacht control points, and served as excellent camouflage for me. I was cheered and welcomed as a Swede and continually asked for my autograph. I felt rather uncomfortable.

I arrived at Copenhagen at one o'clock on May 3, and my conversation with Herr von Post and Herr Ostroem took place at four. I explained the situation, and told them that Admiral Doenitz had ordered the military and civilian authorities of Denmark and Norway to report to him for a conference. There were good grounds for assuming that, backed by the influence of Count Schwerin von Krosigk and Himmler, my plan for surrender would be agreed upon.

Herr von Post said he was no longer in a position to make any binding agreements. A general capitulation was inevitable within the next few days, and at that moment the surrender of Denmark and Norway was a purely academic question. However, he was still willing to pursue our old plan, and I should immediately forward any offer from the new German government to him. We agreed that I should return as quickly as possible, and I arranged to communicate with him by telephone, using the following code words: "I should be very happy to see the gentlemen again"—which would mean there had been a binding proposal on the part of the Reich government with regard to Norway; the words "—and report to you" added would mean that the proposal would also cover Denmark.

Herr von Post and Herr Ostroem emphasized that they could no longer remain in Copenhagen—the maintenance of secrecy necessitated their departure, for, of course, the negotiations were being conducted in the strictest secrecy. So I returned to Flensburg that night and started for Ploen early the next morning.

The journey was one of the most difficult and dangerous I have ever undertaken. On the relatively short distance of about fifty-five miles, there were more than twelve strafing attacks on roads which were completely jammed with retreating army columns and immobilized transport. There were long lines of burned-out lorries, corpses covered the roads, and here and there were the ruins of tanks. We had to fight our way through all this, periodically taking cover in ditches and fields from strafing by low-flying aircraft.

When we did arrive at Ploen, the guards informed us that the seat of the government had been transferred to the Marine School at Muerwick, near Flensburg. As my mission would not brook an hour's delay, I had to turn round at once and make my way back through the holo-

caust from which I had just emerged. However, I managed
to arrive at Muerwick at five o'clock in the afternoon,
and ten minutes later I was reporting to the Foreign Minister and Himmler.

Again I stressed that, in spite of the continuing deterioration of the situation, a solution in the Scandinavian area,
through the help of Sweden, would be of the greatest
importance. Then I spoke with von Krosigk alone. He told
me that if I would stay with him, he would appoint me his
first assistant. On the other hand, he considered it was
important for me to go to Stockholm. We agreed that
time was of the utmost importance, for a total capitulation could not be far off. The only thing that was holding
it up was the fact that in the Bohemian-Moravian area the
army groups of Field Marshal Schoerner and Generaloberst Rendulic, consisting of almost a million men
supplied with munitions and provisions for seven weeks,
were still intact. They were doing a more than adequate
job of defending the eastern front.

At about eight o'clock in the evening I reported to
Admiral Doenitz. At first he would hear nothing about
lifting the occupation of Norway or the internment of
German troops in Sweden. Obviously his military advisers
had pointed out to him the excellent strategic position of
General Boehme's army. Even after I had proved to him
the political importance of a peaceful solution, and of the
intervention of Sweden, he still demanded to know what
immediate gain it would bring to Germany. I explained to
him that it was a question of long-term political prospects,
apart, of course, from the saving of a large number of
German lives. It would ameliorate world opinion toward
us, and in the near future it might be of some importance
for a defeated Germany to have support from a neutral
country like Sweden. In view of Germany's collapse, to
continue fighting in Norway and Denmark was not only
misguided, it was utterly futile.

At this point the meeting was broken off, and I went to
dinner with von Krosigk, Keitel, and Jodl. At the table we
continued the discussion. Both Keitel and Jodl wanted me
to remain with them, as I had the most experience in
matters of foreign policy. However, I pointed out the
importance of my mission to Stockholm, and in the end
Jodl at least seemed to understand.

Afterward I spoke again to von Krosigk and advised

him to induce Doenitz to follow my suggestions to dissolve the Party, the Gestapo, and the SD as soon as possible. We then discussed in which capacity it would be best for me to go to Stockholm. Von Krosigk offered to make me Ambassador, Special Plenipotentiary, Representative, or whatever I preferred. I suggested that he should appoint me Envoy, for this corresponded accurately to the tasks upon which I was embarking. That night Secretary of State Steengracht and Henke were called over by the Foreign Minister, and together they prepared the documents authorizing my appointment as Envoy. Doenitz signed these the next morning, May 5, and after reporting to Krosigk at ten o'clock, I bade farewell to Himmler and left for Copenhagen.

A few days later Himmler committed suicide.

Arriving at Copenhagen, I went to the Dagmarhus, for I wanted to inform Dr. Best of my mission. While I was waiting for him, a huge crowd gathered in the town square in expectation of the impending surrender of Germany. Shots were fired and police vans and ambulances drove up, the crowd growing meanwhile until it must have reached tens of thousands. It was obvious that Dr. Best would not be able to make his way through the tumult. I could not wait as it was imperative for me to get to the Swedish Embassy right away, for apparently they had not received my telephone message from the frontier.

After a long discussion with the SS guard at the Dagmarhus, an opening was made in the barbed-wire barrier, and I was able to drive through in Count Bernadotte's car. Though the driver tried to avoid the crowded streets, we suddenly found ourselves surrounded by thousands of people. They recognized the Count's car and pressed round it until we could move neither forward nor backward. Fortunately I had locked the door from the inside and closed the windows, otherwise they would have pulled me out. I ordered the driver to push on, come what may, and slowly we inched our way through the solid mass of human beings. Those immediately next to the car began to cry out as those behind them kept on pushing forward, gesticulating with wild enthusiasm. By now there were about thirty people all over the car, on the running boards, on the roof, on the bonnet, and only the calm and skill of the driver kept it moving. Meanwhile both he and I, in order to placate the wild demonstrators, kept nodding and saying *"Tak, tak,"* and taking off our hats. When eventually we reached the Swedish Embassy, after an hour and a half of this, it was like coming out of a steam bath.

But even while I was greeting Herr von Dardel and his wife, the demonstrators were gathering outside the Embassy singing the Danish and the Swedish national anthems. Eventually the singing and shouting became so loud that we could hardly hear ourselves speak.

Arrangements were made for my trip to Stockholm, and then I returned to the Hotel d'Angleterre to rest for a few hours. In front of the hotel I was stopped once more by Danish partisans, but when they recognized the car and the driver told them that I was a Swede, they let me pass.

On the morning of May 6, after encountering considerable difficulties with the control post of the Danish partisans and with the German airport guards, I took off from Copenhagen in one of Count Bernadotte's Red Cross aircraft. We landed at Malmo at seven-fifteen and I was told that a Swedish military aircraft was ready to take me to Stockholm. I strapped on an oxygen mask and a parachute, and after a smooth flight of hardly more than two hours, the Swedish bomber landed at Broma. Herr von Ostroem met me at the airport and took me to the house of Count Bernadotte, where talks with Herr von Post and State Secretary Bohemann were begun at once.

I presented my credentials and explained my mission. After a heated conversation, the gentlemen decided that, in view of the state of developments in Germany, they would discuss the whole matter with the representatives of the Western Powers in Stockholm. However, we could not get a definite answer but only a vague promise that a special Allied commission might be sent to Stockholm by General Eisenhower.

The next day, Monday, May 7, the point was raised as to whether General Boehme, who commanded the German troops in Norway, would recognize my authority and conform to any agreements I might reach with the Swedish government. I decided to send Ambassador Thomsen and the Military Attaché, General Utmann, to the Norwegian frontier to discuss my mission with General Boehme. On the morning of the 8th Ambassador Thomsen flew there in a Swedish bomber and met a leading officer of General Boehme's staff. Thomsen telephoned me at noon and said there was some conflict of opinion which he could not discuss in detail on the telephone, but he would be back in Stockholm at six o'clock.

I had a meeting with Herr von Post and Count Bernadotte and was advised to get in touch with Doenitz and report to him that General Boehme had not been informed of my authorization. We then drew up a lengthy message to the Admiral, and General Utmann managed to arrange a telephone conversation with him via Oslo, but it was of little use because connections were so bad. We got through a second time, however, and I talked with von Krosigk.

He explained to me that during the previous night Germany had made a declaration of total capitulation, and that negotiations were still in progress. I should be careful, therefore, not to annoy any of General Eisenhower's representatives, who were now also involved in negotiations on the Norwegian question. He suggested that if the Swedish government were still interested in intervening, they should contact the Western Allies at once.

The Swedes, however, now declared that there was nothing to be done, for obviously both the Norwegian and the Danish problems were part of the surrender negotiations as a whole. They would wait to see whether the Western Allies on their part had any intention of asking them to mediate.

On May 9 a last telephone conversation with Flensburg made it quite clear to me that any intervention by the Swedish Red Cross with regard to the internment of the German forces in Norway was not desired by the British military authorities.

For the time being my services were no longer required.

Are you missing out on some great Jove/HBJ books?

"You can have any title in print at Jove/HBJ delivered right to your door! To receive your Jove/HBJ Shop-At-Home Catalog, send us 25¢ together with the label below showing your name and address.

JOVE PUBLICATIONS, INC.
Harcourt Brace Jovanovich, Inc.
Dept. M.O., 757 Third Avenue, New York, N.Y. 10017

NAME_____

ADDRESS_____

CITY_____STATE_____

NT-1   ZIP_____